Gender, Sex and Translation

The Manipulation of Identities

Edited by

José Santaemilia

ST JEROME
PUBLISHING
St. Jerome Publishing
Manchester, UK & Northampton MA

Published by
St. Jerome Publishing (Manchester, UK & Northampton, USA)
2 Maple Road West, Brooklands
Manchester, M23 9HH, United Kingdom
Tel +44 161 973 9856 / Fax +44 161 905 3498
stjerome@compuserve.com
http://www.stjerome.co.uk

ISBN 1-900650-68-1 (pbk)

Printed and bound in Great Britain by
Antony Rowe Ltd., Chippenham, UK

Typeset by
Delta Typesetters, Cairo, Egypt
Email: hilali1945@yahoo.co.uk

British Library Cataloguing in Publication Data
A catalogue record of this book is available from the British Library

Library of Congress Cataloging-in-Publication Data
Gender, sex and translation: the manipulation of identities / edited
by José Santaemilia.
    p. cm.
Includes bibliographical references and index.
ISBN 1-900650-68-1 (pbk. : alk. paper)
1. Translating and interpreting. 2. Sex role in literature. 3. Women
translators. I. Santaemilia, José.
PN241.G45 2005
418'.02—dc22
                            2005001004

Contents

Introduction

JOSÉ SANTAEMILIA

The idea of 'manipulation' is inherent to the phenomenon of 'translation'. Both *manipulare* and *translatare* share a common lexical ground: an (artful) adaptation, change, transformation, transmission – to suit one's purpose or advantage. In some sense, the two terms are quasi synonyms, which are also associated with transgression, perversion or subversion. In spite of its widespread critical presence, 'fidelity' is a rather useless term, since all texts are both faithful and unfaithful – faithful to some interests and unfaithful to others. Besides, all of us share a cultural fascination with marginal ideas like betrayal, difference or manipulation, because they allow us to live experiences contradictorily: a translator *creates* but *copies* (or *rewrites*), reproduces *faithfully* but has scope for *intervention*, aims at *equivalence* but ends up producing *difference*.

Very few books bear the term 'manipulation' on their covers,[1] undoubtedly because most recent approaches take this manipulation for granted. *Manipulare* is a Latin term meaning 'to handle': to operate with the hands, in a skilful manner. And this is probably the aptest metaphor for a civilization of words such as ours: our languages, literary traditions, canonical texts and ideologies are *in the hands of translators*.

This volume offers twelve articles on diverse aspects of the manipulation of identities (gendered or sexual) operated through translation. They were presented at the *First International Seminar on Gender and Language (The Gender of Translation ~ The Translation of Gender)* which was held in Valencia on 16-18 October 2002.[2]

In the first article, **Pilar Godayol** examines translation as a feminist practice. The work of feminist subjects in translation is a marginal or borderland experience and, hence, translating as/like a woman involves a deep revaluation of margins and a celebration of heterogeneity and of

---

[1] With the popular exceptions of Hermans (1985) and Lefevere (1992).
[2] I wish to thank the *Universitat de València,* the Ministerio de Ciencia y Tecnología and the Instituto de la Mujer (Ministerio de Asuntos Sociales) for their support: research projects "Género y cortesía: Estudio pragmático-discursivo (inglés/castellano/ catalán)" [UV 20020787], "Discurso, (des)cortesía y género: Estudio contrastivo inglés/castellano/catalán [BFF2003-07662] and "Interacción institucional y género: La participación de mujeres y hombres en la comunicación desarrollada en el seno de las instituciones" [I+D+I n° exp. 26/02].

unstable identity categories. Thanks to their work, concepts such as 'women', 'gender', 'sex' or 'identity' are viewed as problematic and unstable categories, and as open to redefinition.

Michaela Wolf studies two examples of 18th-century German female translators (Therese Huber and Luise Gottsched). Despite their self-confidence, both women had to cope with enormous physical and mental strain and to assert their individuality. Against this backdrop of 18th century realities, Wolf situates today's process of female individuality through translation. Although much work has been done and institutions are increasingly aware of the need to strengthen women's visibility in all kinds of texts, skepticism and mysoginistic attitudes still seem to be the norm.

M. Rosario Martín revises translation studies vis-à-vis basic developments in feminism: the analogy between women and translation, the feminization of translations, the relation between original and copy – and so on. Feminist translation, in particular, is fostering a broad crossdisciplinary reconceptualization – of unpredictable consequences – of concepts such as gender, sex, identity, textual authority or cultural practices. Feminism – together with other cultural and/or ideological paradigms – is helping to invalidate the tacit ideals of translation as neutral, unbiased sexual/textual fidelity.

Luise von Flotow explores the importance of gender-related contexts in translation. In fact, it is context (the conditions surrounding the production, reception or revival of a text, the way a translation is studied or evaluated, the ideology of the translator, etc.) which makes translations possible. Recent paradigms such as deconstruction, post-structuralism or gender studies are fragmenting traditional notions of fidelity or authority, of originality or equivalence. Translation is a deliberate and political act whose only horizon is difference, subjectivity, plurality. Flotow concludes that the late 20th century – with its thorough exploration of gender, identity, language and power – has been a very fruitful one for translation studies.

Nicole Baumgarten compares the varying strategies of textualizing the construction of gender in the James Bond movies, both in the original English and in the German versions. The James Bond adventures are only one instance of both the pervasive presence of Anglo-American products in the Western world and of the textualizing of women as marketable products ready for popular consumption. This study evinces that, while the original Bond films show a patronizing character, the German translations – through 'cultural filtering' – try to cut away their most discriminating aspects towards women.

Carmen Ríos and **Manuela Palacios** explore, from a feminist perspective, the connections between translation, nationalism and gender. The Irish writers studied (and the translations into Galician carried out in the early 20th century) show a similar symbolic construction of the nation as feminine. Both nationalist projects – those of Ireland and Galicia – seem to be in the hands of men: the nation is a woman with virgin-like features, while heroism is constructed in masculine terms. We see the masculine appropriation of the discourse on nationalism.

Rosemary Arrojo illustrates – in Moacyr Scliar's *Notas ao Pé da Página* (Footnotes, 1995) and in Italo Calvino's *Se una notte di inverno un viaggiatore* (If on a Winter's Night a Traveller, 1979) – how the ancient theme of betrayal in translation has been charged with sexual overtones. Both Calvino and Scliar build up their stories as competitions between men for the attention of a woman. Both (male) authors establish associations between 'woman' and 'text' – thus confirming the 'gender metaphorics' advocated by Chamberlain (1992 [1988]) – and their plots revolve playfully around the readers' textual/sexual expectations. Although both Calvino and Scliar seem to challenge the love triangle denounced by Chamberlain (author/text/translator), in the end neither of them does so – the (Barthesian) pleasure of productive reading/translating and the authorial power remain masculine privileges, part and parcel of Western culture.

The article written by **Janet S. Shibamoto Smith** shows the extent to which translations from English are such powerful cross-cultural instruments as to help to naturalize and introduce new literary or sexual conventions into non-English cultures. This is illustrated with examples from Harlequin translations into Japanese, which have transformed the Japanese romance fiction, providing Japanese readers with new – and often conflicting – discourses about romance (affecting the physical presence of lovers, their interactional styles and the construction of the hero/ heroine).

Translating sexual language is a challenging affair – sometimes extremely risky – with deep personal, political and ideological underpinnings. **José Santaemilia** compares the four extant translations of John Cleland's *Fanny Hill* into Spanish, paying special attention to the solutions given to highly sensitive sex-related terms. Sex is one of the most sensitive areas in any given culture, constituting an index of the state of the translating culture. A preliminary conclusion out of women's and men's translations seems to indicate that women as translators seem to show a tendency towards the softening – and even desexualization – of sexual references but, when women's status is at stake, they rather tend (mildly) towards dysphemism and moral censure.

The study by **Orest Weber**, **Pascal Singy** and **Patrice Guex** focuses on socio-medical encounters in Lausanne hospitals, between medical professionals and migrant patients, through cultural mediators/interpreters. One of the most conspicuous gendered factors is the proximity between women in medical encounters. When male intermediaries are present, women patients feel severely constrained when talking about certain topics (AIDS, rape, family violence or sexuality in general) and important communication difficulties are likely to arise. The sex of migrant patients and interpreters, then, proves to be a key factor in the success of medical encounters.

Ulrika Orloff analyses the way in which gender struggles convince us of the fragility of such seemingly stable concepts and social institutions as motherhood or the family. The emergence in recent years of NRTs (New Reproductive Technologies) is bringing about sudden – and unforeseen – changes in the perception of *creativity* and *procreation* as male domains. This male supremacy in art, language or literature is further eroded by, for example, current performative views of gender (see Butler 1990) whereby gender is 'drag' and gender(ed) and sexual identities are no longer stable ontologies but rather the results of repeated and conscious imitations. Both NRTs and translation represent a challenge to the notion of male-associated creativity/authority, to the marital contract as a material proof of fatherhood, and to the cultural obsession with originality, biological origin or even identity.

The closing article, by **Şebnem Susam-Sarajeva**, revolves around the advantages and disadvantages found in a course on gender and translation, taught at the University of Helsinki. As is widely known, most research in the field has had an overt feminist bias; today, however, there is a conscious move towards broadening the scope and including also research into how other gender(ed) and sexual identities – female as well as male, homosexual, transgender, etc. – are constructed. From a Finnish perspective, the combativeness of American or European feminist translators is met with strong resistance. Students do not find it appropriate to manipulate texts to further a feminist agenda. In their opinion, feminist 'intervention' should be more accurate and respectful, and also limited to academic circles. While not denying the immense popularity of gender-related approaches to practically all disciplines, there is sometimes a widespread feeling that they are a mere passing fashion.

The idea of translation as a consciously manipulative activity has not escaped the attention of translators and translation scholars across time, and is variously present in such historically loaded concepts as 'adaptation', 'hermeneutics', 'metaphrase', 'imitation', *'belles infidèles'*, 'paraphrase', 'scandal', and so on. More recently, a group of scholars based mainly in Belgium and the Netherlands (Lambert, Hermans, Holmes, Toury, etc.) adopted the name of *manipulation school* because they were convinced that "all translation implies a degree of manipulation of the source text for a certain purpose" (Hermans 1985: 11), with particular references to the manipulation of literary traditions. In fact, few will dispute the fact that translation – though ideally in pursuit of such romantic fallacies as truth, fidelity or accuracy – always ends up being a source – or a reflection – of difference and a distorting lens which tailors realities and/or identities to suit conscious ideological needs.

Both translation studies and gender/sex studies are giving a new thrust to the analyses not only of manipulation of literary traditions, texts or genres, but also of gender(ed) or sexual identities and stereotypes. Manipulation is a broad concept including, among other things, the rewriting of others' lives (as in *spiritual lives* i.e. nuns' narratives recounting their religious experiences), or in the reversal of moral or ethical issues (see Orloff, this volume), or the perverse translation of reality (as exemplified in the military world-scale redefinition of such basic concepts as 'liberty', 'evil' vs 'good', 'terrorism', etc.). Behind all manipulation there is always a *translating* process, a process which necessarily affects identity and which, most likely, starts with identity.

Without a doubt, *gender, sex*[3] and *translation* are among the most widely used terms in the domains of human communication. The three terms are sites of critical and ideological contention, of practical as well as theoretical (dis)agreements, of projection/rejection of individual and collective identities – in fact, they have today become challenging discourses against which we can measure the unstable construction of human identities. They will help us understand that manipulation is intrinsically connected to power, to a desire to redefine reality, to a desire to control behaviour and to shape identities (or entire literary or cultural traditions)

---

[3] Although usually taken as a complementary pair of terms, *gender* and *sex* are developing today into highly diversified and specific epistemologies and methodologies. See Butler (1990, 1993); Talbot (1998); Cameron and Kulick (2003); Eckert and McConnell-Ginet (2003).

to particular ideological expectations. We should not be so naïve as to deny that translators – and particularly feminist translators – manipulate reality. Yes, they do manipulate realities and identities – as much as politicians, bank managers, flower-sellers or TV freaks do.

We should do our best to transform gender/sex and translation studies into an antidote to fight the belligerent attitudes against truth represented by world politicians or multinational companies in (in)famous episodes – like the war in Iraq – which have shown, on both sides of the conflict, unprecedented attacks against and limitations to freedom of speech and thought. All translation is, I agree, a restriction on truth, but not on one's personal or ethical freedom. Translation seems to me one of the most privileged loci for the (re)production and (re)negotiation of identities, because it makes them visible or invisible, worthy or unworthy, etc.

Certainly, the translation of gender or sex is not an innocent affair, and it involves not only a cross-cultural transfer but a cross-ideological one. The intersection between translation (which is contradictory and multiple *per se* – subservient and subversive at the same time) and gender/sex makes possible phenomena such as the imposition of a state ideological censorship (see Rabadán 2000b); the misrepresentation of reality (as can be seen in the sexualization of literature, cinema or erotica – see Arrojo, Baumgarten and Santaemilia, this volume); the translation of political or social aspirations in gender(ed) terms (see Ríos and Palacios, this volume); the rewriting of whole literary traditions in moral terms; or even the unceasing moral(istic) rewritings of individual writers, traditions, lifestyles, sexual options, ethical attitudes, etc. (see Shibamoto, Flotow, Weber *et al.*, this volume).

As we know (Simon 1996; Flotow 1997; Godayol 2000), translation is an archetypically 'feminine' activity, one which has been sexualized as 'woman' (let us remember the *'belles infidèles'* paradigm or the ideas held by Schleiermarcher or Steiner). Translation is not (and will not be) a neutral affair – it is always provisional, fragmentary, contradictory, polemical, political. A translation always adds something: ideology, political (in)correction, urgency or restraint, etc. All translating projects are manipulatory – including feminist translation. The feminist translation project tries to transcend the metaphorical boundaries set by tradition on women, which Chamberlain (1992[1988]) calls 'gender metaphorics', i.e. a sort of 'metaphorical trap' which subverts all gender-related or sex-related identities. Publications by Arrojo and Flotow bear witness to the fact that there is a heated debate around feminist translation because it is possibly the most explicitly controversial approach, the only one which tries to (re)engender reality along feminist lines and to coin new metaphors and de-gender old (patriarchal) metaphors.

Translation studies as well as gender/sex studies evoke the on-going discursive conflict which is always present in the interaction between men and women. The presentation, representation or version of any gender-related or sex-related issues demands a strong and renewed ethics in favour of a militant respect for all gender and sexual options. We must recognize the immense capabilities of gender/sex and translation studies for generating debates of a fundamentally cross-disciplinary nature within more egalitarian parameters.

As we can see, most of the articles focus on women as an object of study. There is still an urge to rediscover the female words and texts, the female images and their history. There has been over the past few years a serious attempt to rewrite women's participation in history, literature, holy texts, etc. Some would say that this is a passing fashion – reanalyzing women's presence in literature or cinema may be a compensatory attitude but it certainly is not a negative fashion. Let us make this fashion a cultural and ideological necessity. Both translation and gender/sex studies can only make us more aware of the fluidity of meaning(s) and identity(ies), as well as of the complex workings of language, culture and power.

I include here twelve articles on gender, sex and translation. They are, I believe, visible proof of the vitality of an interdisciplinary field of research which is questioning its own practice and which places itself at the centre of an on-going discursive conflict (Cameron 1998; Santaemilia 2000, 2002) that may help us understand the complexity of reality.

I wish to thank Patricia Bou, Sergio Maruenda and Peter Vickers for their help, support and – most important of all – their friendship.

Frontera Spaces
Translating as/like a Woman

PILAR GODAYOL
Universitat de Vic, Spain

Abstract. The theory and practice of translating as/like a woman,
being a political and social discourse that criticizes and subverts
the patriarchal practices which render women invisible, assumes
a feminine subjectivity. That is, it makes plain that the common
basis of its activity is a subject who lives in a feminine body. However, despite sharing a common politics of identity, the different
feminisms, among them those in the field of translation, interpret
feminine subjectivity in different ways. Similarly, they also differ
in their definitions of their universal categories, such as 'women',
'identity', 'gender', 'sex', 'experience' and 'history'. As a result,
some translators cast doubt on the possibility of building a feminist theory of translation given the contingency and mobility of
its universal categories. This raises an urgent question: how can a
politics of identity survive if it does not take into account the idea
that its universal categories must be permanently open and questioning in order to lay the ground for the inclusions or exclusions
of its future demands? This paper attempts to move closer to the
unresolved question of the feminine subject in the practice of translation as/like a woman, as well as in all fields of general feminist
study.

A borderland is a vague and undetermined place created by the emo-
tional residue of an unnatural boundary. It is a constant state of
transition. The prohibited and forbidden are its inhabitants. Los
Atravesados live here: the squint-eyed, the perverse, the queer, the
troublesome, the mongrel, the mulatto, the half-breed, the half-dead;
in short, those who cross over, pass over, or go through the confines
of the "normal". (Anzaldúa 1987: 3)

I think of my own people, the only people I can think of as my own
are transitionals, liminals, border-dwellers, 'world'-travellers, be-
ings in the middle of either/or. (Lugones 1994: 469)

Commenting on these two epigraphs, which reflect on the problems deriving from cultural transmission, is perhaps the best way to introduce the

concept-metaphor of 'Frontera Spaces'. These reflections mark the beginning of a journey which will lead us on to dialogue and discussion about the borderland experience, that liminal existence which characterizes the work of all feminine subjects in translation, and which, as we proceed to study the matter, will spark moments of reflection and self-criticism.

Boundaries, says Gloria Anzaldúa in the first of the epigraphs, have been established throughout history with the objective of distancing those who live inside from those who live outside, separating us from them. Those who create boundaries maintain their integrity by differentiating themselves and their space from that which lies beyond their limits, at the same time expelling all signs of strangeness from their territory. For the person who dwells on the inside, everything that is from outside is strange and foreign. The exclusion of these distorting elements and their banishment to alien lands is then the way of maintaining the power of insiders and legitimizing its expression. In precisely this way, the dominant cultural discourses have constructed and sustained the marginality of feminine intellectuals down through the course of history.

For Maria Lugones, the author of the second of the epigraphs which open this paper, only those who reside in borderland states, and who therefore feel obliged to build bridges of communication between the variant positions they occupy, live in open and heterogeneous structures. Contrary to those who see borderlands as arid and unsafe areas, Lugones claims that it is only in these borderland situations that the best cultural interchanges are produced. However, as Anzaldúa points out in the first epigraph, only *los atravesados* (the daring) dwell in the borderlands. Only those who have no fear of occupying indeterminate positions and who celebrate the opportunity to travel, evolve, mutate, metamorphoze, adopt new 'disguises' and abandon fixed identities, only those people live with the knowledge that they are neither inside nor outside.

The positions of Anzaldúa and Lugones, with whom we have begun this textual journey, are based on the conviction that it is possible to construct a cultural object from the borderlands, from a space in which both subject and object sense themselves to be in contact and in mutual contamination. In large part, this is also the conviction of the person who translates as/like a woman. What, however, does translating as/like a woman mean? Does it imply a non-stable subject who is at home in all those borderland states found in life? Is it possible to construct a politics of identity that presents an absolute, immobile, silent subject? Above all, how can a translation survive if it does not question its subject?

The theory and practice of translating as/like a woman, being a political and social discourse that criticizes and subverts the patriarchal practices which render women invisible, assumes a feminine subjectivity. That is, it makes plain that the common basis of its activity is a subject who, in the words of Milagros Rivera (1994: 62), "vive en un cuerpo sexuado en femenino" (lives in a feminine body). However, despite sharing a common politics of identity, the different feminisms, among them those in the field of translation, interpret and express feminine subjectivity, also known as feminine identification (Fuss 1995), in different ways. Similarly, they also differ in their definitions of their universal categories, such as 'women', 'identity', 'gender', 'sex', 'experience' and 'history'. As a result, some translators, like Lori Chamberlain (1988) and Amy Kaminsky (1993), suggest that these are unstable starting points for developing either a theory or a practice of translation. For this reason, they cast doubt on the possibility of building a feminist theory of translation given the contingency and mobility of its universal categories.

This raises an urgent question: is it feasible to believe in a politics of identity which, in its definition of itself, claims that its categories are premises which are neither problematic nor questionable? How can a politics of identity survive if it does not take into account the idea that its universal categories must be permanently open? Thus, if we wish to move closer to the unresolved question of the feminine subject in the practice of translation as/like a woman, as well as in all fields of general feminist study, we must first inquire into the theoretical problems and the practical limitations of the concept itself.

The first problem challenging any attempt to establish the concept 'feminine subject translator' is the essentialism into which the intersection gender/translation falls. Were a stable subject to become the starting point for a social and political theory, such as the practice of translating as/like a woman, this would imply the irrevocable closing of the debate regarding the construction of the subject itself, and, therefore, the immobilization of the subject/object relationship. The desire to elaborate a more definitive theory embracing a more definitive subject in order to facilitate the reconstruction of textual complexity in a translation is easily understood. However, there are several advantages in reading the feminine subject as a permanently contingent and contentious territory, one which shuns the immobility of fundamentalist formulations and categorical universalities. Only in this way can we avoid falling into a dangerous homogenization and simplification of the hermeneutic processes of translation. For this reason, I believe that the fact of questioning and problematizing the feminine subject in the practice of translating as/like a woman means accepting that contingency can never be eliminated in the interweaving of gender and translation. Consequently, no translation can ever share the same feminine subjectivity as another since this would involve the stabilization of its meaning. Translating as/like a woman implies, then, proposing a non-stable and contingent representation of the feminine subject, recognizing, at the same time, that one cannot write about a subject without essentializing it (Scott 1992: 33). Nevertheless, it is easy to imagine the difficulties such an approach entails. How, for example, can we reconcile the representation of heterogeneous subjects with the universality of their social contract? How can we lay claim to a general politics of identity without eliminating difference?

Singularity and plurality in feminist study practices are terms which are in constant conflict (Cixous 1986; Kaminsky 1993; Scott 1992, 1996; Suleri 1992). It is important, then, that the universal category 'women', being both a particular and shared representation, be kept completely open. Even so, one of the most important problems faced by feminisms is the fact that the category 'women' seems to have to describe the base of its social and cultural identity. This has given rise to debates among the advocates of essentialist and constructionist postures (Fuss 1989, 1995). On one hand, the essentialists maintain that there is a feminine essence which lies outside social and cultural limits. The constructionists, on the other hand, insist that the feminine identity is a historical construct and that therefore the category 'women' is the result of complex discursive processes.

This paradox regarding the status of woman, which has for many years been the cause of ideological conflicts among feminisms, cannot be made non-problematic. Rather, we should embrace it as a concept which involves constant transfer, and in this way avoid the polarization of feminist study into antagonistic camps. Only by accepting that the category 'women' represents the fluid base of its practices can translation as/like a woman free the concept from the binary notions which currently frame all discussion. In this way, the category 'women' may be used in future discourses, including those of translators, as one which is open to revision and (re)signification. Only if, in contrast to the static meanings of hegemonic discourses, the idea frees itself from formulation in terms of dichotomies where, mistakenly, binary oppositions are simply mutually exclusive and never mutually communicative, will we be able to speak and reflect about the (im)possibilities of identifying the feminine subject in translation.

If the feminine subject translator eludes definition due to its mobility, in this sense we may also add that believing in a stable reference point in order to create a theory of translation which is non-problematic amounts to paralyzing the (re)signification of the concept itself, throwing up a hurdle to dialogue between the subject and object of translation. Further, the feminine subject translator can never be fully represented, a fact which brings to the fore the multifaceted character of its existence. The true representation of the feminine subject translator is, then, the space which is difference. That is, the definition which is at once included in and excluded from the representation itself – the space which permits (re)consideration, (re)modeling and (re)formulation of the previous configurations of meanings.

We should remember that the practice of translation as/like a woman – and here lies the heart of the controversy between feminist translation theorists – must be based on a permanent criticism of the subject itself since, as Carol Maier (1994: 67) points out "translation must problematize identity". Translation as/like a woman does not mean translating bearing in mind the multiple identities the translator has accumulated throughout her professional career, but rather translating from a borderland, a reflective and self-critical space in which the representations of the feminine subject translator are constantly modified and recreated. Perhaps, translating as/like a woman should not be understood as a utopian or chimerical space of political and social emancipation. Perhaps, instead, we should begin to read it as a borderland in which identity and textuality are constantly (re)written from a point of view of commitment and negotiation.

It is important to bear in mind that the existence of a feminine subject translator, albeit complex, spontaneous, contingent and dynamic, cannot ascertain the truth of the translated text, but neither can it fail completely to ascertain it. In reality, translating as/like a woman means accepting the implications of reading and interpreting from the interweaving of gender/ text in which every sign of gender is negotiable and every translation of a text is unique and unrepeatable. Thus, if gender is not fixed in the text, we may say that all hermeneutic translation practice as/like a woman carries with it a tug-of-war between text and author, between text and translator. The gender signs shape the work, which is, on the one hand, a source of tension which problematizes, and on the other, a negotiable practice on which we can (re)conduct our own reading.

For this reason, if we remove the conventional baggage from the concepts of 'gender', 'sex' and 'women', treating them instead as points which are open to political debate, the translator can opt for a form of translation which not only questions identity but also problematizes it. The person who translates as/like a woman refuses to view her practices in terms of constructing normative, static meanings. Rather, she seeks to ensure that her style of work embraces the implications of reading and interpreting the interaction of gender/text, keeping in mind that all texts and all subjects say what they say on the basis of what they do not say. Both a translated text and feminine subjectivity must be described not only in terms of the content of their discourse, but also in terms of what is excluded.

If the process of translating as/like a woman avoids postulating the existence of a feminine subject translator as a fixed, immobile, absolute category – as the traditional ontological arguments do (Butler 1990: 1-34), this means it can never ascertain the absolute truth of any translation. This in turn implies that feminist translation can only aim for permanent reflection and self-criticism in its representations, its methods, applications, focalizations, textual processes and provisional tactical decisions.

Finally, to return to the concept-metaphor of the borderlands with which we began since it has served as guide throughout this textual journey. 'Frontera Spaces' is an allegory for translating as/like a woman. In the end, what is translating as/like a woman if not situating oneself in an indeterminate space, neither inside nor outside, questioning and problematizing one's own identity? It is an activity that involves making use not of speciously neutral, so-called objective strategies, but rather dynamic procedures and tactics, which negotiate and are negotiable, open and contingent, which never assume the absolute totality of a feminine subjectivity in translation. Thus the non-absolute and non-categorical representation of the feminine subject in the practice of translating as/like a woman neither means the collapse of nor demonstrates the utopian nature of its politics of identity. Rather, it means the demand for a kind of subjectivity different from the conventional, predetermined and immobilized subjectivity of patriarchal discourses. It is a question of a feminine subjectivity which demands openness in readings and meanings, which makes plain that both text and translator say what they say on the basis of what they do not say, and which implies that all feminine subjects neither entail nor deny textual truth in translation. This means to assert our claim to difference, to the feminine, on the basis of questioning and problematising identity in translation. This is tantamount to living the possible impossibility of translating on the border.

The Creation of a "Room of One's Own"

Feminist Translators as Mediators between
Cultures and Genders

MICHAELA WOLF
Universität Graz, Austria

Abstract. In the course of the 18th century, an increasing number of women tried to create their own space both through the formation of a specific literary discourse and the formation of a new professional group, the female writer. This paper discusses the way in which female translators – in a historical as well as in a contemporary context – can 'gender' their social and intellectual environment, thus contributing to the formation of female individuality through translation. Within the broader context of women's constitution of a 'female image' in the period of the Enlightenment, and drawing on the biographies of two German translators, Luise Gottsched and Therese Huber, the paper will illustrate the ways in which these two translators subverted contemporary men-made translation practices and translation theories. In the second part of the paper it will be shown that to a certain extent, even though under obviously different conditions, women are still struggling for a "room of one's own" in the translational domain. This is highlighted by the presentation of the results of a research project which was carried out in Austria three years ago and which focused on a comprehensive record of the state of the art of feminist translation in the various fields of research, teaching and practice in German-speaking countries. The emphasis of the project was on a theoretical survey of the fields of feminist translation and feminist translation studies, detailed surveys conducted in publishing houses concerning their 'policies' in relation to feminist translation, enquiries into guidelines for non-sexist language use in national and international institutions dealing with translation as well as in translation agencies, and interviews with feminist translators focusing on their working conditions.

In the 18th century, in the wake of the ideas of the Enlightenment, we can witness an increasing number of women who created their own space through the formation of a specific literary discourse, and, in institutional terms, through the formation of a quite new professional group – the female writer.

This paper will discuss the role of women translators in such a new context and the way in which they were able to 'gender' their social and intellectual environment. These questions will be discussed by referring to two translators: Therese Huber and Luise Gottsched. The discussion of their life and work will show the different degrees of resistance they were able to manifest towards contemporary men-made translation practices and translation theories. The illustration of this continuous process of formation of female individuality through translation will lead into a discussion of the female translator's situation at the beginning of this century. Three years ago, we carried out a project focusing on a comprehensive record of the state of the art of feminist translation in the various fields of research, teaching and practice in German speaking countries. The major results of this research project will be discussed in the second part of the paper and will illustrate how these developments which took shape 200 years ago are still under way.

1. The constitution of a 'female image' in the 18th century

It has been shown that 18th century Western society, for the first time and under various aspects, engaged with the nature of woman, with her opportunities and limits as well as her 'gender character'. This can be attributed to the insights of the Enlightenment, which dealt primarily with the discussion of the rights and duties of mankind in society in terms of natural right. This does not mean, however, that women were involved in these new discussions, although they were the object of the reflections on newly constructed social conditions. Diderot's definition of 'woman' as 'the man's female' perpetuated woman's image distorted by male projections and continued to hinder the creation of female individuality. Equally, the texts written in this period 'on women' ('Über die Weiber') were not intended for women, but for a small circle of – male – representatives of the Enlightenment movement. Nevertheless, it cannot be denied that the majority of the bourgeoisie attributed some mental abilities to women and that the so-called "optimism in terms of education" of the period also included the figure of the woman (Dülmen 1992: 21f.). The new discourse on MANkind developed during the Enlightenment, however, was bound to contribute in the longer run to the constitution of an image of – at least intellectual – women, which in the 19th century would gain more importance for the whole of society. The female translator's role in this context should not be underestimated.

It was mainly within literary discourse that women were able to create their own space, a "room of one's own", as Virginia Woolf called it, where they could articulate themselves. As a matter of fact, the activities of writers and translators were – with a few exceptions – the only possibilities for women to exercise an employment. In some cases writing activity was even the basis for financial independence from male relatives and as such a form of emancipation of the typical female role in 18th century society (see Walter 2002: 25).

2. Luise Adelgunde Victorie Gottsched, geb. Kulmus (1713-1762)

The example of Luise Gottsched shows the problems a well-educated, self-conscious woman was confronted with when she started to think against the grain of society's conventions with regard to the intellectual woman's behaviour in general and her husband's expectations towards his intellectual wife in particular. Luise came from an enlightened bourgeois family. After her marriage with Johann Christoph Gottsched, she became the fellow crusader of her husband – a 'Reformer of German literature', who tried to import French theatre models to Germany via translation, in order to instrumentalize them for his own comedy concept. This can be viewed as a programmatic attempt to boost German literature through French models with the intention to prove Germany's literary equality of value.

Luise, who became known to posterity with the feminine form of her husband's name – Gottschedin – produced a great number of translations, adaptations and own pieces. In her translations of pieces written by Molière, Destouches or Pope, according to her husband's theatre reform, she carried out cuts and re-writings and inserted new figures. Her interventions in the texts did not stand for the enforcement of female individuality, nevertheless her activities as a woman in terms of translation sociology can be traced on two levels. First, for various of her translations she wrote prefaces in which she commented on the formation of her translations, pointing for example to satirical elements (see Grimberg 1998: 17 and Hinck 1965: 202). The self-confidence of her argumentation in these paratexts is in sharp contrast with the canon predominant at the time, which favoured the humble translator who modestly and discreetly presented her or his œuvre and slavishly asked the readers for recognition. On the other hand, after breaking with her husband, she self-consciously selected the texts she intended to translate. As a result, after a hard working period of ten years, in 1757 she concluded the translation of eleven volumes on the "History of the Royal Academy of Science at Paris". Generally speaking, Luise Gottsched stands for a self-confident woman with a broad education, who matured from an anonymous writer to a partner with – at least intellectually – equal rights in her husband's theatre project and who, finally, through her gradually gained independence, could claim social and cultural recognition in the German literary world.

3.   Therese Huber, née Heyne (1764-1829)

A quite different example for the formation of a female personality is Therese Huber. She seemed to have become active in translation through her two husbands, the well-known circumnavigator of the earth Georg Forster, and Ludwig Ferdinand Huber, literary critic and translator himself. It was mainly financial need as a permanent feature of her second marriage, which forced her to resort to mass produced translations. Therese seemed to have had a hard time while she learned the translation craft, as is proved by one of her letters to an old friend – a fact that seemed to be constitutive for female activity *extra muros* in the 18th century:

> I tried to translate Louvets 'divorcé necessaire'. Huber read the text, shook his head, and cancelled the whole passage. I cried – and translated again, and again, and in the end I learnt it. (Huber, letter to Reinhold, 4.7.1805, in Hahn & Fischer 1993: 56, my translation)

Therese's translation activity, despite its great importance in nearly every phase of her life, is not explicitly documented. The relevant literature points to her important contribution in her two husbands' translation production (Roche 1994: 103f and 1997: 337; Leuschner 1995: 17) as well as to the use of Ferdinand Huber's name as pseudonym (Hahn 1993: 54). Two points seem to be decisive for this 'invisibility'. On the one hand, anonymity of female translators is still widespread in the 18th century. This is mostly due to the fact that the translations produced by women were exclusively distributed through men (editors, booksellers, etc.) (Gokhale 1996: 39). Equally, the fact that the activities of female writers and translators were socially frowned upon plays an important role. On the other hand, the almost symbiotic collaboration with her husbands makes it generally very difficult to distinguish the contribution of the partners involved. As hinted in various letters written by Therese, the work done by the husband and wife had a character of completion and reciprocal enrichment – a fact which somewhat relativizes the question of the identification of authorship (Roche 1997: 343). As far as the translation strategies adopted by the Hubers is concerned, Therese, in her biography on Huber, mentions his 'faithful' translation manner, which seems to have caused him problems with his editors and which she, too, obviously criticized (Roche 1997: 335). The employment of a gendered language, on the other hand, was still not a question for women translators in the 18th century. The feminist literary scholar Sigrid Weigel explains this 'shortcoming':

> [T]hey had to make use of a language regulated by men in order to escape their roles determined by men. (Weigel 1985, in Gokhale 1996: 49)

Although Therese – contrary to many women translators of her time – did not comment on her translations, some parts of her literary production repeatedly criticize existing social prejudices against women, such as those against unmarried mothers or against mistresses of nobility (Köpke 1988: 128). Equally, marriage should not remain the only sanctioned form of existence for women (Hahn and Fischer 1993: 62). It is also interesting to note that the recognition gained by Therese when she was still alive, clearly distances her from her husband's qualifications. Nevertheless, her social and intellectual reputation – according to contemporary tradition – was nearly exclusively seen in relationship to her husband. In 1804, Benjamin Constant, for instance, writes in his diary: "I visited Huber; his wife is much more witty than he is" (quoted in Roche 1997: 359, my translation).

4. The female translator's daily life in the 18th century

In what follows, two aspects which have already been touched on before, will be discussed in more detail in order to shed light on the female translator's activity in the 18th century. First, the question of payment is a central one, especially in view of the relative economic independence aimed at by many translators, and second – in close relationship with the first one – the problem of self-exploitation will be discussed, which in some cases led to a complete physical and mental exhaustiveness of the women.

As far as payment is concerned, most women who translated together with their husbands, were not directly paid for their activity, but at the best on behalf of their husband. Nevertheless, women obviously were not paid less than men: for one sheet (today 8 pages) they were paid between 3 and 4 German thaler; the minimum salary of a worker's family at the beginning of the 19th century was about 100 thaler (Bachleitner 1989: 28f.; Roche 1994: 107f.). Especially renowned translators, who had made themselves known as authors or scientists, could even get 10 thaler. Discrimination against women, in this respect, refers only indirectly to their activity as translator, as they had only limited opportunities to become famous writers, securing themselves in this way a chance for better payment. Basically, it cannot be said that women in the 18th century gained economic independence which was not dictated – as in the case of Therese Huber, Caroline Schlegel-Schelling and others – by financial need. The constraint to independence was thus not necessarily accompanied by the social acceptance of this independence. This makes Therese's efforts to stress her prioritizing of domestic and family duties rather than of her intellectual duties understandable. Luise Gottsched, too, was aware of her unloved, although necessary domestic duties when she wrote:

> Every day I have to fill my head with bagatelles, with domestic
> and economic troubles, which I have always disdained as the most
> miserable human duties [...]. (letter to Dorothee Henriette von
> Runckel, quoted in Dülmen 1992: 103, my translation)

The exhaustion of women from different social settings, including female translators, is another feature repeatedly dealt with in literature. The overburdening of women, on the one hand, was due to the multiplicity of functions most of the women had to exercise simultaneously. This is also shown in a letter written by Therese Huber:

> I write my things in the hustle and bustle of my children, tired
> from servants' labour, from sitting up with my sick children [...].
> (Huber 1810, quoted in Roche 1997: 340, my translation)

In addition, the enormous physical and mental strain, to which (also) female translators were disposed, was stressed through the pressure put on women who appeared in public. In the tense relationship between the danger of being kept away from certain circles and ambiences, on the one hand, and the independence which was often forced upon women and sometimes even longed-for, on the other hand, female translators were often doomed to failure. Luise Gottsched's life for example, sacrificed for the sake of her husband's intellectual edifying nature, had to pay a high price. In a letter to her friend Dorothee Henriette von Runckel, Luise wrote shortly before her death:

> You ask for the reason of my illness? Here it is. 28 years of unin-terrupted work, grief in secrecy, six years of uncountable tears whose flow only God has seen. (Gottsched 1762, quoted in Dülmen 1992: 379, my translation)

As has been seen, women translating in history were always forced to posit themselves in terms of society and intellect, while male translators, as social protagonists, mostly were not exposed to these constraints. The insight into the lack of "a room of one's own" as well as the social contextualization of female translators in the 18th century entails an interpretative view of their activity. Such a view questions, beyond aesthetic criteria, the conditions of the formation of their translations and analyzes their texts in the light of the social and material criteria under which they were created. In such a perspective the long-term impact of their activity gains relevance, which documents the necessary re-determination of the female subject and which, in the final analysis, continually contributes to an image of women which can be opinion-forming for society. In order to achieve these goals, the historical conditions responsible for the creation and fixing of such oppressive situations have to be detected. Interdisciplinary research of course is indispensable for this task.

5. Feminist translation in theory and practice today

During the last 10 or 15 years, the discussion of the process of formation of female individuality through translation has become an important issue in translation studies. Two years ago, we started a project at our department to investigate the situation of female translators as well as the state of the art of feminist translation in research and teaching in German speaking countries (see Messner and Wolf 2000). The emphasis of the project was on a theoretical survey of the fields of feminist translation and feminist translation studies, detailed interviews conducted in publishing houses concerning their 'policies' in feminist translation, enquiries into guidelines for non-sexist language use in national and international institutions dealing with translation as well as in translation agencies, and interviews with feminist translators focusing on their working conditions. In what follows I would like to present some of the most crucial results of this project, which was concluded with an international conference on feminist translation (see Messner and Wolf 2001).

The following questions have been at the basis of our project:

- Is it true that today so-called 'feminist language and discourse' is being widely adopted in translation, and that obviously female translators have a stronger gender consciousness than 10 or 15 years ago? If this is the case, what are the factors responsible for the reception of such translations on the translation market? Is it a specific training at the various translation studies departments? Or is it a more constructive co-operation between clients, commissioners, translators and, eventually, readers? Or is it both?
- Another question is: is there a – scientifically consolidated – exchange between translators practising feminist translation?
- Has the interest in gender-based language in general created a new market for translations?
- Have translation strategies been developed which feminist oriented translators can resort to for various text types?

5.1. Feminist translation studies → *in the beginning not yet institutionalized*

First inquiries with questionnaires and interviews have shown that as a discipline feminist translation studies is only in its beginnings as far as its institutionalization is concerned. Nevertheless, a great variety of research fields are being pursued on: historical topics, Bible translation, translation as contribution to the formation of feminist consciousness and translation in the perspective of feminist linguistics. What is striking is the interdisciplinary character of the activities in research and teaching as well as the obvious lack of specific research projects. What is even more striking is that in German speaking countries as well as in most other European countries, research is almost exclusively done through the individual initiatives of engaged female translation scholars.

5.2. Feminist translation practice

For the survey of the working conditions of feminist translators we tried to approach the latter through professional associations, publishing houses, several networks such as 'BücherFrauen', 'Sisters in Crime', 'Werkstatt Frauensprache' as well as mailing lists. The reports gave an interesting account of the feminist approaches in the translators' practical work as well as of the problems they are confronted with.

5.2.1. Working conditions

As far as the working conditions are concerned, the statements of 46 translators could be analyzed, out of which 85 % work as translators of literary and scientific texts for publishing houses, and only 15 % translate 'pragmatic texts' for translation agencies and firms. The generally bad image of the translator's profession in the public, which becomes apparent through the disregard of their work as well as the phenomenon of invisibility, might also be due to the fact that most of the women translators for obvious reasons carry out their activities at home. This is particularly true for the domains of literary translation and the translation of non-fictional books. Internet and telecommunication largely facilitate the job of the freelancers, but it is not isolation which is regarded as the main disadvantage of their profession by translators. The exchange between translators mainly takes place on a virtual basis, a fact which contributes to the decrease of social contacts. In addition, many translators do not leave their homes for days due to time pressure.

Regarding co-operation with publishing houses in general, the situation continues to be precarious. According to the opinion of most of the translators, the issue of inclusive language is simply ignored by most of the publishing houses. Translations are still expected to be 'fluently written and discreet': they therefore should pretend to be originals, and translators should not be too much in evidence with their own comments. As a consequence, the insertion of forewords, afterwords, footnotes etc. still seems to be an exception. Even renowned translators with a long professional experience find disapproval with proof readers, if they do not produce 'fluent' translations. Nevertheless, most of the committed feminist translators do not give in and struggle for a space of visibility.

80 % of the women who participated in our survey had already translated for publishers concentrating on or dealing exclusively with women literature. The co-operation with this specific type of publishing houses proved to be quite complex. On the one hand, publishers expect translators to use a so-called 'female language', on the other, they do not really decide to opt in favour of the consequent adoption of inclusive language and discourse in translation. One exception is the series *Ariadne* of the

Argument Verlag, which produces mainly detective stories and gives out a style sheet for translators, which includes feminist language use in translations.

The genres where feminist translation is mostly practised is belles lettres (mainly lesbian novels and female detective novels), specialist feminist texts and texts in general which address women as readers. In the last few years, translators of cultural political texts or even advertisements have become increasingly aware of political correctness and repeatedly aim at adopting it also in translation.

5.2.2. Situation in publishing houses

An important point in the survey were the questionnaires sent to 56 publishing houses calling themselves 'women publishers' or which publish 'women's series' in translation. The response rate was 41 %. 30 % of the literature published by these publishing houses are translations, about 3 % of all books are multilingual editions, and about 67 % are German originals. The period considered was 1998 to 2000.

In the women publishers' lists, the translators' name shows up in nearly 69 % of all cases, clearly more than in publishing houses with women's series. In the latter, translators were mentioned by name in only 17 % of all cases. 91 % of all translations for women publishing houses are done by women, only 3 % by men, whereas in women's series only 50 % are done by women and 33 % by men.

5.2.3. Professional associations

Professional associations are generally sceptical about feminist translation, and many of them directly or indirectly reject them for the sake of 'legibility' or 'linguistic aesthetics', as they call it. The respect of the 'holy original' is obviously still stubbornly stuck in many heads. Although most of the associations do not want to close their eyes to changing conditions in language use as well as changing views in society, they are obviously afraid of excessively 'radical' measures and suggest rather half-hearted solutions: inclusive language should be used, but in a way that nobody notices.

Another field we touched on in our inquiries was translation offices and agencies. These results will not be presented here, however, because they are not really revealing for the questions we posed for this paper.

5.2.4. Guidelines for inclusive translations

Manuals, handbooks, guidelines, thesauri or feminist dictionaries are valuable tools for feminist translators at least on a lexical level. In order to investigate the adoption of such tools in organisations and institutions, which deal with translation, we sent questionnaires to 102 institutions in Austria, Germany and Switzerland. The result was quite surprising, as there seems to be a rethinking in many organisations, mostly those active internationally: they are becoming increasingly aware of the necessity to make women more visible in texts – a fact that is at least proved by the use of in-house style sheets for inclusive language. On the other hand, feminist dictionaries, feminist encyclopaedias and other pertinent literature, serve in some institutions as means of orientation and sensitizing for the composition of feminist translations.

6. Conclusion

If, by way of conclusion, we compare the working conditions and the image of female translators in the 18th century and today, we realize that a re-orientation is under way. Today the question of the translator's identity in the translation process is no longer a no-man's or no-woman's land, and the translator's activity is continuously being re-evaluated. The increasing awareness that translation activity is being carried out in the context of the gender and the social role of the female translator, despite numerous setbacks, has led to a more intensive perception of feminist translators as well as feminist translation among the public. Nevertheless, the contribution of feminist translators in the process of raising awareness and consequently of the formation of critical attitudes in the production and consumption of feminist texts in general, in some countries – like in Austria at the moment, seems to be in danger in view of misogynistic social and cultural politics which are calling women back into the kitchen. Generally speaking, however, we can say that the developments initiated about 200 years ago are the beginning of a process where the female subject *qua* translator can be seen as both a structured and a structuring agent in society.

Gender(ing) Theory
Rethinking the Targets of Translation Studies in Parallel with Recent Developments in Feminism[1]

M. ROSARIO MARTÍN
Universidad de Salamanca, Spain

Abstract. This paper grew out of the conviction that drawing parallels between the evolution of gender studies and translation studies may be enlightening in order to foster new developments in our discipline. Firstly, comparing the evolution in the definition of the objects which are at the very basis of these two movements, i.e., the concepts of 'woman' and 'translation', allows us to posit that translation studies could enlarge its horizon by revising and de-essentializing (emulating the move in gender studies in relation to the concept of 'woman') both the ideal definition of translation that has traditionally been in force and the social yet biased definition of translation which descriptive translation studies claims as the (only) point of departure. In the second place, the comparison seems to be helpful not only in discovering the flaws of descriptivist approaches but also in questioning and problematizing the core assumptions of mainstream feminist translation theories. Gender studies, in short, proves to be instructive not only for redefining the general targets of the discipline but also for inspiring new feminist translation agendas which aim to circumvent the risk of essentialism.

In the last two decades, a considerable number of publications have looked into the analogy that can most apparently be established between 'women' and 'translation' on the grounds of their common historical position of inferiority; in other words, into the various dimensions which add to what Lori Chamberlain diagnosed as the 'feminization of translation' in her now classic essay ([1988]1992). In this regard, translation, like women, has been perceived to have been historically neglected and devalued, the 'weak' term in a hierarchical and somehow gendered cultural system privileging a 'strong' and 'active' (masculine) conception of authorship;

[1] This essay is part of the research project "El lenguaje de las artes visuales: terminología, traducción, normalización", PB 98-0272, financed by the Spanish Ministry of Culture and Education.

translators, for their part, have also been seen to have been invisible, merely expected to perform a reproductive function or, in any event, an activity denigrated as 'inferior', 'secondary' or simply 'feminine'. Undoubtedly, this type of work comparing and identifying 'translation' and 'woman' on the basis of their traditional oppressed and devalued status has been extremely productive, inasmuch as it has shed new light on the profound underestimation of the profession and prompted the desire to challenge it. In this paper, nevertheless, we will try to extrapolate the parallel to the meta-level, to the discourses that in our day and age deal with translation and women, and more precisely to their evolution in time. In *Translation and Gender* (1997: 1), Luise von Flotow observes that "although gender studies and translation studies may be contemporaneous fields of scholarship, their development has not been parallel". It is our contention nevertheless that Translation Studies may productively benefit from looking at the development seen in the concepts and basic tenets used by feminism. The larger tradition of this vindicative movement, in our opinion, may well teach us about some of the flaws to be avoided in the process of reevaluating and affirming translation in which Translation Studies has (either openly or incidentally) played a major role. One area in which the parallel may prove instructive is the presumed nature of the object (or *subject*) which is at the basis of vindications, that is to say, the very definition accorded to 'woman' and 'translation'.

Needless to say, one of the tasks which feminist theory first undertook was to demystify, to use Linda Bell's title (1983), the *visions of women* prevailing in society, to unearth the concept of 'woman', the point of departure for any feminist theory and politics. As women have always occupied the position of the Object, the concept in which our self-definition was to be grounded appeared to be mainly an invention by others, a definition developed by, and in any event to the benefit of, a patriarchal system. As Linda Alcoff puts it, the concept proved to be radically problematic as "it is crowded with the overdeterminations of male supremacy" (1988: 405). The definition of translation has also traditionally been controlled by and subject to the interests of other cultural institutions in relation to which it is supposed to have played a merely subservient role. Translation has always been predetermined by the expectations and suspicions of a cultural system indisputably granting an absolute authority to the concept of 'Original', either the Original Text or the Original Author; expectations thus based on the ideals of Sameness and Mimesis, and suspicions (which are at basis of a whole popular imagery about translators as betrayers) that translations systematically flouted these ideals. Even the first attempts to *conceptualize* translation scientifically (undertaken in the 60s and 70s by scholars concerned with the translation of the Holy Scripture), far from explaining what translation really does and is, devoted themselves to the task of outlining what it ought to be in order to claim 'faithfulness' or 'equivalence' to the Original. And even the first attempts to *describe* translation scientifically (carried out by the first linguistics-oriented approaches to translation), far from enquiring into the reasons for the evident shifts and transformations visible in any translation, limited themselves to pointing out the differences in grammar, nuances or details in which translations incurred. Measured as they were against the intouchable and worshipped ideal of the sacrosanct Original Text, existing translations appeared to be irrevocably flawed, imperfect and faulty, even unworthy of being called translations. As Franco Aixelà concludes, prescriptivism, inasmuch as it predetermines the limits of what translation is, inevitably leads to the rejection from the object of study of multiple actualizations of the phenomenon, the understanding of which is radically hampered (2000: 34).

As is widely accepted today (see Venuti 1998: 25-30; Baker 1998: 163-165; Hermans 1999: 31-45), the emergence of Translation Studies as a new discipline owes much to the general acceptance of a descriptive paradigm, as articulated in Gideon Toury's seminal work, which intends to explore and assess translations in their own terms, not as they should be but as they are and do, on account of their actual role and cultural significance in the interaction between cultures. In the light of the enormous contribution of descriptive-oriented research to our current knowledge about the real nature and procedure of translation, there can be no doubt about the importance of this paradigm self-proclaimed to be 'target-oriented' and intended to infer 'norms', 'regularities of behaviour' and even 'predictable laws' of translation departing from a definition that equals 'translation' to the texts *regarded* as such in the target system (Toury 1980: 43). This approach has been extremely useful inasmuch as it has provided irrefutable evidence supporting the claim that translations are not merely a reproduction of the Original and do not only involve a metamorphosis at the linguistic level; rather, embedded as they are in the intricacies of intercultural traffic, where convoluted issues concerning competing ideologies and institutions, cultural representation and power relations obtain, they entail a complex cultural negotiation and an active, productive presence on the part of translators largely exceeding their traditional invisible role. But however fruitful it has proved to be, it is precisely this definition of translation currently accepted in our field that, in our view, is today in need of further revision. The opinion of scholars in the discipline like José Lambert, Clem Robyns, Ovidi Carbonell or Michaela Wolf and, more important, the parallel which can be established with the ontological progression seen in recent trends in feminism leads us to argue that the shift from an ideal to a *social* definition of translation as the point of departure for descriptive research in our field, although productive, is insufficient. Let us not forget that the *social* definition of translation is precisely the source of the invisibility of translation and translators that Translation Studies nowadays seeks to eradicate.

If feminism, or other emancipatory social movements, can teach us something in this regard, it is precisely that claims for visibility cannot be based exclusively on definitions which are the result, or even the cause, of historical subordination. This is precisely the criticism levelled by recent post-structuralist feminist thought at their predecessor: a wave of feminism focused on a politics of 'difference' – 'cultural feminism' in Linda Alcoff's terminology. This trend, aware of the negative interpretation by patriarchy of the attributes linked to 'femininity', devoted their efforts to reappropriate those traditional 'feminine' traits (e.g., passivity, sentimentality, subjectiveness) in order to reappraise them affirmatively (as peacefulness, proclivity to nurture and advanced self-awareness, respectively) (Alcoff 1988: 407). As Alcoff notes, "[c]ultural feminists have not challenged the defining of woman but only that definition given by men" (*Id.*). It could be argued, in this regard, that the descriptive paradigm takes a stance similar to that of the above-mentioned cultural feminism, in that it claims the reevaluation of established translation models, shedding light on their complexity (Toury invites us to take the mission to extremes, towards the formulation of the laws governing translation behaviour [Toury 1991: 186; 1995: 16]) without questioning them at all (indeed, Toury implicitly attributes these laws a normative role when he claims that these should eventually help predict future translation behaviour [Toury 1997: 79-80]). If we are to take advantage of the outcome of the internal debates in feminist theory, it seems that, as the basis of any claim for recognition, this stance proves to be radically problematic by virtue of its essentialist bias and its backward-looking projection. The equation of the behaviours socially expected of the object of vindications with its 'essence' or 'nature', and of its 'normal behaviour' with its 'norms' or 'laws', results in an implicit promotion of the established modes and practices and a tacit rejection of unconventional or subversive behaviour.

Cultural feminism has been seen to perpetuate dominant cultural assumptions about women by rediscovering the notion of 'femininity' as linked to a series of (positively understood) attributes nevertheless developed under oppression, thus questioning the applicability of this category to female behaviour challenging dominant expectations. In parallel, Descriptive Translation Studies, to the extent that they postulate the deduction of the definition of translation from its regular behaviour, can be seen to restrict the category to long-established translation models, to the detriment of experimental approaches and practices dissenting from hegemonic assumptions. It could be argued, in this regard, that in the long run descriptivism falls prey to precisely the same wrong prescriptivism was blamed for, to wit promoting the exclusion from the definition of translation of a whole series of translative practices, in this case those not recognized as such in the social domain. For, if it is the case that translation is largely an invisible phenomenon, it seems at least short-sighted to base the study of trans-lation exclusively on a working definition corresponding to its social perception.

This is precisely the claim that José Lambert (1993, 1995) has put forward to the discipline in the light of his intuitions about the operation of translation in our time, in the epoch of mass communication and the internationalization of discourses. If translation has always been unseen, it is all the more so today, Lambert suggests, as it is ubiquitous (1993: 19). In effect, in our global world, and as illustrated exemplarily in the case in point of international news, the activity of translation pervades all communication, although most commonly it tends to conceal its presence disguised as or mixed with original discourse (*ibid.*: 15). Even though we are on the whole unaware of this fact, our own words are nourished by and packed with translated discourse: concepts, terms and clichés born in other cultures. In this new context translation not only produces what is commonly understood by translation(s), *i.e.*, entire translated text(s); rather, translation (dis)appears in segments, expressions, buzz words, camouflaged as a *fragment* in other texts. This is why Lambert urges us to abandon the idea that, in his opinion, most translation scholars have implicitly adopted, i.e., "that whatever is NOT considered to be translation by a given society would hence not be translation for the scholar either" (1995: 99). If we are really interested in gaining insight into the complexities of the phenomenon of translation, Lambert says, "[w]e have no formal nor rational reasons for excluding text *fragments* from the realm of Translation Studies nor for reducing the concept of translation to autonomous, entire and

well-identified texts" (*ibid.*). Moreover, he thinks, "[w]e are totally wrong
in reducing translations to [...] texts produced by individual writers and
individual translators".

This opinion is coincidental with Sager's (1994) or that shared by some
of the contributors to the special issue entitled *Translation in the Global
Village* (Schäffner 1999), who clearly see that, in a period bearing the
phenomenon of globalization and the emergence of big corporations in
the field of communication, translators rarely work in solitude and are
now (required to be) involved in intercultural practices largely exceeding
the traditional concept of translation based on a text-to-text relation. And
while, faced against this undeniable gap, there are some who think that
"we need to make a clear distinction between the nature of translation on
the one hand and the activites of a translator on the other hand" (Newmark
1999: 152), in our opinion, grounded upon the belief that translation is
less an essence than a contingent construct, this distinction appears to be
a dangerous pretext to broaden the invisibility of translation and translators *qua* translators in the context of computer-mediated communication.
For in a moment when the increase of cross-cultural textual traffic and the
revolution that information technology has introduced to traditional forms
of textuality and text processing have prompted and required a radical
transformation and diversification of the profession and its products, the
insistence on exclusively recognizing the translator's activities as translation when matching its rudimentary definition and therefore on denying
the consideration of translation status to a multiplicity of translative activities, precisely those clearly revealing the immense complexities,
responsibilities and exigencies of intercultural mediation in our times,
seems most paradoxical, even suspicious, albeit hardly surprising: the fact
that translation is only acknowledged when limited to its expected behaviour of being a servile reproduction, an automatic, mechanical task – "manual
labor", in Venuti's words (1992: 2) – serves as a confirmation of the workings of the powerful mechanisms controlling the order of culture and its
hierarchies; an order, by the way, one may attempt to intervene in and
challenge. Revising accepted elementary definitions of our object of study
seems to be a good field to start – especially in the light of Teresa de Lau-
retis' extrapolative conviction that a major asset of feminist theory lies in
those self-analyzing, reflective practices by which the subject can be
rearticulated relationally (cf. Alcoff 1988: 22-25). Even at the risk of finishing up empty-handed, presuming the existence of more 'translation'
than that within the reach of our eyes or the always perfectible spyglass of

social definitions might not be preposterous, and going into unmapped and unexplored territory may turn out to be worth the effort. Perhaps at the end we find nothing; perhaps beyond the *finis terrae* we may discover *terra incognita,* the world *continuing.* Not incidentally, the continuity (of discourse) is, for Lambert (1995: 99), precisely what current notions of translation (based exclusively on separate, autonomous texts) prevent from observing, as well as the premise which should underlie any new, extensive definition of translation aimed at explaining the phenomenon in all its complexity, including its disperse and fragmentary occurrence.

Some tentative definitions in this regard include Ovidi Carbonell's conception of translation as paradigm of cultural contact (1997: 103-9) and more precisely as "a superior level of interaction [that] takes place whenever an alien experience is internalized and rewritten in the culture where that experience is received" (1996: 81); Michaela Wolf's understanding of translation "in a broader sense, which means it is used in the sense of *'rewriting'* or even *'cultural textualization'*", not necessarily implying the "exist[ence of] an original text that is to be translated into a target language and target culture" (1997: 122); or Clem Robyns' broad definition of translation as "the migration and transformation of discursive elements between different discourses" or, more briefly, "discursive migration", a definition, in any event, which requires a shift in the focus of attention "from individual texts or linguistic features in translation [...] to interference between discourses and discursive structures and strategies" (1994: 408, 405, 406). As can be seen, common to these various approaches is the conviction that translation can hardly be thought of nowadays as one of the terms in a one-to-one relation if that relation is conceived between individual, clearly identifiable, ultimately tangible *texts.* And it may be argued that the radicalism of this view lies not so much in the recognition that translations are diffuse than in the claim that their source is equally vague, perhaps no more than indeterminate fragments floating undecidably in the ethereal level of discourse(s). In a way, and to proceed with our parallel, this view questions the tacit assumption that translation(s) can only stem from a concrete, ultimately material and physical original text just as most recent feminist thought has challenged cultural feminism's assumption that the essence of women is rooted in another materiality, the body. In effect, the concept of (female) gender has evolved from a biological determination which presumed us diametrically different from males to a cultural construction involving a series of habits, practices and discourses not necessarily seen in opposition to those predicated of a supposedly essential 'masculine identity' (if there was such a thing). This move being acknowledged today as probably one of the most productive advances in feminist theory; orientations such as those taken in the work by Carbonell, Robyns or Wolf seem to be worth looking at and developing, for they can be seen as emulating the progression in feminism, as attempting to deconstruct and de-essentialize the radical and unquestionned concepts of a discipline on the whole, according to Susan Bassnett's assessment, "far too obsessed with binary oppositions within the translation model and [...] too concerned with defining and redefining the relationship between translation and original" (1998: 30).

By the way, and in order to introduce a new dimension in our discussion, it may be argued that the deconstruction and de-essentialization of concepts like 'text' or 'gender' seems to be beneficial not only to the approaches closer to what Theo Hermans calls 'the disciplinary matrix' of (Descriptive) Translation Studies but also to theoretical directions that, to some extent, have helped revise its tenets, including the 'disciplinary matrix' of the so-called feminist translation theories. These must be acknowledged to have largely contributed to invalidating the tacit ideal of the neutral, unbiased *fidus interpres* and thus to disputing the validity of conventional translation models attached to or claiming an absolute notion of fidelity. Both their theoretical contribution and their experimental practices have revealed new conceptions of translation exceeding or questioning those existing in the social domain. Their definitions of translation as "production rather than reproduction" (Banting 1994: 178), transformation and/as performance (Godard [1990] 1995: 89) or simply "transformance" (*Id.*), "a political activity aimed at making language speak for women" (de Lotbinière-Harwood 1989: 9), "rewriting in the feminine" (*Id.*) or "womanhandling the text" (Godard [1990] 1995: 94), to mention just a few, call existing assumptions and expectations about translation into question insofar as they problematize the relation linking the original and translated texts. In any event, feminist translation theories still construe translation in terms of *texts*. As Susan Bassnett concludes in indirect reference to, among others, feminist contributions, "[e]ven where the model of dominant original and subservient translation has been challenged, the idea of some kind of hegemonic original still remains" (1998: 39). It is our contention that a methodological shift from text level to discourse as repository of translation(s) may prove productive for feminist approaches to translation and feminism as such, as this is an international/ized discourse exposed to the strategies of mass communication. Let us

not forget that, according to Lambert, those strategies, "where translations are used as (the hidden) part of the game, are never and can never be
innocent. Whether intentionally or not, they redefine discourse principles
and hence also societies" (1993: 19). In this regard, the various sorts of
manipulation to which feminist ideas, concepts or values are prone and
subjected in those undeniable yet covert processes of 'discursive migration' are still to be investigated.

Nevertheless, it is not this aspect which most interests us here. If mainstream feminist translation theories are likely to profit from dematerializing
the notion of translation currently understood as derived from another
text, nowadays it seems certain that they need to revise both the argumentation alleged in support of what it means translating as a woman (or as a
feminist) and the ensuing strategies they endorse or put into practice. As
argued in recent work by Arrojo, Maier, Massardier-Kenney or von Flotow,
feminist translation theories are not free from essentialist temptations and/
or bias. Luise von Flotow indeed identifies a whole (first) paradigm approach to gender issues in translation arising from

> the 'conventional' feminist view of female gender as a category
> that can in some respects be applied to all women, and its corollary
> that women are a special case in any society; they represent deval-
> ued difference in most existing socio-political systems (1999: 281)

The pioneering work by a series of Canadian translators which has
come to be generally accepted to constitute the core of feminist translation theories is on the whole grounded in a universalized definition of
'women' as generically oppressed by and opposed to males and their patriarchal language and system; it is mainly devoted to the (re)construction
of a genuinely distinctive female culture, an aim clearly in line with the
proposals of cultural feminism. This unproblematic conceptualization of
(female) gender and the adhesion to an ultimately essentialist project are
evident in the work by de Lotbinière-Harwood. In *The Body Bilingual.
Translation as a Rewriting in the Feminine* (a title which also reveals an
anatomical understanding of gender), this translator and theorist empha-
sizes the alienation imposed on women by a male-made culture when
declaring "I am a Translation / Because I am a Woman" (1991: 95). Moreover, for de Lotbinière-Harwood, liberation seems to require the rejection
of all links with masculinity: "That was the last time I translated literary
work by a male writer. I soon became a feminist and, some time later,
started calling myself a feminist translator" (*Ibid.*: 97). Her practice is

based on and at the same time conceived to be extending a culture exclusively of our own, "an emerging women's culture" (*apud* Homel and Simon 1988: 44), a dream somehow reviving the radical feminist dream of creating a 'separate reality' – a project, according to Deborah Cameron (1992: 156), which succeeds as a source of group solidarity but fails as a form of real resistance. Not surprisingly, the translation strategies applied and proposed by de Lotbinière-Harwood and other translators belonging to the 'first paradigm' are in consonance with a project conceived in terms of binary oppositions. As their aim is to reverse the existing order and to resex language, their main method is complete feminization. In her translator preface to Lise Gauvin's *Letters from an Other,* she states that:

> this translation has used every possible translation strategy to make the feminine visible in language. Because making the feminine visible in language means making women seen and heard in the real world. Which is what feminism is all about. (de Lotbinière-Harwood 1989: 9)

In fact, according to recent post-structuralist feminist theories, feminism is much more than a project focusing exclusively on the feminine. Perhaps because 'the feminine' as such, in the singular, has turned out to be considered a radically suspect concept and the possibility of making women seen and heard in the real world all at once a most homogenizing pretension, more and more feminist trends would agree on a self-definition as 'gender-conscious' rather than simply 'woman-centered'. In the realm of Translation Studies, these ideas are gaining momentum among a number of theoreticians preferring a self-definition as 'woman-identified translator' over 'feminist translator' (Maier in Godayol 1998: 161) and in any event constituting a still tentative 'second paradigm' working, to use the title of Massardier-Kenney's 1997 essay, 'towards a redefinition of feminist translation practice'. These theoreticians depart from prior monolithic visions of gender, either by questioning the oppositional character of femininity vs. masculinity – Maier and Massardier-Kenney (1996: 225), in this regard, understand "gender as the locus where not only femininity but also masculinity enters into the conceptualization of difference" –, or by challenging the uniformity of all women, for instance as far as sexual orientation (see Parker 1993 for an advocacy of polysexual and multi-gendered approaches to translation), intellectual formation (see Arrojo 1994; Leonardi n.d.; von Flotow 1998: 5 for a critique of elitism in feminist translation practices) or position in/of culture (see Spivak 1993, and

Maier and Massardier Kenney 1996 for a condemnation of ethnocentric standardization of cultural difference) is concerned. The acknowledgment of differences among women goes hand in hand with the recognition of a plural meaning in 'translating in the feminine', or at least with a sceptical attitude about the universal validity of 'canonical' or 'established' feminist practices – that is to say, those used and supported by the first paradigm –, including the emblematic claim for feminizing language whenever possible. Carol Maier, for instance, faced with the subtitle of María Zambrano's work, *Veinte años en la vida de una española*, refuses to maintain a clear allusion to the femininity of a philosopher, as she explains to Pilar Godayol (1998: 158), who never made an issue of the fact that she was a woman. If in this case feminization seems to Maier inopportune for very precise reasons, in Riabova's opinion (2001: 144), it may prove counterproductive when used as a general strategy, as the use of certain feminine gender-coded words in cultures where gender consciousness is underdeveloped may be understood derogatorily, given usual asymmetries in the social perception of masculine forms and their feminine counterparts.

In brief, these practices represent a move from an ultimately prescriptive project ('making the feminine visible in language') to new feminist translation politics and poetics based on a flexible ethics of location and on an awareness of the importance of positionality (Alcoff 1988). There is much work to be done within the frame of this 'second paradigm' of feminist approaches to translation which is currently only emerging and which, in any event, is called to be always emerging to prove fruitful. For the main asset of the theoretical background informing this paradigm – the acknowledgment of the impossibility of attaining atemporal conclusions – is precisely its main exigency: the request to constantly reinterpret our concepts and strategies relationally. Our attempt at (en)gendering new translation theory by translating current theorizations on gender is just a modest and necessarily limited contribution in that direction.

⇒ follow up ideas of
describing feminist trsl.
practice & theory as

* first paradigm
 – early interventionist work
* second paradigm
 – less politically-separatist

Tracing the Context of Translation
The Example of Gender

LUISE VON FLOTOW
University of Ottawa, Canada

Abstract. Starting from the premise that the contexts in which translations and translation studies are produced are of paramount
importance (Lefevere 1992), this article looks at a number of instances where gender has played an important role – in the process
of translation and/or in the studies of a translated text. It begins
with the work of Julia Evelina Smith, Bible translator in the 1850s
and suffragette in the 1870s, moves on to the challenges encoun-
tered when translating the eighteenth-century abolitionist discourse
of French intellectual women for twentieth-century America, turns
to gay writing and its translation in the 1990s, and returns to the
Bible at the turn of the new century – the Vatican's *Liturgiam
authenticam* instructions on Bible translation and the new French
Bible 2001.

Contexts are of paramount importance when we produce translations, and
when we study them; they shape, influence, permit or prohibit certain
versions of certain texts at certain times. They make translation, *and translation studies*, possible,[1] or impossible – or allow work on a cline between
these two extremes. Translation is a deliberate act, eminently social, historical, and personal – a hugely variable, opportunistic act – and as such it
is context-bound. Translation is planned rewriting; it produces a deliberately and inevitably different version of an already existing text –
prepared under specific conditions, to reach a specific readership. Similarly, studies of translations are deliberate activities, carried out in specific
socio-political, economic, and cultural contexts, which affect the outcome
of the study. André Lefevere has often pointed out this contextual aspect
of translation, or rewriting, most polemically in the introduction to his
Translation, Rewriting and the Manipulation of Literary Fame (1992).
Arguing that 'rewritings'/translations are the most widely available versions of texts, he asserts that their study should not be neglected; and

---

[1] In 1990 graduate students in the USA were discouraged from studying translation
which was seen as 'academic suicide.' Today, there are translation studies all across Europe, in Asia, South America, Canada, and in some of the best American universities.

those who study rewritings "will have to ask themselves who rewrites, why, under what circumstances, for which audience" (7) the work was done. A study of translation that addresses these points, Lefevere and many others, have shown, will take into account many, if not all, of the contextual elements that shape a rewritten text, and "restore to a certain study of literature some of the more immediate *social relevance* the study of literature as a whole has lost" (9) [my emphasis]. Lefevere is as much concerned with the social relevance of translation studies as with that of translation, and he firmly locates both in social contexts. In this, his work foreshadows the current trend to use Bourdieu's sociological concepts of "habitus" and "champ/field" to study translations, and translators (Gouanvic 1999; Simeoni 1998), and to develop work on the 'ethics' of translation,[2] clearly also a socio-political thrust in the discipline.

Using gender as a frame of reference, this article explores the importance of contexts in translation. One of the more important determinants in the Anglo-American (and wider Western) academic contexts of the past thirty years, gender has not left translation studies untouched. A number of recent books and many articles[3] attest to this situation, and changes in research direction – from feminist, to 'woman-interrogated', to gay or queer approaches – show how flexible conceptions of gender have become,[4] and how flexibly translation studies research has responded. Further, the spread of gender approaches from the Anglo-American translation studies realm into the academic endeavours of researchers in Austria, Spain, Italy, Mexico, Turkey, Czechoslovakia, Brazil, China,[5] and many other cultures/countries is a further indication of the flexibility, mobility, and therefore, viability of the topic. Much as different contexts will affect the translated versions of a text, so these different research contexts will affect the gender topics addressed, and the findings. This is made clear by Beverley Allen (1999) who argues that a term as basic to gender discussions as 'mother' cannot be translated with impunity from Italian to English. *Madre* in Milano is not the same as *mother* in New York: cultural and

---

[2] See the special issue of *The Translator*, "The Return to Ethics" (Pym 2001).
[3] See my overview article "Translation and Gender Paradigms: From Identities to Pluralities" (Flotow forthcoming).
[4] I discuss some of these changes/developments in "Genders and the Translated Text: Developments in Transformance" in *Textus* (Flotow 1999).
[5] Conferences and research projects related to gender and translation have recently developed in all these countries – in Graz, Austria (2001), in Valencia, Spain (2002), in Mexico (2002), in Gargano, Italy (2003), in Istanbul (2003), etc.

contextual differences impose themselves, making *difference*, and not equivalence, the constant of translation.

1. A translation narrative – in context

In the following, I recount the story of a translation – its inception and its aftermaths – in order to demonstrate the vital importance of context.[6] In the 1840s, the Northwestern United States experienced a religious movement named Millerism after William Miller, the man who had calculated that the world was about to end, and was preaching this throughout the region. Huge prayer and revival meetings were held in the early part of the decade to spread the happy news, and help prepare people for the day. Mr. Miller, a gifted orator and self-styled preacher, traveled widely and convinced thousands of their imminent ascension to heaven. In the fall of 1843, as the appointed day came closer, normal life changed significantly: people lived only for the prayer meetings, they spurned decoration in their homes and of their persons (covering the pictures on their walls, and their musical instruments with black cloths, for example), and farmers didn't take in their crops, since they knew they would soon be going to heaven. The appointed day in October 1843 came and went, and nothing happened. The 'Great Disappointment' followed. As for Miller, he blamed his miscalculation on the interpreters of God's word who had evidently made mistakes when they wrote down the prophecies.

Out of this curious context, a translation developed. A learned spinster by the name of Julia Evelina Smith, who was probably not untouched by Millerism herself, speculated that the problem might lie less in the *interpretation* of God's word by the prophets than in the *translation* of the biblical texts Miller had used for his prediction. She therefore decided to translate the entire Bible from the original Hebrew and Greek into English, and to do so as literally as possible. Unlike many of her less educated contemporaries, she could see that the King James Version that Miller had referred to deviated substantially from the Hebrew and, in line with the thinking of the Sandemanian sect to which she belonged, she decided to re-translate the Bible, staying as close to the Word as she could. Only this method would yield an answer to the question of dates and numbers. When her translation was completed about eight years later, in 1855, she

---

[6] I have discussed this translation event elsewhere; see bibliographical references Flotow (2000b) and (2002).

put it aside, as a bundle of about 10,000 sheets of manuscript.

Many years later, in the 1870s, Smith decided to publish the transla-tion. Again, the context was decisive, if peculiar: as an old lady of about 80 she had become involved in the movement for women's suffrage – the movement seeking women's right to vote. Due to her struggles in response to mistreatment at the hands of local tax authorities, Julia Smith had be-come quite visible. Together with a younger sister in her mid-70s, she had already appeared before the US Senate and regularly traveled throughout New England to speak at women's meetings. After losing a number of court cases against the tax authorities because she was a woman, she de-cided to publish her translation "to show that one woman can do what no man has ever done" (i.e. translate the entire Bible single-handedly from the original languages). We can assume, I think, that if the women's move-ment had not been such a strong social force, and provided this context, the work would never have appeared. It is now available in the archives of the American Bible Society, New York.

A further contextual development made this translation an important artifact and authority. The project to produce *The Woman's Bible* headed by Elizabeth Cady Stanton, a fiery suffragette, was a largely joint effort that brought together suffragette scholars and Bible experts to comment on those passages of the Bible most important to women, and to women's inferior position in American society. Throughout the 19th century, the Bible had served politicians and other public figures in the USA as a political instrument to justify all manner of political, civil, and social in-equality for women. *The Woman's Bible* extracts pertinent passages, comments on them, and demonstrates to what extent both the Bible and its interpreters are misogynist. Throughout the ten-year duration of this project, which caused important political rifts within the women's move-ment, Julia Smith's literal translation served as the authoritative text. The commentators wrote *about* the King James Version, since that was the main Bible in use in English, but they knew how important the 'transla-tion effect' could be – the ideological twist that any translation can give to a text – and so they used Smith's version as the most appropriate and literal reference work. After all, she translates 'Hawwa', the word nor-mally rendered as 'Eve' and the name for the first woman on Earth, as 'Life', in line with the meaning of the word in Hebrew[7]. Elizabeth Stanton's

---

[7] With regard to translating 'Hawwa' as 'Life' rather than 'Eve', this innovation has been corroborated in the late 20th century work of Mary Phil Korsak in *At the Start*.

comment on this is

> It is a pity that all versions of the Bible do not give this word in-
> stead of the Hebrew Eve. She was Life, the eternal mother, the
> first representative of the more valuable and important half of the
> human race (*The Woman's Bible*, 27).

After this brief moment of glory which lasted about 20 years, Smith's Bible fell into disuse and oblivion, much like *The Woman's Bible*, which was considered too aggressive and polemical for the large majority of mainstream women that the movement wanted to represent. Both texts were revived, however, and again the context was decisive: the second women's movement dating from the 1960s onward. Further, in the United States, two books (both published in 1993) have focused on Smith's religious life and her work as a Bible translator, and a number of articles written in the 1970s claimed her for feminism. I have just published the first article on her in French – in a book entitled *Portraits de traductrices* (Flotow 2002). In other words, this 20th century context that spawned a huge interest in women's writing of all kinds, and in issues of gender and identity more generally, also brought these 19th century materials back into the public, academic eye.

In regard to the ideological import of Smith's work, I am not sure that she actually produced what might be called a feminist translation, as the enthusiastic articles of the 1970s claim. Her work hardly even fit the agenda of the suffragette movement of the late 19th century, though she was able to gain notoriety and support from the movement. She was interested in seeking and revealing the 'Word' of God, in an approach we might now term fundamentalist. Yet, her intellectual achievement is impressive and as such considered noteworthy: she fits into the category of important, intellectual women forebears of the feminist movement whose work un-justifiably lapsed into oblivion.

The story of Julia Smith with some of its contextual details and follow-ups is not only picturesque; it is useful as a demonstration of how important *context* is for all aspects of translation, and for translation stud-ies. Smith **produced** her translation because of the religious fervour of the 1840s and the aftermath of this social movement; she was searching

---

Genesis Made New (1992). In Korsak's words, it places the focus on women as 'life' and not as mothers/madres.

for an explanation for the events of the early 1840s that had moved thousands of people. She **published** the translation in order to make a point regarding her own socio-legal situation in the 1870s; the publication would demonstrate that a woman could far surpass the achievements of a man and that therefore discrimination against women was unjustifiable. The translation was **well-received and used** as an authoritative text by thinkers within the women's suffrage movement for about twenty years because it was considered more literal, and therefore true or honest or trustworthy, than other versions, and therefore served their purpose. It **dropped out of sight** because the aggressive critique of the Bible published in *The Woman's Bible* was considered politically harmful. It was **revived** as an example of a woman's intellectual accomplishment in the 1970s when researchers and scholars working in the context of a new women's movement were looking for important women whose work had been dropped from the canon, and lost to subsequent generations. And I am reviving interest in the work of Julia Evelina Smith (translator) at a time when it has become fashionable to unearth and publicize the achievements of women intellectuals and translators. The fact that *Portraits de traductrices,* edited by Jean Delisle (2002) should be awarded the prize for best book of the year by the Canadian Association of Translation Studies is a further sign of this contextually opportune moment.

Context in translation involves all the conditions affecting the production, the publication, the dissemination, the reception, the lack of reception, and the revival of a text. And it affects the way a translation is studied and evaluated – even centuries later. It is a vast field that also comprises the subjectivity and the personal politics of the translator (and the translation researcher), an aspect that is garnering more and more interest. It means studying a translation in order to understand it, and formulate a coherent, reasoned, understanding of it – as an artifact of its time. It means examining a translation in the environment in which it was produced and, if possible, not imposing the aesthetic or ideological or practical demands of another era upon it or judging it from some vague personal aesthetic. It is an approach that expects difference in translation and seeks to account for it. Specifically, it means studying 'l'horizon de la traduction' (Berman 1995) – the personal, political, social, aesthetic conditions under which a translation is produced and received.

This is not a new idea, but it is one that regained importance in the late 20th century for a number of contextual reasons. One is the impact of the relativistic thinking that came with post-structuralist theories undermining the authority of any text and thus valorizing the slippery, subjective, opportunist, *partisan* (Tymozcko 2000) aspects of meaning and meaningfulness, as typified by translation. As Edwin Gentzler (2002: 195) puts it, deconstructive and post-structuralist thinking on translation, "challenge[s] privileged concepts of the sanctity of the source text and originality of the author", and has focused on the changeable, flexible translation effect. In this environment there is no ultimate authority, no originality, only difference and change. Further, the once solid link between language and nationality/nation has been systematically eroded through massive increases in mobility and in communications in the late 20th century (Potter 2002). In translation, where a text is produced through a malleable, flexible process, and is as indefinite as any source text, and where cultural and contextual adjustments need to be made even at the level of *madre* and *mother*, this additional lack of territorially-defined linguistic spaces enhances the influence and importance of contingent contexts.

2. Opportunism in translation

Returning to the work done in translation and translation studies under the sway of gender interests in the last decades of the 20th century, it is easy to see the impact of context. Perhaps the most immediate development as a result of the second women's movement (from 1960s) was production. As in the case of Julia Smith's translation, the socio-political moment, a very fecund moment, was vital. It led to vast amounts of translation, with highly motivated and educated women gaining the power to impose their work and their ideas. The translation market in anthologies of women's writing boomed in all the European languages, and English as well. In many publishing houses lists and series of women's writing were created and entirely new publishers, producing only books written by women, sprang up. One prime example is the German *Frauenoffensive*, a small collective of women in the mid-1970s which published Verena Stefan's *Häutungen* (*Mues* in French, *Shedding* in English). When the book became a cult hit, the publishing house was born, and its politics established. The presence of a huge reading public of women with a great appetite for new materials that might reflect aspects of their own lives, made these business ventures possible. This burst of production was not due to any change in the intrinsic value of the texts; indeed, as Lefevere claims, there may be little intrinsic value in any text. What there is though, is context: conventions, traditions, trends, fashions, power plays that any social context will bring and that will determine what publishers sell and people read.[8]

Inevitably and logically then, there is room for aggressive and opportunist activity in such a dynamic environment. With regard to gender issues in translation, the 'hijacking' of texts has been seen as a part of 'feminist translation', at least in North America. This refers to the deliberate intervention in a text in order to incorporate contemporary feminist politics, where there are none, or nothing very visible, in the source text. Obviously, such activity is very context-dependent – relying on friendly publishing houses and readers to support it.

A good example of this practice of **'hijacking' into context** can be taken from a book published in 1994 in the United States, *Translating Slavery: Gender and Race in French Women's Writing – 1783-1823*, edited by Doris Kadish and Françoise Massardier-Kenney. It presents a number of abolitionist texts written by French women just before and just after the French Revolution in 1789. These texts had never before been translated into English, and were viewed by the editors of the book as work by important intellectual women forebears, ancestors of the women's movement, so to speak. The fact that they had never been made available or read in English was seen as typical of the treatment of work by intellectual (and therefore intimidating and uncomfortable) women: Mme de Stael, Mme de Gouges, and Mme de Duras.

The translation of this material from late 18th century France to late 20th century United States, however, posed a series of problems. One of the most serious was the language used for the black heroines and for Blacks in general. The word 'savage', for instance, was a part of the normal lexicon of the French texts, and often used to refer to the slaves that were to be freed. It could not appear in late 20th century American translations. These were adjusted, and not only because the word itself is now considered offensive, but because the writers (Stael, Gouges, and Duras) were to be viewed as important libertarian forerunners of the women's

---

[8] In an ongoing research project that I am heading and that investigates the German translations of Canadian writing, it has been found that, opportunistically, throughout the 1980s, the translation of contemporary writing by Canadian *women* was far more important than the translation of male authors in Germany, most likely in response to the huge interest in women's texts. When this abated, and difficult social issues arose after the unification of the two Germanies in 1990, Canadian texts by so-called 'multikulti' (multicultural authors – members of visible minorities) predominated.

movement. They could not be given the language of rightwing racists. Similarly, the black heroines who appeared too weak, or did not reflect the characteristics that late 20th century readers might expect, had their language adjusted. The translators "purposefully heighten[ed] the eloquence of the black female character" and "effaced what sometimes appeared [...] as the whining undertones of the character Ourika" (16). In other words, the feminist American context into which these texts were being translated strongly affected the translations. They were produced and published at a time and in an environment that welcomed such material, but required important changes in the text. The 'otherness' of the late 18th century was obscured, and the text was 'hijacked' through translation, for a very specific use in the late 20th century.

3. Subjectivity and translation

One of the most interesting recent contextual developments in translation, and in translation studies, is the focus on the translator as subject. A champion of the personal aspects of translation, Antoine Berman (1995) has sought to develop a flexible method with which to understand and criticize literary translations. This puts considerable emphasis on studying the translator as an important actor in the work of translation. The focus is on that person's literary and cultural background, on their 'position traductive', and finally on their 'pulsion à traduire', the force that drives them to translate. In this, Berman is clearly referring to personal context, and to a confluence of factors: personal taste and connections, cultural traditions, trends and fashions, education, financial concerns, and so on. In terms of gender, his work was foreshadowed by the famous slogan "the personal is political" that galvanized so many women in the 1970s and 1980s, and also connects the subject position with its sociopolitical context. It is adapted by translation studies scholars who locate and understand translations in very specific personal environments, comparing and contrasting them with other versions of the same text or the same author, done by another translating individual, informed and formed by other contexts.

A good example of an adapted Bermanien approach that works within the current climate of changing gender politics is work by Keith Harvey (1998, 2000). As ideas about gender have undergone important changes, moving from polarized to pluralized positions, translation scholars such as Harvey have followed suit, exploring gay writing and the translation of gay texts. Again, the social context allows this; but a very personal need to gain access to certain texts or make materials accessible to others is also apparent. Keith Harvey studies gay American writing, its stylistic and semantic features, and its translations into French, and compares these with similar aspects of French gay writing in American/English transla-tion. He makes this study very personal, describing how as a young man he searched through gay writing in order to understand his own feelings, and how he sought out foreign writers such as Marcel Proust and André Gide. He describes his disappointment in reading the English translations of these French authors as underlying his subsequent motivation to re-search the importance of gay community and context in translation. He discovers that these communities, as reflected in the translations they pro-duce and consume, are very different. In the French world, for example, there is far less of a community that will support gay writing *as* gay writ-ing. The French translations of Gore Vidal, say, or of Tony Kushner seem not to be produced for a French community of gay men; they are mainstreamed, much like Proust and Gide were in English translation a few generations ago. On the other hand, certain American translations of gay texts from France are clearly "gayed" for the more assertive Anglo-American gay community. Eric Keenaghan's work (2000) on an American version of Federico García Lorca corroborates this American translation tendency. Indeed, both Harvey and Keenaghan show that the differences between an American translation (or hijacking, in the case of Lorca) of gay materials is dependent on the context that places emphasis on per-sonal identity politics, on the community that will read the translation, and on the "subjectivité du traducteur".

4.   Controlling the context

The focus on gender, and more recently, on its diversification or plu-ralization, may be attractive and stimulating for some; for others, it threatens unity, tradition, belief systems, and power structures. Predict-ably, there are attempts to control the contexts in which certain texts are translated. And this brings us back to the Bible. A current publication from the Vatican, entitled *Liturgiam Authenticam,* is a good example of such an attempt to control translation. This publication gives directions about how to translate the Bible, and prepare texts for congregations and church services. Specifically, for my interests in gender and translation, it cracks down on 'gender-neutral, inclusive' liturgy. This refers to the recent work done by many institutions, committees, and translators to adapt the language of the Scriptures to the social situations in which they are used, and to recognize the fact that gender has become an important category according to which people identify, and live.[9] The Vatican condemns translations that might have Jesus telling his disciples to become 'fishers of people' rather than 'fishers of men' or that might refer to God as the 'Father and Mother'. On the Vatican website, and in a text segment clearly entitled 'Gender', the authors of the *Liturgiam authenticam* insist that:

30.   In many languages there exist nouns and pronouns denoting both genders, masculine and feminine, together in a single term. The insistence that such a usage should be changed is not necessarily to be regarded as the effect or the manifestation of an authentic development of the language as such. Even if it may be necessary by means of catechesis to ensure that such words continue to be understood in the "inclusive" sense just described, it may not be possible to employ different words in the translations themselves without detriment to the precise intended meaning of the text, the correlation of its various words or expressions, or its aesthetic qualities. When the original text, for example, employs a single term in expressing the interplay between the individual and the universality and unity of the human family or community (such as the Hebrew word *'adam*, the Greek *anthropos*, or the Latin *homo*), this property of the language of the original text should be maintained in the translation. Just as has occurred at other times in history, the Church herself must freely decide upon the system of language that will serve her doctrinal mission most effectively, and should not be subject to externally imposed linguistic norms that are detrimental to that mission.

31.   In particular: to be avoided is the systematic resort to imprudent solutions such as a mechanical substitution of words, the transition from the singular to the plural, the splitting of a unitary collective term into masculine and feminine parts, or the introduction of impersonal or abstract words, all of which may impede the communication of the true and integral sense of a word or an expression in the original text. Such measures introduce theological and anthropological problems into the translation. Some particular norms are the following:

   a)   In referring to almighty God or the individual persons of the Most Holy Trinity, the truth of tradition as well as the established gender usage of each respective language are to be maintained.

---

[9] See Sherry Simon (1996: 111-133) for a comprehensive overview of feminist approaches to Bible translation.

b) Particular care is to be taken to ensure that the fixed expression "Son of Man" be rendered faithfully and exactly. The great Christological and typological significance of this expression requires that there should also be employed throughout the translation a rule of language that will ensure that the fixed expression remain comprehensible in the context of the whole translation.

c) The term "fathers", found in many biblical passages and liturgical texts of ecclesiastical composition, is to be rendered by the corresponding masculine word into vernacular languages insofar as it may be seen to refer to the Patriarchs or the kings of the chosen people in the Old Testament, or to the Fathers of the Church.

d) Insofar as possible in a given vernacular language, the use of the feminine pronoun, rather than the neuter, is to be maintained in referring to the Church.

e) Words which express consanguinity or other important types of relationship, such as "brother", "sister", etc., which are clearly masculine or feminine by virtue of the context, are to be maintained as such in the translation.

f) The grammatical gender of angels, demons, and pagan gods or goddesses, according to the original texts, is to be maintained in the vernacular language insofar as possible.

Basing its instructions on arguments such as 'lack of precision', 'inauthenticity', 'aesthetics' and a 'doctrinal mission', this document calls for a return to the use of masculine terms as the generic for human being, designating words such as 'man', 'adam', 'anthropos', 'homo' and pronouns such as 'ils' in French or 'ellos' in Spanish as being inclusive, i.e. referring to all humans. This, of course, runs counter to all the work done by feminist and other linguists to individualize and personalize language along gender lines since the 1970s. Further, the document reinstates the predominance of masculine references to various characters in the Christian belief system, the 'Filius homini' (Son of Man) and the 'Patres' (Fathers) of the Church, a tendency of Church language that was much attenuated in publications such as the *Inclusive Language Lectionary*. The feminine pronoun, on the other hand, is exclusively reserved for the institution: the Church itself. The purpose of this return to 'traditions' is stated to be twofold: it seeks to maintain the "interplay between the individual and the universality and unity of the human family and community". Secondly, it re-implements a "system of language that will serve her [the Church's] doctrinal mission most effectively". This mission is not spelled out, nor is the abstraction of individual human and universal human family made very clear; but the intent is clear enough: to re-instate a 'pre-gendered', patriarchal approach to the language of the Bible and control its translation.

Foreshadowing, or coinciding with, a general move toward more traditional thinking, this decree seeks to regain authority over the contexts of Bible translation. It comes at a time when there is renewed interest in Bible translations, as exemplified by the new French *Bible* (*La nouvelle traduction* 2001). This work was created through a double effort of translation: exegetes working directly from the Biblical languages first produced literal versions, and then writers from various French-speaking cultures turned these into literary texts. These texts constitute both a return to the original Biblical writings (via the exegetes) and a reformulation of the old material in the French of the late 20th century – for a reading public of believers and non-believers. The results, finalized in "soixante-treize séminaires de traduction – autant que de livres bibliques" (24) [seventy-three translation seminars, as many as there are books of the Bible, *my translation*], consist of many compromises.[10] One of the more interesting, given the new 'traditionalist' environment and the array of exegetes and translators involved, in other words the complex context, is a compromise that resonates with Julia Evelina Smith's version. It is the translation of the name of Adam's wife. She is 'Eve la Vivante/ la mère de tous les vivants' [Eve the Living/the mother of all the living], a translation that is not quite as radical or disconcerting as Smith's stark 'Life' but still less traditional than what the Vatican might have preferred.

The **context** of this past 'fin de siècle', the late 20th century, with its focus on gender, subjectivity and personal politics, with its critical interest in the power of language and its critical focus on the language of power has been very fruitful for translation. It has not only refocused the attention of academics and institutions on the phenomenon, but seen the production of many new works in translation. Most importantly, it has made the figure of the translator, and often the translation researcher, stand out as that of a individual clearly affected by the context in which they are working, and equally implicated in the text: a translator who leaves a trace in every text. This is the trace of context.

---

[10] Anne Marie Lamontagne, one of the Canadian writers participating, has described this work of discussion and compromise in a number of talks, maintaining however, that in the end, each team of exegete and writer take responsibility for the final published version of their text.

On the Women's Service?
Gender-conscious Language in Dubbed James Bond Movies

NICOLE BAUMGARTEN
Universität Hamburg, Germany

Abstract. This paper deals with the construction of social gender through spoken language in film. The investigation of language in film and film translation has been a hitherto largely ignored field of enquiry. Before proceeding to present a concrete example of the type of cross-linguistic analysis undertaken on the basis of a large corpus of multimodal texts, the paper gives an outline of a model for the analysis of language in film and translated film dialogue ('the dubbed text'), which is based on a broadly systemic-functional theoretical framework. Drawing on current research into the notion of cultural specificity in original and translated texts, the paper aims at describing the forms and functions of language-specific textualization of 'extralinguistic concepts'.

The paper examines varying strategies of textualizing social gender in the original and the German-language versions of James Bond movies.[1] I want to show how lexicogrammatical changes in the translation with respect to the corresponding structures in the English text carry with them changes in the depiction of gender and gender relations. The social role relationships – the 'tenor of the discourse', in Hallidayan terms – in the translation text seem to qualitatively depart from that of the original language version. The instances of linguistic construction of social gender in an English original and its German translation text are embedded in a larger frame of current research into the effects of the translation relation English-German on German preferences in language use. The paper is structured as follows: I will start by pointing out the relevance of research into translation relations for contrastive (socio-)linguistics. Secondly, I will give a brief account of the idea of language change in German through translational language contact with English. Thirdly, I will describe the particular nature of the texts that are investigated and the method of analysis that is

[1] I am grateful to Deborah Cameron for her comments on an earlier version of this paper.

applied. Fourthly, I will describe how cultural specificity comes into play in original and translation text production. It is within this contextualizing framework that I will then present and discuss examples of textualizing gender in English and German film texts.

1. The relevance of translation research for contrastive linguistics

Contrastive linguistic analysis of translations and their original texts is a prime way of investigating the parallel or as it were 'co-occurring' ways and strategies of constructing social reality in texts across cultures. Investigation into translation relations makes the significance of the notion of linguistic choice in textualising meaning particularly obvious: what linguistic resources does each text in each language resort to in handling the essentially same task of social semiotic representation?

Unlike original text production, a translation is always in a double bind: the re-instantiation of form and content of the original in the target language is constrained by the textual function of the original text and the conditions of language use put down in its semantic and grammatical structure, and it is constrained by the conditions of text reception in the target language environment, that is the cultural context of the addressee, hearer, reader, spectator, audience. The notion of the double bind is constitutive for any claim to translation equivalence or functional equivalence between source and target language text (Koller 2001[1979]; House 1981[1977]). How the translation negotiates the constraints with respect to the thematic and linguistic aspects of the texts can be revealing of cross-linguistic differences and cross-cultural preferences.

2. Shifts in communicative preferences

This paper presents work in progress of a larger study that looks into the dynamics of social semiotics in film translation. The study is part of a larger project[2] which investigates language change in German in the context of English-German language contact in translation. The assumption

---

[2] The project "Covert Translation" is currently carried out inside the Research Center on Multilingualism at the University of Hamburg. The Center is funded by the Deutsche Forschungsgemeinschaft (DFG).

is that ongoing processes of globalization and internationalization, the pervasive presence of products of Anglo-American culture and the concurrent status of the English language as a global *lingua franca* in key areas of cultural life such as science, entertainment, economy or information technology, impact on language specific norms and conventions of translations from English into German and monolingual text production in German. The purpose of the analyses is to find out whether and in what respect cultural specificity in communicative conventions and preferences of German target and parallel texts are giving way to Anglophone textual norms.

Preliminary results from the synchronic analyses of computer manuals, popular science articles and certain types of written business communication point to the fact that this influence is most marked in texts that display a very pronounced interpersonal functional component (Halliday 1994; House 1997). This is expressed linguistically in the specific realization of (inter-) subjectivity and addressee orientation. The quality and scope of this interlanguage influence seems to be collateral with two other functional characteristics: first, the degree to which the texts can be counted as being oriented towards "popular culture", and secondly, the degree to which they show signs of prototypical "involved" or "oral" text production and communicative purpose (Biber 1988).

As Doherty (1995) points out, lexicogrammatical differences in textualization between an English source language text and the German target language text often amount to stylistic preferences (and notions of 'wellformedness') on the basis of differences in language typology, which determine for instance information structure at sentence level. The "Analogvariante", that is, the translation which closely imitates the information structure of the English sentence, is, in most cases, possible and not ungrammatical. But, Doherty claims, it would often be less acceptable in terms of what a native speaker of German intuitively would consider as good style and wellformedness. If our assumption of shifting preferences in textual norms and communicative conventions is right, translation realizations of specific lexicogrammatical phenomena, which at one point are or were considered stylistically flawed because of violating language-specific parameters and 'sticking' too close to the source text, would gradually become acceptable and sanctioned – if they are employed to textualize textual aspects which are in the process of convergence, such as intersubjectivity and addressee orientation. The specific linguistic structure could then proliferate uninhibitedly in translation text production and possibly make its way into monolingual text production. Changes in communicative preferences which involve e.g. the specific use of process types, deictics, theme structures or mood choices would then affect the representation of gender or any other thematic aspect of the text. If we consider gender relations as being constructed within the more general semiotic frame of addressee orientation, and if we simultaneously assume that the verbalization of gender in texts depends on constructions of subjectivity for the speaking subject, the linguistic dimension of their representation could be suspected to change too.

3.   The text basis and the method of analysis

Evidence for changing communicative preferences in German seems to be most frequent in translations of written texts that are oriented toward general, non-specialized audiences. Typically, such texts incorporate linguistic features of prototypically 'spoken' and 'involved' text production. These features are generally used to suggest an affective edge in the text and evoke various constellations of interpersonal closeness. It is this 'vulnerability' of all things expressing 'spokenness' and interpersonal involvement in German that suggests, to my mind, a closer look at texts that lie at the interface of spoken and written genres. They should provide a clearer view on the functions of medium-mixing and its behaviour in translation.

The multimodality of film texts (visual, phonic channels) and its essential mimetic character has placed the medium at the centre of popular text reception. The present study therefore traces language use in the translation relation English-German through what I have called the Wor(l)d of Bond Corpus of Fictional Spoken Discourse (WOB). It consists of transcriptions of the original English film soundtracks and their corresponding official German dubbed versions. It comprises at the moment 11 hours of transcribed spoken discourse from a principled selection of scenes. The transcriptions are minimally annotated for references to extralinguistic visual co-text, paralinguistic and non-verbal features, and they are also prepended by relevant narrative context.

'Bond' is a pivotal product of 20th century popular mainstream culture. The James Bond movie series stretches from 1962 to the present, featuring a new movie release approximately every two years. At present this amounts to 21 major film productions, which means that 'James Bond' *is*, compared to many other genres, very consistent text production over time. The series also features a synchronous,[3] stable, intertextually bound, translation relation English-German. Furthermore, by virtue of its medial form and the mimetic character of narration the texts rely heavily on creating text-internal as well as text-external interpersonal relations. This is to say that the simultaneous levels of communication – between characters in the film and between the film and the spectator in the audience – both presuppose animate, subjective, cognitively engaged social beings as speaker and addressee. And, the film uses language that is written to be spoken as if not written: i.e., it displays the characteristics of involved and oral communication without being spontaneous speech. Therefore, if the degree of 'spokenness', 'involvement' and interpersonal focus, really is a qualitative factor in determining the pace and the effects of the evolution of language contact between English and German in translation, this process should show in the linguistic preferences of dubbing practice – in the way it affects the linguistic construction of extralinguistic concepts, such as gender.

A film text is made up of different layers of meaning. Meaning is constructed on the interconnecting levels of the word, image, scene, film text, film series, genre, film medium, etc. The enumeration is not exhaustive. It is important to note that each of these levels relate to the others in specific ways; each provides the context for the previous one. One could say that the terms stand in a text-context relation to each other; they can be said to be in a meta-redundancy relation (cf. Lemke 1995). Word, image, scene, etc. are interwoven in a relational-contextual constellation of meaning. The question is how the different layers map to make particular instances of meaning in a text, e.g. that of the sequence of utterances when a character in the film speaks to another character about a certain topic. The challenge for analysis is how to methodically decompose meaning, to open up the context of the text, so to speak, to arrive at a functional interpretation of the use of lexicogrammatical devices in that particular situation.

At the core of the analysis lies the meaning that is made by words and their contextualization in film. The analysis is grounded in the framework of systemic-functional theory. The mode of analysis revolves around the application of House's model for text analysis and translation evaluation

---

[3] Synchronous in the sense that the translations are produced immediately after the completion of the film.

(House 1981[1977];1997) which is based on Hallidayan systemic-functional theory, register linguistics, discourse analysis and text linguistics.[4] The ultimate goal of the analysis is the reconstruction of the types of motivated choices the text producer made in order to create this and only this particular text for a particular effect in the 'context of situation' enveloping and conditioning the text formation.

4. Film texts and cultural specificity

Converging evidence from a series of empirical German-English contrastive pragmatic analyses (see House 1998 for a summary) lead to the abstraction of the following dimensions of communicative preferences between English and German:

> Indirectness – Directness
> Orientation towards other – Orientation towards self
> Orientation towards persons – Orientation towards content
> Implicitness – Explicitness
> Use of verbal routines – Ad-hoc-formulation

These are, of course, clines rather than clear-cut-dichotomies with absolute values. One can say, however, that in general in written and spoken discourse, native speakers of German tend to realize lexicogrammatical devices which are associated with the values on the right. Native speakers of English, in the same situations, prefer linguistic structures which are associated with the values on the left.

An analogous tendency has been observed in translations (cf. Baumgarten 2003; Böttger and Probst 2001). Translations from English into German tend to be adapted according to the above dimensions: linguistic features which convey 'implicitness' in English are changed into linguistic features that express 'explicitness' in German. That means, for instance, that in the German translation we would find more lexicalization of the situational context. An effect of this is that the source text and the translation text may be grammatically and semantically quite different, but pragmatically equivalent. The formal divergence between an acceptable English and acceptable German expression of the same logical content

---

[4] These are the main *linguistic* frameworks of the study. I also include theories and models of (mimetic) narrative and cinematic representation, cf. e.g. Branigan (1984).

would attest to a translator's attempts to accommodate the target culture's presuppositions about cultural norms and conventions. As a result of this process of adaptation, the translation does not appear to be a translation at all, but an authentic German text: the translation is "covert" (House 1981) and the text has the status of an 'original text' in the receiving culture. The procedure by which this 'inconspicuousness' of the translation is achieved is called "cultural filtering" or "applying a cultural filter" (House 1997). Cultural filtering means translating culturally and situationally defined linguistic structures by replacing them with culturally defined, contextually appropriate linguistic material in the target language in order to compensate for cultural specificity in texts. Obviously, the complexity of this process increases with the quantity of culture-specific elements in a text, and the extent to which they are foregrounded as meaningful structures. In visual media e.g., there is always the image that cannot be 'filtered away'. It needs to be integrated in the mode of cultural filtering. The application of a cultural filter is also the moment at which the verbalization of extralinguistic concepts may be changed – to the extent as they are determined through linguistic structures – according to the prevalent social discourses in the target culture. On the one hand, there could be conscious changes in linguistic devices with regard to a specific topic, on the other hand, such changes can be inadvertent side-effects of an overarching shift toward target cultural conventions in textualization.

5. Depicting gender in Bond

In this chapter I am going to describe how the linguistic representation of gender is affected by changes in discourse semantics in the process of translation. Before I present some examples from a pair of scenes from a 1960s James Bond film, *From Russia with Love*, [5] I will give a rough outline of the role of 'women' in Bond: women figure prominently in the James Bond film series. One of the billboard promotion texts for *From Russia with Love* reads: "Meet James Bond, secret agent 007. His new incredible women ... His new incredible enemies ... His new incredible adventures ..." (cited in: Lane and Simpson 1998: 139). The construction of gender in the films is obviously a constitutive factor in the production

---

[5] *From Russia with Love* (E) – *Liebesgrüße aus Moskau* (G), UK 1963. This film is the second release of the movie series.

and consequently for the narration[6] of the films. In the narratives, women occur in a set of predictable characters which are enacted in a recurring set of scenes and situations which, over the time, have come to have predictable significance within the course of narrative.

Probability and notions of what can be expected play an important role for the films as communication with a spectator/audience. The predictability of the realization of the main aspects of the plot – 'women', 'enemies', 'adventures' – develops out of the dense intertextuality of the film texts. This be may the reason why promotion for later films seemingly does not explicitly, lexically advertise any of these three concepts,[7] although they still can be said to be the abstraction at the basis of each film. But as we are considering here only the second film, and these features are advertised as the main attractions, it is possible to assume that women, enemies and adventures in the context of "James Bond, secret agent 007" are textualized in a particular, popular fashion. The terms must have been thought by the text producer to have a recognizable, marketable meaning in their context. Accordingly, one could hypothesize that the pictorial and linguistic construction of women, enemies and adventures, made special, probably favourable connections with the prevalent social discourses of gender, enmity and personal experience. The imperative "meet" furthermore is an offer of social contact. It propels the reader of the text and prospective spectator of the film into the position of a privileged observer/witness of James Bond's experience of the key concepts of the film.

Gender in Bond can be considered from several different perspectives. Among these are: talking about women; talking with women; how women talk in general; how women talk to men; how women talk to women, which they generally do not. Note that for the overwhelming part of the entirety of the James Bond films conversation between man and woman means conversation between 007 and a woman. The discourse on female gender in the films is thus, almost exclusively, subjectively constructed as a feature of the character "007". Note also that the centrality of the character "007" – there are very few scenes in which he is not present – provides him with the privileged voice in the text. In the following exam-

---

[6] "Narration" refers to the process of telling; "narrative" refers to what is told.
[7] This refers to promotion for the US and UK film releases. Information on German language promotion was not available to the author at the time this paper was completed.

ples I want to illustrate 'man-talk about the absent woman' in English and German.

In the first example, 007 and the local liaison officer in Istanbul, Kerim Bey, are observing a house. It is night, the street is deserted. The men hide in a doorway. The whole front of the house they are watching is plastered with a billboard advertising a film starring Bob Hope and Anita Ekberg. The billboard shows a painted portrait of the head of what could be inferred to be a voluptuous, blond woman, representing the actual, non-fictional actress Anita Ekberg. The mouth is laughing and opened. Where her teeth and tongue are, there is a secret exit door in the house front.

	12	13	14
Kerim Bey [v]	Do you notice anything?		She has a lovely mouth that Anita.
Kerim Bey [German]	**Fällt Ihnen irgendetwas auf?**		**Diese Anita hat einen wunderschönen großen Mund.**
007 [v]		Not yet.	
007 [German]		Nein.	
Desc [nv]			[That Anita has a beautiful, large mouth]

In section 14 Kerim Bey draws the attention to the mouth of the billboard. The English text uses the demonstrative pronoun "that" to realize a clarifying extension to the main clause "She has a lovely mouth". "That Anita" serves as an anaphoric identification of the sentence-initial personal pronoun "she". "That Anita" maps the pictorial information (the billboard) of the situational context on the propositional content of the utterance. In the clause "she has a lovely mouth", mouth is rhematic. By using the "that"-extension as a kind of postmodification of "mouth", mouth loses, to my mind, (some of) its rhematic status to the following "Anita". At the same time, the "that"-extension refocuses and elaborates the theme

"She". The effect is that at the end of the processing of the sentence, "Anita" would remain as the new information in focus, inviting whatever associations spring to mind on the part of the audience with respect to the actual, living actress Anita Ekberg and the more or less sexually defined image that surrounded her public persona at the time of the films' initial release (cf. Baumgarten 1998). Furthermore, "that" is usually regarded as a deictic device for 'distant' reference within the extralinguistic situational context. Using "that" would distance the speaker from the object he is referring to. In this sentence the distancing effect could be seen as mitigated by the initial use of the personal pronoun, which is unmarked for distance and makes the referent appear as given and familiar, and possibly spatially more immediate. The use of the personal pronoun can be considered a marked choice, because up to that point in the text, the billboard is only present in the visual context and has not been referred to before. An explanation might be that it is a strategy of referring the spectator to the mental processes of Kerim Bey. It may be that he is meant to be understood as having considered the billboard for a while before he starts to speak. That is, he has been thinking precisely how to direct the attention towards that part of the building where the hidden door is. He has been familiarizing himself with the information in picture and formulates the sentence on the basis of information that is already 'given' in his mind. He therefore starts his utterance with the undetermined "She". The marked structuring of the sentence also supports the notion of a highly subjective utterance. The deictic "that" could also be read as a marker for familiarity and givenness in the sense of: *"that Anita" Ekberg, who we all recognize and know about*. The deictic device would then point to presupposed hearer knowledge of the public persona of Anita Ekberg. This kind of familiarity might be further qualified when we consider that "that Anita" can be seen as an example of a disparaging use of "that" (Quirk *et al.* 1985: 289), indicating a subjective, negative evaluation. The referent for "that" in this respect would be the extrafilmic, social discourse on the image, the star persona of Anita Ekberg. The exact quality of the evaluation – sexual or other – has to be inferred on the basis of contextual information.

Apart from realizing this kind of discourse which seems to be defined by the male gaze (cf. e.g. Sturken and Cartwright 2001), the sentence has also the function of telling 007 and the audience where the secret exit door is. It is the latter information which is relevant in terms of the logical-temporal sequence of the narrative.

In the German translation the "Mund" (mouth) is the rhematic element and as such remains the main new information on which basis the hearer processes the following information. The German uses the demonstrative pronoun "diese" in a straightforward way of connecting the pictorial information of the billboard to the propositional content of the sentence. As a deictic device "diese" orients speaker and hearer in the situational context and in physical space. The distancing effect is, in the German translation, not mediated by any other linguistic feature. The utterance is an unmarked simple sentence, that does not draw attention to its own structure. Accordingly, the hearer is not invited to draw special attention to the speaker of the utterance. The utterance appears more depersonalized and less subjective. Also, "diese" does not necessarily invoke a particular aspect of the social discourse on the star persona. The hearer is instead referred to the mouth on the billboard, where the secret exit door is located. The German translation, in contrast to the English original, much more underscores the logical-temporal function of the utterance, and textualizes less sexualized discoursal surplus.

The context for the second example is the following: Kerim Bey and 007 have just shot dead a man that tried to leave the house through the secret exit door mentioned above. Pictorially, he came out of the mouth of the Anita Ekberg likeness on the billboard. Section 25 below is the scene-closing comment by 007. It is not directed at Kerim Bey although he is within earshot. The primary function of the remark therefore probably is characterizing 007. It serves to support the image the character has with the film spectator. The utterance can be seen as more immediately oriented towards the film audience than his turns in conversation with other characters: Kerim Bey does not react in any way and does not show any signs of acknowledgement which would convey that he received the information. Again, we may say that the hearer is admitted to the 'mind' of the character. The utterance can be read as a verbalization of mental processes. As such it is an indicator of highly subjective discourse. This is comparable to the dramatic convention of soliloquy: the character verbalizes his or her innermost thoughts. The utterance(s) are solely directed at the present audience in the theatre, other characters onstage do not take notice of the character's speech.

In the English version the utterance has a patronizing, admonishing character. This is primarily achieved by the use of the modal verb "should". "Should" implies two related ideas. First, the socially determined authority of the speaker to recommend, suggest, or order a certain course of

	25
Kerim Bey [v]	
Kerim Bey [German]	
007 [v]	She should have kept her mouth shut.
007 [German]	**Sie hat wirklich einen hübschen Mund.**
Desc [nv]	[She really has a pretty mouth.]

action: in particular, doing things or refrain from doing things. Second, "should" implies that a recommendation has not been carried out, which had consequences, usually of a negative kind (Quirk *et al.* 1985). On a more content-oriented level of analysis, one could argue that the question of granting somebody the floor, i.e. the right to speak, is played at. In the context of the representation gender this gains particular significance, since the right and the opportunity for women to express themselves verbally (and otherwise) has never been an uncontested matter in the cultural context of Western society that the film depicts as well as represents. The utterance can be read as a punch-line in form of a sexist joke. It functions overtly as a humorous element and belongs to a category of 'quip'-routines that over time have become a distinctive feature of the character 007. Taken literally, this quip serves to minimize 007's role in the killing. "She should have kept her mouth shut" could be paraphrased as: "If the woman had kept her mouth shut the man would not have died – therefore she is to blame for what happened".

The German translation links 007's utterance to Kerim Bey's utterance in section 14, discussed above. The text uses lexical repetition of the adjective "hübsch" to form a cohesive tie with the "wunder*hübsch*en" in section 14. The adverb "wirklich" in its affirmative and intensifying function also contributes to the cohesion between the utterances. In other words, at the end of the scene, the German translation is picking up a thematic element from the preceding discourse that orients the hearer backwards in the structure of the text. One effect is that the intermittent action – the killing – becomes embedded in an anaphoric structure. The English original, by contrast, does not display that kind of circularity but a linear sequence of themes which corresponds to the logical-linear sequencing of events. It could be argued then, that in the German text the killing gains a different informational quality by ending the scene on refocusing the point in time before the killing. From the point of view of sexualized discourse, however, the German translation is inconspicuous. It would be straining grammar and semantics to read for any other information than that the subjective attitude of 007 towards the present situational context is one of considering the mouth on the billboard pretty. There is ambiguity left whether he thinks it pretty because of aesthetic reasons, or whether its attractiveness lies in the fact the he completed one part of his mission there. Finally, the German utterance does not come across as a joke but more as an almost polite voicing of a personal opinion. This is because in contrast to the English version, the combination of the situational context and the lexicogrammatical realization of the remark is unmarked, that is, there is no equivalent discrepancy between the meaningful elements in the setting of the scene, which is the precondition for funniness.

To sum up, in the German translation the semantic resources are almost exclusively used to verbalize and support the action, that is, the event structure of the text. In the English version we find again the splitting of the text into two discourse strands: one that is referring to the logical linear sequencing of the action and one that is textualizing gender. First, female gender is textualized semantically in a negative, derogatory way. In the second place, the texts constructs a hierarchical relationship between male and female gender roles with the prerogative of power to recommend and evaluate actions on the side of the male speaking subject.[8]

The last example in this chapter deals with functional variation in the use of paralinguistic devices. Kerim Bey and 007 have been discussing the role of the prospective defector from the KGB, Tatjana Romanova. The exchange starting in section 7 below, deals with the implications of 007's having sex with her for the course of Kerim Bey's and 007's professional plans and goals.

Preceding this situation, there is a scene which shows 007 and the woman in bed together. On the basis of the information that the narrative of the film provides as given, Kerim Bey's utterance "[…] your not using

---

[8] One could further argue that by not realizing the gender discourse in an equivalent way the German translation also deflects a third discourse strand: humour. The 'fun' in the English version is instantiated in a sexist joke. A qualitatively different approach is taken in the translation, where the 'fun' has to be derived from the fact that 007 pays a compliment to a picture. However, degrees of funniness are impossible to measure, hard to pinpoint and hard to relate functionally to the lexicogrammatical features, so this has to remain a tentative suggestion.

	7	8
Kerim Bey [v]	How is she gonna get the machine over to us?	
Kerim Bey [German]	**Und wie will sie die Maschine zu uns bringen?**	
007 [v]		She's leaving that to me. She'll do anything I say.
007 [German]		**Das soll ich machen. Sie will alles tun was ich sage.**
Desc [nv]		

	9	10
Kerim Bey [v]	Hehehe . my dear James, you're not using this.	It all sounds too easy to me. We don't even know if she's telling the truth.
Kerim Bey [German]	**Hahaha. . Alles? He. . Mein lieber Freund . Sie müssen einmal nachdenken . Sie müssen einmal nachdenken .**	**Die Sache kommt mir zu einfach vor. Woher wollen Sie denn wissen dass sie die Wahrheit sagt.**
007 [v]		
007 [German]		
Desc [nv]	*points with his finger to his head* [Hahaha. Anything? Heh. My dear friend. You have to think.]	

this.", obviously invites hearer associations what other body part 007 actually might be using in this particular strand – the 'women-plot' (cf. the discussion of "women-enemies-adventures" above) – of the overall narrative. The pointing character of "this" is underscored by Kerim Bey's movement. It is the movement that clarifies the referent of "this". At the same time, the negative construction "not [...] this" might trigger hearer inferences within the context that would provide the implicit 'positive counterpart' "but that". Kerim Bey's utterance is a playful but unequivocal evaluation of the character of 007 by hinting at a problem at one of the cornerstones in the construction of the character, namely, 'simultaneous sexual control over women and control over the course of action'. In this context then, Kerim Bey's utterance becomes potentially disruptive for the 007-image, because it questions his being in control.

The utterance is an assertion in the form of a routine formula. The routine implies that something irrational (emotions, passions) is overriding the individual's rational reason. Again, on the basis of the information given about the character 007 up to that point, it seems clear that Kerim Bey insinuates that 007's behaviour is governed by his sexual interest in the prospective defector, and that 007 gives precedence to that part of his body that figures prominently in that respect. Substituting a gesture for the explicit lexicalization of "head" or "mind" makes the statement more implicit. Thus, the gesture is also a means of evading the utterance of a potentially face-threatening act against 007.

The German translation on the other hand, realizes a request instead of an assertion: "Mein lieber Freund Sie müssen einmal nachdenken." (My dear friend you have to think.). The modal verb "müssen" (must) indicates the obligation for 007 to act in a certain way ('think') as well as Kerim Bey's authority in advocating this particular behaviour on the part of 007. The force of the obligation is mitigated by Kerim Bey's chuckling, which opens his turn. The paralinguistic gesture here coincides with the word "nachdenken" (think). The gesture underscores the significance the speaker places on the mental activity and the concept of rationality that is connoted by "nachdenken". The implication is that 007, up to this point, has not been thinking enough or not at all, which is strengthened by the use of "einmal". "Einmal" in this context has no equivalent in English, but it implies that the following action is either new to begin or has to be pursued more thoroughly from now on. Overall, the sentence leaves little room for inferences concerning 007's male gender role, and there is no implication of an evaluation of the character of 007 via questioning his male gender role. Also, the sentence is a fully explicit structure. The ad-hoc-formulation is made up of the present situational context and preceding information. Although the request to think is very direct, the quality of the face-threatening is different from that of the English sentence, because the

German realization does not involve key concepts of the construction of the character of 007.

Textually, the English utterance marks a break in the conversation. In the preceding turns, 007 and Kerim Bey exchanged details which are action-oriented, i.e. information that supports the overall event structure of the film narrative. During the conversation, Kerim Bey adopts a critical stance towards the topics that are discussed. In section 9 of the example he unexpectedly enters into an evaluation of these 'professional' topics via an evaluation of 007's behaviour as a 'private', sexual being. The German translation marks no equivalent break in the conversational structure. On the contrary, the lexical repetition of "Alles?" serves as a cohesive device that connects the propositional content of Kerim Bey's turn to the content of 007's utterance in section 8: "She'll do *anything* I say." In addition to that, "Alles?" in its function as rhetorical question explicitly addresses the hearer and refers him backwards to the information on which the question was formed. The desexualized request for rationality is also a coherent continuation of the criticism that Kerim Bey has been voicing throughout the scene.

To summarize, in this example, the German translation deflects textualising gender by lexicalizing a direct, explicit attempt to initiate an action on the part of 007 that concerns the special significance of the 'professional' events in the narrative. Again, the translation seems to be focused on realizing the logical event structure of the text.

5. Conclusion

In the examples discussed above, the German translations feature gender-conscious language in the sense that potentially socially discriminating aspects of the discourse are cut away. Changes in lexicogrammatical devices deflect the realization of a second strand of discourse that textualizes gender in the original English version. There are several possible explanations for why this is. First, the marked departure of the German textualizations may be evidence for the existence of so called translation universals (cf. Laviosa-Braithwaite 1998). Phenomena such as "normalization" might, on a discourse level, account for 'normalizing' discourses that have overtones that are unwelcome in the receiving culture. On a more particular linguistic level, shifts in cohesion and coherence, which are also regarded as universal features of translations (Blum-Kulka 1986), change the semantic relations in the text. The resulting changes e.g. in the chains of reference consequently effect qualitative differences in the target-language discourse. Secondly, the greater content-orientedness, in the sense of a stronger focusing of the event structure of the narrative, could be interpreted as typically German use of language, in line with the dimensions of cross-cultural differences between English and German. The same interpretation would be valid for the concurring non-focusing of interpersonal issues that the narrative brings forward. Personal issues and subjective attitudes are textualized to a far lesser extent than in the corresponding English texts. Thirdly, the reason for the differences might be sought in the particular type of translation. Multimodal translation poses the problem of mapping several, parallel discourses as well as the storyline on only one set of linguistic structures. However, technically, an analogous German translation such as "Sie hätte ihren Mund halten sollen." (for "She should have kept her mouth shut.") would have been possible. Hence, it seems fair to suggest that German translation has been *chosen*. Finally, I did not analyze the texts for their relation to the overarching social discourses that surrounded this James Bond movie at the point of its initial release: for instance, the social discourses on Bond in the source language culture and the target language culture. I also did not include the intertextual relations that connect *Form Russia with Love* with its predecessor *Dr. No*. Analyses of these contexts would offer additional perspectives on the construction of gender in the film.

To conclude, whether or not the use of language in the English and German versions of the film part have consistent patterns – each language one of its own, and one for the relation between the two – needs to be further investigated (Baumgarten forthcoming). To my mind, this is relevant because film is not just a phenomenon of pop culture, and language in film is not just a matter of linguistics. Both integrate in processes of social semiosis. When we look for the ways how social situations and social roles are constructed and instituted across languages, the potential of multimodal mass media in depicting and verbalizing modes of social interaction appears to be very significant.

Translation, Nationalism and Gender Bias

CARMEN RÍOS & MANUELA PALACIOS
Universidade de Santiago de Compostela, Spain

Abstract. The analysis of the connections between nationalism and translation allows for new perspectives on the issues of gender and language. An example of this is represented by the project undertaken by the Galician group *Xeración Nós* in the 1920s, as can be gathered from their translations into Galician of Irish texts which are concerned with nationalist issues. It seems that there is a gender bias in these translations, as both writers of the source texts and translators are usually men, whereas the nation is most often constructed in feminine terms. However, in order to avoid charges of essentialism, both source and target texts have been thoroughly analyzed to see how nationalist discourse constructs masculinity and femininity, as well as the degrees of appropriation of these patterns that translation may implement. The results of these analyses suggest that Galician translations of Irish nationalist texts in the 1920s have functioned as perpetuators of the gender bias of the source texts, maintaining all the stereotypes around masculinity and femininity which were characteristic of the Irish originals.

The present paper aims to explore the connections between translation, nationalism and gender. To do so, we shall focus on a particular period in Galician literature, the first decades of the twentieth century, when the members of the *Xeración Nós* – a group of nationalist intellectuals concerned with the refurbishing of the Galician literary system – translated various texts from other European literary systems. Among all the translations they produced, the ones that are more relevant for our present purposes are those of Irish texts, which at that time were highly concerned with the literary representation of the nation.

Our choice of both literary period and corpus of texts has a great significance in terms of gender. Díaz-Diocaretz suggests that feminist analysis should outline the woman's presence or absence as translator, as character and also as reader. Besides, it should provide a historical account of the woman's function in the corresponding cultures (1985: 155). Along this line, we have found that both the Irish authors selected for translation and their Galician translators are all men. As for the woman as a textual component, we have noticed that the allegorical construction of the nation implemented in our corpus is most often done in feminine terms.

Our perspective as female readers is indebted to feminist analysis, so we intend to interrogate the connections between sex and ideology as well as between patriarchal discourse on nationalism and the symbolic construction of the nation as feminine. Feminism provides us with an adequate theoretical framework because it calls our attention to the linguistic and social complexities of the speaking subject. Furthermore, feminism, as a political project, exposes the ideological dimension of translation. The interface between feminist and translation studies reveals, as Nikolaidou and López Villalba suggest, that neither writer nor translator are a universal, ahistorical essence, but sexed bodies in specific and historical contexts (1997: 91). In the light of these tenets, one further objective of our study is to explore whether the receptor-texts in Galician perpetuate or challenge the gender bias of the source-texts and to scrutinize the reasons for this.

In order to understand the reasons that moved Galician intellectuals to be so deeply interested in the literature that was being written in Ireland at the time, we must take into account the proposals of theories of reception such as the Konstanz School as well as the Polysystem theory designed by Itamar Even-Zohar. We should not forget that translation is a privileged field for the study of the reception of literary texts between cultures. Reception Theory, for instance, presents the work of art as a product related to the social and historical reality of its producers and consumers. This explains the fact that new translations are demanded with the pass of time since, following Sherry Simon, each literary generation brings with it different problems of translatability (Homel and Simon 1988: 54). The cultural gap between our twenty-first-century perspective on gender issues and that of Galician or Irish nationalism from the early twentieth century may account for our voluntary role as resisting readers.

As for Polysystem theory, we find particularly useful Even-Zohar's study of dependent literary systems. Especially relevant are his laws of literary interference (1978), since they provide the patterns followed by dependent systems in the establishment of contacts with other more developed systems. The Galician literary system of the first decades of the twentieth century was in a situation of dependence and weakness. It was dependent on the more developed Spanish literary system and had an internal weakness due to its lack of a proper repertoire. In order to overcome their weakness, literary systems tend to search for contacts with those systems that are closer in geographical terms. However, Galician nationalist writers avoided contacts with the Spanish literary system, which they saw as an oppressive force, and looked for contacts with other developed European literary systems with which they had affinities in historical and ideological terms.

Even-Zohar pays thorough attention to the role of translated texts and their effect on the target literature, especially when the target polysystem is not a stable one:

> For such [peripheral] literatures, translated literature is not only a major channel through which fashionable repertoire is brought home, but also a source of reshuffling and supplying alternatives. Thus, whereas richer or stronger literatures may have the option to adopt novelties from some periphery within the indigenous borders, "weak" literatures in such situations often depend on import alone. (1991: 48)

It is often acknowledged that smaller cultures produce and consume more translations (Homel and Simon 1988: 55). What needs to be further analysed is why the *Xeración Nós* chose certain texts and authors in particular, since theirs cannot be considered as an innocent choice. As Nikolaidou and López Villalba put it in their discussion of feminist translators: "la *selección* de escritoras (o escritores) que traducen no puede considerarse ni casual, ni inocente, ni neutral, sino coherente con sus propias premisas teóricas e ideológicas (...)" (1997: 95). Both nationalists and feminists have their respective strong ideological commitments. The former are deeply aware of the institutional role played by literary translation in the construction of the nationalist self-image. The latter insist on making the feminine subject visible. Álvarez and Vidal also stress the relevance of ideology to translation:

> If we are aware that translating is not merely passing from one text to another, transferring words from one container to another, but rather transporting one entire culture to another with all that this entails, we realize just how important it is to become conscious of the ideology that underlies a translation. (1996: 5)

The choice by the *Xeración Nós* of well-known Irish authors to be translated, such as W.B. Yeats and James Joyce is due to their project to renovate the Galician literary system from an aesthetic and ideological point of view. This twofold motivation is described by Caneda Cabrera as an interest in the "dignificación e o desenvolvemento da cultura autóctona que queren conectar directamente con Europa", which is combined with their "particular e apaixonado compromiso de descolonizar Galicia política e culturalmente" (1998: 90). The interest that Galician nationalist writers of the 1920s and 1930s had in Irish literature is related to the fact that the Anglophone system in Ireland had wider international recognition and to the existence of a feeling of communion with Ireland, a communion that Galician intellectuals labelled as the "Brotherhood of the Celtic Race".

However, it is mandatory to study also the reasons that moved the members of the *Xeración Nós* to ignore[1] an Irish woman that was very important in the Irish literary system of the time. We are thinking here of Lady Gregory, whose literary production and personal interests were deeply connected with the kind of nationalist program defended by the intellectuals of the *Xeración Nós*. It is rather surprising that, in the series of articles written by Vicente Risco under the title "A Moderna Literatura Irlandesa", he deals with authors of less importance or with a less active role in terms of their commitment to the nationalist cause, while Lady Gregory only appears mentioned in discussions of W.B. Yeats, as his collaborator in the Irish Literary Theatre. The omission of Lady Gregory is even more significant when we take into account all the debates around the authorship of "Cathleen ni Houlihan", a play that we shall come back to later. In this respect, James Pethica has highlighted the role of Lady Gregory in the composition of this play on the grounds that "the accounts both Yeats and Lady Gregory gave of their partnership in playwriting make clear that their collaboration on *Cathleen ni Houlihan* must have involved greater degrees of mutuality (…)" (Pethica 1988: 5).

The relevance of Lady Gregory to the development of the Irish Literary Renaissance invites comparisons with other movements in search for a national identity such as the Galician one in the 1920s and 1930s. In contrast to the presence of this leading female writer in the Irish movement,[2] we notice that the role of women intellectuals around the *Xeración Nós* was at best tangential. Why was this so? The nationalist project launched by the *Xeración Nós* was almost exclusively in the hands of

---

[1] In the sense that women are neither translated nor even dealt with in the articles they wrote on foreign literatures.

[2] However, it has to be acknowledged that the role played by Lady Gregory in the Irish Literary Renaissance must be understood only in terms of her nationalist convictions, since there are no hints of a committed feminism on her part.

men. Our question, which breaks fresh ground for further research, is whether this relegation of Galician women writers is basically due to the patriarchal control of culture in this period, or whether the nationalist agenda was hostile to the active presence of women in their struggle.

W.B. Yeats's "Cathleen ni Houlihan" constructs an allegorical representation of the Irish nation as an Old Woman. This play was performed in the Irish Literary Theatre in 1902. The debut was very successful and its revolutionary message was well received by militants. Yeats's portrayal of Ireland as the traditional wronged old woman calling on her children for help was seen as an invitation to political action. This play was translated in *Revista Nós*[3] in 1921 by Antón Villar Ponte, one of the most active members of the Galician cultural movement, founder of the so-called "Irmandades da Fala"[4] in 1916 and co-founder of the political and cultural magazine *A Nosa Terra*. This translation was not accompanied by any introduction or preface on the part of the translator where he might explain the reasons for the choice of this particular text. This play was translated again into Galician some years later, in 1935, by Plácido R. Castro and the brothers Villar Ponte. This second translation was published under the title *Dous dramas populares de W.B. Yeats. Vertidos á lingua galega directamente do inglés por Plácido R. Castro e os irmáns Villar Ponte, con licencia do autor.* Apart from "Cathleen ni Houlihan" ("Catuxa ni Houlihan"), this edition included also "The land of Heart's Desire" ("O país da saudade"). The 1935 edition was accompanied by an introduction by Plácido R. Castro and Antón Villar Ponte, where they explain the reasons that led them to translate these plays: Yeats's fame in his homeland and the favourable reception of the plays in Ireland, together with the significance of the theme for the Galician audience, parallel to the effect that the plays had on the Irish audience when they were performed in Ireland. It is quite surprising that the 1935 edition has not the slightest mention to the previous translation of "Cathleen ni Houlihan" published in 1921, above all when we do not find many discrepancies between the two Galician texts. Some of the differences have to do with the choice of particular words, in a way that the second translation seems to have chosen terms that sound more Galician, as if looking for a greater

---

[3] The literary magazine published by the members of the *Xeración Nós* from October 1920 until the outbreak of the civil war in 1936.

[4] A cultural movement similar to the "Gaelic League" in its aim to defend the Galician language against the overwhelming presence of the Spanish language.

differentiation from the Spanish language. We also find a higher frequency of words with religious connotations that were absent in the 1921 version.

In our analysis of both translations of Yeats's text, we feel some uncertainty about the source language used by the Galician translators. Though the 1935 translation insists in its very title on the fact that the text was directly translated from English, there are hints that make us suspect that the translators may have used an intermediary language, such as French, since there are passages where the two Galician versions add adjectives or entire sentences that do not appear in Yeats's original text written in English. The English version we have worked with belongs to the 1982 edition of W.B. Yeats's *Collected Poems*, published for the first time in 1934. There is a preface written by Yeats himself, where there is no evidence that may lead us to think that this version differs from the one performed at the Irish Literary Theatre in 1902. Thus, it is plausible to think that the Galician translations may have been made via another translation. It is a well-known fact that the members of the *Xeración Nós* had a deep command of the French language and that they were acquainted with the main French magazines of the period, which were the site for the publication of many translations at that time. This fact is more important than it may seem, as we might be dealing with translations of translations, a fact that endows the analysis of the translated texts with a further complexity.

The analysis of the construction of the feminine in the source-text – by feminine we refer both to the female characters in the play and to the metaphors and other images that are constructed in feminine terms – reveals that the female protagonist of "Cathleen ni Houlihan", the one who gives its title to the play, cannot be understood as a real character but as the allegorical representation of the nation, that is, of Ireland. Though we have a female protagonist, she is not a flesh and blood character and, therefore, she does not have a voice of her own. She is only relevant inasmuch as she stands for something else. Something similar happens with the other female characters in the text, who are only valued in terms of the dowry they can offer to their husbands or of the children they can give birth to. Cathleen is the icon used by Irish nationalists to represent the nation: Ireland as an Old Woman, forced to wander across the country after suffering all sorts of outrages.

This representation of the nation in feminine terms is consonant with other nationalist symbols in Irish texts of the period, which were also translated by the members of the *Xeración Nós*. For instance, in Yeats's,

"Our Lady of the Hills",[5] one of the main ideologies constitutive of the Irish nation, religion, is embodied as a woman, in this case the Virgin. This is a very significant type of representation: on the one hand, one symbol of national identity is once again constructed in feminine terms and, on the other hand, the Virgin, rather than a flesh and blood woman, is a dehumanized icon of unattainable perfection. These representations of the nation and of national identity through female characters can be contrasted with other examples of Irish literature, where the heroism needed to save the nation is constructed in masculine terms.

The poem by Yeats "The Rose Tree"[6] praises the heroism of the Irish people through historical characters such as Patrick Pearse and James Connolly. This poem by Yeats, collected in *Michael Robartes and the Dancer* (1921), is one of the texts of the Irish Literary Tradition that best exposes the kind of patriarchal tradition to which this movement is to be ascribed. On the one hand, traditionally masculine values such as heroism and force are represented by men, while the nation is once again inscribed in terms often associated with patriarchal views of femininity: in this case, a beautiful rosebush that needs to be watered by those heroic men for its subsistence. In her discussion of the work of the Indian political philosopher Ashis Nandy, Gerardine Meaney remarks that colonized nations are often characterized as feminine, whereas the forces that claim independence usually aspire to a traditionally masculine role of power. The anxiety that derives from a history of defeat is assuaged by the assumption of sexual dominance (1991: 6-7).

These symbolic representations of the nation in the texts of the members of the Irish Literary Renaissance are to be understood as part of the patriarchal tradition to which its authors belonged. What is more important for our study is our verification of the fact that the same patriarchal values are to be found in the translations by the members of the *Xeración Nós*. The perpetuation of gender bias in the translated text has been widely discussed in recent debates on the role of feminist translation. We find theoreticians of translation, such as Barbara Godard, for whom translation should not be understood as a mere act of reproduction but as an active process of production. Godard backs up her thesis with the following statement:

---

[5] This play was translated by Vicente Risco and published in *Revista Nós* in 1923 as "Nosa Señora dos Outeiros".

[6] This poem was translated by Vicente Risco in 1926, in the series of articles he wrote on Modern Irish Literature.

> This theory of translation as production, not reproduction, focus-
> ing on the feminist discourse as it works through the problematic
> notions of identity and reference, is at odds with the long-dominant
> theory of translation as equivalence and transparency which de-
> scribes the translator as an invisible hand mechanically turning the
> words of one language into another [...] Here, translation rejoins femi-
> nist textual theory in emphasizing the polyphony and self-reflexive
> elements of the translator's / rewriter's discourse. (1988: 50)

For Godard, as for many other female theoreticians of translation, feminist discourse offers the possibility to subvert and challenge patriarchal
discourse, so that the source-text can be manipulated in accordance with
the particular ideology of the translator. But this manipulation or any similar
space for subversion is absent in the Galician translations of Irish texts in
the 1920s. The same constructions of the nation in patriarchal terms are
maintained in the translated texts, and besides, since Galician is a language with a visible morphological mark for gender, the relegation of the
feminine to symbolic representations is even more explicit in the translated versions than in the source-texts. The following is an example from
"Cathleen ni Houlihan": in the source-text, the Old Woman declares that
one of her main sorrows is the loss of her land ("My land that was taken
away from me" (Yeats 1935: 81)), with 'land' used as a metonymy for the
country of Ireland. This sentence was translated into Galician as "A miña
ter*ra* que me teñen roubado" (Villar Ponte 1921: 10 and Castro and Villar
Ponte 1935: 32) (the italics are ours). Thus, the translated version has
wider resources to insist on the construction of the nation in feminine
terms, so that not only does it not subvert the kind of representation we
found in the source-text, but reinforces it.

This presence of the feminine can by no means be understood in positive terms from a feminist perspective, since these patriarchal and
nationalist traditions relegate women to mere symbols of the nation. The
relations between Irish nationalism and feminism have been widely discussed by Gerardine Meaney, for whom nationalism is one oppressive
force that has often worked against women and feminism in Ireland. Symbolic representations of the nation, such as those we find in "Dark
Rosaleen" or "Cathleen ni Houlihan" are for Meaney constant reminders
of the invisibility of real Irish women in the literary and cultural tradition
of their country (Meaney 1991: 17). She proposes a way out of this traditional obliteration of women in the following terms:

> Feminism cannot, in attempting to see women outside their tradi-
> tional role as symbols of the nation, be content to merely impose a
> revised role on them, a role as victims of the nation or of history.
> The work of contemporary continental feminist thinkers, with its
> emphasis on the way in which we are produced by and produce the
> dominant culture and the internal complexities of any programme
> of cultural and psychological change, may offer a way out of the
> twin stereotypes into which any analysis of women in Irish culture
> so easily falls. (1991: 14-15)

In our analysis of certain Irish texts and their respective Galician translations, we have noticed that the stereotypes around masculinity and
femininity are maintained in the receptor-texts. A feminist approach to
both the source-text and its translations should attempt to criticize the
kind of metaphoric language that presents women as icons with no active
role in real life. The use of imagery along patriarchal gender lines has
been present in the very history of translation studies, as the activity of
translation has been often understood in feminine terms, in opposition to
the masculinity of the source-text. As Lori Chamberlain argues in this
respect, "the sexualization of translation appears most familiarly in the
tag *les belles infidèles* – like women, the adage goes, translations should
be either beautiful or faithful" (Chamberlain 1988: 455).

In order to subvert this perpetuation of gender bias, translators should
make use of the spaces that are available for them to deconstruct those
images that trap women within patriarchal appropriation of language. These
spaces are, as Barbara Godard has noted, italics, footnotes or even prefaces to the translations (Godard 1988: 51). These are also the spaces that
we miss in the Galician translations of Irish texts in the 1920s and that
would have served as a challenge to the gender bias of the source-texts.

The Gendering of Translation in Fiction
Translators, Authors, and Women/Texts in Scliar and Calvino

ROSEMARY ARROJO
Binghamton University, USA

Abstract. This paper focuses on how the theme of betrayal in translation (or interpretation) is often treated in fiction in terms of love
triangles in which the interpreter's 'betrayal' of the original is associated with some form of competition (between an interpreter
and an author) for the love of a woman. The objects of analysis are
the following works of fiction: Italo Calvino's *Se una notte
d'inverno un viaggiatore* (first published in Italy in 1979), and
Moacyr Scliar's short story entitled 'Notas ao Pé da Página' (published in Brazil in 1995). This type of analysis may help us further
understand the often negative reputation translators seem to have
in a culture that worships originals and tends to reject any activity
that somehow 'touches' them. It may also help us reflect on why
mainstream translation theories have always been so interested in
controlling and disciplining translators and their 'subversive' interventions in the texts they necessarily have to rewrite.

Common sense has often associated both translations and translators with
different forms of betrayal, as some well-known aphorisms (*"traduttori-
traditori," "les belles infidèles"*) clearly show. In previous texts I have
examined how a few selected works of fiction represent the complex
relationship generally established between originals and their reproduc-
tions, as well as between authors, translators, interpreters or readers
(Arrojo 1986, 1993, 2001-2002, 2002, 2003a, 2003b). My general assumption is that the views on texts and their derivations and on those in
charge of producing them, which are implicitly or explicitly interwoven
in the plots developed in works of fiction from different literary traditions
(by authors such as Borges, Poe, Kafka, Kosztolányi, and Saramago), are
ultimately a faithful reflection of the ways in which culture tends to deal
with the reproduction of originals and with those who are dedicated to
this kind of textual activity.

In this essay I intend to focus on how the age-old theme of betrayal in
translation has been charged with explicitly sexual overtones as it is associated with some form of competition between men for the attention of a

woman in an intriguing short story entitled *"Notas ao Pé da Página"* ("Footnotes"),[1] by Brazilian author Moacyr Scliar (1995),[2] as well as in Italo Calvino's novel, *Se una notte di inverno un viaggiatore* (1979), which I will be reading in its English version, *If on a Winter's Night a Traveler* (1981).[3] It is my assumption that the intertextual dialogue that I plan to establish between Scliar's and Calvino's texts will bring some light to the intricate triangular relationship which seems to trap translators, writers, and originals in the imaginary of a patriarchal culture that associates the writing of originals and authorship with notions of property (and, of course, which views creation and ownership as male prerogatives). I also believe that such readings may help us further understand the often negative reputation translators tend to have in an ideological context that privileges originals as the allegedly stable containers of authorial meaning and is, thus, inclined to distrust any activity that seems to destabilize them. It may also help us reflect on why both common sense and mainstream translation theories are usually quite keen on 'protecting' originals from translators, and on finding ways to discipline them and their 'unwelcome' interventions in the texts they necessarily have to interpret and rewrite.

In a groundbreaking essay, "Gender and the Metaphorics of Translation", Lori Chamberlain introduces her discussion on the sexualization of translation by calling her readers' attention to the notion of *"les belles infidèles"* that compares translations to women: "like women, the adage goes, translations should be either beautiful or faithful" (1992: 58). As Chamberlain aptly observes, this tag

> owes its longevity – it was coined in the seventeenth century – to more than phonetic similarity: what gives it the appearance of truth is that it has captured a cultural complicity between the issues of fidelity in translation and in marriage. For les *belles infidèles*, fidelity is defined by an implicit contract between translation (as woman) and original (as husband, father, or author). (*Ibid.*)

What interests Chamberlain in exploring the implications of this comparison is the basic asymmetry of power that constitutes the relationship

---

[1] I want to thank my former student Maria Aparecida Fernandes for having brought this text to my attention.

[2] There is no English version available, and the translations of quotes will be mine.

[3] Most of the comments presented here will be revisions of the arguments first proposed in Arrojo (1995), with an emphasis on gender issues.

between "translation (as woman) and original (as husband, father, or au-thor)". As she argues, "the infamous 'double standard' operates here as it might have in traditional marriages: the 'unfaithful' wife/translation is publicly tried for crimes the husband/original is by law incapable of com-mitting" (*ibid.*).

It is precisely an expansion (and a reinterpretation) of this love trian-gle, involving text (as woman), author and translator, that is the main foundation of Scliar's "*Notas ao Pé da Página*" ("Footnotes") (1995). As its title suggests, the story is composed of footnotes, five of them, which appear at the bottom of the five empty pages where the 'invisible' trans-lated original is supposed to be. While the translation and, consequently, while the original and its author are not accessible to us, readers, it is the translator's writing that constitutes the actual text of Scliar's story. And yet, even though Scliar's narrator/translator represents the only authorial voice in the story, he is definitely 'speaking' within the only textual space that is usually granted to translators: the bottom of the page. Through his footnotes we learn that they refer to his translation of a poet's diaries. Allegedly it is in order to clarify some points of the poet's narrative that the translator's footnotes end up telling us (inappropriate) details of his author's biography. We learn, for example, that the poet, who is now dead, used to be ungrateful, immensely ambitious, and difficult to relate to. We also learn of his 'anxiety' to have his work translated by our narrator/translator, and of his humiliating efforts to achieve just that. We are told, for instance, that the last time they both met, the poet, as usual, overpraised the translator's work and confessed that he even liked the latter's foot-notes (275). More importantly, we are exposed to details of the love triangle that involved the poet, the translator, and N., the poet's mistress, who left the latter in order to marry the translator. It is also through such footnotes that we learn that the poet, the 'invisible', 'dead' author, was not only a helpless, lonely man who got desperate as he lost his mistress, but who also had to credit most of his 'relative' success to the translator's talent and compassion.

What seems particularly intriguing about Scliar's plot is the fact that we are faced with a translator who, according to his own account, is quite competent and, we may infer, quite efficient in achieving adequate 'fidel-ity' to his originals or, at least, that is what we are led to believe considering the poet's alleged insistence in having his work translated by him. And yet, the translator certainly misuses (and virtually abuses) the space that is conventionally given to him at the bottom of his translation of someone

else's text. We are thus dealing with a translator who is, at best, both faithful and unfaithful – supposedly faithful to the poet's originals, but unfaithful
nonetheless. Considering such circumstances, how are we, readers, expected to react to Scliar's translator/narrator? Are we supposed to consider
that some form of 'infidelity' or 'abuse' is the inescapable fate of translators, even of those who seem to do their job adequately? Or is Scliar perhaps
celebrating the sheer 'visibility' of his empowered translator/narrator? One
might ask, after all, what kind of professional ethics is Scliar's story implicitly or explicitly defending for translation and translators.

Before I try to elaborate on a possible answer, it seems clear that the
story is humorously playing with the basic, old clichés that involve the
notions of property, fidelity and betrayal, as they bind together authors,
originals, translators and translations. The underlying power relations that
generally organize such notions in clear-cut hierarchies seem to be radically reversed in Scliar's plot. While common sense generally expects of
translators (and particularly of those involved with literary texts) to do
their (hopefully) 'invisible' work in the shadow of the writers to whom
they are supposed to be blindly faithful, Scliar's narrator/translator takes
a clearly authorial stance. Furthermore, he presents himself as the powerful male figure in the love triangle that defines the story, and in which N.
plays the obvious *belle infidèle* who, in spite of her betrayals[4] to the poet,
ends up happily married to the translator. Thus, we are confronted with a
resourceful, self-assured, influential, utterly 'visible' translator who not
only overpowers the weak, insecure poet to whom he is supposed to be
faithful, but who is also largely responsible for the latter's modest success. In other words, it is the translator, and not the author of the original,
who ends up (legitimately) 'possessing' the text as woman. Moreover, in
such a plot, it is the poet who begs the translator to pay attention to his
work and who depends upon such attention, and not the other way around,
as tradition generally teaches us. In Scliar's story, it is the 'dead' author
who loses his right to the woman/text and who owes his recognition as a
published poet to the translator's talent and alleged generosity (and to his

---

[4] As we learn, when N. met the poet in France, she was working as a secretary in the
small publishing house that finally agreed to publish the poet's first collection of
poems. According to the narrator/translator, "the relative success of such a work should
be attributed, at least partially, to N.'s own efforts. She was the one who managed to
obtain from the publisher (and for that she had to grant him certain favors) his reluctant approval for an enterprise which, from the market's point of view, represented a
venture of unpredictable outcome" (1995: 371).

mistress's sexual favors to his first publisher, as we may well remember).

Readers who are familiar with contemporary translation theories might associate Scliar's plot with some often quoted contemporary texts on interpretation, reading and translation. Lawrence Venuti's work on the translator's (in)visibility is probably the first one that comes to mind. As it has been widely known among translation scholars in recent years, Venuti's main theoretical focus has been the exploration of what he sees as the "eclipse of the translator's labor", and, as he has often argued, translation continues to be "an invisible practice, everywhere around us, inescapably present, but rarely acknowledged, almost never figured into discussions of the translations we all inevitably read" (1992: 1). Venuti has been particularly interested in unveiling the "asymmetries" involving translation practice. As he writes in the introduction to *The Scandals of Translation – Towards an Ethics of Difference*, his "overriding assumption" is perhaps "the greatest scandal of translation: asymmetries, inequities, relations of domination and dependence [,which] exist in every act of translating, of putting the translated in the service of the translating culture" (1998: 4). Furthermore, the main goal of his work has been not only to make translators and translation scholars aware of such "scandals", but also to propose and defend translation strategies that might contribute to change the *status quo*.

One can also think of some of the most prominent thinkers usually associated with poststructuralist textual theories. Michel Foucault's and Roland Barthes' explorations of the notions of the 'dead' author and the productive reader are appropriate examples. In his post-Nietzschean celebration of the 'death' of the author and the reader's newly acquired power, Barthes argues that "no vital 'respect' is owed to the Text [...] it can be read without the guarantee of its father, the restitution of the inter-text paradoxically abolishing any legacy" (1977a: 161). And as the Text's father becomes an unnecessary presence in the scene of reading, it is the reader's prerogative to decide what to do about the role of the powerless author, who can only "come back" into his Text as a "guest" that the reader may, or may not, wish to entertain: "he becomes, as it were, a paper-author: his life is no longer the origin of his fictions but a fiction contributing to his work" (*ibid.*). In a similar fashion, Michel Foucault has turned the once all-powerful Author into a mere "function", or a "certain functional principle by which, in our culture, one limits, excludes, and chooses; in short, by which one impedes the free circulation, the free manipulation, the free composition, decomposition, and recomposition of fiction" (1979: 159). From such a perspective, the author is viewed as a mere strategy of reading, that is, as an "ideological figure by which one marks the manner in which we fear the proliferation of meaning" (*ibid.*).

Another appropriate example is Jacques Derrida's reading of Walter Benjamin's "The Task of the Translator", in which the French philosopher elaborates on Benjamin's radical revision of the traditional relationship generally established between originals and translations. As Derrida deconstructs the logocentric notion of the original as presence, and as he expands Benjamin's notion of translation as survival, he argues that to the extent that "the structure of the work is 'survival'", the translator's "debt"

> does not engage in relation to a hypothetical subject-author of the original text – dead or mortal, the dead man, or "dummy," of the text – but to something else that represents the formal law in the immanence of the original text. Then the debt does not involve restitution of a copy or a good image, a faithful representation of the original: the latter, the survivor, is itself in the process of trans-formation. (1985: 182-183)

Would such associations between Scliar's plot and postmodern notions of text and translation suggest that the story is somehow defending the translator's 'visibility' and proposing a reconfiguration of the power relations that usually bind together originals and translations, authors and translators? In other words, is it appropriate for the translator to take over and for the "*belle infidèle*" to leave the 'dummy' author and marry the empowered translator?

In order to attempt to answer this inescapable question, I propose to bring to our discussion another plot that also plays with the relationships generally established between readers, authors, editors, and translators, at the same time that it explicitly colors them with sexual overtones. I refer to Italo Calvino's (and his translator's) *If on a Winter's Night a Traveler* (1981).[5] As in Scliar's story, Calvino's intricate plot establishes a clear

---

[5] The following is a brief summary of Calvino's plot: because of what seems to be an error in the binding of a new book (entitled *If on a winter's night a traveler*, by Italo Calvino), the male protagonist simply referred to as "Reader" returns to the bookstore and discovers that all the remaining copies contain the same 'mistake'. In his search for the continuation of the book, he accidentally meets a female reader, Ludmilla, who has rushed to the bookstore for the same reason. From then on the plot revolves around the Reader's quest for the true 'original' and his pursuit of Ludmilla. In his

association between woman and text, in which reading, apparently celebrated as a true form of text production (or as a truly legitimate strategy
of pursuing the original), coincides with the pursuit of an attractive female reader (the "*Lettrice*") named Ludmilla, who becomes the "Other
Reader" in the English version.

As one might predict, the Reader, Calvino's protagonist, is not alone
in his quest for the ultimate possession of the woman as text. There are at
least two other characters drawn to Ludmilla: Silas Flannery, an Irish nov-
elist who is now able to write only a personal diary, and Ermes Marana,
the translator/'swindler' who manipulates and misplaces originals and
translations, and who is responsible for the truncated texts we actually
read in Calvino's novel. Flannery is an exemplary personification of the
'dead' author of poststructuralist textual theories,[6] as he is reduced to a
mere shadow that is under the control of powerful readers. Moreover, in
Calvino's plot, being a 'dummy' author also seems to imply some form of
textual/sexual impotence since Flannery's inability to write is paralleled
to his inability to approach the woman/reader he desires. He can only
watch her from afar through a (phallic) telescope:

> "She's there every day," the writer says. "Every time I'm about to
> sit down at my desk I feel the need to look at her. Who knows
> what she's reading? I know it isn't a book of mine, and instinc-
> tively I suffer at the thought, I feel the jealousy of my books, which
> would like to be read the way she reads. I never tire of watching
> her: she seems to live in a sphere suspended in another time and
> another space. I sit down at the desk, but no story I invent corre-
> sponds to what I would like to convey." (126)

Ludmilla is also the very reason why Ermes Marana has decided to
misplace texts and their translations. As we learn, "the secret spring that
set [his machinations] in motion was his jealousy of the invisible rival
[any author she might read] who came constantly between him and
Ludmilla" (158-159).

---

search, he is faced with books that are interrupted and misplaced, other readers and,
particularly, with references to a mysterious 'swindler', a translator named Ermes
Marana, founder of Apocryphal Power and a representative of the OEPHLW of New
York (Organization for the Electronic Production of Homogenized Literary Works).
[6] Calvino's familiarity with French intellectuals associated with structuralism and
poststructuralism has been documented in biographical accounts. See, for example,
Bloom (2001: 113).

While Flannery personifies the author as an impotent 'dummy', Ermes Marana is the unscrupulous translator who does not hide or shy away from his authorial/sexual desire. Even a brief exam of the most obvious associations suggested by his name can tell us a lot about the nature of his 'character'. "Ermes", of course, is also "Hermes", the Greek god, usually associated with interpretation ('hermeneutics') and mediation. Paul Friedrich, for example, has discussed the "multiple liminality of Hermes and his links with Aphrodite". In his synthesis of Hermes' most prominent attributes, we will certainly find appropriate associations with Calvino's translator:

> 1. Hermes moves by night, the time of love, dreams, and theft; 2. he is the master of cunning and deceit, the marginality of illusions and tricks; 3. he has magical powers, the margin between the natural and the supernatural; 4. he is the patron of all occupations that occupy margins or involve mediation: traders, thieves, shepherds, and heralds; 5. his mobility makes him a creature betwixt and between; 6. his marginality is indicated by the location of his phallic herms not just anywhere but on roads, at crossroads, and in groves; 7. even his eroticism is not oriented to fertility or maintaining the family but is basically aphroditic – stealthy, sly, and amoral, a love gained by theft without moral concern for consequences; and finally, 8. Hermes is a guide across boundaries, including the boundary between earth and Hades, that is, life and death. (1978: 205)

We can also relate our translator (as well as his aphroditic 'eroticism' and his morals) to Don Juan de Marana, Alexandre Dumas' 1837 version of the widely known playboy character – the relentless, amoral, cynical seducer of women – whose emergence in literature is usually traced back to Tirso de Molina's *El Burlador de Sevilla*. As a translation of multiple other translations, the very proper name "Ermes Marana" functions as an efficient synthesis of the character it names: a sly, deceitful, predatory manipulator of authors, texts, and women, who has no scruples and, of course, who could never be faithful to anybody or anything.

In this Barthesian comedy of intrigue, which fictionalizes the pleasures (and the disappointments) of textual/sexual relationships, authorial power is somehow granted only to those male characters that actually have the strength and the courage to pursue and 'possess' Ludmilla. And it is certainly significant that while the translator-character and the Reader actually have sex with her, the 'paper author' Flannery, barely reduced to a ghostly presence, can only resort to voyeurism. It is appropriate to note that both in Barthes' texts on reading (1974 and 1977b, for example), and in Calvino's plot, even though the author (or, at least, the author as character in *If on a Winter's Night a Traveler*) has lost his paternal control over his texts, the pleasure (and the alleged power) of the 'productive' reader or translator is essentially related to masculinity. The pleasure of reading is, as Barthes suggests, "an Oedipal pleasure (to denude, to know, to learn the origin and the end)": "the entire excitation takes refuge in the *hope* of seeing the sexual organ (schoolboy's dream) or in knowing the end of the story (novelistic satisfaction)" (1974: 10). Conversely, Ludmilla, the female reader, finds pleasure in a very different approach to reading. In contrast with the male Reader, who actively sets out to build his reading out of the fragments he finds, the "Other Reader" chooses to remain simply a reader. As she declares, she does not want to cross the "boundary line" that separates "those who make books" from "those who read them": "I want to remain one of those who read them, so I take care always to remain on my side of the line. Otherwise, the unsullied pleasure of reading ends, or at least is transformed into something else, which is not what I want" (93). It is her non-aggressive, 'feminine' way of reading, which is precisely what seems to make her attractive to Calvino's male characters, that also distinguishes her from her sister, Lotaria, a reader whose reductive, computer-assisted approach is associated with the academic world and the university, "where books are analyzed according to all Codes, Conscious and Unconscious, and in which all Taboos are eliminated, the ones imposed by the dominant Sex, Class, and Culture" (45). Lotaria's assertive, ridiculous, somewhat 'feminist' approach not only sterilizes authors and books, but also turns her into an unattractive female. As we are told, Ludmilla always gives Lotaria's phone number to the people she does not know because Lotaria manages to keep them "at a distance" (45).

In *If on a Winter's Night a Traveler*, as in Scliar's story, authorial power is definitely a masculine privilege, which is apparently (or temporarily) granted to translators. In both texts, we are faced with shadowy authorial figures whose writing abilities are somehow questioned, and with translators who take on a truly authorial role to the point that they are the actual 'authors' of the very texts we are offered to read. Furthermore, Marana, like Scliar's narrator/translator, is not only 'visible' and powerful, but also morally objectionable. After all, Calvino's translator cannot help stealing and faking manuscripts, at the same time that he 'possesses' the woman/text (another "*belle infidèle*"?) without being married to her. In fact, the major difference regarding Calvino's and Scliar's translator-characters, which might be relevant for my present discussion, is that while Scliar's "*belle infidèle*" ends up married to the translator, in Calvino's plot it is the male Reader who is apparently given the privilege of legitimately possessing the desired woman/text.

This intertextual dialogue between Scliar and Calvino may help us speculate on what might be going on behind the main scenes of both plots. Starting with Calvino's text, we may wonder, for example, whether the myth of the author's absolute paternal authority has really been overthrown in the Italian novel. In other words, is the author really 'dead' in Calvino's novel? And, also, if the author were truly 'dead', and if Calvino's plot were truly celebrating the (male) pleasure of productive interpretations, why does his enterprising, aggressive translator-character have such a bad reputation?

As one may argue, although Calvino actually seems to fictionalize the main traits of a caricatural postmodern textual theory in his plot, in which the woman as text ends up 'belonging' to the Reader, most of such traits get to be subtly (and also not so subtly) deconstructed in other networks of meaning throughout the novel. Behind Calvino's apparent celebration of poststructuralist theories of language, text, and authorship, we "find that this is the gambit of an intricate game, a game that cannot be played without the reader but is set up to trick him/her into realizing that it is always [he], Calvino, who is in total control of the situation" (Fink 1991: 94). It seems that even though the novel's author-character, Silas Flannery, is a caricatural personification of the 'dead' author theorized by poststructuralists, the actual author behind the plot, Calvino's narrator (or Calvino himself), does not give up the traditional role of the story-teller as the controlling voice of his fiction. In the very first paragraph of the novel, for example, in the very first contact between Calvino's narrator and the Reader and, consequently, also with us, as we inevitably identify with the "You" that opens the novel, we (and the Reader-character) get to receive instructions on how to read his book, and on how to turn this reading into the very center of our lives:

> You are about to begin reading Italo Calvino's new novel, *If on a Winter's Night a Traveler*. Relax. Concentrate. Dispel every other thought. Let the world around you fade. Best to close the door; the TV is always on in the next room. Tell the others right away, "No,

I don't want to watch TV!" Raise your voice – they won't hear you otherwise – "I'm reading! I don't want to be disturbed! (3)

Calvino's narrator proceeds to indicate "the most comfortable position" and circumstances in which his own book should be read and often interrupts the narrative to let the Reader know who is in control of the plot. As Fink points out, "there is no freedom for the Reader-character because he can only seemingly escape the grasp of the author, who makes up the rules of the game" (1991: 99). Calvino's narrator even warns his Reader against his controlling strategies in more than one passage. For example, just a few pages after the beginning of the novel, he tells us:

> For a couple of pages now you have been reading on, and this would be the time to tell you clearly whether this station where I have got off is a station of the past or a station of today; instead the sentences continue to move in vagueness, grayness, in a kind of no man's land of experience reduced to the lowest common denominator. Watch out: it is surely a method of involving you gradually, capturing you in the story before you realize it – a trap.[7] (12)

Thus, the "Reader," who seems to play an authorial role in the reading of someone else's text, is in fact a puppet in the narrator's hands. As Ian Rankin points out, the purpose of Calvino's novel seems to be two-fold:

> The author gives us a breathtaking, magical read, and at the same time he draws lines of demarcation. This is your role, he tells us in the numbered chapters, your job is reading, while in the titled chapters he shows us his own role, that of a storyteller. Calvino is not about to "die" in order that the real reader may live [...] and he is not about to hand over the responsibility of the creative act to his audience, for he is in no doubt that it is the author who is in charge of the literature-making process. (1986: 129).

---

[7] In an interview that appeared soon after the publication of the English version of his novel, Calvino makes it clear that his game-playing in *If on a winter's night a traveler* is not accidental and comes from yet another kind of (textual/sexual) pleasure: "And of course there is always something sadistic in the relationship between writer and reader. In *If on a Winter's Night a Traveler* I may be a more sadistic lover than ever. I constantly play cat and mouse with the reader, letting the reader briefly enjoy the illusion that he's free for a little while, that he's in control. And then I quickly take the rug out from under him; he realizes with a shock that he is not in control, that it is always I, Calvino, who is in total control of the situation" (in Du Plessix Gray 1981: 23).

The (real) author's pleasure is, therefore, comparable to that of a 'sadistic lover' who gives his Reader the illusion of being involved in a reading
that may take initiatives in the construction of the text, which are, however, predicted and controlled by the guiding hand of an omniscient
narrator. Mary McCarthy calls our attention to the "permissive" *ars amoris*
that seems to underlie the relationship that takes place between the Reader
and the narrator in Calvino's plot. While the whole first chapter seems to
function as a prolonged "foreplay", in which we can witness the Reader's
anxious "anticipation", the powerful author-lover "withholds consumma-
tion" as he offers the Reader a series of ten beginnings, ten novels that
break off precisely as they become interesting, which McCarthy associates with instances of "*coitus interruptus*" in the art and practice of fiction
(1981: 3). It is from this perspective that we may try to understand why
the "ideal reader" in Calvino's novel is not the male Reader, but a passive, attractive female who refuses the male Reader's invitation to join
him in finding "the thread [of the narrative] that has been lost" on the
grounds that, "on principle", she wants to remain simply a "reader" who
is happy to be guided by the novel's controlling narrator (93). In fact, as
the author marries both Readers at the end of the novel, there seems to be
a suggestion that those two different strategies of reading could (or should)
be somehow reconciled. What matters, though, in the end, is that both
Readers, "now man and wife", are together in their "great double bed"
reading "If on a Winter's Night a Traveler" (260).

It is also along the same lines that we can try to explain why Marana
is, at the same time, both an authorial figure and a 'swindler'. After all, it
is as a result of his direct interventions that the Reader ends up with ten
incipit novels, which actually constitute most of the text of *If on a Winter's
Night a Traveler*. That is, the very text we read is, figuratively speaking,
the result of an unwelcome intervention attributed to the translator-
character – "a serpent who injects his malice into the paradise of reading"
(125) – who 'takes over' the place of the 'real' author. But who is the
'real' author and who is the 'thief'? It is particularly revealing that
Calvino's strategy in this novel is also the strategy devised by Marana in
the Sultana's episode. As we learn, in a sultanate of the Persian Gulf, the
Sultan's wife "must never remain without books that please her: a clause
in the marriage contract is involved, a condition the bride imposed on her
august suitor before agreeing to the wedding" (123). Since the Sultan fears,
"apparently with reason, a revolutionary plot", as well as a betrayal by his
wife (another *belle infidèle*?), he hires Marana to translate all the books

the sultana is about to read so that "if a coded message were hidden in the succession of words or letters of the original, it would be irretrievable" after translation (124). What Marana proposes to the sultan is a "stratagem prompted by the literary tradition of the Orient":

> He will break off this translation at the moment of greatest suspense and will start translating another novel, inserting it into the first through some rudimentary expedient; for example, a character in the first novel opens a book and starts reading. The second novel will also break off to yield to a third, which will not proceed very far before opening into a fourth, and so on... (125)

The translator-character repeats, of course, Scheherazade, one of the greatest authorial figures of all times, whose ability to tell a story changes her fate and postpones death. If Marana's authorial strategy is also Calvino's, and if Marana is a manipulative thief for faking originals and for misguiding readers, isn't the author also guilty of similar sins?

What I am trying to suggest is that at the same time that Calvino's plot offers us an intriguing illustration of the feelings of rivalry and jealousy that seem to haunt the often delicate relationship that can be established between authors and translators, it also shows us the difficulty of drawing a definite line that could separate them in clear-cut categories. Even though Calvino's novel only gives us caricatural portraits of an author, a translator and a few readers, it does allow us to reflect on the inextricable connections that can be found between the translator's age-old reputation as an incorrigible traitor and the relationship that seems to trap translators/interpreters, authors, and originals in a complex triangle. At the same time, it gives us an acute perspective on the author's desire to control his readers and the fate of his texts, as well as his emphatic refusal to become a mere 'shadow' in the (poststructuralist) scene of reading. As it blatantly sexualizes textual relations and activities, Calvino's novel also exposes in an exemplary fashion how the association between creative power and masculinity is (still) deeply inscribed in a culture that insists in establishing definite, hierarchical oppositions between male and female roles, writing and reading, originals and translations, subject and object, and which (still) relates property rights exclusively to men.

Similarly, as we go back to Scliar's plot after our incursion into Calvino's book, what the Brazilian author seems to be offering us in his unusual piece is also a rare glimpse into the highly emotional conflict that often underlies the ambivalent relationship that both separates and brings together writers and translators (see also Arrojo 1993, 2001-2002, and 2002). Unlike Calvino's plot, however, Scliar's story (apparently) gives us a translator's perspective on such a relationship, as we are exposed exclusively to the translator-narrator's voice. And yet, could we really trust such a perspective? The sheer absence of the translated poet's voice and the translator-narrator's outrageously inadequate use of his textual space seem to hint at the translator's negative feelings for having such a limited space and such a marginal role in the literary world. In other words, even though Scliar's story allegedly offers us a translator's point of view, it seems to be implicitly defending the absent author-character from his inadequately 'visible' translator. After all, how can we possibly trust Scliar's narrator as we witness the unprofessional manner in which he treats his author? How can we not sympathize with the 'dead' poet whose mistress the translator ends up seducing and marrying? Like Ermes Marana, Scliar's translator gives us a perverse perspective on the translator's al- leged desire to take over someone else's beloved property, a perspective that is inevitably filtered by the author's underlying concern regarding the protection of his texts from external interferences. In both plots, how- ever, no matter how negatively the translator's reputation is portrayed, there is an explicit recognition of the translator's authorial role. In fact, one may argue that it is precisely because such a role is acknowledged that there is so much concern.

It is also the highly sensitive nature of such a concern that seems to be at stake in the clear associations that both Calvino's and Scliar's texts efficiently weave between texts and women. That is, one of their underly- ing messages seems to be that an author's desire to protect his texts from the interference of others is as strong as a man's desire to keep his women away from any other man's influence. Unfortunately, though, such a mes- sage is not merely about concerned authors and consciously predatory translators. It is also about women who are not only trapped as men's objects in their fictions, but who are, in such a position, comparable to texts, particularly as they are conceived in the age of poststructuralism, that is, fickle, unstable, and necessarily unfaithful until they find power- ful men who manage to stabilize them in marriage, as it is the case with both Calvino's Ludmilla and Scliar's N.

Finally, even though such texts portray translators as explicitly nega- tive authorial figures, it is undeniable that behind Scliar's and Calvino's humorous, sexist fictions there are a lot of (productive) readings in trans- lation and, thus, a lot of good, reliable work done by countless anonymous translators. At the same time, in spite of the fact that in their stories the role of women has been limited to that of secretaries, 'naïve' readers, or ridiculous feminists, it is the example of a very powerful woman/author figure such as Scheherazade that seems to have been the ultimate model (at least) of Calvino's novel. As translation scholars, one of our important tasks should be the unveiling of what goes on behind the scenes of the main plots that have defined the roles of translation and translators in our culture, at the same time that we become aware of how such scenes, to the extent that they reveal markedly asymmetrical relationships between authors and translators, originals and translations, are also intimately linked to other similarly asymmetrical plots such as those that have defined gender relations in a culture obsessed with the possibility of original meanings and binary oppositions.

Translating True Love
Japanese Romance Fiction, Harlequin-Style

JANET S. SHIBAMOTO SMITH
University of California, Davis, U.S.A.

Abstract. Japanese preferences for fictionalized love affairs depicted in category romance fiction have been significantly affected by translated Harlequin-style western romance novels. Harlequins have been immensely popular since their introduction in the early 1980s, even to the point of triggering a 'Harle-quinization' of Japanese *ren'ai shôsetsu* 'romance novels'. Harlequin translations are thus one important site for displaying the qualities and behaviours associated with portraits of desirable femininity and masculinity. This paper presents an analysis of three aspects of interactional style between the Harlequin hero and heroine that differ substantially from the typical styles of Japanese category romance novels. Dialogue drawn from the Harlequin lovers' interactions is analyzed and interpreted against native Japanese norms for the appropriate expression of emotion and against the speech and actions of counterpart lovers drawn from a sample of contemporary native Japanese category romances. Of the differences found, two serve primarily to construct a different kind of heroine, the third, a different hero. Together, they provide new spaces for imagined female equality and emotional helplessness, on the one hand, and for male verbal expressivity, on the other. Japanese-language Harlequins offer linguistic portraits of 'true' lovers inhabiting very different worlds of heterosexual desirability from their domestic Japanese fictional lover counterparts. The imported 'messages' about ideal heroines and heroes may not always flatter Western-style lovers, but they provide alternative ways of imagining loverly behaviour for the Japanese reader.

Since the moment in 1979 that Harlequin translations hit the bookstores in Tokyo and other urban centers, they have transformed the Japanese 'romance fiction' market. By 1998, Harlequin Tokyo employed four hundred English-to-Japanese translators and was advertising production levels of 16,000,000 volumes annually. Their effects are visible. Once, romance novels had to be culled from sections labeled, e.g., *shinkan* 'current releases', *joryuu shoosetsu* 'women's novels',[1] or the large and largely undifferentiated sections of paperback fiction (*bunkobon*).[2] Now, romances are positioned in highly visible Romance Corners quite often centered around a Harlequin-provided revolving bookstand. Romance fiction has, in effect, been constituted as a popular genre, one centered around translations of North American and western European category romance fiction exemplars.

The types of novels produced domestically have also been affected by the introduction and popularity of Western category romances. For the romance readers among women of my generation, coming to adulthood before, during, or immediately after World War II, the best romance was the tragic romance, the story of *hiren* 'blighted love'. A novel was, in essence, only *romantic* if it made the reader cry. Likewise for movies, where the 'three handkerchief' movie drew large female audiences. And for *enka*, a lyric-based song genre focused on nostalgia and lost love.

McKinstry and McKinstry (1991: 157-8) note that "love stories in novels and movies in which romance is portrayed as bringing people together *for marriage* – in other words, love as part of the preliminary marriage process, rather than extraneous to marriage – have only been prevalent for three or four decades. This concept was imported into Japan along with many other innovations after World War II; its major advocates are people under thirty". It is hardly surprising, then, that younger Japanese women readers, affected by the newer discourses of romance circulating in contemporary Japan and by the Harlequinization of romantic fiction more specifically, prefer the happy ending.[3] Although the Harlequin phe-

---

[1] Which include a wide range of genres, such as history, fantasy, and mystery, as well as love (see, for example, the listings of *joryuu shoosetu* at http://www.geocities.co.jp/Milkyway-Cassiopeia/9000/my/book2.htm). Often, this category seems to be defined by *joryuu sakka* 'female authors' rather than by genre.

[2] Romances could even be found in the *suiri* 'mystery' section, for those mysteries which included just that 'touch' of romance. Here one would find mysteries in which the 'touch' of romance swamped the mystery as, for example, Akagawa Jiro's *Futari no Koibito* 'Two Lovers' (Akagawa 1996), advertised on Yahoo! Japan's Books Shopping website as a *romantic suspense* [novel] by Akagawa Jiro for the reader [lit., you] who wants two lovers (*koibito o futari hoshii anata ni...Akagawa Jiroo ga okuru saikookyuu no romantikku sasupensu*). The first romance novels in my corpus, in fact, were 'donated' to this project by a former master's student who read Akagawa and other mystery writers precisely *for* the romance they contained.

[3] When they do not shun this genre entirely, or are not drawn to one of two other categories of 'relationship' fiction – the ironic ending kind (exemplified in much of the work of Hayashi Mariko) and the sado-masochistic, (quasi-)pornographic kind

nomenon is by no means the sole influence on this shift in preference, then, their effect on the romance fiction *industry* has been strong enough for at least two series, modeled on the Harlequin type romance, to have been launched since 1980: Sanrio's New Romance series in the 1980s and Oto Shobo's short-lived Crystal Romance series, launched in 1996. We may say, then, that Harlequin romances have had a profound effect on the category romance industry, the romance 'product' (i.e., the novel itself), and the romance reader.

Nonetheless, one thing is certain. The reader of a translated Harlequin is *not* reading a Japanese romance. The characters are depicted in Japanese, to be sure; they speak to each other and to other characters in Japanese, and they come to a mutual recognition of their attraction and true love in Japanese. But they inhabit 'western' social fields and react in ways that – whatever their suitability in those social fields – are not the ways that Japanese true lovers speak, behave, and come to their own *happii-endingu* 'happy ending' in domestically produced romance novels. What, then, are the differences?

1.   Lookin' good, Lookin' loveable

I have treated elsewhere the differences in the ways that Harlequin lovers and Japanese romance fiction lovers are described in terms of physical appearance and general demeanor (Shibamoto Smith 2004), and will not dwell on these differences here. It is sufficient to say that, like Radway (1984), I found that Harlequin men were described as spectacularly masculine, sexually hyper-experienced, and reserved, if not cold. The Harlequin hero is seemingly indifferent to the heroine, until the end of the novel, when his hitherto well-hidden feelings burst forth. His heroine is unusually intelligent and/or unusually honest and moral. She often has a fiery disposition, but even when she does not, is generally given to impulsive albeit well-intentioned actions. She invariably has a childlike innocence and is sexually inexperienced.[4] Above all, however, she is extraordinarily beautiful and extraordinarily unaware of her beauty.

These women and men stand in stark contrast to the women and men of the domestic Japanese category romance. Japanese heroes, when they

---

(e.g., *Vaajin Byuuti* 'Virgin Beauty" by Saito Ayako). These latter two types of fiction lie outside the scope of the present study.

[4] Or, has little experience with 'good' sex.

are described, tend to be described as more average than Harlequin heroes. They are, to be sure, sometimes depicted as 'special'; they are often
rich, or tall, robust, and they may even seem arrogant or sardonic. But
most of them are just ordinary, nice men, who act in relatively ordinary
ways.[5] The Japanese heroine, too, as noted by Mulhern (1989) is neither
socially isolated, as Western heroines often are, nor sexually repressed.
She is generally self-confident, often enjoys a career, and she is not necessarily a great, sexually compelling beauty. Japanese heroines are as often
described in terms of relatively realistic self-evaluation, suggesting a more
down-to-earth self-awareness on the part of the Japanese heroine than is
the norm for the Harlequin-style women.

A very obvious difference, then, between these category romance styles
is the very physical presence of the lovers. But there is more to love than
looks, and there are more differences between our lovers than their physical personae. There are substantial differences in interactional style as
well. Here, I provide a preliminary analysis of three. Two of these differences most noticeably affect the presentation of the heroine as an
appropriate candidate for being in 'true' love; the third differentially affects the construction of the hero. These three differences are: a pattern of
insistent overfamiliarity and erasure of status asymmetries (a pattern of
presumption), a pattern of excessive self-disclosure and emotionality (a
pattern of extended juvenility), and a tendency to make lengthy and detailed declarations of love (a pattern of extended personal disclosure).

2. Getting to know you: the pattern of presumption

Let us take a look at the first verbal interchange between *Jenifaa* 'Jennifer',
a salesgirl in the housewares department of a major Chicago department
store and *Chaaruzu* 'Charles', the young company president of the store
(Herter/Minami 1996/1998). Jennifer has been selected to participate in a
'live' show window Christmas display, and Charles approaches her to

---

[5] With one exception, having to do with the erasure of class boundaries that is possible in category romances in ways not at all possible in 'real' romantic life. Men in
professions that are unlikely to be stable or that are unlikely to provide an adequate
economic base of support for a family are frequently heroes in category romances.
That they would not be generally viewed as 'heroes' by contemporary Japanese women
is well-documented.

talk to her about it. Jennifer has been told of her selection and informed
that Charles has arranged for them to talk over the details of the assign-
ment over lunch. In (1), Charles arrives at Jennifer's counter.

(1)[6] Charles   Itsu mo no koto nagara yoku hataraku ne.
        Jennifer   Ee, **shachoo** ni inshoo-zukeyoo <u>to omotte</u>.
        Charles   Aa, nakanaka ii taido da. (then, jokingly)
                   De mo kimi no baai wa, tokidoki hame o
                   hazushite moratte mo ii yo.
        Jennifer   Mata, shigoto ni muchuu de asonde inai <u>to o-
                   sekkyoo shitai no</u>? Ranchi ni sasoi ni kite kudasatta
                   n deshoo?
        Charles   Soo da yo. Okotte iru no kai?
        Jennifer   Doo <u>kashira</u>.
        Charles   Burasseri wa doo?
        Jennifer   Ee, <u>ii wa</u>.

               ....they walk to the bistro...

        Charles   Sate, uindoo reedii ni erabareta kansoo wa?
        Jennifer   Shoojiki ni itte, kangeki wa shite imasen.
                   Dooshite watashi ga erabareta n desu ka?
        Charles   Dooshite? Soo da na....Seikaku na riyuu wa
                   oboete inai. Maaketingu-bu ya keshoohin no
                   senmonka ni makasete ita n da. Karera wa josei
                   juugyooin subete o kentoo shi, kimi ni kimeta to
                   itte ita yo. Misutaa jeemuzu wa kimi no kokkaku
                   ga ki ni itta yoo datta na. Maaketingu-bu no dare
                   ka wa, kimi wa kono depaato no shoochoo de aru
                   chisei o kanjisaseru to itte ita yo.
        Jennifer   Tsumari, **anata** ga eranda <u>wake de wa nai no ne</u>?
        Charles   Boku ga? Masaka! De mo kimi ga erabareta to
                   kiite hotto shita kedo ne.
        Jennifer   Hotto shita tte <u>doo iu koto</u>?
        Charles   Boku datte ishuukan mo issho ni sugosu josei
                   wa, kigokoro no shireta..
        Jennifer   **Anata** ga shoo uindoo ni <u>hairu no</u>?

----

[6] Forms in boldface are the pronoun forms that I discuss following the example. Un-
derlined elements are the sentence endings used by Jennifer, and these are discussed
after the section on pronoun use.

Charles	As usual, you're working hard, aren't you?
Jennifer	Yes, thinking to make a good impression on you (lit., on shachô 'company president').
Charles	Ah, that's a good attitude. (then, jokingly) But sometimes it would be okay for you to slip the traces.
Jennifer	Do you want to scold me again for being wrapped up in work and not having fun? You came to invite me to lunch, didn't you?
Charles	Yes. Are you angry?
Jennifer	I wonder.
Charles	How's the Brasserie?
Jennifer	Okay.

....they walk to the bistro...

Charles	Well, how do you feel about being chosen 'window lady'?
Jennifer	To tell you the truth, I'm not very thrilled about it. Why was I chosen?
Charles	Why? Well,... I don't remember the exact reason. I left it up to the Marketing Division and the cosmetic people. They reviewed all the women employees and said they had selected you. Mr. James seemed to like your build.[7] Someone in the Marketing Division said that you conveyed 'class' (lit., chisei 'intelligence') that symbolizes this store.
Jennifer	Then, it's not that you chose me, right?
Charles	Me? Of course not! But, when I heard you had been selected, I was relieved.
Jennifer	What do you mean, you were relieved?
Charles	Well, if I'm going to spend a whole week with a woman, a reliable one.....
Jennifer	You're going in [the window]?

In this very long example, what, precisely, do we see as constructing our heroine as 'different', as unlike the Japanese heroine, with respect to overfamiliar behaviour? There are three aspects of Jennifer's speaking

---

[7] This remark could, of course, be taken as suggestive; in terms of the unfolding of Charles and Jennifer's story, however, it appears to refer to her 'build' as a good scaffolding for the display of clothing (merchandise).

pattern that are characteristic of Harlequin heroines and unlike Japanese heroines in this regard. Taken together, I argue that they construct a pattern of an 'overfamiliar' and presumptuous female.

The first has to do with Jennifer's use of forms of address, most particularly, her use of the second-person pronoun *anata* to address Charles. There are many first- and second-pronoun forms to choose from in Japanese, each with particular connotative or indexical association with the age/sex/class of the speaker, the relationship to the addressee, and the formality of the context of use. Their role in gendered language is substantial; indeed, first- and second-person pronouns have been one of the centerpieces of the literature on language and gender in Japanese. Their utility in indexing interpersonal status relationships interacts with gender in interesting ways. This is particularly true of second-person pronoun options. Women and men share the second-person pronoun form *anata*, whereas typically only men have use of the less formal and more condescending *kimi* and *omae*. Like first-person pronouns, second-person pronouns are significantly marked for gender and for status. Status considerations dictate that second-person pronouns are avoided by subordinate members of status asymmetric dyads. It will hardly surprise us that cultural models of male superiority over women are evidenced in these texts, leading women in domestically produced romances to be represented in both blighted love and happy ending texts as avoiding second-person pronouns, in just the way subordinate members of dyads properly should. And, in Japanese terms, Charles, as the president of the store where Jennifer is employed should not be addressed as *anata* either, but rather by title (*shachoo*) or by last name + *san* 'Mr.'. To be sure, there are also conventions for the ways husbands and wives (or, male and female lovers) address each other. Although many young couples today call each other by their first names, without *-san*, or by nicknames, older conventions still seem to obtain to a reasonable degree in romance novels generally, and in Harlequins in particular. According to these conventions, wives *would* use *anata* to address husbands, while husbands would respond with *kimi* or *omae*. Jennifer might, then, use *anata* to her lover (which Charles will become) or her spouse (which he will ultimately aspire to become), but it is unlikely that as female employee – her status at the time of this interchange – she would use this form to her boss.

In Harlequin translations, however, *anata* is used regularly and very, very often. Pronominal usage is fixed as follows: heroes use *boku* for self-reference and *kimi* 'you' to address heroines; heroines use *watashi* for self-reference and *anata* 'you' to the heroes. The dictates of English-language pronoun use, coupled with the apparent requirement that these dialogues use pronouns in Japanese where they appear in English, construct heroines who through their very speech seem pushy (through too much overt self-reference) and impertinent (through too-frequent and inappropriate second-person address).

The second element of Jennifer's self-presentation in this initial passage of dialogue between the lovers that fits the pattern of presumption is the use of informal verbs, coupled with stereotypically feminine sentence final particles. Japanese verbs are morphologically marked for social distance between interlocutors, a 'distance' which is sometimes dictated by context. social distance is indexed by the use of *desu* 'is' following a plain verb form or by the verbal suffix *-masu* and its conjugated variants. These forms are often terms politeness markers. Verbs may also be marked for relative status of speaker and addressee, through use of one of a number of morphological devices which indicate speaker's on-record assessment of a status asymmetry; together these latter devices are termed honorifics. Both the underlying gender hierarchy in Japan and the specifics of the workplace relationship between Jennifer and Charles dictate that one or another – if not both – devices be employed by Jennifer. The workplace itself is, moreover, a context which typically calls for 'politeness' marking on verbs, particularly in utterances produced by the subordinate member of a conversational pair. And Jennifer does, indeed produce utterances marked appropriately with a *desu* or *-masu*, the verbal politeness marker, as in her response to Charles' question about her reaction to being selected as the "window lady": *Shoojiki ni itte, kangeki wa shite* _imasen_. *Dôshite watashi ga* _erabareta n desu_ *ka?* Both *shite imasen* '[I] am not' and *erabareta n desu ka* '... was it that [I] was chosen' are adequately 'polite' for a workplace conversation between non-intimate employer and employee. But Jennifer uses no honorifics at all, and also uses many non-polite, or plain forms: *o-sekkyoo* _shitai_ *no?, doo Æ kashira,* _ii_ *wa, wake de wa* _nai_ *no ne?, doo iu koto Æ,* and _hairu_ *no?,* the casual, familiar tone of which utterances is intensified by the use of sentence final particles *no?, kashira, wa,* and *no ne?* Sentence final particles, which follow the verbal (and all other post-verbal) morphology in Japanese, serve to indicate the speaker's stance with respect to the proposition with which it is associated. There are numerous sentence final particle forms either used exclusively by one sex of speaker or the other, or strongly associated with one gender or the other (Shibamoto 1985; McGloin 1997; Shibamoto Smith

2003); all Jennifer's sentence final particles in this (and virtually all other other) passages are characteristically 'feminine'. And this, too, is worthy of passing comment. Previous research has shown that romance heroines across the board construct femininity by using relatively high frequencies of 'feminine' sentence final particles. However, it turns out that Japanese heroines are *less* likely to use high frequencies of feminine sentence final particles than are heroines in domestically produced romances. This particular sort of hyper-feminine encoding, then, constructs a rather different heroine than a reader might be led to expect, one who is persistent – not to say *in*sistent – on calling attention to her femininity. Returning to the issue of excessive familiarity, however, it must be admitted that we soon learn that the encounter above is not Jennifer and Charles' first encounter. They worked together in the housewares department when Charles was in the early stages of his training to take over the family store. Nonetheless, the linguistic style, compounding informal verb forms and context-inappropriate sentence final particle use, results in a conversation between an employer and one of his (rather low-status) employees, conducted in the workplace, about a work-related issue that leaves Jennifer looking not very socially adept and pretty presumptuous.

The impression is exacerbated by a third element of Jennifer's dialogue, having to do more with her role in the conduct of the interchange than with its form. In her second turn, in which she responds to Charles' comment that she could relax sometimes, she responds: *Mata, shigoto ni muchuu de asonde inai to o-sekkyoo shitai no? Ranchi ni sasoi ni kite kudasatta n deshoo?* 'Do you want to lecture me again about working too hard? You came to invite me to lunch, didn't you?' What is 'wrong' with these remarks? Well, there are two things wrong, from the Japanese conversational perspective, in addition to the forms of the utterances. Jennifer accuses Charles *directly* of wanting to lecture her, a violation of general conversational preference for indirect encoding of negative information or evaluation. Then, she takes control of topic management in an abrupt shift from her work habits to what Charles is 'supposed' to do next. In neither case is Jennifer responsive to the normative social needs of the situation (Maynard 1997). I argue, then, that with respect to the first point of difference, the Harlequin novels of which these Japanese versions are translated construct a romantic heroine who, in her dialogue at least, acts in unawareness or defiance of social prescriptions to mark respectful social distance and social status asymmetry, both pronominally and verbally.

It is certainly not the case that no pushy female characters appear in

Japanese category romances. They do, to be sure. Sometimes they are friends, sometimes workmates, sometimes even relatives of the heroine. But it must be emphasized that they never *are* the heroine, and they never succeed in attracting the hero.

3. Emotional maturity *vs.* extended juvenility: The Harlequin heroine

Maturity in Japan consists, in part, of a public muting of affect. Where Americans, ideologically at least, follow norms of direct, open expression of feelings, in Japan, more favourable judgements are attributed to moderated expressivity, reflecting a greater degree of control (Matsumoto 1996: 157). It is instructive, then, to see how Harlequin heroes and, especially, heroines manage their emotions. *Guen* 'Gwen' and *Mitcheru* 'Mitchell' (Browning/Nakagawa 1985/1987) meet when their cars collide on a remote West Virginia mountain road (2).

(2) Mitchell   Daijoobu ka? Ugokeru kai? Doko ka kega shita no ka?

Gwen   Itsu datte, onna no hoo ga warui to iwareru n da wa. Onna wa itsu mo sukeepugooto nan da wa.

   .... after several exchanges about names and insurance companies, Gwen starts a series of exchanges about who is to blame for the accident....

Gwen   De mo, kono jiko ga watashi no sei da to itteru wake ja nai no yo. Anata wa ano kaabu o marude...

Mitchell   Baka na koto o iwanai de kure. Zenpoo o mi mo shinai de yokomichi kara tobidashite kita no wa, kimi ja nai ka? Futari to mo shinanakatta no wa kiseki datta.

Gwen   Zenpoo fuchuui wa, anata no hoo ja nai! Uesuto-baajinia no yama no naka de, nukarumi ni hamatta mama, isshoo o oero to de mo iu no?

Mitchell   Nee, reedii, boku wa kimi ga kore kara isshoo, doro no naka ni kubi made tsukatte sugosoo to kamawanai yo. Kimi ga haiuei ni chikazukanai

	de ite kureru nara ne. Ittai doo yatte unten menkyo o totta n dai?
Gwen	Anata ni sonna ni fuyukai na koto o iwareru sujiai wa nai wa. Watashi wa waza to tobidashita wake je nai n da mono. Moshi anata ga anna supiido de...
Mitchell	Are you all right? Can you move? Are you hurt somewhere?
Gwen	Whenever [something happens], the woman is blamed. Women are always the scapegoats.

....exchanges of names and insurance companies....

Gwen	But I'm not saying that this accident was my fault. You were [coming around] that curve just like a....
Mitchell	Don't be ridiculous. Wasn't it you who just burst out onto the road from a side road without even looking where you were going? It was a miracle we both weren't killed.
Gwen	Wasn't it you who weren't paying attention to what was in front of you? Are you saying that I should just end my life stuck in the mud of the mountains of West Virginia?
Mitchell	Hey, lady, I don't care if you do life out your life stuck up to your neck in mud. As long as you don't come anywhere near the highway, you know? Where on earth did you get a driver's license?
Gwen	There's no reason for you to be so mean to me. I didn't jump out onto the road on purpose (da mono). If you hadn't been speeding...

We need first to be absolutely clear on the fact that this whole thing was Gwen's fault. Gwen is, we have already learned, a sad case. Her father had no respect for girls, thus no respect for her. Her husband, from whom she has just been divorced, shared her father's lack of respect for her. Socially isolated, untrained for employment, with all her possessions packed into the trunk of her car, Gwen has chosen to spend the day in the West Virginia mountains, off the main road, collecting wild flowers. Upon returning to her car, she found that she had parked it in a muddy patch

and was now stuck. In a panic, she guns the car and quite literally erupts
onto the main highway, to collide with Mitchell's car as he rounds a bend
in the road. When Mitchell, concerned for injuries, approaches her car
and asks if she is injured, Gwen's pent-up frustrations with her history of
being disrespected and disregarded (and, in fact, discarded) are expressed
without restraint to this perfect stranger: "Whenever [something happens],
the woman is always blamed. Women are always the scapegoats...". Her
emotional outbursts continue, as she tries to blame Mitchell for the accident and, when she fails to convince him of his fault, accuses him of being
mean to her (*Anata ni sonna ni fuyukai na koto o iwareru sujiai wa nai
wa. Watashi wa waza to tobidashita wake je nai n da mono*). Here, in
addition to the use of the familiar *anata* and the non-polite verb forms, we
have Gwen ending her self-justificatory statement "I didn't do it on purpose" with *da mono*, a sentence final form used by young girls and young
women which carries the connotations of surprised perplexity and an over-
tone of "poor little me". This flies in the face of what Mulhern (1989)
claims for Japanese heroines, which is that they are neither socially isolated nor socially insensitive, that they are generally self-confident and
that they participate in the privileging of public muting of affect. Gwen,
as she present herself to Mitchell (and us) on this and many more occasions, is clearly not a Japanese heroine.

Again, I stress that depressed and 'helpless' women characters, women
who wear their emotions on their sleeves appear in Japanese-produced
category romances as well as in Harlequins.[8] And they do sometimes find
men to love them. But, it is never the case that such women are at the
center of the novel. They may – like the overly familiar women described
above – be friends, workmates, relatives, or the like of the heroine. She
often worries about them, and it may be a matter of relief that they find
someone to 'take care of' them. But their 'someone' is never the hero,
who does not find such women appealing.

In the case of Gwen and Mitchell, the timing and degree of personal
disclosure and expression of emotion is, perhaps, particularly unfortu-
nate. Irrespective of timing, however, the significant difference in the
manner – most particularly, the linguistic manner – of personal disclo-

---

[8] A particularly good example of such a character is Hisayo in *Saredo, kasumisoo*
'Baby's Breath' (Todo 1992), whose habits of rescuing boyfriends from their own
improvidence has left her penniless – constantly cold, hungry, and miserable –, but
who is always ready to go further into debt in order to rescue a new lover.

sure distinguishes Harlequin heroines from their Japanese counterparts. To illustrate this, and to bring home the connection of control of the expression of emotion with maturity, I turn to a Japanese pair of lovers, Yuri and Hiroshi (Hanai 1989). As college students, Yuri and Hiroshi dated, argued, and broke up. In fact, their last fight – and their relationship – ended when Yuri, in her own words, *hisuterii okoshite kuruma kara tobidashite tta* 'threw a fit and jumped out of the car' (Hanai 1989: 158). The fight begins when Yuri asks Hiroshi what they are to each other, and is not satisfied with the answer.

(3) Yuri   Watashi no koto, suki ja nai no!?
     Hiroshi   Otoko wa, sô iu mon da yo.
     Yuri   Katte ne.
     Hiroshi   Docchi ga katte nan da yo. Suki da to ka, kanojo to ka, oshitsukegamashii no meiwaku da.
     Yuri   Meiwaku!? Are dake watashi ni nan da kan da chûmon tsuketa kuse ni.
     Hiroshi   Dakara katte ni omoikomu na yo na?! Boku no konomi ni awasero nante tanonda oboe wa issai nai n dakara ne.
     Yuri   Oriru wa.
     Hiroshi   Suki ni shiro yo.
     Yuri   Suru wa yo. Baibai.

     Yuri   You don't love me?!
     Hiroshi   Men are like that.
     Yuri   Self, right?
     Hiroshi   Who's selfish? Pushing that stuff, "I love you" or "my girlfriend" onto me that way is a nuisance.
     Yuri   A nuisance! After all the demands you made of me.
     Hiroshi   Don't just think stuff up on your own and try to put it on me! I don't remember ever telling you to change for me.
     Yuri   I'm getting out.
     Hiroshi   Do whatever you want.
     Yuri   I will. Good-bye.

Space precludes a detailed examination of the linguistic forms that support the charged and mutually self-disclosing nature of this dialogue; we will have to be content to accept it as frankly confrontational. In the end, Yuri does get out of the car at a stop light, and Hiroshi drives off, ending their relationship. This is fine, as these are immature lovers; college students are not, in Japan, considered to be truly adult. Some years later, however, both are finished with college and have achieved some measures of success as a professional writer and photographer, respectively. They are brought together again over a book project. Each retains feelings for the other. However, unlike Gwen and Mitchell, who continue on as they began, Yuri and Hiroshi attempt to 'make up for' their youthful lack of control over their emotions and lack of discretion in expressing their feelings by speaking throughout the book in the most linguistically and discursively respectful ways possible. They address each other by Last Name + *san*; they use polite (*desu/-masu*) language forms; they conduct conversations by continually and overtly attempting to cede topic control and floor to the other; and they take great pains not to show any uncontrolled emotion. Even at the end of their story, in fact, when they are expressing mutual attraction and affection, they remain very much less self-revealing than their Harlequin counterparts (4).

(4)	Hiroshi	Tokoro de, Niimi-san.
	Yuri	Hai?
	Hiroshi	Koibito wa?
	Yuri	Imasen. Katagiri-san wa?
	Hiroshi	Imasen.
	Yuri	Onnatomodachi wa?
	Hiroshi	Sore nara nannin ka.
	Yuri	Dattara watashi mo, sono uchi no hitori ni mazete moraemasu?
	Hiroshi	Unnn...
	Yuri	Dame desu ka?
	Hiroshi	Ie. (to himself) Uun, mujaki, mujaki!
	Yuri	Ha?
	Hiroshi	Koibito kôho no tsumori datta n desu kedo. Niimi-san ni sono ki ga nai n nara.
	Yuri	Tonde me nai!
	Hiroshi	Sotchi no hoo ga ureshii na.
	Yuri	A, yokatta.
	Hiroshi	By the way, Miss Niimi.
	Yuri	Yes?
	Hiroshi	[Do you have] a boyfriend (lit., 'lover')?
	Yuri	No. [How about you], Mr. Katagiri?
	Hiroshi	No.

Yuri	A woman friend?
Hiroshi	Yes, several.
Yuri	In that case, could I be included among them?
Hiroshi	Well...
Yuri	No?
Hiroshi	No (to himself) [Be] Open! open! (lit., 'guileless').
Yuri	What?
Hiroshi	I was thinking as a prospective lover, but if
	you (Miss Niimi) isn't interested...
Yuri	Not at all! [of course I am]
Hiroshi	I'd be happier with that.
Yuri	Oh, that's good.

In this example, we see love being declared, an emotional topic and one to which we return below. The import of the dialogue is clear, but the emotion is confined within the semantics of *koibito* 'lover' versus *tomodachi* 'friend'. Neither in the language forms, nor in expanded discussions of feelings is emotion allowed much room. The very abilities to continue to use last name + *san*, polite *desu/-masu* verb endings almost to the very end, and to defer to the interests of the other rather than to focus on one's own feelings construct a mature pair of adults, able to regulate and control their emotions in ways that Harlequin couples cannot. And, indeed, should not. An American model of true love developed by metaphor theorist Zoltán Kövecses suggests that true love follows precisely along a path toward loss of control: "True love comes along; the other attracts me irresistibly. The attraction reaches the limit point on the intensity scale at once. The intensity of the attraction goes beyond the limit point. I am in a state of lack of control" (Kövecses 1988: 58-59). And, indeed, we find that, compared to Japanese heroes and heroines, Harlequin lovers regulate or hedge their verbal disclosures of emotion much less. Which brings us to our final difference, a difference in how – and how much – love is declared.

4. Declarations of love

Theo and Jane(y) (Donald/Kato 1981), are getting ready to make a mutual disclosure of love. Theo is in his early thirties, highly successful and overwhelmingly masculine, while Janey is very young, under twenty, and was, at the beginning of their story, very naive. After a stormy series of encounters, Theo left the small town where Jane(y) had always lived.

Desperate and desperately unhappy, Jane(y) moves to the big city, takes employment, and 'grows up', under the auspices of a favorite aunt. At this point, when Jane is 'ready' to experience true love,[9] Theo reappears and they meet (5).

(5)	Theo	*(who has rushed toward Jane and embraced her tightly)* Kurushiku nai kai?
	Jane	Iie, anata ga watashi o kurushimeru nante dekik-konai wa. De mo sukoshi yurumete kudasattara... Ee, sore de ii wa.
	Theo	Yokatta. Ayauku nozomi o suteru tokoro datta. Nikurashii yatsume, kimi wa noonoo to kurashinagara, boku o jigoku ni tojikomete ita n da zo.
	Jane	Watashi ga? Sonna, anata koso...anata koso...

....they embrace again and things get a bit out of hand....

	Theo	Boku o yuwaku shinai de kure yo, Jeen. Ima wa mada sono toki ja nai n da.
	Jane	Wakatta wa.
	Theo	Sonna kimi ga daisuki dakedo... *(they start to embrace again)* Iya, dame da, hayaku fuku o kichin to naoshite kurenai to yuwaki ni makete shimaisoo da. Soo nareba, kimi wa jibun no meiyoo o mamoru tame ni boku to kekkon sezaru o enai hame ni oikomareru n da yo!
	Jane	Teo, anata wa watashi to kekkon shitai to omotte iru no? Hontoo ni?
	Theo	Mochiron.
	Jane	Teo, dooshite anna ni tsurenaku watashi kara hanarete itta no? Anata ni hajimete atte shibaraku tatta koro kara, moo sukkari anata ni muchuu datta koto wa wakatte ta hazu yo.
	Theo	Mochiron wakatte ta sa. Kimi jishin yori mo hayaku ki ga tsuite ta kurai da yo. Minato o dete tta no wa, kimi ga boku no jinsei o kuruwaseta kara da.
	Jane	Anata o kuruwaseta, desutte? Hanashite, Teo! Donna fuu ni watasi ga anata o kuruwaseta tte iu

---

[9] The very form of her name changes in recognition of her new maturity.

| | no? Itsu mo anata ga yuui ni tatte ita ja nai. |
| Theo | Soo ka na? Boku wa oroka ni mo kimi ni koi o shite shimatta n da. Shoojiki itte, jibun no i no mama ni naranakatta no wa umarete hajimete no koto datta.... Fuyukai na kibun datta yo, mattaku. Kimi o nokoshite dete iku beki da to iu koto wa hayaku kara wakatte ita n da ga, hatashite jibun ga sonna kurushimi ni taerareru ka doo ka ga wakaranakatta. |

Theo	Are you uncomfortable?
Jane	No, you couldn't possibly make me uncomfortable. But if you would just loosen your grip. Yes, that's good.
Theo	This is good. I was on the verge of giving up hope [of your returning]. You wretch, while you were off carefree, living your life, you had imprisoned me in hell.
Jane	Me? That's impossible, it was you, you...

....embrace...

Theo	Please don't seduce me, Jane. This isn't the time.
Jane	I know.
Theo	I like that (i.e., the seductive] you, but (embrace) No, this is no good. If you don't straighten out [button, zip,...] your clothes, I'm going to be defeated by your seduction. Then, you would be put in the position of having to marry me for the sake of your own honor.
Jane	Theo, are you thinking you want to marry me? Really?
Theo	Of course.
Jane	Theo, why did you take yourself away from me so heartlessly? You must have known that I was in love with you from the first time we met.
Theo	Of course, I knew. Probably I was aware of it before you yourself know it. I left the harbor [of Jane's town] because you had turned my life upside down.
Jane	I turned your life upside down? Theo, tell me! How did *I* turn *you* inside out? You always had the advantage.
Theo	Is that so? I foolishly fell in love with you. To be honest, it was the first time things didn't go as I

planned. It was distressing, completely [distress
ing]. I knew I should leave you and simply leave,
but I didn't know if I would, in the end, be able to
bear that much pain.

Let us compare Theo's declaration with that of Tooru in (6). Tooru
has been traveling in northern Japan, on a business trip embarked upon
after a serious disagreement with Chikako, his heroine (Yuikawa 1997).
Chikako is waiting for him at the station the night he returns to Tokyo,
and their story ends as they come to a mutual, and mutually expressed,
understanding.

(6)   Chikako   Okaerinasai.
       Tooru   Kite kureta no ka.
       Chikako   Hanashitai koto ga takusan aru no.
       Tooru   Ore mo da yo. Yuki no naka de, zutto kimi no koto
                  o kangaete ta.
       Chikako   Sore, kikitai.
       Tooru   Ore mo kikitai. Kaeroo.
       Chikako   Ee.
              (and she leans her body against him)

       Chikako   Welcome back.
       Tooru   You came to greet me?
       Chikako   I have a lot I want to tell you.
       Tooru   Me, too. I thought of you constantly in the snow.
       Chikako   I'd like to hear about that.
       Tooru   I'd like to hear [what you have to say], too.
                  Let's go home.
       Chikako   Yes.
              (and she leans her body against him)

Our first comparison is just in terms of a very crude measure: length.
Theo, like most of his Harlequin cohort of heroes, declares his love at
length. He explains the past, explains his feelings, and explains the logic
for his actions. He details his understanding of Jane's attraction to him
and her confusion over his actions. He returns to his own emotions, elabo-
rating on their development throughout the course of the relationship.
Japanese heroes, in contrast, generally declare their love once if at all,
with no explanation of how they fell in love or any elaboration of what
that love actually *feels* like. Short speech, or no speeches, are the order of
the day.

Further, the content of a Harlequin man's declaration of love is quite different from the Japanese hero's sense of what needs to be said.

Tooru says, in response to Chikako's (unexpected) appearance at the station, "Oh, you came to greet me". When Chikako says that she has some things she wants to talk to him about, Tooru replies – and here's the romantic bit – "I do, too. In the snow [in the north of Japan], I thought about you all the time". Chikako says she'd like to hear about that, and Tooru replies that he'd like to hear what she has to say, too. So, they should go home.

Theo, on the other hand, had this to say to Jane: *Ayauku nozomi o suteru tokoro datta. Nikurashii yatsume, kimi wa noonoo to kurashinagara, boku o jigoku ni tojikomete ita n da zo.* "I was about to give up hope [that you'd return to me]. You wretch, while you were off carefree, living your life, you had imprisoned me in hell". After this promising start, he and Jane can hardly help embracing again, but Theo puts her aside before things get too far out of hand and says that if they were, in fact, to have sex, Jane would *have to* marry him simply to save her honor. Jane, surprised, asks if Theo wants to marry her, to which Theo replies that of course he does, and always has. Continuing, he points out that he had even had to leave her town because she, at a point when she was unready to experience true love, had turned his life upside down (*Minato o dete tta no wa, kimi ga boku no jinsei o kuruwaseta kara da*). He goes on to say how: "I foolishly fell in love with you. To be honest, it was the first time things didn't go as I planned". The use of *i* 'mind' here provides a significant contrast to feeling. He knew, he explains, that he should leave, since she really was too young and inexperienced for romance, but didn't know if he could bear the pain that a separation from her would cause him: *hatashite jibun ga sonna kurushimi ni taerareru ka doo ka ga wakaranakatta* 'I didn't know if I could stand that much pain'.

Pretty intense stuff. And, perhaps, we here get a hint of the tremendous appeal that Harlequin translations have for romance readers in Japan. At least in this instance, the difference between Japanese and Harlequin heroes may attract a reader in the same way the work in foreign corporations and/or in foreign places and real-life relationships with Western men are claimed by Kelsky (2001) to represent a sort of 'occidental longing', here not a longing to *be* in the social field of the Western, but to imagine a romantic partner *from* the Western, one who is attentive to the emotional, social, and – yes – economic needs of his true love and who will not balk at telling her so. A longing for a fictional dip, at least, into love 'Western-style'.

5. The Harlequin Romance and Japanese cultural logics of femininity and masculinity

We have seen, then, that Harlequin romances present a very different picture of women and men finding and enacting true love. The imported
'messages' about ideal heroines and heroes are not always flattering to
Western-style lovers, but they provide alternative, and in the case of heroes, I would argue attractive alternative ways of imagining loverly
behaviour for the Japanese reader.

As translation encodes one language into another, we often assume
that there is a reality 'out there' that simply is transferred from the first
language to the other. But we cannot assume a culture-free, non-semiotic
world serving as ground for [...] interpretation" (Becker and Mannheim
1995: 238). Japanese-language Harlequins offer linguistic portraits of 'true'
lovers inhabiting very different worlds of heterosexual desirability both
from the English originals and from their domestic Japanese fictional lover
counterparts.

The effects on reading audiences are, at this point, only to be guessed
at. But the romantic imagined (or imaginable) spaces for female equality,
emotionality and helplessness and for male verbal expressivity in Harlequin translations, spaces that were inhabited – in the case of heroines –
only by women destined not to 'win' at love and – in the case of heroes –
inhabited not at all, provide new discourses that embody different sets of
values from the dominant Japanese discourses about romance. How these
will interact with, provide alternatives to, or simply render more complex
the 'ideal' Japanese romantic model is a focus of future research.

The Translation of Sex/The Sex of Translation

Fanny Hill in Spanish

JOSÉ SANTAEMILIA

Universitat de València, Spain

Abstract. Sex is, without a doubt, one of the most intimate indicators of identity, as it conjures up images of sexual activity,
eroticism, pleasure, taboo, fantasies, desire, etc. Likewise, language is the most intimate way of expressing sex. John Cleland's
Memoirs of a Woman of Pleasure (1748-49) is the most famous
erotic novel written in English: it is both a pornographic work
and a philosophico-rhetorical exploration of sex and sexuality as
a key discourse in eighteenth-century England. It also offers provocative and mixed-up perspectives: a male (Cleland's) fantasy
about female (Fanny Hill's) sexuality for a predominantly male
audience. This wealth of perspectives places a great deal of importance on translation – the translation of sex becomes a political
act, with important rhetorical and ideological implications. Since
its publication *Fanny Hill* has been an enormously popular novel,
which has enjoyed innumerable translations into the major European languages. The earliest documented translations into Spanish,
however, come from the 1920s. In this paper I examine four Spanish translations of *Fanny Hill* from the late 1970s, after Spanish
dictator Franco died: three of these translations were carried out
by men (Lane 1977; Martínez Fariñas 1978; Santaemilia and
Pruñonosa 2000) and one by a woman (Podestá 1980). The main
objective is to test whether translating sexual language and imagery suggests different strategies for either male or female
translators, whether there is any gender-associated struggle for
rewriting the erotic into a different language.

Let me start by introducing two key concepts seemingly at odds: *sex*
and *translation*. Without a doubt, sex is one of the most intimate indicators of identity. It conjures up images of sexual activity, both physiological
and affective, of pleasure, of taboo, of fantasies, of desire, etc. *Sex* is an
ambiguous term, a rich term which has given rise to very different interpretations, attitudes, public or private censure. However ambiguous it may

be, it leaves no one indifferent because its study offers enriching insights into ourselves. Sex is the most profoundly human personal experience. It is not only a physical reality but – especially – a cultural one. Culture is firmly entrenched in sexual ideals or sex habits, as can be seen in extreme manifestations such as erotic literature or porn cinema, but also in the cultural production of taboos, in conversational habits or in the rules of politeness. Sex has to do with human biology, with the mechanics of human and animal life, but also – and more importantly – with the mechanics of human culture. Sex-related language, experiences, routines or taboos are among the basic icons of today's cultural representations.

If sex is the most intimate indicator of identity, language is likewise the most intimate way of expressing sexual experience, because language acts repeatedly as a site for the enactment of gender identities and sexual conflicts. Sexual anxieties, experiences or aspirations may be shown through a variety of expressive means: painting, sculpture, cinematic images, etc. And, above all, through language: through the whole discourse but also through metaphors, euphemisms, synonyms, syntactic structures, ellisions, or even punctuation.

Over the past years gender issues have become entangled with issues of language: both sex and language are the two most intimate and pleasurable things in life. Roland Barthes rightly said: "Le langage est une peau: je frotte mon langage contre l'autre. C'est comme si j'avais des mots en guise de doigts, ou des doigts au bout de mes mots. Mon langage tremble de désir" (Barthes 1977: 87). And he was right: language offers unique access to the secrets of self, to the most recondite fears and anxieties. In literary creation – one of the most artistic uses of language – sex is an essential factor for the plot, atmosphere and human conflicts of every good literary work. The erotic motive is pervasive in every good novel or poem. In erotic literature, in particular, the verbalization of sex is an unavoidable element, althought not the only one. Erotism must be integrated in a human web of feelings, passions and words.

This paper will also focus on *translation*, an enriching experience with obscure origins and motivations. Translating sexual language is a challenging affair, both at a personal and (an) academic level, as will be seen in the following sections. Both sex and translation share more than a whiff of transgression and self-discovery, of deep passion and serious discursive construction, of identity and manipulation.

1. The translation of sex: John Cleland's *Memoirs of a Woman of Pleasure* and the Spanish translations

1.1. The translation of sex

John Cleland's *Memoirs of a Woman of Pleasure* (1748-9) is possibly the only English *erotic* novel worthy of this name. It is a modestly porno-graphic work but, above all, it is a philosophico-rhetorical exploration of sex and sexuality as an important discourse in 18th-century England. Be-sides, it offers provocative and mixed-up perspectives: a male (Cleland's) fantasy about female (Fanny Hill's) sexuality for a predominantly male audience. Whether a purely erotic or a deeply pornographic novel – a somewhat sterile debate for our purposes – *Fanny Hill* asserts the un-controvertible importance of sex in literary and vital experience. Cleland's book is a celebration, at times naïve and at times parodic, of erotic pleas-ure, both in life and in realist literature.

Translation is – by definition and traditionally – an almost impossible task. Complex works like *Ulysses, Cien años de soledad* or *Tristram Shandy* are constant reminders that translating any text into another lan-guage can only give us a dim version of the original. Once acknowledged the impossibility of perfect translation, we are in a period of revaluation of translation as a cultural construct, as a mediation strategy, as an imper-fect but essential language transfer. Translating sex, in particular, is a highly sensitive area in language (and culture) transfer: it constitutes a powerful index of the translator's linguistico-cultural competence, preju-dices, taboos or ideological assumptions.

There is a large, and growing, body of translations which are being made under the label of 'feminist translation': their practitioners examine the special problems posed by the translation of explicitly feminist texts ('women's writing') deriving from the female body or experiences, and propose strategies (or 'interventions') of a political or ideological nature – dignification of women's experiences, reversal or challenge of gender-biased references, omission of words or expressions that are likely to offend women's dignity or to strengthen patriarchal values, etc. (see Simon 1996 or Flotow 1997).

Authors and translators/translatresses such as Suzanne de Lotbinière-Harwood (1994) or Nicole Brossard point in their writings or translations

to the existence of sexism in language, to the asymmetry of sexual references in language, to the damage this is causing to women, etc. A whole
range of compensatory strategies (mostly 'feminist') are being put forward – from a strong resexualization of translation designed at increasing
public awareness of women's subordinate status to milder attempts towards politically correct or even desexualized versions.

To prove the importance of the issue, we can have a passing glance at
a recent (1999) commercial Spanish translation of Helen Fielding's *Bridget
Jones's Diary* (1996). The whole book is based on the war of sexes, and
on different attitudes towards life and relationships between women and
men. One of Bridget's New Year Resolutions is:

(1)   Behave sluttishly around the house, (2)
(1a)   Pasear por la casa como una zarrapastrosa, (9)

Bridget's sexual life is downplayed in Spanish, thus losing force and
producing a more conventional – though equally funny – text. (1a) is an
understatement which weakens the original. 'Slut' is applied to women
who are dirty, untidy and/or very immoral in their sexual behaviour;
'zarrapastroso' or 'zarrapastrosa' ('shabby' or 'scruffy') can only be applied to dirty or untidy women and men. The original text, then, has been
desexualized. Another of Bridget's resolutions is:

(2)   Have crushes on men, (2)
(2a)   Enamorarme de hombres, (9)

An 'enamoramiento' ('passing infatuation') is a weak and formal version for 'crush' or 'crushes', which refer to a strong (and sudden) feeling
of attraction or love for someone, and which is much more physical than
the Spanish term. A misplaced tone of formality in translation may somewhat spoil the original's playful tone. Also, in the following example,

(3)   Jude arrived in vixen-from-hell fury ... (187)
(3a)   Jude llegó hecha una auténtica furia ... (195)

the sex-related comic effect is somewhat lost in translation. Although more
politically correct (3a) is not a faithful translation. Either a man or a woman
can arrive 'hecho(a) una furia' ('furious'), but only a woman can do it 'in
a vixen-from-hell fury', adding connotations of unpleasantness, bad tem-
per and bitchiness. It is well worth quoting a sex-related phonetic pun:

(4)   'Why don't you interview Joanna Trollope?' I said. 'A trollop?' he
        said, staring at me blankly. 'What trollop?' 'Joanna Trollope. The
        woman who wrote *The Rector's Wife* that was on the telly. *The Rec-*
        tor's Wife. She would know.' (210)

(4a)   –¿Por qué no entrevistas a Joanna Trollope? –dije.–¿A una puta? –me
        dijo, mirándome sin comprender–. ¿Qué puta?–Joanna Trollope. La
        mujer que escribió *La esposa del Rector*, la dieron por la tele. *La esposa*
        del Rector. Ella debería saberlo. (220)

The pun is completely lost in Spanish; the retort '¿A una puta?' is
likely to confuse readers – they may even believe Joanna Trollope is a
reputed trollop herself! The homophonous pair *Trollope/trollop* is missing in Spanish and the translator has not made the effort to find a similar
phonic pattern. You can well imagine the confusion of a Spanish reader.
A last example from *Bridget Jones's Diary* will introduce us to questions
of sexism in translation:

(5)   I could hear Richard over my earpiece going, 'Bridget… where the
        fuck…? Dole Youths.' Then I spotted a cashpoint machine on the wall.
        (215)

(5a)   Podía oír a Richard en mi oreja diciendo: "Bridget… ¿dónde coño…?
        Jóvenes Parados." Entonces vi un cajero automático en lapared. (225)

Although perfectly translated, and conveying the same vulgar tone,
(5a) reinforces sexism and denigrates the female body – in Spanish 'coño'
(*cunt*) is abundantly used derogatorily and as a vulgar emphasizer.

It is an undeniable fact that sexual habits or sex-related behaviours
affect us all at a very deep level. Examples from (1) to (5) show that sex is
variously translated, depending on a number of factors: the historical period, the presence/absence of a certain concept of 'morality', the author's
own morality, the translating fashion, the publishing house's policy, the
ideological conditions of the recipient culture, personal options, the pres-
ence/absence of censorship, etc.

There is, we believe, a more or less general axiom at work that pre-
scribes that translation of sex, more than any other aspect, is likely to be
'defensive' or conservative, tends to soften or downplay sexual references,
and also tends to make translations more 'formal' than their originals, in a
sort of 'hypercorrection' strategy. What else can we say of Mary Lamb's

19th-century 'adaptations' of Shakespeare (which in fact suppressed references to sex and bodily functions), or of the non-translation of certain authors, or of literary or political censorship? All these examples constitute one and the same phenomenon: sex as a translated experience is often downplayed, censored, eliminated or ignored, but very rarely emphasized or celebrated, the only exceptions being possibly the historical periods immediately following political or ideological repression.

1.2. Translations of 'Fanny Hill' in Spanish

All the above points towards an extreme ideologization of the sexual experience in our society. The writing of sex is rarely an instinctual or emotional response but a complex ideological rhetoric emmeshed with the prevailing social values. Ortega y Gasset used to say that love is, above all, a literary genre – sex is, similary, a *translated* experience, an experience which has to be tolerated, sanctioned by or approved of by society and thus constituting an accepted *rhetoric* in itself. It will be worthwhile discovering what happens when translating *Fanny Hill* into Spanish: a man's (Cleland's) writing the feminine body and sexuality (Fanny Hill's). Cleland's book is to a large extent already a translation of a woman's experience. This complicates the picture but may give us an enormous wealth of perspectives: we are faced with the work of a male author about a female character who exposes her sexuality, which is translated into Spanish by a man (or by a woman). The multiplicity of angles and, sometimes, contradictory insights offered by writer, character and translator(s) may be, if not an illuminating experience, at least a challenging and enriching cultural one.

The four Spanish translations of *Memoirs of a Woman of Pleasure* we are going to analyse are:

> (**L**): John Cleland, *Fanny Hill: Memorias de una mujer galante*. Madrid: Akal, 1985, translated by Frank Lane. This translation was originally published in 1977.
> (**MF**): John Cleland, *Fanny Hill: Memorias de una cortesana*. Barcelona: Ediciones 1984 S.A., 1984, translation by Enrique Martínez Fariñas. This translation had already been published by Producciones Editoriales (Barcelona) in 1978, and has been frequently reproduced.
> (**P**): John Cleland, *Fanny Hill*. Barcelona: Editorial Bruguera, 1980 translated by de Beatriz Podestá.
> (**S&P**): John Cleland, *Fanny Hill: Memorias de una mujer de*

placer. Madrid: Cátedra, 2000, edition and translation by José Santaemilia and José Pruñonosa.

I will use the translators' initials (**L, MF, P** or **S&P**) to refer to these texts throughout my paper; also the page numbers refer to the editions mentioned above. Three of the translations (**L, MF** and **S&P**) have been done by men and one (**P**) by a woman.

The first three translations (**L, MF** and **P**) have a clear historical origin: they were published in the late 1970s. The Spanish dictator Francisco Franco died on 20 November 1975 and a new era was about to begin. New horizons in political or cultural spheres opened up: in books, films or magazines, sexual matters started to be depicted with unprecedented freedom and with a sort of frenziness. In cinema, especially, sex scenes were generously and gratuitously multiplied, bearing little or no relation to the plot of the films in question. A colloquial Spanish term came to represent this newly-regained freedom: *'destape'*. It is a term which did not enter the dictionaries of the Spanish language but which did enter the hearts and skins of a whole generation: it means something like sudden revelation or 'exposure' of erogenous zones (especially female's) on the cinema screens, in magazines catering for the general public or in literature.[1]

---

[1] This new climate started, in fact, in the 10-year period preceding Franco's death, with a 'sexy' sort of comedy films which constituted a bold version of traditional comedies, fuelled by the new social realities such as the beginning in the late 60s of large-scale tourism from abroad, which brought a gush of fresh wind to political, social or sexual attitudes. It all crystallized in a series of pseudo-erotic films along this line, based on puerile off-colour sexual innuendoes which ultimately attempted to reinforce the regime's moral values (the repentant sinner, the unaccomplished temptation, the constant frustration of the sexual act). In a word, the *status quo* was preserved at the expense of a few equivocal situations and sex is not dignified but hypocritically celebrated. The 1965-1975 period in cinema is characterized by mild eroticism which conceals more than it reveals, and which is accompanied by an extraodinary onomastic pleasure; a succint list of film titles will suffice to demonstrate it: *No somos de piedra* ('We're only too human!') (1968), *No desearás a la mujer de tu prójimo* ('You shall not covet your neighbour's wife') (1968), *Los novios de mi mujer* ('My wife's boyfriends') (1972), *Lo verde empieza en los Pirineos* ('Bawdy begins in the Pyrenees') (1973), *El reprimido* ('The sexually repressed man') (1974), *Mi mujer es muy decente dentro de lo que cabe* ('All things considered, my wife is rather decent') (1974), *Dormir y ligar todo es empezar* ('Sleeping and flirting – once you start you can't stop!') (1974), *Zorrita Martínez* ('Zorrita (= diminutive for tart) Martínez') (1975), *La zorrita en bikini* ('The little tart wears a bikini') (1975), *La mujer es cosa de hombres* ('Woman is man's affair') (1976).

When Franco died, it was as if Spaniards suddenly had to make up for lost time. During the period of *'destape'* – which was, understandably, a short-lived period – an urgent need to enlarge the 'repertoire' of erotic works was felt. Classical Spanish erotic works were reprinted (*La lozana andaluza*, *El libro de Buen Amor*, etc.) and, especially, foreign erotic books and films were hurriedly released (*Emmanuelle*, …). **L**, **MF** and **P** may be said to stem from that need: a classical work or erotic fiction like *Memoirs of a Woman of Pleasure*, variously popularized as "mujer galante", "cortesana" or simply "Fanny Hill" (a highly evocative name). *Fanny Hill* has been immensely popular in all major European languages, with dozens of translations into French, German or Italian. In Spanish, however, before **L**, only four translations are documented (1918, 1921, 1924, 1927).[2] It is, however, extremely surprising that, apart from uncredited or clandestine printings, *Fanny Hill* was not translated into Spanish until 1918!

Unlike the other three translations, **S&P** has a very different origin: it stems from the need to retranslate a classical erotic work and, especially, from the need to recontextualize it, in terms of the cultural and sexual contexts in which the novel was published. This need to revaluate gender and cultural perspectives made a new (academic) translation necessary. A key difference this translation presents us with is the use of explanatory notes which try to contextualize the linguistic, social or sexual references.

All four translations are, I believe, very faithful to the original text – if this is not surprising in **S&P**, which is a critical edition, it is more so in **L**, **MF** or **P**. Except for **L**, the other translations follow the unexpurgated text of *Memoirs* which was restored by the 1963 G.P. Putnam's Sons edition.

When I decided to analyze these translations, a few questions and concerns came to my mind: how have they translated sexual language into Spanish? Do the original and the translations convey the same sexual urgency or suggestion? What are the main translators's challenges in attempting women's sexual experiences? Are there any gender-associated strategies? Is the translation of sex a gendered type of cultural or political rewriting? One has to be very cautious when dealing with these and similar questions: "the entire semantic field around issues of sexuality has caused serious problems for translators", is Flotow's serious

---

[2] Carmen Toledano (2002) documents the translations of *Fanny Hill* into Spanish. Curiously enough – although it is not uncommon with erotic or pornographic literature – the earliest copies registered at the Biblioteca Nacional in Madrid are missing from its shelves.

warning (Flotow 1997: 18).

We are in an 'era of feminism', of acute gender consciousness, which renders all translations not a transparent or impersonal activity, but a significant one. Translating today we cannot ignore the hidden gendered meanings and potentialities in any text. Beyond the fact that translations might be good or bad, translating sexual imagery or language is becoming more and more a political act.

We know that the erotic is an ideal site for differing political and ideological sensitivities to be projected on. Translating the erotic is thus always a risqué political act, which is entirely subservient to sociohistorical and ideological influences, and highly dependent – more than other genres – on extralinguistic and extratextual factors. "Translators live between two cultures, and women translators live between at least three, patriachy (public life) being the omnipresent third", claims Flotow (1997: 36). Translators of erotic texts, as 'gendered' beings, might experience what has been called an 'ambivalence of identity' which would in all likelihood modify their final work.

In this paper we examine four Spanish translations of *Fanny Hill*, a good site to test not only linguistic/rhetorical expertise or command of translation techniques but especially the gender-sensitive (or rather sex-sensitive) processes which are actually internalized by translators. Our comparative analysis does not presuppose or preclude any *a priori* hypothesis or conclusion on the matter, nor does it even assume the importance of the pursuit. It rather opens up a far-reaching inquiry into the general nature of translating: does the act of translating evince fears of transgressing linguistico-social boundaries? Does translating raise issues of decorum or self-censorship? What is the process through which translation maintains (or reverses) gender constructs? Are gender differences played out in actual practices of translation? Are there politically active (or reactive) 'feminine' or 'masculine' translations? Can we speak of – to simplify – a 'masculine' or a 'feminine' approach in translating?

2. The sex of translation: *Fanny Hill* in Spanish

Translation is a useful metaphor of the struggle to transfer from one identity to another. Furthermore, Cleland's *Fanny Hill* is also an apt metaphor of cross-sex writing, of translating female experience into male writing for male audiences. We believe that analyzing the sex of translation has an unbounded potential for destabilizing identities. If the expression of sex is of prime importance to understand the intimate impulses of a given literary – and historical – period, then the translation of sex becomes a political act, with important rhetorical and ideological implications.

When we are actually translating, it is unlikely that we are aware of any gender-related mechanisms activated or relied on; once the translation is a finished or published product, we may begin to wonder whether our options were the best ones. Nevertheless, there are instinctual reactions or attitudes towards the most intimate concerns (sex) that are depicted in a given literary or artistic work.

I study four translations of *Fanny Hill* into Spanish, three by men and one by a woman – I am interested both in textual and meta-textual divergences in these translations with a view to analyzing whether there is a – conscious or unconscious – gendering of the erotic in translation. My main objective is to test whether translating sexual language and imagery suggests different strategies for either male or female translators, whether there is any gender-associated struggle for rewriting the erotic into a different language. I have carefully analyzed the translations mentioned and I have identified three main general tendencies in the work of **P**, the only female translator of *Memoirs* into Spanish:

1. Softening or downplaying of sexual references.
2. Desexualization of sexual references.
3. Tendency towards dysphemism and moral censure when women's status is at stake.

2.1. Downplaying of sexual reference

In **P**, we can observe from time to time a significant softening or downplaying of references to sex:

(6)   amidst the whirl of loose pleasures I had been tossed in, (39)

(6a)   ... en el torbellino de placeres deshonestos en que me vi sumida. (L, 5)
(6b)   en el centro del torbellino de placeres desatados al que me habían arrojado, ... (MF, 19)
(6c)   en aquel torbellino de placer y ligerezas al cual me vi abocada, ... (S&P, 61)
(6d)   dentro del torbellino de placeres relajados en el que me vi envuelta, ... (P, 7)

This would be consistent with the stereotype of women as speaking a hesitant, deferential and powerless language. In translating the phrase 'loose pleasures', (6d) offers a more neutral translation ('placeres relajados', 'relaxed pleasures') while (6a) offers even a strong tone of moral censure ('placeres deshonestos', 'dishonest pleasures'). A similar example can be found in:

(7)   Truth! stark, naked truth, is the word, and I will not so much as take the pains to bestow the strip of a gauze-wrapper on it, but paint situations such as they actually rose to me in nature, careless of violating those laws of decency, that were never made for such unreserved intimacies as ours; ... (39)

(7a)   La verdad: la verdad monda y escueta. [...] intimidades tan poco recatadas como las nuestras, ... (L, 5-6)

(7b)   ¡La verdad!, una verdad completa y desnuda, [...] intimidades tan irrefrenadas como las nuestras; ...(MF, 19)

(7c)   ¡La verdad! La verdad, monda y desnuda. [...] intimidades tan impúdicas como las nuestras. (S&P, 62)

(7d)   ¡Verdad! La verdad cruda y desnuda es la palabra, [...] intimidades tan candorosas como las nuestras, ... (P, 7-8)

All (7a), (7b) and (7c) add a moral comment ('intimidades tan poco recatadas como las nuestras' ('immodest'), 'intimidades tan irrefrenadas como las nuestras' ('uncontrolled'), 'intimidades tan impúdicas como las nuestras' ('shameless, indecent') lacking in the original. Only (7d) avoids sexual overtones, softening sexual references ('intimidades tan candorosas como las nuestras', 'innocent, naïve'). Again in the translations of (8) as well explicit sexual references are softened:

(8)   ... one of her favourite girls, a notable manager of her house, and whose business it was to prepare and break such young fillies as I was to the mounting-block: (47)

(8a)   una de sus muchachas preferidas, muy dispuesta administradora de la casa, cuyo cometido era preparar y desbravar a potrancas como yo y habituarlas al poyo del picadero ['exercise ring' but also 'bachelor pad'], (F, 14)

(8b)   ... una de sus muchachas predilectas, notable administradora de su casa, cuya tarea consistía en preparar y domar para el cabalgadero ['mount'] jóvenes potrancas de mi estilo; (MF, 26)

(8c)   una de sus favoritas, apreciable gobernanta de su casa, cuyo cometido
       consistía en preparar y acostumbrar a las potrancas como yo a los
       aparejos de la monta ['mount']; (S&P, 73)

(8d)   ... una de sus chicas favoritas, una notable administradora de su casa
       cuyo oficio era preparar y domar a las potrancas jóvenes para que se
       avinieran a la montura ['saddle' or 'mount']. (P, 17)

In the choice of adjectives used to describe sexual experience in translations, **P** tends to use softer and less explicit ones. Let us see it in (9):

(9)   ... with her busy fingers fell to visit and explore that part of me where
       now the heat and irritations were so violent that I was perfectly sick
       and ready to die with desire: that the bare touch of her finger in that
       critical place had the effect of a fire to a train, and her hand instantly
       made her sensible to what a pitch I was wound up, and melted by the
       sight she had thus procured me. (69)

(9a)   [...] hasta qué punto me encontraba excitada y desmadejada ['excited
       and exhausted'] por el espectáculo que de tal manera me había ofrecido.
       (L, 41)

(9b)   [...] hasta qué punto estaba yo de acabada y derretida ['finished and
       melted'] por el espectáculo que me había proporcionado. (MF, 47)

(9c)   [...] hasta qué extremo me hallaba excitada y derretida ['excited and
       melted'] por el panorama que me había brindado. (S&P, 103-4)

(9d)   [...] hasta qué punto estaba yo herida y ablandada ['hurt and softened']
       por la visión que me había procurado. (P, 48)

(9a), (9b) and (9c) provide sexually-explicit adjectives ('excitada y
desmadejada', 'acabada y derretida' and 'excitada y derretida') while (9d)
shows much more restraint, and even sexual ambiguity ('herida y
ablandada'). In the translations given for:

(10)   I wanted more society, more dissipation. (103)

(10a) ... apetecía más sociedad y distracciones ['entertainment']. (L, 80)
(10b) ... necesitaba más sociedad y más disipación ['dissipation']. (MF, 78)
(10c) ... necesitaba más compañía y más disipación ['dissipation']. (S&P, 148)
(10d) ... anhelaba más compañía, más diversiones ['entertainment']. (P, 93)

we find in (10d) both a softening of the sexual reference and a desexualization strategy – if not an outright euphemism or simply a mistranslation

('diversiones' ('entertainment')) is, at least, a poor counterpart for 'dissipation'). Also, the sexual climax reached at the end of:

(11)   I saw with wonder and surprise, what? not the plaything of a boy, not the weapon of a man, but a maypole of so enormous a standard that, had proportions been observed, it must have belonged to a young giant; its prodigious size made me shrink again. (109)

(11a) [...] Su prodigioso tamaño me infundió temor ['fear'], (L, 88)

(11b) [...] su enorme tamaño me hizo nuevamente estremecer ['shudder']. (MF, 84)

(11c) [...] Aquel portento de tamaño me hizo encogerme de miedo ['shrink in fear'] otra vez, (S&P, 155)

(11d) [...] Su prodigioso tamaño me hizo dudar ['doubt'], (P, 101)

is abruptly brought to an end in translation (11d), in which **P** chooses a wrong verb ('dudar', 'doubt') – it is wrong because it mistranslates the original verb ('shrink') and because it desexualizes the whole passage. Similarly, in

(12)   I guided gently with my hand this furious fescue to where my young novice was now to be taught his first lesson of pleasure. (110)

(12a) ... guié con la mano dulcemente aquel frenético ['frenzied'] instrumento al lugar en donde el joven novato recibió su primera lección de placer. (L, 88)

(12b) ... guié dulcemente con la mano el aparato furioso ['furious'] hasta donde mi joven novicio había de aprender ahora su primera lección de placer. (MF, 85)

(12c) ... delicadamente guié con mi mano este ariete furioso ['furious'] al punto donde había de enseñar a mi joven aprendiz su primera lección de placer. (S&P, 156)

(12d) ... guié suavemente con la mano el irritado ['annoyed'] puntero hacia el sitio donde mi joven novicio no necesitaría que le enseñaran su primera lección de placer. (P, 102)

it is the woman translator, in (12d) who softens or downplays the strength of the adjective 'furious' (in 'this furious fescue') into 'irritado' ('annoyed'), which is an obvious mistranslation and, especially, deprives the sexual weapon ('fescue') of its agency. The same logic can be found in:

(13)   ... that instrument of the mischief ... (143)

(13a)   ... el instrumento del agravio ['affront'], ... (L, 123)
(13b)   ... aquel instrumento de agravio ['affront']... (MF, 113)
(13c)   ... aquel arma del delito ['crime, offense']... (S&P, 197)
(13d)   ... ese instrumento dañino ['harmful']... (P, 145)

where the sexually-connotated 'instrument of mischief' is equally downplayed as 'ese instrumento dañino' ('this harmful instrument') (13d) which might even express a negative attitude towards male sexuality.

Fanny Hill is, among other things, an undisguised celebration of male sexuality and of the male sexual member (see Santaemilia 2001). Al-though **P** translates all these references to the male organ, in cases such as:

(14)   Without more ado, he plants me with my back standing against the wall, and my petticoats up; and coming out with a splitter indeed, made it shine, as he brandished it, ... (178)

(14a)   [...] llegándose a mí con una verdadera pica ['a spear indeed'] de abordaje que blandió ante mis ojos ... (L, 163)
(14b)   [...] entonces avanza hacia mí blandiendo su verga ['prick'] ... (MF, 145)
(14c)   [...] se sacó una verga ['prick'] seca que, según empuñaba, lució ante mis ojos primero ... (S&P, 242)
(14d)   [...] sacando una verdadera maravilla ['a wonder indeed'] la lució, blandiéndola, ante mis ojos; ... (P, 191)

this rule is broken: (14d) omits the reference to the male member, and provides a weaker – but highly idiomatic – alternative ('una verdadera maravilla', 'a wonder indeed') which somewhat resists Cleland's constant glorification of the male member in terms of physical strength, sexual power and moral authority (see Markley 1984).

2.2. Desexualization of sexual references

Another tendency that seems to emerge from the translations we have studied is that **P** has a sharper tendency towards hyperonymy, the use of softer synonyms and the omission of sexually explicit terms here and there. They all contribute towards a certain desexualization of texts translated by women, at least in **P**'s case. In (15):

(15)   ... her hands became extremely free, and wandered over my whole body,
with touches, squeezes, pressures that rather warmed and surprised me
with their novelty than they either shocked or alarmed me. (48)

(15a)   ... movió las manos con gran libertad a todo lo largo de su cuerpo,
tocando, pellizcando o apretando ['touching, pinching or hugging'],
cosas todas nuevas para mí que me causaron más calorcillo que susto o
recelo. (L, 15)

(15b)   ... sus manos se volvieron excesivamente libres y se pusieron a recorrer
todo mi cuerpo con toques, pellizcos, presiones ['touches, pinches,
hugs'] cuya novedad me asombró en vez de alarmarmeo escanda-
lizarme. (MF, 27)

(15c)   ... las manos de Phoebe tornáronse ágiles en extremo y recorrieron mi
cuerpo todo con roces, apretones, pellizcos ['feeling someone up, hugging, pinching'] que antes me confortaban y sorprendían por su novedad
que me turbaban o escandalizaban. (S&P, 75)

(15d)   ... sus manos se volvieron muy libres y recorrieron todo mi cuerpo
con toques, apretones y presiones ['touches and hugs'] que más me
entusiasmaron y sorprendieron por su novedad que me chocaron o
alarmaron. (P, 19)

while all translations mostly coincide, only (15d) eliminates 'pellizcos'
or 'pellizcando' ('pinches' or 'pinching') – with its playful connotations
of sexuality – and prefers instead more neutral and nearly-synonymous
terms like 'apretones' and 'presiones' (both mean 'hugs').

P, in some cases, desexualizes sex-related terms. and, in some others,
simply omits or excludes whole sections with details of a sexual nature,
as in the following example:

(16)   ... giving me to feel the titillating inspersion of balsamic sweets, drew
from me the delicious return, and brought down all my passion, that I
arrived at excess of pleasure through excess of pain; but when succes-
sive engagements had broken and inured me, I began to enter into the
true anallayed relish of that pleasure of pleasures, when the warm gush
darts through all the ravished inwards. (80)

(16a)   ... me hicieron sentir el cosquilleo de su suave bálsamo, que me hizo
corresponderle debidamente y apasionarme, no alcancé el inefable
placer que me llegó luego del dolor extremado. Pero cuando los
sucesivos encuentros me quebrantaron y habituaron, comencé a conocer
el verdadero y puro deleite del placer de los placeres, cuando el
templado manatial fluye impetuoso a través de las violadas entrañas.
(L, 54)

(16b) ... me hubieran dado la sensación de una aspersión cosquilleante de
dulzuras balsámicas me sentí volver deliciosamente y prolongar toda
mi pasión, llegando a excesos de placer a través de dolores excesivos.
Pero cuando encuentros sucesivos me hubieron habituado y endurecido,
empecé a disfrutar el verdadero deleite sin mezcla de ese placer de los
placeres, cuando calientes oleadas se precipitan por las entrañas
maravilladas [...] (MF, 57)

(16c) ... dándome a probar un cosquilleo de balsámicas dulzuras, extrajeron
de mí la deliciosa respuesta y apaciguaron mi pasión, que arribé al
exceso del placer por un exceso de dolor. Y cuando sucesivos lances
hubiéronme domado y acostumbrado, comencé a degustar el sabor
verdadero y puro del placer de los placeres, un vez el cálido torrente
inundó en riada mis arrebatadas entrañas. [...] (S&P, 117)

(16d) [...] Pero cuando sucesivos encuentros me endurecieron y habituaron,
comencé a entrar en el puro y verdadero disfrute de ese placer de los
placeres, cuando la cálida efusión atraviesa las arrebatadas vísceras.
[...] (P, 62)

In (16d), apart from the omission of a whole sentence ('giving me to
feel ... excess of pain'), we also observe the desexualization of sexual
feelings: instead of 'entrañas' ('womb') (16a, 16b and 16c) and its associations with motherhood and basic instincts, we are offered 'vísceras'
('entrails'), with its connotations of animality and even bestiality. A profound sexual feeling in women is not only desexualized but also
dehumanized. Furthermore, in one of the main declarations of principles
of *Memoirs*:

(17)   ... the amazing, pleasing object of all my wishes, all my dreams, all
my love, the king-member indeed! (147-8)

(17a) ... el asombroso y amable objeto de mis deseos, de mis ensueños, de
mi amor, el miembro soberano ['the sovereign member'] en verdad.
(L, 128-9)

(17b) ... el asombroso y placentero objeto de todos mis deseos, mis sueños,
mi amor, ¡el miembro rey ['the king-member'], en verdad! (MF, 118)

(17c) ... el encantador y asombroso objeto de mis deseos todos, de mis sueños
todos, de todo mi amor: ¡el miembro rey ['the king-member'] por
excelencia! (S&P, 203)

(17d) ... el asombroso y placentero objeto de todos mis deseos, todos mis
sueños, todo mi amor, ¡el rey de los miembros! [the king of members!]
(P, 152)

it is only (17d) in which – through mistranslation – the woman translator desexualizes the patriarchal implications present. Similary, as with the male sexual member, the reference to the profession of Fanny Hill and of the other *women of pleasure* ('the little troop of love') is also desexualized. Let us see it in:

(18)   ... the little troop of love, the girls my companions, (162)

(18a) ... la tropa del placer ['troop of pleasure'], mis compañeras, ... (L, 146)
(18b) ... la pequeña tropa de amor ['little love's troop'], las muchachas compañeras mías ... (MF, 131)
(18c) ... la pequeña tropa del amor ['little troop of love'], mis jóvenes compañeras, ... (S&P, 222)
(18d) ... la pequeña tropilla amorosa ['little loving troop'], mis compañeras, ... (P, 171)

The use of the adjective 'amorosa' ('loving') in (18d) – as opposed to the noun phrases 'del placer' ('of pleasure') or 'del amor' ('of love') – turns away the reader's attention from their profession (prostitution), and presents it rather humorously ('tropilla amorosa', 'little loving troop').

2.3. Tendency to dysphemism and moral censure

In the following example,

(19)   She was about five and twenty, by her most suspicious account, in which, according to all appearances, she must have sunk at least ten good years, allowance too being made for the havoc which a long course of hackneyship and hot waters must have made of her constitution, (47)

(19a) [...] Era menester tener en cuenta asimismo el daño que una larga carrera alquilona y de años de azarosa vida hubieron de causar a su constitución. (L, 15)
(19b) [...] teniendo en cuenta los estragos que una larga carrera de monta y agua caliente tiene que haber hecho en su constitución. (MF, 27)
(19c) [...] a juzgar por los estragos que una larga carrera de vicio y aguas calientes. (S&P, 74-5)
(19d) [...] también había que tomar en cuenta los estragos que había realizado en su constitución una larga carrera de mercenaria. (P, 19)

when referring to women's status as a sex object, (19a), (19b) and (19c) resort to traditional images and idiomatic expressions of the field of prostitution ('una larga carrera alquilona y de azarosa vida', 'a long and eventful life on hire'; 'una larga carrera de monta y aguas calientes', 'a long course of hackneyship and hot waters'; and 'una larga carrera de vicio y aguas calientes', 'a long course of vice and hot waters') and only (19d) is clearly dysphemistic although ambiguous ('una larga carrera de mercenaria', 'a long course as a mercenary'). Besides, only (19c) introduces a footnote to make explicit the metonymic connection between 'hackneyship and hot waters' and prostitution.

In example (20):

(20)   Phoebe herself, the hackneyed, thoroughbred Phoebe, to whom all modes and devices of pleasure were known and familiar, (49)

(20a)   Phoebe, la yegua alquilona de pura sangre ['thoroughbred mare'], harto conocedora de toda forma de placer y de sus artimañas, (L, 17)

(20b)   Al parecer la propia Febe, pura sangre ['thoroughbred (mare)'], jineteada, familiarizada con todos los modos y dispositivos del placer, (MF, 29)

(20c)   La misma Phoebe, Phoebe la curtida, la pura sangre ['thoroughbred (mare)'], para quien todas las formas y mecanismos del placer resultaban conocidos y familiares, (S&P, 77)

(20d)   La misma Phoebe, la ramera ['prostitute'] de pura raza para quien todas las formas y recursos del placer eran conocidos y familiares, (P, 20)

only (20d) uses dysphemism ('ramera', 'prostitute') to convey, possibly, an explicit note of contempt at women's status in *Fanny Hill*. Similarly, in

(21)   ... that brutal ravisher, the author of my disorder, ... (59)

(21a)   ... al bestial ultrajador ['offender'] causa de mi dolencia, ... (L, 29)

(21b)   ... aquel brutal estuprador ['ravisher'], causante de mis males, ... (MF, 38)

(21c)   ... este primer, brutal y horripilante invasor ['invader'] de mi tierna inocencia. (S&P, 88)

(21d) ... ese brutal violador ['rapist'] , el culpable de mi enfermedad, ... (P, 34)

(21d) is again the most radical option. It is again **P**, the woman translator who shows in her translation the most moral and human contempt for those who abuse women. When the book revolves around questions connected with women's status, the versions offered by **P** (the female translator) seem to throw a fiercer moral comment on the unpleasant reality of women's lives in *Fanny Hill*. These versions (more than those offered by **L**, **MF** or **S&P**) eschew questions of power and authority.

3. Conclusion: sexing the translation of the erotic?

This is the first attempt to try to suggest a discursive and ideological connection between the translation of sex and the construction of gender identities. We need, however, many more examples and a varied range of analyses – from language to ideology, from mental processes to sexualizing strategies.

So far we have been looking for evidence as to divergent or distinctive strategies which characterize female from male translators when dealing with sex-related language and, sometimes, a single example is more revealing than countless others. Nearly at the end of the book, Fanny Hill broods over the importance of the male sexual member for women in:

(22)   … the feel of that favourite piece of manhood has, in the very nature of it, something inimitably pathetic. Nothing can be dearer to the touch, or can affect it with a more delicious sensation. Think then! as a lover thinks, what must be the consummate transport of that quickest of our senses, in their central seat too! when, after so long a deprival, it felt itself re-inflamed under the pressure of that peculiar scepter-member which commands us all, but especially my darling elect from the face of the whole earth. (219)

(22a) [...] bajo la presión de ese miembro cetro que a todos nos manda, [...] (L, 209)
(22b) [...] bajo la presión de ese miembro-cetro peculiar que nos dirige a todos; [...] (MF, 182)
(22c) [...] bajo la presión de ese peculiar cetro que a todos nos gobierna, [...] (S&P, 295-6)
(22d) [...] la presión de ese miembro coronado que manda en todas nosotras; [...] (P, 243-244)

Understandably, (22a), (22b) and (22c) have translated 'that peculiar scepter-member which commands us all' as 'ese miembro cetro que a todos nos manda' (all of us, men and women), 'ese miembro-cetro peculiar que nos dirige a todos' (all of us, men and women) and 'ese peculiar cetro que a todos nos gobierna' (all of us, men and women), respectively, but only (22d) has considered the most obvious version: 'ese miembro coronado que manda en todas nosotras' (all of us women). Only a woman translator could have produced such an immediate and authentic identification!

When we venture into an analysis of the sex of translation, we are also dealing with questions of power and authority, of version and subversion, of legitimation and intervention, of identity construction and resistance to it. Because of the tight web of personal, political and ideological interdictions associated with it, I believe that the translation of the erotic is an ideal site for testing the complex rewriting(s) of identity in sociohistorical terms.

Erotic texts have historically been written for male consumption, but (male and female) translators have very much to say when it comes to retextualizing sexuality in another language.

Gender and Interpreting in the Medical Sphere
What is at Stake?

OREST WEBER, PASCAL SINGY & PATRICE GUEX
University Hospital, Lausanne, Switzerland

Abstract. Like other Swiss urban centers, Lausanne has a high foreign population which includes a significant number of recent arrivals making use of the health care system. When medical specialists and migrants meet in this context, they often have little knowledge of the sociolinguistic and sociocultural systems used by their interlocutor. Recourse to a translator seems to be the only solution enabling the two parties to achieve mutual understanding. Traditionally, this third person is one of the patient's relatives or acquaintances. Due to the problematic nature of this practice, a group of Lausanne health care providers initiated a pluridisciplinary action-research. The major objective of this study was to advocate the introduction of professional *Cultural Mediators/ Interpreters* (CMIs) and to measure the effects of this change on the representations made by the persons involved: patients, health care providers and CMIs. Data were collected in focus groups and interviews and subjected to qualitative analysis. The investigation of linguistic and social representations has revealed diverging views regarding the role of participants' gender in translated medical consultations. There seems to be a general consensus as to the existence of taboos linked to gender roles, whereas there are significant differences in opinion on the importance of choosing the health care provider and the translator/ress according to the patient's gender. Further analysis of this controversy reveals that underlying the question of gender, the place of a new group of actors (CMIs) in the medical field is being negotiated. Grasping the stakes of the discourses on gender of translators/resses implies considering them in their broader context because the hierarchy of this field rests on principles other than solely gender domination.

A great amount of research ascertains the existence of complex relationships (Singy 1998) between language use and gender, defined as a socially constructed (Beauvoir 1949), asymmetrical opposition linked to a difference in sex. Deborah Cameron (1995: 33) argues that the studies establishing that women and men tend to adopt differing conversational styles are based on three main explanatory models. The *deficit model* describes the language women learn as hesitant and as having less impact than that of men (Lakoff 1975), whereas the *dominance model* views women in a continuous negotiation of their relatively powerless position compared to men, whose social privilege is constantly corroborated by the dominant patterns of language use. According to this second model, the attested fact that in some specific contexts women ask more opening questions than men and interrupt their conversational partners less often (Fishman 1983) is seen as typical behaviour of socially dominated persons trying to be listened to despite their lack of authority. Finally, the *cultural difference model* draws some parallels between gender and other social divisions like, for instance, ethnicity. According to this model, the differing conversational styles of women and men are explained by a relative segregation between a masculine and a feminine world during childhood and youth (Maltz and Borker 1982; Coates 1995).

Besides this research on conversational styles, other linguists work on the role linguistic systems and their use play in discrimination against women. Problematic fields such as the invisibility of women in profession names or in generic pronouns have been widely discussed (Houdebine 1998).

The links between gender and language use mentioned so far are likely to affect, in one way or another, all situations where gendered human beings interact verbally, including the one this paper focuses on: the interpreted medical encounter. As a matter of fact, all the patients, interpreters and medical professionals taking part in these consultations are women or men. This raises the question to what extent and in what manner their communicative behaviour is influenced by their gender identity.

This question is as pertinent where interpreters are concerned as it is for the other participants. Indeed, recent studies of interpreted face-to-face interactions of several types have seriously challenged tenacious common sense opinions of the medical sphere (Weiss and Stuker 1998: 44): they provide evidence that interpreters are never mere "word-to-word translating machines" whose behaviour is in no way likely to vary under the influence of identity matters. Obviously interpreters always play an active role in the interactions (Wadensjö 1998: 278) and they are to be considered as historical agents and social intermediaries (Davidson 2000) who have to deal with pressures of their working environment (Roy 2000: 123-124).

Moreover, the activities of interpreting and translation bring two linguistic systems into contact. Each system analyzes human experience in different ways (Mounin 1963), including concerns of maleness and femaleness, masculinity and femininity. In this context, the transition from one language to another often offers a possibility to render women more or less visible in the linguistic forms of the target language. In the literary domain some translatresses have shown particular sensitivity to these potentially discriminating aspects of language and its use. Claiming the need for a feminist translation, they have worked towards an active *visibilization* of women referred to by translated texts (Simon 2000).

How about men and women interpreting in medical contexts? How do they perceive the influence of gender upon their interactions? And what about the other participants in interpreted encounters? A recent action-research (Lewin 1947) in Lausanne provides a partial answer to these questions.

1. Methodology

The field of this study[1] was limited to five social-sanitary structures in Lausanne[2] particularly involved in the care of migrant patients. The general hypotheses of the project assumed that the relationship between the migrant patient and the medical professional is an asymmetrical one (Bourdieu 1987; West & Frankel 1991; Heath 1993; Goffman 1975). It further stated that the use of cultural mediators/interpreters (abbrev. MCI, from *médiateur culturel interprète*) reduces communicational difficulties between medical professionals and migrant patients. MCIs are trained interpreters who provide culture related information and explanations to improve mutual understanding (Weiss & Stuker 1998).

To test our hypotheses one of the things we observed was the evolution of the representations the interacting persons have of their encounters. Patients, MCIs and medical professionals were invited to

---

[1] Swiss National Foundation N° 4039-44832, PNR 39 'Migration et relations interculturelles'.

[2] The different structures are the Département universitaire de psychiatrie adulte (adult psychiatry), the Policlinique médicale universitaire (medical policlinic), the Département de gynécologie et obstétrique of the Centre hospitalier universitaire vaudois (gynaecology and obstetrics), and the association Appartenances (private socio-sanitary institution offering psychosocial care to migrant patients) and the Service de soins infirmiers de la Fondation vaudoise pour l'accueil des requérants d'asile (nursery service for asylum seekers).

express themselves in focus groups of about one hour. The data discussed in this paper are extracted from four of these focus groups. The *MCIs-time 1* focus group assembled interpreters who were already trained but who had not had much practice yet. Another focus group called *MCIs-time 2* was conducted one year later, after an active intervention of the research team to enhance the use of MCIs in the medical sphere; this offered interpreters the opportunity to increase their working experience. The patients were interviewed in two focus groups: *patients without MCI*, composed of persons who had never had an MCI during their consultations, and *patients with MCI*, who had experienced professional MCI-interpreting at least once. The two patient focus groups were conducted in Albanian – all members were Kosovars, Macedonian or Albanian – and translated by interpreters before the transcription.

The four above-mentioned focus groups enabled a comparison of discourses produced by social actors in different situations: persons playing different roles in the medical encounter (MCIs vs. patients); and persons with different levels of experience with MCI-interpreting (MCIs: *time 1* vs. *time 2*; patients: *without MCI* vs. *with MCI*). In each of the focus groups, 10 minutes were devoted to a discussion about the importance of gender in the consultations.[3]

The tape-recorded discourse of the focus groups was transcribed and submitted to a content analysis (Morgan 1997), completed by some elements of discourse analysis (privileged linguistic forms, thematization, argumentation, etc.) and computational analysis. The content analysis resulted namely in a category of content called 'gender'. This paper offers a possible interpretation of the part of this content category that specifically addresses interpreting-related issues.

2. Selected results

2.1. The incidence of the interpreter's gender: an overview

First of all, the analysis of the discourse about gender and interpreting shows that the interviewed MCIs and patients do not even mention that

---

[3] According to the identity of the members of the focus group, the formulation of the initial question was: *Quelle importance attribuez-vous à la différence ou à la concordance de sexe entre le patient/MCI/soignant et vous-mêmes?* (what importance do you attach to the sex difference or concordance between yourself and the patient/MCI/medical professional?)

the lexical and grammatical systems of the different languages render sex-differences in different manners. The discourse they develop does not contain any perceptible sign of a reflection about the potentially discriminating role of languages and their use. When the patients and the interpreters speak about gender in the interpreting practice, they always focus on the gender of the participants and its influence upon the interactions. In this matter, each of the four focus groups has an overriding opinion.

The *patients without MCI* unanimously claim that the 'sex' of the interpreter and the medical professional does not 'play an important role' in the encounter:

> H : Il n'y a pas de différence, il faut qu'ils nous comprennent, et c'est tout. Bien sûr, il faut un interprète aussi.
> H : L'important, c'est de se comprendre, et le sexe ne détermine pas ça, mais quand on sait pas la langue, là, c'est vraiment difficile.
> F : L'important c'est de résoudre le problème, d'aider. Le sexe ne joue pas un rôle important.

> (H : There is no difference, they have to understand us, that's all. Of course, there has to be an interpreter too.
> H : The important thing is to understand each other, and the sex doesn't determine that, but when you don't know the language, then it's really difficult.
> F : The important thing is to solve the problem, to help. The sex doesn't play an important role.)

On the other hand, the majority of the patients with MCI focus group considers that it is easier for women patients when the interpreter – respectively the medical professional – is a woman. This opinion can be illustrated by the following excerpt:

> F : Pour les femmes, c'est toujours mieux d'avoir une interprète ou une doctoresse, que un interprète et un médecin.
> F : C'est normal, là on se sent très bien.

> (F : For women, it's always better to have a women interpreter and a woman physician rather than a man interpreter and a man physician
> F : It's normal, it makes you feel very comfortable.)

Consequently, it seems that the *patients with MCI* are far more sensitive to the difficulties raised by cross-gender interpreter/migrant patient relationships than the *patients without MCI*. This increased awareness is perhaps partially due to awkward situations that patients had previously experienced in consultations interpreted by a professional of the opposite gender.

The general evolution of the opinions the MCIs express in their focus groups is contrary to the one observed among the patients. This time, it's the *MCI-time 1* group – with little practice of MCI-interpreting – which seems to fear that the gender difference could obstruct communication:

> F : [...] s'il s'agit des, euh, ou des maladies qui touchent plus, par rapport au sexe, ou, dans, dans la plupart, le psychiatre, euh, s'il s'agit des femmes qui ont été violées, bien sûr que, il faut que surtout le traducteur, si possible le soignant c'est aussi le même sexe [...]

> (F : [...] If, um, or diseases that are related more to sexuality, or, in, in most of, psychiatrist, um, if raped women are concerned, of course, there is a need for, above all, the interpreter, and if possible, the medical professional, that they are of the same sex too. [...])

As the next example illustrates, this position is strongly challenged or even negated by the MCIs interviewed at *time 2*:

> F : [...] moi la patiente, je vois la période de la maternité, vous voyez, le patient je vois au planning familial, pour moi il y a aucune différence, [...]
> Female Interviewer : Mais par rapport à vos expériences, le fait que vous soyez un homme ou une femme, vous dites que ça n'a pas d'incidence?
> F : Pas de problèmes.
> H : Moi non plus.

> (F : [...] I see female patients at the birth clinic, you see, and male patients, I see them for family planning consultations, for me, there is no difference [...]
> F-Int : But according to your experience, the fact that you're a man or a woman, you say there's no consequences?
> F : No problem.
> M : For me neither.)

Thus, it seems that the MCIs are minimizing the importance of gender in interpreted consultations as their experience in the field increases, whereas among the patients, the actual confrontation with MCIs leads to a greater awareness of the difficulties of cross-gender communication in this specific context. To gain a better understanding of these opposed dynamics, it might be useful to take a closer look at the arguments the patients and the MCIs develop for and against taking gender into account in the interpreters practice.

2.2. Typical arguments of the discourse that recognizes and stresses the incidence of gender

The discourse by which the interviewed persons assert the importance of gender for the interpreted consultation comprises two major thematic categories.

The first category contains utterances according to which, in some cases, privileged relationships between women contribute to an easier contact between migrant women and the medical sphere. This kind of discourse is produced only by women. A female interpreter of *time 1* explains this position as follows:

> F : [...] j'ai traduit avant en gynécologie-obstétrique. Là on ne peut pas demander à un homme de venir traduire, mais en pédiatrie non plus, [...] dans notre communauté c'est le père qui travaille, les mamans restent à la maison, s'occuper de l'éducation de tout un peu, de ce qui concerne les enfants, et là je crois c'est, elles ont tellement, je sais pas une autre confiance si c'est une autre femme, une autre mère qui traduit pour elle. Je peux partager mon expérience.

> (F : [...] Before, I used to translate in gynaecology. Here, you can't ask a man to translate, but neither can you in paediatrics [...] in our community, the fathers work and the mothers stay at home, take care of upbringing, and everything that involves children. And I think it's, they have such, I don't know, they trust more if it's another woman translating for her. I can share my experience.)

In the *patients with MCI* focus group we find a similar explanation of the proximity between women in medical encounters. This time a female patient is speaking about a "world of children" that a female physician knows better than a male physician. This, in turn, leads to a better under-standing:

> F : Je pense que si le pédiatre est une femme, elle a le sentiment
> d'une mère, elle comprendra plus de choses qu'un pédiatre. Dans
> la vie, il me semble que la mère est plus attachée aux enfants que
> le père. C'est pour ça que, quand une pédiatre traite un enfant, elle
> comprend mieux le monde des enfants.

> (F : I think that if the paediatrician is a women, she has the feeling
> of a mother, she'll understand more than a male paediatrician. In
> life, it seems to me that the mother is more attached to the children
> than the father. That's why, when a female paediatrician treats a
> child, she understands the world of the children better.)

The second category of discourse stressing the need for gender to be taken into account focuses on taboos. Here, the interacting persons' gen-der is perceived as a factor which leads to communication difficulties when, for instance, sexuality has to be tackled.

Two excerpts from the *patients with MCI* focus group illustrate the problem:

> F : Oui, c'est vrai ça, parce que des fois on a dans une situation
> qu'on dit plus rien, donc entre nous et un interprète, parce que on
> veut découvrir des choses d'intimité, là on est pas libre, si c'est
> une femme c'est tout à fait autrement.
> F : Oui, c'est vrai, parce que même quand le médecin est une femme
> et l'interprète est un homme, j'ai des difficultés de répondre comme
> je veux simplement à cause de lui.

> (F : Yes, that's true, because sometimes we are in situations where
> we don't say anything anymore, between us and the male inter-
> preter, because we want to reveal things of intimacy, so we're not
> free, if it's a woman, it's different.
> F : Yes, that's true, because even if the physician is a woman and
> the interpreter is a man, I have difficulties answering as I'd like,
> simply because of him.)

These two quotations describe the presence of a male intermediary as a constraint on the production of utterances on certain topics. Actually, this constraint appears to limit the women's possibility to tell the doctor what they initially intended to.

Among the MCIs interviewed at the two times of the study, there are women and men who claim to perceive communicational impediments when they have to talk about sex with a patient of the opposite gender. One female MCI at *time 1* declares that she is unable to translate information about Aids to male patients. She says:

> F : Il faut pas oublier qu'il y a pas mal de tabous aussi, moi je pourrais jamais aller traduire, je me sens pas libre, pour aller traduire, pour un jeune homme euh concernant la prévention du sida, je peux pas, j'ai essayé, mais j'ai pas pu aller jusqu'au bout de parce que je vois déjà, que le client était déjà tellement mal à l'aise d'entendre de la bouche d'une femme tout ça de recevoir, c'était pas évident, alors c'est vraiment quelque chose, et pour nous et pour le patient à respecter.

> (F : One shouldn't forget that there are quite a lot of taboos, as well. I could never translate, I don't feel free to go and translate for a young man, um, about Aids-prevention. I can't. I tried, but I couldn't do it to the end because I see already that the client is so ill at ease to hear all that from [lit. the mouth of] a woman. It's not easy, so that's really something, for us and for the patient, we have to respect.)

The topics that MCIs and patients consider as difficult to address when conversational partners are of differing gender include sexuality in general, Aids, rape and violence in the couple. Medical and psychosocial support to raped women in particular, is viewed as the case *par excellence* where gender concordance between the interpreter and the patient is required.

2.3. Typical arguments of the discourse that negates or minimizes the incidence of gender

The discourse that contests or minimizes the influence of gender upon the consultation contains several thematic categories. Only one of them can be discussed here. The utterances belonging to this category argue that it would be inappropriate to exclude the interpreter without replacement, solely in order to achieve gender concordance in the consultation. This position can be illustrated by a proverb cited by an MCI at *time 2*:

H : Moi j'utilise toujours le même proverbe : quand il y a pas du beurre ça va la margarine [...]

(M : I always use the same proverb : when there is no butter, margarine will do [...])

This opinion is defended with emphasis by the *MCIs-time 2*. The energy they spend fighting for a more systematic use of professional interpreters has a particular value. One could say, an existential one : it is clearly their presence in the medical sphere and their professional future that is involved. The interpreters' insistence thus suggests that they are presently caught up in a struggle for a more widespread presence in encounters from which they are frightened to be excluded.

Other results of our study show that the MCIs' fear of exclusion is far from unfounded. Some of the interviewed physicians[4] produce, for instance, a strongly ambivalent discourse about the usefulness of interpreters. Some of them even glorify the virtues of a physician/patient contact without any common language and without an interpreter.

3. Conclusion

The analysis of a part of our data shows a relative lack of diversity of the gender related questions discussed by the persons attending the focus groups. None of them mention, for instance, problems caused by the fact that different languages – as instituted and instituting vectors of communication – operate divergent analyses of the male and the female in their grammatical and lexical structures. The focus group members talk mainly about taboos and about how women-specific 'worlds' can facilitate mutual understanding between women.

It does not come as a great surprise that the range of aspects discussed by the patients is not very large, since they mostly have little experience with professionally interpreted medical encounters. The small variety of topics is, on the contrary, more striking in the discourse of the MCIs. Not only do they have more practice, but they also underwent a training course. One could have expected this course to be a place where the MCIs would have discussed and reflected upon the social implications of their com-

---

[4] A short report of the results of our study has been published (Singy, Guex & Weber 2003).

municational activities, including gender related aspects. Our data suggest that the obviously increasing trend of the interpreter to negate or minimize gender influence is due to the struggle for their presence as professionals in the medical sphere. The interpreters probably fear that if they accord too much importance to gender related questions, they are giving weapons to the people trying to exclude them from the medical encounters.

It seems, nevertheless, that it would make sense to reopen the discussion among the interpreters about gender issues in their professional practice once their position is no longer threatened. The existing scientific evidence suggests that in such a debate it would be worth transcending the *cultural difference* perspective, which is already tackled in our data ('worlds' and 'common experience' making mutual understanding in interactions easier).

Some *dominance model* work has shown how questions of power and authority play a critical part in the ways women and men interact in medical encounters. It has, for instance, been demonstrated that in some contexts, women physicians are interrupted far more frequently by their male patients than male physicians (West 1984). Furthermore, women and men physicians appear to resort to differing discursive and conversational strategies using, namely, more opening questions than men (West 1990; Singy 2002). Considering these results, it seems reasonable to assume that women and men working as interpreters in the medical sphere cannot stay out of reach of gender related hierarchical phenomena.

Who Wrote This Text and Who Cares?

Translation, Intentional 'Parenthood' and New Reproductive Technologies

ULRIKA ORLOFF
University College London, United Kingdom

Abstract. This article makes a connection between the ideologies forming the Western conception of human reproduction on the one hand and literary production on the other. By presenting the contingent, arbitrary and outdated foundation on which those ideologies are built the purpose is to pave the way to an alternative manner of perceiving creativity and the well-being of its offspring. Ultimately, to discuss the ability of a translator from the point of view of gender or the suitability of a parent from the point of view of sex would become superfluous. The opportunity for the latter and, consequently, the former has presented itself in the form of New Reproductive Technologies (NRTs) and their influence on how the notion of procreativity and parenthood is perceived in the eyes of the individual and, most significantly, the law. The concept of originality in the shape of artistic genius and units of transferable genes could be replaced by the idea that whoever is the best provider of care for the text or the child is also its rightful 'custodian'.

Keeping in mind Lori Chamberlain's famous texts on the gendered metaphorics of translation (1988 & 1998) this paper will develop a few points regarding prospective changes in the discourse of literary translation and relate them to a more general social construct of sex/gender and the ideology of human (pro-)creation. I intend to draw attention to some very important developments within the field of natural science and, specifically, the so-called New Reproductive Technologies (NRTs), involving surrogacy, egg and sperm donation, *in vitro* fertilization, etc. There is a close relationship between how we perceive and describe artistic creativity and originality on the one hand and parenthood on the other, not least in relation to legal issues – which, of course, is something Chamberlain describes in her essay. The 'emergence' of NRTs and the consequential focusing on what constitutes parenthood and kinship elucidates the fragility of presumed stable concepts and social institutions such as 'motherhood' or 'the family'.

I suggest that NRTs further undermine the prejudicial mystification and 'mythification' of procreation, a fact that can only be of advantage to present and future analyses regarding 'natural' and/or 'cultural' (re-) production. Consequently, these changes will weaken the ancient and persistent perception of creativity and procreativity as something closely connected to *male* genius under the phallocentric rule of *logos spermatikos* – "the spermatic word" (Battersby 1989: 7 and *passim*) or "generative intelligence" (Dent 1995: 512). Such arguments will also be useful in discussions concerning contemporary feminist approaches to writing and translating, for instance when *female* genius or female bodily and/or maternal specificity are presented as important qualities for literary production.

Further, I will in this paper give a couple of examples of court cases concerning NRTs and parenthood and where (at least in one of the cases) intellectual property law (copyright) rather than family law has assisted the court in their rulings. In these cases the intellectual initiative and *intentions* to produce a child (rather than to *care* for it) of the involved parties have been investigated to help reach a decision regarding who is the rightful parent and 'owner' of that child. Taking these legal 'confusions' into consideration my conclusion will be that financial settlements and critical evaluations regarding written material in general and literature in particular would have plenty to gain from using the concept of care and the willingness to bring up and forth a text ('family' law) rather than merely looking at original authorship and production ('property' law). I argue that translators play an important part as caretakers/custodians of texts and their efforts should be recognized accordingly.

1.   Gender, sex and (re-)production

Arguably there is a connection between the conventional metaphorical language used for describing the 'derivative' character of translations and the stereotypical language frequently used to describe women (and mothers) in relation to men (and fathers). Even if there have been several changes in the general (Western) social and cultural structure as well as in the everyday lives of individuals regarding family formations and sexuality, the so-called biological, natural and allegedly inescapable procreative division between female and male human beings still dominates the picture and needs to be discussed. Undoubtedly, heterosexuality's warrant of sexual correctness has, to a large extent, been justified because of its connection with the notion of human survival *per se*. Not surprisingly, then, many still believe that every society must and does distinguish at least two kinds of body, under the presently unavoidable constraints of human REPRODUCTIVE exigencies. All peoples erect a vast superstructure of cultural meanings around this *socially* necessary distinction between the sexes (Andermahr, Lovell & Wolkowitz 1997: 85).

Notwithstanding, Judith Butler is one of several feminist critics who has questioned the established functions of sex and gender. Gender is 'drag' – which repeatedly imitates and performs identity structures. Normative, heterosexual, structures are themselves the result of this manner of persistent repetition rather than representatives of some ontological originality (1991: 21). What Butler claims is that every gender identity is no more than skin deep and the belief in an 'inner sex' and 'inner depth' is a product of the ruling discourse of gender. Thus, sexuality and gender could even be described as socially constructed phenomena founded on and naturalized through an *illusion* "of an inner psychic or physical *necessity*" (1991: 28). Furthermore, to found a political agenda on these, 'inescapable', necessities as in the case of, for instance, radical essentialist feminism, is counterproductive. Because, as Butler suggests:

> There is no ontology of gender on which we might construct a politics, for gender ontologies always operate within established political contexts as normative injunctions, determining what qualifies as intelligible sex, invoking and consolidating the reproductive constraints on sexuality, setting the prescriptive requirements whereby sexed or gendered bodies come into cultural intelligibility. Ontology is, thus, not a foundation, but a normative injunction that operates insidiously by installing itself into political discourse as its necessary ground. The deconstruction of identity is not the deconstruction of politics; rather, it establishes as political the very terms through which identity is articulated. This kind of critique brings into question the foundationalist frame in which feminism as an identity politics has been articulated. The internal paradox of this foundationalism is that it presumes, fixes, and constrains the very 'subjects' that it hopes to represent and liberate. The task here is not to celebrate each and every new possibility *qua* possibility, but to redescribe those possibilities that *already* exist, but which exist within cultural domains designated as culturally unintelligible and impossible. (1990: 148-49)

The incentive to use certain females' capability of giving birth as a fundamental definition of women's identity *per se*, whether in a 'positive' or 'negative' sense, is inevitably on the decrease. Moreover, to adhere to the idea of a fundamental ontological possibility of, exclusively, belonging to *either* the female or the male sex (and the impossibility of belonging to neither) is to acknowledge the intelligibility and fundamental *necessity* of what is being attacked – the woman vs. man polarity. This is the case even if the actual purpose of the attack is to criticize the assumed, gendered, behaviour attached to such a division. If dualistic thinking is a metaphorical construct then polarities such as man vs. woman, creation or production vs. reproduction, heterosexuality vs. homosexuality and original vs. translation can be not only contested, deconstructed and reconsidered but even, in a 'final' analysis, ignored.

For a long time human reproduction and heterosexuality have been viewed as eternally linked to certain physical attributes and patterns of behaviour and it has been assumed that the very survival of humanity has depended upon (and, indeed, been impossible without) them. Of course, both the formation and interpretation of those attributes and patterns have always been contingent but, importantly, they have avoided harsh criticism since they have actually worked well enough for quite a few individuals. Moreover, convincing alternatives have been scarce. Not anymore. In my view the development of NRTs offers a political and ideological opportunity for change. Because of NRTs we have entered into an actual age of 'mechanical' human reproduction and there is no looking back.[1] Instead of being based on the ideal of *automatic* rights, duties and responsibilities caused by heterosexual necessity and a romantic/sentimental ideology of biological kinship, parenthood can be based on the

---

[1]Already in the beginning of the 1970's Shulamith Firestone in *The Dialectic of Sex* (1970) predicted how NRTs could change women's position in society. For, according to Nancy Lublin's interpretation, Firestone proclaimed that,

> Once the reproductive meaning of sexual difference is erased, equality
> (of result) can be established. Women will not become men; rather, these
> distinctions will be completely destroyed, and people will be recognized
> only as human beings. Sex as an activity might still be practiced, but it
> will be void of any reproductive meaning. (Lublin 1998: 30)

Firestone's conclusion may seem to be oversimplifying questions of power, production and pleasure. However, it is also an important example of a feminist viewpoint that does not, automatically, perceive science and technology as a patriarchal enemy of her 'people'. Moreover, it is vital to remember that the original *reasons* for undertaking certain scientific projects and producing technological inventions (if, indeed, they can be defined at all) may be of little significance when the results/products are actually incorporated into the 'real' and changing world.

notion of *care*, that is to say, on the intention of giving care (not of producing or owning) and on the activity of caring. Possible parental alternatives
and 'family' constellations that have been judged as, using Butler's words,
"culturally unintelligible and impossible" will be redescribed and move
into the sphere of discursive acceptability.

Through the possibilties of NRTs the heterosexual *myth* – nourished
also in homosexual and transsexual discourse – involving the figures of
an active, virile, aggressive and penetrating male and a passive, fertile,
submissive and receptive female is effectively undermined. The implications this will have for our notion of sexuality and, consequently, any
kind of production vs. reproduction, active vs. passive constellation are
numerous – for instance within the field of literature. As noted, stereotypical terms such as 'lacking', 'subordinate' and 'faithful' quite easily
present themselves when a conventional metaphorical link between women
and translations is considered. There are, of course, quite limited assumptions regarding production and reproduction involved in this type of
terminology. Moreover, such assumptions have helped to sustain an ideology of original creativity and the empowering idea of (usually male)
artistic genius.

The trope of the 'book of nature', and the metaphor of a book as a
child or a creative idea as a brainchild are all ancient figures of speech
dating back to (at least) Plato and Aristotle. Remembering that the male
role in human procreation has, until fairly recently in social and scientific
history, been seen as both the active force and the spiritual contribution to
that (re-)productive process presents an opportunity to see the link between literary, authorial, original production and a phal(logo)centric picture
of parenthood. Aristotle's "form and matter' theory of generation' has
had a strong impact on subsequent conceptions of (pro-creativity (Rose
1998: 223-24). According to Aristotle,

> The male [...] is like a carpenter whose intellect shapes the matter
> according to his idea of what it should be; *the female merely pro-
> vides the physical substance.* No material part of the carpenter
> enters his work. Likewise, no material part of the male is incorpo-
> rated in the embryo; nevertheless, *the male provides the active
> principle that forms the child in the father's image.* (Rose 1998:
> 224, my italics)

Furthermore, Aristotle held the attitude that women could not produce
(male) soul-containing semen but only a second-rate, 'soul-less' type of

semen (menstrual blood) which was a sign of their inferiority (Norris 1998: 139-40; see also Battersby 1989: 29). This, in turn, resulted in his peculiar description of the conception process where the unique form and soul of the child is provided by the male genius through intellectual, procreative, action. The alleged 'mindlessness' of women and, consequently, of the female role in reproduction confines that role to *un*intentional and passive mater-iality.

Needless to say, in a modern context Aristotle's views appear highly degrading towards women (as well as plain ridiculous). However, instead of dwelling upon (or laughing at) these ancient phallocentric misconceptions it could also simply be noted that parenthood has been connected to such misleading abstractions because of a fundamental and long-lasting scientific *ignorance* regarding human anatomy. It was Aristotle's lack of a certain type of important knowledge that made him found a theory of reproduction purely on ideological and philosophical speculation. And yet, even though most of us now know about and believe in the 'true' scientific story of human procreation the concept of (male) genius is still being used in the discourse of art and literature and functions as a strong indicator of, so-called, creative excellence and artistic originality. According to Christine Battersby, in her book *Gender and Genius*, it was actually not until the Romantic period that the concept of genius directly was linked to *artistic* originality and creativity rather than human procreativity. As we shall see, this connection was closely related to the rise of the book 'industry', with the literary world as a prospective lucrative market, emerging at that time. The 'business' of literature was entering the age of mechanical reproduction and there was money to be made.

2.   Intentional authorship – the owner(s) of the text

> The distinguishing characteristic of the modern author [...] is that he is conceived as the originator and therefore the owner of a special kind of commodity, the 'work.' And a crucial institutional embodiment of the author-work relation is copyright, which not only makes possible the profitable publishing of books but, also, by endowing it with legal reality, produces and affirms the very identity of the author as author (Rose 1988: 54).

The modern picture of the author as an original creator, an individual who realizes his spiritual and artistic *intentions* in a unique piece of literature started to develop in the late 18th-century together with important

developments regarding copyright and property law. As Martha Woodmansee has pointed out, writers in 18th-century Europe began to realize
how the rapidly increasing number of readers could be lucrative in a scale
never previously experienced. For the author's input on the production of
a book to be more highly regarded, and subsequently financially rewarded,
it became necessary to stress the spiritual and intellectual uniqueness that,
allegedly, only the author could provide. Not surprisingly, the old Aristotelian division between reproducible material and unique form became
useful in developing what we today conceive of as '*authorship*' (Woodmansee 1984: 426, 443-48. See also Rose 1988 and 1993; Chartier 1994:
29-34) – a fact taken up and criticized by Lawrence Venuti when he
presents the alternative notion of 'collective' authorship and the trans-
forming abilities of the translator (1995: 13-14).

The modern notion of the author's work is highly influenced by the
Aristotelian conception of (male, intellectual) form as superior to (female,
physical) matter as well as on a Romantic connection between literary
creativity and genius. This notion, in turn, has had an important impact on
copyright law and the status of the original and, consequently, on the translations of the same. As Chamberlain notes, the need for patrimonial
legitimacy through matrimony is founded on a quest for male power which,
historically, has forced women into a situation where their fidelity constantly has been questioned and demanded (Chamberlain 1988: 465). The
marital contract, and the moral and legal requests attached to it, has functioned as an unequal seal of female accountability and subordination.[2]
Similarly, in copyright law the translator is morally accountable to the author, not vice versa. Even if the translator's 'moral rights', the 'right of
paternity' for instance, are as valid and secured as the author's in the eyes
of the law, it is still expected of the translation to be *faithful* to the original
(The Society of Authors 1995: 4 & 1996: 7; The Translators' Association
1994: 3). Copyright law, therefore, can be said to primarily secure the
interests of the author, the father of the original and 'legitimate' text just

---

[2] Barbara Johnson in her essay "Taking Fidelity Philosophically" also stresses the
supposed analogy between matrimony and translation and she focuses on linguistic
faithfulness. Even though her text is full of gendered metaphors she does not make a
connection between sex/gender and fidelity. However, some of Johnson's arguments
clearly indicate a (psychoanalytical) gender-bias regarding language and translation:
"[I]ncest [...] is at stake in the enterprise of translation. Through the foreign language
we renew our love-hate intimacy with our mother tongue". She continues, "If we are
impotent, it is because Mother is inadequate" (1985: 144-45).

as the marital contract has been seen as a legal solution to a physical 'problem' – the uncertainty of fatherhood.

The anxiety of influence and infidelity in the name of necessary patrimonial legitimacy is based on the (material/physical) self-evidence of maternity and expressed in legal terms as *"Mater semper certa est: pater is est quem nuptiae demonstrant"* / "The mother is always certain. The father is he to whom the marriage points" (O'Brien 1989: 20-21; see also Marsiglio 1995: 161-62). Such an anxiety can be paralleled with the general obsession with authenticity regarding creative production that has prevailed, especially during the past two centuries (cf. e.g. Maier and Massardier-Kenney 1996: 237; Chamberlain 1988: *passim*). Marriage, a social 'institution' traditionally induced by a contractual agreement (oral and/or written) between a man and a woman and sustained by the nuclear family model has been made into a 'necessary' criterion for creating a stable and secure environment for the children to thrive in. Theoretically, this implies that it is only when the father can be certain about his kinship to the children in a family unit that he ought to provide and *care* for them. His emotional and financial investment will be profitable, as it were, because he will have regenerated through his offspring. Similarly, it appears that the immortality of the author is preserved and justified through copyright law. Copyright law has created an illusion of the necessity for the work of art to be 'legitimate'.

3. Intentional parenthood- the owner(s) of the child

The conclusions reached thus far regarding the formation of the discourse of literary production are of utmost importance for a discussion on how and why the notion of what translation is/does (in relation to the original) appears to be more mobile than ever. As noted, scientific development – New Reproductive Technologies – plays a vital part here since it undermines fixed, polarized, ideas of how and by whom human beings are *created*. Seemingly, the marital contract as a tangible proof of fatherhood (provided the wife is good and faithful), as described by Chamberlain, becomes redundant in cases of *in vitro* Fertilization (IVF), for instance. The request for ('physical') fidelity would be directed towards the doctor who would have to insure that the correct sperm had been 'mixed' with the correct egg – which could be ascertained by a simple DNA-test. The conventional feminization of fidelity is, thus, displaced since doctors/scientists can be seen as either gender-'neutral' or as patriarchal authority figures.

Yet, the "legal dimension to the concept of fidelity" (Chamberlain 1988: 465) – be it to legitimatize the offspring of the father (through marriage) or of the author (through copyright) – is firmly based on a production vs. reproduction constellation which is not easily disrupted. The complexity and persistence of that dualistic construct is revealingly presented by Mark Rose when he discusses one of the many legal cases dealing with the validity of surrogate contracts. Different countries have different rules regarding these issues but this specific case refers to the American judicial system. The case, *Johnson v. Calvert*, concerns the question regarding who should be declared the 'natural' mother of a child born in September 1990 (1998: 219-22). In January that year the two parties involved, Mark and Crispina Calvert (the genetic parents) and Anna Johnson (the gestational surrogate/parent) signed a surrogacy contract stating that Anna Johnson would bear the Calverts' child to term and would in return receive a life insurance policy and $10,000. However, relations broke down and both parties brought a lawsuit against the other regarding motherhood (1998: 219; see also Schwartz 1996: 342 & 344). In the first trial Anna Johnson was dismissed as the child's natural mother since she was not genetically related to it and "her relationship to the boy, if indeed she had any, was analogous to that of a foster parent"(1998: 220). The appeals court also declared Crispina Calvert the mother of the child on genetic grounds.

In contrast, the majority of the California Supreme Court decided that *either* woman could, biologically, be granted natural motherhood and that, in biologically (in)-dubitable cases like this, "motherhood was ultimately a matter of *intention*"(1998: 220-21, my italics). Since the Calverts had *conceived* the idea of a child – they had mentally initiated (intended) the child's existence, as it were – they were also the rightful parents/owners of the boy. Crispina Calvert was the mother not for genetical/biological reasons but because the court applied intellectual property law – copyright – to the issue of human procreation. Moreover, as Rose puts it, such a ruling involved an "implicit equation of mothers and authors" – quite an unusual, almost 'oxymoronic', connection in itself (1998: 218 & 225). Crispina Calvert was judged to be an active producer and creator (author) whereas Anna Johnson remained on the negative side of the persistent metaphor of dualism as a passive reproducer and 'carrier' – a translator in the most limited sense.

The perseverance of dualistic thinking and of the concept of natural-ness is evident even in a *bio-illogical* case such as this. The court swiftly dismissed the suggestion that *both* women were the child's mothers – not, it claimed, because multiple parenthood was impossible but because the combination of parental intentions and genetic kinship of Crispina Cal-vert made such an arrangement redundant.[3] One of the most intriguing aspects of the courts ruling is that to avoid the arguably challenging pros-pect of dual biological motherhood it on the one hand had to reinforce a patriarchal attitude of women/mothers as passive and on the other ascribe to mothers an active role as creators and originators.

The decision that motherhood (and fatherhood) was a question of in-tention was not reached without some disagreements. It is noteworthy that the only woman on the court, Justice Joyce Kennard, protested against using intellectual property law as a guideline instead of family law where the object of consideration would have been the child's well-being and the respective adults' suitability for raising the child. Kennard also pointed out that a pregnancy in itself was a matter of intention and a "pregnant woman [...] a conscious agent of creation" (Rose 1998: 221; cf. Schwartz 1996: 344). The lawyers of Anna Johnson also stressed that the genetic make-up was not the only factor forming the unborn child – the shape and size of certain parts of the body (the brain, for instance) are often linked to the gestational mother (Rose 1998: 228).[4] Nevertheless, the Calverts 'won' the case and gestation, it was decided, "was not 'the *sine qua non* of motherhood'" (Schwartz 1996: 344).

---

[3] Rose notes how in the question of dual motherhood the court resumed the geneti-cally based arguments that had been conclusive evidence of parenthood in the previous trials. In a later case, *Belsito v. Clark* (Ohio, 1994), the court rejected the 'intention-ality test' since it could lead to the "unacceptable" consequence of dual motherhood and referred to a hypothetical case where two lesbian women together decided (in-tended) to have a child (1998: 228-29 & 232). The obvious difficulties with accepting multiple parenthood (of a child or, as I suggest, a piece of literature) are logical if situated within a persistent dualistic framework. The dominant ideal of stable nuclear families (with two married and different sexed parents at its centre) makes itself heard in both the *Johnson v. Calvert* and in the *Belsito v. Clark* case.

[4] Rose points out how Kennard protested against the long tradition of abstracting procreation and that she also (together with Johnson's lawyers) refused to accept 'genetic essentialism'. The lawyers' argument, however, must be said to be based on *gestational* essentialism.

4. Translation as care-taking in an age of mechanical human reproduction

Our socially constructed notion of what constitutes not only 'social' but also biological motherhood and fatherhood respectively, is rapidly changing. Almost every week there are reports in the newspapers on new parental constellations in connection with New Reproductive Technologies. One such case concerns a British male gay couple who, by an American court, have both been granted parenthood ('parent one' and 'parent two') to twins that were conceived *in vitro* using an egg from a donor who was not the subsequent gestational mother. The San Diego court "in October ruled that both [men] could be listed as *'intended* parents'"(Allen 1999, my emphasis; see also Hartley-Brewer 1999).

For the first time in history the "organic unity of fetus and mother can no longer be assumed" (Martin 1987: 20; cf. Ragoné 1994:110). At the same time the intentionality of parenthood previously associated with male procreative activity has dispersed into a variable and highly context bound concept. Aristotle's view that it is the (male) intellectual 'idea' that creates the child presents a phallocentric standpoint that, in various forms, has been extremely persistent. As we have seen, women/mothers too can now pass the 'intentionality-test'. Yet, it could also be argued that such rulings are still male-oriented and, therefore, based on an intentional 'phallacy' which assumes positive, assertive and constant control from the point of view of the individual parent regarding what her/his intentions might be and what they will result in. In her book, *Surrogate Motherhood: Conception in the Heart*, Helena Ragoné explains how surrogates often justify their decision to bear a child who, subsequently, will be brought up by someone else by believing "that motherhood is composed of two separable components: the biological process, conception, pregnancy and delivery; and the social process, intentionality, love, and nurturance" (1994: 127). The distinction may seem far too simple and clear-cut. There is of course the possibility that such an argument would deem the gestational part of parenthood *negatively* finite and emotionally detached and therefore, yet again, putting the pressure of the 'sacred bond' attachment between mother and child on women who may view their pregnancy in a different light. Nevertheless, it could also be seen as a point of departure away from a mystification and 'mythification' of procreation and towards the idea of parenthood (to parent in Latin means 'bringing forth') as a contextual relationship between supportive, temporary and *authoritative* caretakers/custodians and a developing and (in-)dependent being, the child.

The written text, also, is a developing work in progress with the translators of that text playing a significant part in bringing it up and forth. The initial writers (the 'authors') and the subsequent writers (the 'translators'), together with any other variety of involved 'writers', will all make decisions that are bound to have an impact on the life (not *after*life) of the text and those decisions will be of relative importance. The authoritative (but not necessarily 'best', most 'fair' or 'wise') decisions made by these custodians will be of relative importance because of how the text reacts to and interacts with them. The success of these text-caring (multiple) parents has little to do with their gender and more with a willingness and aptness to care. Care, in this sense, is not the kind of 'mythified', so called instinctive and unselfish will to nurture that has so often in the past been ascribed to women. A willingness to care (just as the urge to create) may have a number of different reasons, the prospect of fame and acclaim being one and that of financial reward another.

In conclusion, I would like to argue that translation theory, when concerned with the status and role of the translator, would gain from making a *conceptual leap* away from, firstly, the perception that works of literature are properties in which the translator may or may not hold a share and, secondly, the insistence on promoting translation or, in fact, any kind of writing as a 'creative' activity. If writers were to be regarded as temporary but responsible 'caretakers' of words and ideas rather than long-term owners of intellectual offspring, the appeals to increase the appreciation and value of the translator's efforts, both on a discourse level and a financial level, could become more persuasive.

A Course on 'Gender and Translation'
As an Indicator of Certain Gaps in the Research on the Topic

ŞEBNEM SUSAM-SARAJEVA
University of Edinburgh, United Kingdom

Abstract. This essay[1] focuses on the challenges of giving a lecture course on 'gender and translation' and on the insights such a course offers into gender studies and translation studies. Based on the experience of the author in teaching this course in Finland, the essay first examines the advantages and disadvantages of setting up a course on translation specifically from the perspective of gender-oriented approaches. It states that while the course was useful in increasing students' awareness in translational matters and gender-related issues, certain problems arose in relation to addressee, genre, and languages involved, and the feminist interests underlying these approaches. The essay then raises certain questions concerning the present levels of exchange between gender studies and translation studies, and between these disciplines and 'the real world'. It points out certain gaps in the existing research on gender and translation and offers some suggestions for tackling these gaps.

1. Introduction

Although they are relatively young academic disciplines, gender studies and translation studies have already been in close contact for more than a decade. Both interdisciplinary fields, they have been interested in similar areas and have encouraged research into a variety of neighbouring branches, such as language, society, religion, literature, anthropology, and

[1] *Acknowledgements:* I would like to thank the Christina Institute for Women's Studies, University of Helsinki, for providing me the financial support to present this essay as a paper at the *First International Seminar on Gender and Language (The Gender of Translation / The Translation of Gender)*, University of Valencia, 16-18 October 2002, and to the MonAKO Multilingual Communication Programme, University of Helsinki, for providing me the financial support to work on it. Thanks are also due to my students, who with their invaluable feedback, made this essay possible in the first place.

communication. Yet it would be interesting to find out how much exchange actually has taken place between the two disciplines in general. What have they learned from each other until now and what else could have been learned? Also, what sort of impact have they managed to have *outside* their own boundaries, on other scholarly disciplines and on 'the real world'?

These questions are obviously beyond the scope of a single essay. Here I will content myself with concentrating on the 'plusses' and 'minuses' of teaching a course on 'gender and translation' as possible indicators of the extent of such exchange, interaction and impact. The essay may also offer an opportunity for scholars writing on 'gender and translation' to learn something about the repercussions of their work in a language and culture quite different from their own.

2. Background information on the course

2.1. Institutional settings

The course was first taught at the Christina Institute for Women's Studies, University of Helsinki, in autumn 2001. In autumn 2002 it was offered again at the same institute, and also at the University of Jyväskylä under the aegis of the women's studies programme and several philology departments. The reason why the course was set up in the first place was to make use of the theoretical work carried out in the overlapping area of gender and translation, and thus, to establish academic connections between the programme offering translation studies (MonAKO) and the institute focusing on women's studies (Christina) within the one and the same university. The course aimed at encouraging critical thinking on the relationships between translation and gender, and language and gender; at introducing the central concepts of gender-conscious approaches to translation and showing how these approaches could be implemented in terms of certain translation strategies; and at broadening the students' perspectives on a variety of theoretical issues related to the translators' role(s) and the political power of translations.

2.2. Contents of the course

The first lecture (re)introduced the concepts of 'gender' and 'translation', and elaborated on the interrelations between them. For those students who were new to translation studies, a brief overview of research areas in the field was given. The second lecture dealt with gender and language, discussing topics such as surface-level inclusive language, grammatical gender, metaphors, marked vs. unmarked words, cognitive categories, stereotypes, etc. The third lecture focused on Western metaphorical thinking on translation – a thinking laden with patriarchal implications. Notions such as '(in)fidelity' in translation and translation as (re)production were discussed. The fourth lecture introduced the approaches and strategies of certain feminist translators. Ideas presented include translation as rewriting, feminist translation as a political act, 'womanhandling' the texts, and translation as 'transformance' or 'hologram'. In lecture 5 we discussed how to deal with 'offensive' material in translation, i.e. with texts perceived to be derogatory for peripheral groups. Lecture 6 addressed the criticism directed against feminist approaches to translation, pointing especially at certain theoretical contradictions found in these approaches.

In session 7 we concentrated on translation and minority issues: how has translation been used as a means of power to oppress the minorities, and how has translation served the enunciation efforts of these minorities? Relationships between feminist and postcolonial theories of translation were touched upon, as well issues of ethics and cultural difference. In lecture 8, we examined case studies on translations of women writers' works by 'patriarchal' translators, whether male or female, and we tried to understand how these texts had been manipulated. Lecture 9 offered an overview of 'gay' theoretical contributions to translation studies. Feminist approaches to the translation of religious texts were dealt with in lecture 10. Radical and reformist approaches to the translation and interpretation of the Bible were examined, and certain feminist interpretations of the Qur'an were mentioned. Lecture 11 aimed at increasing the students' awareness of the 'translatedness' of 'feminist' theories, and to draw the attention to the role translation plays in their reception. Translation of French feminisms into English was examined as a case study. The final lecture looked back and to the future: what have translation studies and gender studies learned from each other? What can be the future prospects and possible research areas?

The course was carried out in English. For each session, students had to read an article on which group discussions were arranged as part of the lectures. The requirements for the course were two to three lecture diaries and/or one essay, depending on the credits required by the various departments.

2.3. Student backgrounds

The majority of my students in both institutions came from departments
of English philology, partly because they felt more competent in this language compared to students coming from other language departments,
and because their tutors encouraged them to attend courses in English.
Then came other philology students, e.g. Spanish, French, German, Finnish, Hungarian, or more generally students from Romance, Slavonic and
Scandinavian languages and literatures. In addition, I had students whose
main field of study was social politics, social psychology, general linguistics, political science, sociology, cultural anthropology, philosophy,
comparative literature or musicology. Although the great majority of them
were Finns, there were also a few with other nationalities.

The diversity in the students' backgrounds was a welcome experience
indeed. They brought along expertise in a variety of languages and cultures, ranging from Bengali to Bulgarian, enriching the sessions with
interesting examples. However, one major problem was the degree of students' familiarity with translation studies and with gender studies, which
varied considerably (see Table 1).

Institution	Total # of students	# of students who were somewhat familiar with translation	# of students who were somewhat familiar with issues related to gender
Christina Insitute autumn 2001	9	8	5
Christina Insitute autumn 2002	21	12	14
Jyväskylä autumn 2002	27	11	10

Table 1 Degree of familiarity with translation and gender studies

According to the form they filled in at the beginning of the course, 9
of my students in Jyväskylä, i.e. 1/3 of the whole class, had no familiarity
at all with either of the disciplines. In general, some students who had
some familiarity with translation had not been 'exposed' to translation

theories at all, but had attended practice-oriented courses. Some who said they were familiar with these disciplines had only begun to take classes in either of the topics. Furthermore, only a handful of them had ever worked as a translator/interpreter or intended to work as one in the near future.

In section 4 I will come back to the implications of student backgrounds for the teaching of the course, and for the interaction between the two disciplines in question and between these disciplines and 'the real world'.

3. 'Plusses' in teaching 'gender and translation'

The general reaction to the course was a mixture of excitement, interest and frustration (the reason for the latter is explained in section 4). Throughout the course, students displayed a gradually heightening awareness in matters related to translation and to 'life' in general, as summed up below.

3.1. Increased awareness in relation to translational matters

3.1.1. On translation theory and translation ethics
Several of the students who *had* taken courses in translation said that until then their courses had been practically oriented and discussion on theoretical and ethical issues had rarely taken place. For the philology students, translation courses were used as a means to test and enhance their language capabilities. On the other hand, those who were being trained to work as translators were mostly given 'down-to-earth advice' and practical tools, but were not necessarily encouraged 'to do more thinking on translation'. Therefore, they took the course as a positive contribution to their future careers.

3.1.2. On the empowerment of translators
Several students noted that they were glad to be introduced to a topic in which translators were given more authority. They were enthusiastic about the possibility that gender-conscious approaches to translation might have political impacts. They learned to question the authority of the source text, feeling more confident as translators and not necessarily feeling inferior to the 'authors'. They often agreed with the need to change the status of translators and to break the silence and invisibility associated with them, though some of the students claimed that the translators' status is 'not that bad' in Finland.

3.1.3. On 'packaging'

Students noted that they developed a new degree of appreciation and need for 'packaging' (see e.g. Kolias 1990), i.e. the translator's contextualizing efforts in extratextual material, such as prefaces, introductions, footnotes, etc. In fact, they expressed more affinity with 'packaging' than with the actual manipulation of source texts.

3.1.4. As users/readers of translations

Almost all the students showed an increasing understanding of the translation process, even if they were not specifically trained to be translators/ interpreters. They have become more conscious users of translations and have somewhat got used to the idea that translated texts are always shaped by the identity of the translators and the ideologies of the times, that texts are not manipulated only in 'propagandas'.

3.2. Increased awareness in relation to gender and life

3.2.1. On language and gender

The issues related to gender in language found direct repercussions in the daily lives of students. Therefore, they were often quick to contribute with their own examples. Most of the language-related points raised during the course were things they have not thought about or realised before. For example, the gender-sensitive interpretations of religious texts proved to be an important topic for several of the students, who noted that they finally pinned down why they had been put off by religion as they experienced it as a child and adolescent. It was mainly because they had felt disconcerted and excluded by its male-oriented language.

3.2.2. On the construction of gender identities in Finnish society

As a result of the course, students noted that they increased their questioning about the gender issues in Finland, where most of the problems seemed to have been resolved. Although some students claimed that women's position was 'good' in Finland, and that whatever sexism there was, it was only a leftover from earlier days and would eventually disappear, there were others who articulated their disappointment with the more implicit gender-related problems in the Finnish society.

3.2.3. On general theoretical knowledge

The course introduced new theoretical viewpoints to the students. For instance, before starting the course, several of them had only a vague idea about what 'gender' meant. They also started questioning their previous and rather monolithic conceptions of 'feminism', since they were presented with different forms of and approaches to feminism. The references to other literary and cultural theories, such as deconstruction, psychoanalysis, and postcolonial studies were also helpful in initiating them to wider theoretical perspectives, although these references were also frustrating for some who confronted them for the first time.

In short, I believe that the benefits of the course for the students outweighed the disadvantages. As one of my students concluded in her final lecture diary:

> [...] For me, [the course] did definitely raise more questions than offer answers, but I don't think that is necessarily a bad thing in any way. The course turned out both to work as a (re-)introduction to the issues of gender in language and to put translation in general into a new perspective for me – especially by highlighting the ethical questions related to translating, when earlier I've been used to only wondering about how 'correct' a translation might be. (Leea Sokura 2001)

Yet in this essay I will focus more on the problematic points (section 4), with the hope that these issues can point out certain gaps in the research on gender and translation and that these gaps might be discussed more widely and certain solutions might be suggested (section 5).

4.   'Minuses' in teaching 'gender and translation'

4.1. Who is the addressee of the research on 'gender and translation'?

Predictably, student backgrounds have a direct bearing on the issues that can be discussed in the classroom. If several of the students have not heard the expression *les belles infidèles* before, or are not accustomed to the prominence of the Tower of Babel myth within traditional thinking on translation, it is not easy to discuss *alternative* ways of thinking with them. When their background does not include translation studies, I am often left with not much 'to deconstruct'. The majority of scholars who have written on the topic of gender and translation have often targeted translation studies scholars as their intended audience, since they felt the need to challenge the gendered metaphorics prevalent in the traditional thinking on translation. However the *audience of translations* are not limited to translation studies scholars. Future research on the topic may benefit from addressing issues related to a broader readership, both scholarly and popular. As one student notes:

> [...] Perhaps *all* readers – not just translators and scholars – should be made more aware of the different aspects of translation, so that people would more easily remember that when they read a translation, they are not reading a simple 1:1 conversion of the original text. (Leea Sokura 2001)

This issue has direct links with the idea of popularizing academic discourses, which certainly is not a problem only of translation studies or gender studies. Nonetheless, I believe that the relative disinterest and ignorance in matters related to translation in fields other than translation studies and in 'the real world' are due to the 'invisibility' of translation studies as a discipline itself. In the same way as a translation is supposed to 'hide itself' from the eyes of the readers, so that the reader believes that s/he is reading the 'original' text, the discipline which deals with such an elusive topic is also risking being elusive itself. As Michael Cronin has pointed out, translation studies is a rather nomadic discipline (2000: 104). It deals with a wide range of areas, from machine translation to literary translation, from media translation to the translation of religious texts, from cognitive aspects of translation to socio-cultural contexts. Consequently, it often ends up leaving no trace on the areas it investigates into – just as nomads pack up their tents and leave without much trace in history.

4.2. Gender and translation = Literary translation?

This is a related point to the one stated in 4.1., since it again concerns the addressee of 'gender and translation' research. The current emphasis on literary texts in the field puts off several students who are interested in other forms of translation. Even if they come from 'language and literature' departments, for them literature is not the one and the only medium. For instance, they would like to see more examples from media translation. It will probably not be an exaggeration to say that today's gender identities are constructed not through literary texts, which are read less and less, but through films, advertisements, T.V. programs, newspapers, cartoons for children, school textbooks, etc.

Similarly, those who come from a social studies background together with a certain interest in gender studies, regard literature as 'not so relevant' for the purposes of the emancipation of minority groups. In 2.2. I noted that several students from social sciences initially registered for the course. I should add here that the majority of them dropped out after the first one or two courses, because they could not relate the discussion to their own fields of study. This, I believe, points at one of the major 'disconnections' between translation studies and gender studies. While those students had initially registered for the course because of their interest in gender studies, the lack of research on the translations carried out in *their* fields, such as social psychology, sociology, cultural anthropology or philosophy, led them to believe that gender and translation had nothing to do with their own fields of expertise. This is far from true, of course, since these fields are as dependent on translations as any other research field. Nevertheless, the existing research into translation has not adequately addressed the issues in such fields, let alone from a gender-conscious point of view.

At this point, one needs also to ask to what extent translation studies has managed to initiate substantial historical research on the development and spreading of the women's movements around the world *through translation*, and on the role translation plays in the canonization of certain 'feminist' texts. Do the students read certain important figures like Simone de Beauvoir or Hélène Cixous in French, or more likely, do they read them in their own mother tongue? If the latter is the case, how much attention is given to the 'translatedness' of texts in courses related to gender studies? Have studies carried out on the reception of these writers increased awareness on the role translation plays in the travels of theories (see, e.g., Flotow 2000; Freiwald 1991; Simons 1983; Susam-Sarajeva 2002b)? I rather doubt it. Therefore, I believe we need more students coming from areas other than philology departments to a course on 'gender and translation'.

4.3. Gender and translation = Feminist translation?

Another point related to the addressee question: one thing that often bothered me as a teacher, as much as it bothered the students, is that the research on gender and translation has mostly revolved around the issue of feminist writers and their agendas (see Mira 1999 for a similar criticism). This contrasts rather sharply with the initial explanation I give for 'gender' at the very first lecture: that the biological sex distinction is unable to explain the social roles we undertake, hence the socio-cultural construction of sexual identities, etc. I emphasize for them that 'gender' does not cover only female members of a society, and it certainly does not *prima facie* relate to the feminists, although it might have came into existence first as a result of their explorations.

The emphasis in 'gender and translation' on what are called the 'feminist' approaches to translation belies these initial explanations of mine. Those who do not 'adhere to' feminism, including some of the males and the possible gays or lesbians in the classroom, give signs of being rather out of place. In general, male students were already rare creatures in this course. Last year there were none. This year two started at the Christina Institute and four at the University of Jyväsklyä; one of them completed the course at the former and two at the latter. I contend that we need research into how 'male' gender identities are (re)constructed in and through translations, which should be as important a research area as other gender identities. By placing more emphasis on gender issues in general, from a variety of perspectives addressing male students as well as female, the gays as well as the lesbians, and also whatever forms of gender identity exist in between, work on training gender-conscious translators and users of translations can be better conducted.

The foregrounding of 'feminist' approaches to translation has another disadvantage. Because of all the negative connotations that, rightly or wrongly, came to be attached to the label 'feminism', several colleagues working within translation studies tend to regard the topic cautiously, and therefore miss the opportunity of learning from the insights derived from 'gender and translation'. A wider perspective might also appeal to them.

4.4. Dominance of central languages and cultures

This point may also be considered as part of the addressee question. The greater part of the research findings in gender and translation is still limited to an English- or French-speaking world only (maybe also Spanish and German, at best) and this jeopardizes the relevance of the arguments for other languages and cultures. The historical information provided on 'lost' and 'recovered' women writers/translators, the examples of wordplay and experimental language, the challenging of gendered metaphorics related to translation, these all assume a 'central' audience. Recently one of my students was commenting on how talking about translation as a 'woman', as in Lori Chamberlain's work (1992[1988]) or in the example of *les belles infidèles*, went so much against the grain in her mind, since the word for 'translation' in Icelandic, her mother tongue, carries *male* grammatical gender. Similarly, since the Finnish language does not have *grammatical* gender difference, it is often difficult for my students to relate to the examples given in French or English. The 'mainstream' work on gender and translation focuses on the points of view prevalent in the Anglophone and Francophone systems. There is, of course, nothing intrinsically wrong with this, and it is not at all surprising when we take into consideration that translation studies as a whole has long sustained such a centre-oriented approach (see Susam-Sarajeva 2002a). Nevertheless, as a result of such an orientation, students are experiencing difficulties in contextualizing certain arguments into other systems, and therefore they risk concluding that 'gender and translation' cannot offer them much that is relevant to their own languages and cultures.

A related issue arises when dealing with the gender-conscious interpretations of religious texts. Not much work is widely available on religious texts other than the Bible. Despite all my efforts, I could not, for instance, have access to texts on feminist interpretations of the Qur'an, although I am aware of their existence. As for other religious texts, I would have liked to learn more about the work done on them by 'feminist' theologians.

Has gender studies indeed become more sensitive to differences in language, culture and ethnicity among women, since these differences inevitably emerge in translations? If yes, I believe this sensitivity should also be reflected in the research carried out on 'gender and translation'. For instance, there are considerable differences between cultures regarding the appropriateness of writing about one's own work and of degrees of modesty. To risk a generalization, I would contend that in the Finnish culture, drawing attention to one's own work, or to *oneself* for that matter, is rather inappropriate. In a culture where silence, invisibility and submissiveness are almost virtues rather than vices, discussing 'gender and translation' as it currently stands gives rise to different sorts of problems. Students have already expressed their doubts about using extratextual material for emphasizing the translator's presence and agenda, especially if this is done in a very assertive way.

4.5. Theory vs. examples

Students often find the theoretical level of the texts rather high. This obviously has to do with their previous levels of experience in reading theoretical texts and also reading in languages that are not their mother tongue. From the 'double bind' of deconstructionists to the 'subaltern' of the Subaltern Studies group, most of the concepts and ideas have been new for students. In one sense, this is a good thing, since the course adds to their 'intellectual repertoire' so to speak. Yet on the other hand students want examples. They want to see 'concretely' how feminist/woman-oriented translators go about their work, or how female writers' texts have been tampered with, or how gay writers' texts can be reinforced for gay politics. Therefore they welcome reading case studies such as those of Kabi Hartman (1999), Valerie Henitiuk (1999) and Keith Harvey (1998).

'Gender and translation' was a fast evolving field in the 1990s, so it is often difficult to delineate the arguments stated. Several positions remain vague or they clash with each other. Students are quick to point out certain theoretical inconsistencies in the feminist approaches to translation, and when they read texts like Rosemary Arrojo's 1994 article, they often wholeheartedly agree with them. Very few of them justify the manipulation of texts in the name of feminist 'truths', and even those who do so find an inconsistency in sticking to the rhetoric of 'faithfulness' after such manipulation. I should immediately note here that in fact the majority of students are taken aback when I assure them that manipulations of texts have been taking place all the time. They then start wondering about their 'favourite' foreign writers, whom they have read in translation, and they feel visibly uneasy about the idea that those texts too might have been tampered with. For instance, when they learned about the censorship on Simone de Beauvoir's *Le deuxième sexe* in both English and Finnish translations, one of the students noted: "I have always allowed myself to believe that in Finland the liberty of speech is not violated" (Eeva Tervo 2001). My intuition is that age is a major factor here, since my more mature students have been less 'shocked' about issues related to text manipulation.

At this point, one of course ponders about the speed with which academic writings might have any influence at all on 'the real world'. It has been almost two decades that within translation studies such instances of manipulation have been a matter of fact. Yet scholars within the field apparently do not feel the need to communicate these findings to a wider audience, possibly because writing for popular journals does not serve academic promotion.

4.6. Issues of fidelity

Have feminist approaches managed to challenge the ideals of 'equivalence', 'faithfulness', and 'neutrality' deep-rooted in the traditional understanding of translation, within and outside the academia? My answer would be a firm 'no'. Concepts such as 'translation as hologram', translation being (un)faithful, (re)production, (re)constructing the meaning which is not inherent in the source text, etc. do not find easy currency – neither within translation studies, nor on the public platform. People are rather reluctant to accept the 'both/and' logic instead of the more deep-rooted 'either/or' (cf. Littau 1995).

The resistance of students towards the 'feminist manipulation' of texts – both as future translators/interpreters and as readers dependent on translations – is strong indeed. They find it quite impossible to question the notion of 'fidelity' to the author or the source text. Both in their lecture diaries and in the class, they often ask questions like "How far can you go? Is there any limit to subversion? Where can you draw the line between translation and something else that cannot be called a translation anymore, because it deliberately exhibits an agenda of its own?" and so on. Translation for them is a text 'loyal' to the original, conveying 'its specific feelings and thoughts'. They often talk about the 'obligation towards the author' despite any negative feelings due to offensive material. As one of my students put it, in other translation courses they were taught that "a loyal translation is always a good one, you cannot go wrong with it" (Mirka Hypén 2001). They were advised to correct possible spelling mistakes or grammatical errors in the source text, and *maybe* to slightly improve the source text to make it more comprehensible, if need be. Compared to this advice, they claimed that the 'gender and translation' course was a 'refreshing', but probably rather 'far-fetched' experience.

Some students expressed their conviction that feminist intervention should only target one's own scholarly peers and academic circles, but not the general public who are 'innocently' dependent on the translators. This, I believe, is directly related to the situation in Finland, where there is a small readership, as opposed to the wider audience in Anglophone and Francophone contexts. Therefore the students think that they need to please the readers and should not tamper with their expectations (Mirka Hypén 2001). Also the assumed characteristics of the audience make a difference for the students: "I believe that Finnish audience is honest and is entitled to [have access to] the texts as faithful translations" (Eeva Tervo 2001).

4.7. Fashion

This point has more to do with attitudes prevailing among translation studies scholars than among students. Gender-related approaches to translation are regarded as 'yet another passing fashion' which has 'swept through' translation studies, as did postcolonial approaches, deconstructionist approaches, etc. These 'importations' from literary and cultural theories seem to be regarded as periodic reflections of 'foreign' trends coming into fashion in translation studies. The contributions of such approaches are then seen as temporary issues, 'ephemeral, contemporary trends'. Maybe new, interesting and promising at the beginning, but all 'theory' in the end... Only 'practice' is regarded as permanent, i.e. the proper ways of translating, 'good translation', etc.

Gender-related approaches are not very much 'in the air' nowadays within translation studies, and I have occasionally wondered whether it would be seen an anachronistic decision to come up with such a course. Nonetheless one needs to think about what is left behind after this 'passing fad', if it were indeed so. For instance, after all the persuasive argumentation within gender studies challenging dominant groups' knowledge disguised as 'universal' knowledge, how come we find increasingly concerted efforts within translation studies to attain more general 'laws' and 'universals'? Why is 'neutrality' still the unquestioned expectation in interpreting settings (e.g. conference or community interpreting), despite all that has been written on gender, race and class factors affecting the outcome of everyone's work? In short, what have translation studies and gender studies actually learned from each other?

5. Conclusion

In this essay I have tried to share the insights derived from teaching a course on 'gender and translation' and to highlight certain problems found in the research on the topic. I want to conclude by offering some suggestions:

- We (meaning researchers dealing with the topic) need to carry out
  - o More research on non-literary translation, such as media translation, translation of legal texts and medical texts, of school text books, and *especially* of texts in the social sciences.
  - o More research into interpreting situations, where the contexts and requirements are very different from those of translation.

o More research on other languages and systems apart from the dominant ones, e.g. on translations from and into languages with no grammatical gender, such as Finnish or Turkish; on the 'lost' works of female writers/translators in strongly patriarchal societies, etc.

o More research into other gender-related approaches apart from the 'feminist' ones. With a focus shifted slightly from the feminist/woman-oriented angle to wider forms of gender construction, which specifically include men, the findings can be much more convincing and appealing for a wider audience.

- We need to establish better contact with a wider audience, both scholarly and popular. After all, if the 'agency' of translators *and* scholars is in question, aiming at a broader audience will only increase the potential impact of our writings.

- We need to conduct more case studies on actual translation strategies, on the reception of translated texts, etc. to find out how gender is (re)constructed in and through translations. This may require adopting a more descriptive translation studies approach, which could ultimately enhance the theoretical argumentations by providing solid examples.

- We need to arrange for more 'patronage' to be offered to students who wish to pursue the topic. A few of my students expressed their intention to take up matters related to 'gender and translation' as part of their master's theses. Yet, at least in two of these cases, finding a supervisor willing to deal with the subject proved to be impossible and the students had to change topics. Supervisors (female or male) may be reluctant to supervise theses and dissertations in this area, because of its alleged 'unscholarly' and 'subjective' nature, or because of the stigma that goes with 'feminism'. Yet, if enough 'patronage' is not provided to students in a *variety* of countries, research in the field will remain limited to dominant languages and cultures.

- We need to establish
  o A better network among teachers and researchers working on the topic, so that new and diverse material can be easily shared.

For instance, in addition to the material on religious texts, I also had difficulties in locating lesbian approaches to translation. I hope that the First International Seminar on Gender and Language (The Gender of Translation / The Translation of Gender) will be a useful step in this direction.

o   More contact with other scholars working in translation studies and gender studies, so that this 'passing fad' will finally have longer lasting impacts on these two disciplines.

It may be high time that gender and translation *can* offer some answers to the non-expert (including the students), as well as continuing to raise different and interesting questions.

List of contributors

Rosemary Arrojo is currently directing the Center for Research in Translation at Binghamton University USA, where she is Professor of Comparative Literature. She has published widely on the intersections between translation studies and contemporary textual theories, particularly in Brazil, her native country, where she taught translation for over twenty years. Her e-mail address is: rarrojo@binghamton.edu.

Nicole Baumgarten, M.A. is Research Assistant at the Research Center on Multilingualism at the University of Hamburg, Germany. Her research interests include translation theory, social semiotics and multimodal texts, currently focusing on English-German dubbing of mainstream movie productions. Her website is at: http://www.rrz.uni-hamburg.de/SFB538/mitarbeiter/Baumgarten_pers.html. Her email address is: nicole.baumgarten@uni-hamburg.de.

Luise von Flotow is associate professor for translation studies at the University of Ottawa, Canada. Her research interests include gender and other cultural issues in translation, audiovisual translation, translation and cultural diplomacy, and literary translation. She is the author of *Translation and Gender. Translating in the Era of Feminism* (1997), co/editor of *The Politics of Translation in the Middle Ages and the Renaissance* (2001), co-editor and translator of the anthology *The Third Shore. Short Fiction by Women Writers from East Central Europe: 1989-2000* (forthcoming 2003). Her e-mail address is: luisevonflotow@yahoo.ca.

Pilar Godayol (PhD in Translation Theory, Universitat Autònoma de Barcelona) is a certified legal translator and currently teaches in the Translation Studies programme at the Universitat de Vic. She coordinates the 'Biblioteca de Traducció i Interpretació' series published by Eumo Editorial. She has published a book, *Espais de frontera. Gènere i traducció* (2000) (*Spazi de frontiera. Genere e traduzione*, 2002), and several articles and lectured on cultural aspects of translation with emphasis on Theory of Translation, Gender Studies and Chicana Literature. She has also edited and translated a book, *Veus xicanes. Contes* (2001), of Chicana literature. Her new book (*Germanes de Shakespeare. 20 del XX*) is about to be published. Her e-mail is: pgodayol@uvic.es.

Patrice Guex is an ordinary Professor of psychiatry and psychosocial medicine at the Faculty of Medicine of the University of Lausanne and the head of the Department of Psychiatry of the Lausanne University Hospital (CHUV). He is the author of numerous studies and papers on the subjects of the physician/patient relationship, the medical decision and the coping with illness (cancer, pain, transplants). He is the author of *Psychologie et cancer* [Psychology and cancer] that has been translated into several languages. His e-mail address is: Patrice.Guex@chuv.hos-pvd.ch.

M. Rosario Martín is a lecturer in Translation at the Centro de Estudios Superiores "Felipe II" (Universidad Complutense, Spain). Her research interests include translation theory, gender issues and cultural studies. Her publications include *El (des)orden de los discursos: la traducción de lo políticamente correcto* (Granada: Comares, 2003) and *En los límites de la traducción: reflexiones desde el otro lado del espejo* (with África Vidal, Granada: Comares, 2003). She has also coedited *Babel* (special issue on translation in *Debats*, no. 75, 2001-2, with África Vidal and Anne Barr) and *Últimas corrientes en los estudios de traducción y sus aplicaciones* (Salamanca: Ediciones Universidad de Salamanca, 2001, with Anne Barr and Jesús Torres). Her e-mail address is: mrmr@usal.es.

Ulrika Orloff is originally from Sweden where she worked as a teacher and translator. She is currently completing her dissertation in Comparative Literature at University College London (UCL), England. Her thesis, *Challenging the Feminization of Translation: Sex, Lies and the (Re-)Production of Words*, concerns the ideology and discourse of translation, specifically taking issues of cultural and social productivity and gender into consideration. Her research interests include the division between art and science and the politics of gender and difference. She has previously published on M.M. Bakhtin and translation theory. Her e-mail address is: u_orloff@hotmail.com.

Manuela Palacios is a tenured lecturer at the University of Santiago de Compostela. She has translated Virginia Woolf, as well as Estonian poetry, into Galician. She is currently completing an anthology of contemporary Irish women poets, whose work she has also translated. Besides, she has published articles on translation studies in *Babel* and *Translatio*. Other fields of interest are, on the one hand, women studies and the configuration of gender, and, on the other, the relationship between literature and the visual arts. Her e-mail address is: iamapago@usc.es.

Carmen Ríos is a predoctoral student at the University of Santiago de Compostela and is currently working on her PhD dissertation about the reception of Irish literature by Galician nationalism of the early twentieth century. Her publications and former research projects deal with issues of reception, with translation as a key aspect, and national identity. Together with Manuela Palacios, she has written articles on the Galician appropriation of the Irish model of literary nationalism in the 1920s as well as on the reception of the translation of some passages of *Ulysses* by Ramón Otero Pedrayo. Her e-mail address is: carife@usc.es.

José Santaemilia is associate professor of English language and linguistics at the University of Valencia. His main research interests are gender and language, sexual language and legal translation (English-Spanish). He is the author of *Género como conflicto discursivo: La sexualización de los personajes cómicos* (2000) and has also edited several books (*Sexe i llenguatge: La construcció lingüística de les identitats de gènere* (2002) and *Género, lenguaje y traducción* (2003)) and published (with José Pruñonosa) the first critical edition and translation of *Fanny Hill* into Spanish (Madrid: Cátedra 2000). His e-mail address is: jose.santaemilia@uv.es.

Janet S. Shibamoto Smith is a professor in anthropology at the University of California, Davis. Her research interests include the relation of language ideology and language practice; the concept of self –particularly the gendered self–, identities and citizenship; language and emotion; Japan. She is the author of *Japanese Women's Language* (1985), 'Women in Charge' (*Language in Society* 1992), *From Hiren to Happî-endo: Romantic Expression in the Japanese Love Story* (in Palmer & Occhi 1999), and *Japanese Language, Gender, and Ideology: Cultural Models and Real People* (with Shigeko Okamoto, forthcoming from Oxford University Press). Her email address is: jssmith@ucdavis.edu.

Pascal Singy lectures in linguistics at the University of Lausanne. He is the author of *L'image du français en Suisse romande* (Paris, L'Harmattan, 1997) and has edited *Les femmes et la langue* (Paris, Delachaux et Niéstlé, 1998). In addition, Pascal Singy conducts research on the physician/patient relationship at the Lausanne University Hospital (CHUV). His e-mail address is: Pascal.Singy@ling.unil.ch.

Şebnem Susam-Sarajeva is a lecturer in translation studies at the University of Edinburgh. Her research interests include descriptive translation studies, gender studies, research methodology in translation studies, literary and cultural theories, and community interpreting. Her e-mail address is: s.susam-sarajeva@ed.ac.uk.

Orest Weber is a sociolinguist working at the Department of Psychiatry of the Lausanne University Hospital (CHUV). His research interests include interpreting in the medical sphere, sexual identity and aids-preventive discourse in medical consultations, language and ethnic identity in former Soviet states. He is the author of several papers in those three fields of research. His e-mail address is: orestweber@hotmail.com.

Michaela Wolf is assistant professor at the Department of Translation Studies, University of Graz, Austria. Her research interests include cultural aspects of translation, translation history, feminist translation. Presently her research focuses on social aspects of translation which she is investigating on a large corpus of German translations in the Habsburg Monarchy. She has edited various books, e.g. *Übersetzungswissenschaft in Brasilien. Beiträge zum Status von 'Original' und Übersetzung* (1997); *Übersetzung aus aller Frauen Länder. Beiträge zu Theorie und Praxis weiblicher Realität in der Translation* (2001), and has recently organized an international conference on feminist translation. Her e-mail address is: michaela.wolf@uni-graz.at.

Bibliography

Akagawa, Jiro (1996) *Futari no Koibito* ('Two Lovers'), Tokyo: Shuei-sha.

Alcoff, Linda (1988) 'Cultural Feminism *versus* Post-Structuralism: The Identity Crisis in Feminist Theory', *Signs* 13(3): 405-36.

Allen, Beverley (1999) 'Paralysis, Crutches, Wings: Italian Feminisms and Transculturation', http://pum.12.pum.umontreal.ca/revues/ surfaces/vol13/ allen.html, 1-19.

Allen, Richard (1999) 'We'll quit Britain if we are not accepted declare gay fathers', *Evening Standard*, 14 December 1999.

Álvarez Rodríguez, Román and Mª Carmen A. Vidal Claramonte (1996) 'Translating: A Political Act', in Álvarez Rodríguez and Vidal Claramonte (eds.): 1-6.

Álvarez Rodríguez, Román and Mª Carmen A. Vidal Claramonte (eds.) (1996) *Translation, Power, Subversion*, Clevedon: Multilingual Matters.

Andermahr, Sonya, Terry Lovell and Carol Wolkowitz (eds.) (1997) *A Concise Glossary of Feminist Theory*, London: Arnold.

Anzaldúa, Gloria (1987) *Borderlands/La Frontera*, San Francisco: aunt lute books.

Arrojo, Rosemary (1986) *Oficina de Tradução – A Teoria na Prática*, São Paulo: Ática, 11-22.

------ (1993) 'A Tradução e o Flagrante da Transferência: Algumas Aventuras Textuais com Dom Quixote e Pierre Menard', in *Tradução, Desconstrução e Psicanálise*, Rio de Janeiro: Imago, 151-176.

------ (1994) 'Fidelity and the Gendered Translation', *TTR* 7(2): 147-164.

------ (1995) 'Translation and Postmodernism in Calvino's *Se una notte d'inverno un viaggiatore*', *La traduzione: Saggy e documenti II, Libri e riviste d'Italia*, Ministero per i Beni Culturali e Ambientali, divisione Editoria. 41-56.

------ (2001-2002) 'Algunas aventuras textuales con Don Quijote y Pierre Menard', *Debats* 75: 24-35.

------ (2002) 'Writing, Interpreting and the Power Struggle for the Control of Meaning', in M. Tymoczko and E. Gentzler (eds.): 63-79.

------ (2003a) 'The Power of Originals and the Scandal of Translation – A Reading of Edgar Allan Poe's 'The Oval Portrait'', in Maria Calzada Pérez (ed.) *Apropos of Ideology – Translation Studies on Ideology – Ideologies in Translation Studies*, Manchester: St. Jerome, 165-180

------ (2003b) 'A Relação Exemplar entre Autor e Revisor (e Outros Trabalhadores Textuais Semelhantes) e O Mito de Babel: Alguns Comentários sobre *História do Cerco de Lisboa*, de José Saramago', in D.E.L.T.A. (special issue on translation), Catholic University of São Paulo, São Paulo, Brazil, 193-207.

Bachleitner, Norbert (1989) "Übersetzungsfabriken'. Das deutsche Überset-
zungswesen in der ersten Hälfte des 19.Jahrhunderts', *Internationales
Archiv für Sozialgeschichte der deutschen Literatur* 14(1): 1-49.

Baker, Mona (1998) 'Norms', in M. Baker (ed.): 163-165.

------ (ed.) (1998) *Routledge Encyclopedia of Translation Studies*, London &
New York: Routledge.

Banting, Pamela (1994) 'S(m)other Tongue?: Feminism, Academic Discourse,
Translation', in Barbara Godard (ed.) *Collaboration in the Feminine. Writings on Women and Culture from Tessera*, Toronto: Second Story Press,
171-181.

Barthes, Roland (1974) *The Pleasure of the Text*, Trans. Richard Miller, New
York: Hill.

------ (1977a) 'From Work to Text', in *Image, Music, Text*, Trans. Stephen
Heath, New York: Hill and Wang, 155-164.

------ (1977b) *Fragments d'un discours amoureux*, Paris: Éditions du Seuil.

Bassnett, Susan (1998) 'When Is a Translation Not a Translation?', in Susan
Bassnett and André Lefevere (eds.) *Constructing Cultures*, Clevedon:
Multilingual Matters, 25-40.

------ and André Lefevere (eds.) (1990) *Translation, History and Culture*, New
York: Cassell.

Battersby, Christine (1989) *Gender and Genius: Towards a Feminist Aesthetics*, London: The Women's Press.

Baumgarten, Nicole (1998) *Der Starkult im amerikanischen Theater des 19.
Jahrhunderts und im Film des 20. Jahrhunderts: Entstehung und Bedeu-
tung eines nationalen Phänomens*, Unpublished M.A. Thesis, Universität Kiel.

------ (2003) 'Close or distant: Constructions of proximity in translations and
parallel texts', in H. Gerzymisch-Arbogast *et al.* (eds.) *Textology and Translation*, Tübingen: Narr, 17-34.

------, Juliane House and Julia Probst (2004) 'English as *lingua franca* in covert translation processes', *The Translator* 10(1): 83-108.

------, (forthcoming) *The Secret Agent: Film dubbing and the influence of the
English language on German communicative preferences. Towards a
model of analysing language in visual media. The case of James Bond*,
PhD Dissertation, Universität Hamburg.

Beauvoir, Simone de (1949) *Le deuxième sexe*, Paris: Gallimard.

Becker, Alton L. and Bruce Mannheim (1995) 'Culture troping: Languages,
codes, and texts', in Dennis Tedlock and Bruce Mannheim (eds.) *The
Dialogic Emergence of Culture*, Urbana & Chicago: University of Illinois
Press, 237-252.

Bell, Linda (1983) *Visions of Women*, Cifton, N.J.: Humana Press.

Beresford, Sarah (1998) 'The lesbian mother: Questions of gender and sexual
identity', in Leslie J. Moran, Daniel Monk and Sarah Beresford (eds.) *Legal*

queeries: Lesbian, gay and transgender legal studies, London: Cassell, 57-67.

Berman, Antoine (1995) *Pour une critique des traductions: John Donne*, Paris, Seuil.

Biber, Douglas (1988) *Variation across Speech and Writing*, Cambridge: Cambridge University Press.

Bloom, Harold (ed.) (2001) *Italo Calvino*, Broomall: Chelsea House.

Blum-Kulka, Shoshana (1986) 'Shifts in cohesion and coherence in translation', in Shoshana Blum-Kulka and Juliane House (eds.) *Interlingual and Intercultural Communication*, Tübingen: Narr, 17-36.

Bold, Alan (ed.) (1982) *The Sexual Dimension in Literature*, London: Vision and Barnes and Noble.

Böttger, Claudia and Julia Probst (2001) *Adressatenorientierung in englischen und deutschen Texten*, Hamburg: Universität Hamburg, Arbeiten zur Mehrsprachigkeit.

Bourdieu, Pierre (1987) *Choses dites*, Paris: Minuit.

Branigan, Edward (1984) *Point of View in the Cinema: A Theory of Narration and Subjectivity in Classical Film*, Berlin & New York: Mouton.

Brisset, A. (1990) *Sociocritique de la traduction: Théâtre et altérité au Québec (1968-1988)*, Longueil: Le Préambule.

Bristow, Joseph (1997) *Sexuality*, London: Routledge.

Brossard, Nicole (1980) *Amantes*, Montréal: Quinze. [Trans. into English by Barbara Godard as *Lovers*, Montreal: Guernica Editions, 1986].

------ (1987) *Sous la Langue*, Trans. into English by Suzanne de Lotbinière-Harwood as *Under Tongue* (bilingual edition), Montreal: L'Essentielle.

Browning, Dixie (1985) *Something for Herself/Tomadoi no Kisetsu* 'The Lost Season', Trans. by Reiko Nakagawa, Tokyo: Harlequin, 1987.

Butler, Judith (1990) *Gender trouble: Feminism and the subversion of identity*, London & New York: Routledge.

------ (1991) 'Imitation and gender insubordination', in Diana Fuss (ed.) *Inside out: Lesbian theories, gay theories*, New York: Routledge, 13-31.

------ (1993) *Bodies that matter: On the discursive limits of sex*. New York: Routledge.

Calvino, Italo (1979) *Se una notte d'inverno un viaggiatore*, Torino: Giulio Einaudi.

------ (1981) *If on a winter's night a traveler*, Trans. by William Weaver, New York: Harcourt Brace and Company.

Cameron, Deborah (1985) *Feminism and Linguistic Theory*, London: MacMillan Press.

------ (1992) *Feminism and Linguistic Theory*, 2nd edition, London: Macmillan Press.

------ (1995) 'Rethinking language and gender studies: some issues for the 1990s', in S. Mills (ed.): 31-44.

------ (1998) 'Is there any ketchup, Vera?', *Discourse and Society* 9(4): 437-456.

------ and Don Kulick (2003) *Language and Sexuality*, Cambridge & New York: Cambridge University Press

Caneda Cabrera, Teresa (1998) 'Literatura, traducción e reconfiguración da identidade nacional: a 'apropiación' galega do *Ulysses*', *Grial* 137: 87-97.

Carbonell, Ovidi (1996) 'The Exotic Space of Cultural Translation', in R. Álvarez and África Vidal (eds.): 79-98.

------ (1997) *Traducir al Otro. Traducción, exotismo, poscolonialismo*, Cuenca: Ediciones de la Universidad de Castilla-La Mancha.

------ (1999) *Traducción y cultura. De la ideología al texto*, Salamanca: Ediciones Colegio de España.

Castro, Plácido R., Antón Villar Ponte and Ramón Villar Ponte (trans.) (1935) *Dous dramas populares*, by W.B. Yeats, Vigo: Edicións Castrelos.

Chamberlain, Lori ([1988] 1992) 'Gender and the Methaphorics of Translation', *Signs: Journal of Women in Culture and Society* 13(3): 454-472. Rept. in L. Venuti (ed) (1992): 57-74.

------ (1998) 'Gender metaphorics in translation', in M. Baker (ed.): 93-96.

Chartier, Roger (1994) *The order of books: Readers, authors, and libraries in Euorpe between the fourteenth and eighteenth centuries*, Trans. by Lydia G. Cochrane, Cambridge: Polity Press.

Cixous, H. (1986) 'Sorties', in *The Newly Born Woman*, Trans. by B. Wing, Minnesota, Minn.: The University of Minnesota Press. 63-132.

Cleland, John (1980) *Fanny Hill*, Transl. by Beatriz Podestá, Barcelona: Editorial Bruguera.

------ (1984) *Fanny Hill: Memorias de una cortesana*, Transl. by Enrique Martínez Fariñas, Barcelona: Ediciones 1984 S.A.

------ (1985) *Fanny Hill: Memorias de una mujer galante*, Transl. by Frank Lane, Madrid: Akal.

------ (2000) *Fanny Hill: Memorias de una mujer de placer*, Ed. and transl. by José Santaemilia and José Pruñonosa, Madrid: Cátedra.

Coates, Jennifer (1995) 'Language, gender and career', in S. Mills (ed.): 13-30.

Corbett, G. (1991) *Gender*, Cambridge: Cambridge University Press.

Cronin, Michael (2000) *Across the Lines: Travel, Language and Translation*, Cork: Cork University Press.

Davidson, Brad (2000) 'The Interpreter as Institutional Gatekeeper: The Social Role of Interpreters in Spanish-English Medical Discourse', *Journal of Sociolinguistics* 4(3): 379-405.

Dent, Nicholas (1995) 'logos', in Ted Honderich (ed.) *The Oxford companion to philosophy*, Oxford: Oxford University Press, 511-12.

Derrida, Jacques (1985) 'Des Tours de Babel', Trans. by Joseph F. Graham, in Joseph F. Graham (ed.) *Difference in Translation*, Ithaca and London: Cornell University Press, 165-208.

Díaz-Diocaretz, Myriam (1985) *Translating Poetic Discourse: Questions on Feminist Strategies in Adrienne Rich*, Amsterdam & Philadelphia: John Benjamins Publishing Company.

Dixon, R. M. W. (1986) 'Noun classes and Noun classification in Typological Perspective', in C. Craig (ed.) *Noun Classes and Categorization*, Amsterdam & Philadelphia: John Benjamins, 105-112.

Doherty, Monika (1995) 'Prinzipien und Parameter als Grundlagen einer allgemeinen Theorie der vergleichenden Stilistik', in Gerhard Stickel (ed.) *Stilfragen*, Berlin: de Gruyter, 181-197.

Donald, Robyn (1981) *Summer at Awakopa/Umi no Mieru Ie* 'The House with a View of the Ocean', Trans. Shiori Kato, Tokyo: Harlequin, 1981.

Du Plessix Gray, Francine (1981) 'Visiting Italo Calvino', *New York Times Book Review*, 21 June, 22-23.

Dülmen, Andrea van (ed.) (1992) *Frauenleben im 18. Jahrhundert*, München & Leipzig: Beck/Kiepenheuer.

Eckert, Penelope and Sally McConnell-Ginet (2003) *Language and Gender*, New York: Cambridge University Press.

Even-Zohar, Itamar (1978) 'Universals of Literary Contacts', in F. Coppieters and D. L. Goyvaerts (eds.) *Functional Studies in Language and Literature*, Ghent: Stony-Scientia, 5-15.

------ (1991) 'The Position of Translated Literature within the Literary Polysystem', *Poetics Today* 11(1): 45-51.

Felski, R. (1989) *Beyond Feminist Aesthetics. Feminist Literature and Social Change,* Cambridge, Mass.: Harvard University Press.

Fielding, Helen (1996) *Bridget Jones's Diary*, London: Picador.

Fielding, Helen (1999) *El diario de Bridget Jones*, Trans. by Néstor Busquets, Barcelona: Editorial Plaza & Janés.

Fink, Inge (1991) 'The Power Behind the Pronoun: Narrative Games in Calvino's *If on a Winter's Night a Traveler*', *Twentieth Century Literature 1*, vol. 37, 93-104.

Firestone, Shulamith (1970) *The Dialectic of Sex: The Case for a Feminist Revolution*, New York: Marrow.

Fishman, Pamela (1983) 'Interaction: the work women do', in Barrie Thorne and Nancy Henley (eds.) *Language, gender and society*, Rowley: Newbury House, 89-101.

Flotow, Luise von (1991) 'Feminist Translation: Contexts, Practices, Theories', *TTR (Traduction, Terminologie, Rédaction)* 4(2): 69-84.

------ (1997) *Translation and Gender. Translating in the 'Era of Feminism'*, Manchester & Ottawa: St Jerome/University of Ottawa Press.

------ (1998) 'Dis-unity and Diversity: Feminist Approaches to Translation Studies', in Lynne Bowker, Michael Cronin, Dorothy Kenny and Jennifer Pearson (eds.) *Unity in Diversity? Current Trends in Translation Studies,* Manchester: St. Jerome, 3-13.

----- (1999) 'Genders and the Translated Text: Developments in 'Trans-formance'', *Textus* 12: 275-88.

----- (2000a) 'Translation Effects: How Beauvoir Talks Sex in English', in Melanie C. Hawthorne (ed.) *Contingent Loves: Simone de Beauvoir and Sexuality,* Charlottesville, VA: University Press of Virginia, 13-33.

----- (2000b) 'Women, Bibles, Ideologies', *TTR* 13(1): 9-20.

----- (2002) 'Julia E. Smith, traductrice de la Bible à la recherche de la vérité par le littéralisme', in Jean Delisle (ed.) *Portraits de traductrices,* Ottawa & Artois: Presses de l'Université d'Ottawa/Artois Presses Universitaires, 291-320.

----- (2004) 'Translation and Gender Paradigms: From Identities to Pluralities', in Piotr Kuhiwczak and Karin Littau (eds.) *The Companion to Translation Studies,* Clevedon: Multilingual Matters.

Foucault, Michel (1979) 'What Is an Author?', in Josué V. Harari (ed.) *Textual Strategies – Perspectives in Post-Structuralist Criticism,* Ithaca: Cornell University Press, 141-160.

Franco Aixelà, Javier (2000) *La traducción condicionada de los nombres propios (inglés-español),* Salamanca: Ediciones Almar.

Freiwald, Bina (1991) 'The Problem of Trans-lation: Reading French Feminisms', *TTR (Traduction, Terminologie, Redaction)* 4(2): 55-68.

Friedrich, Paul (1978) *The Meaning of Aphrodite,* Chicago: University of Chicago Press.

Fusco, C. (1995) *English is broken here,* New York: The New Press.

Fuss, D. (1989) *Essentially speaking,* London: Routledge.

----- (1995) *Identification papers,* London: Routledge.

Gentzler, Edwin (2002) 'Translation, Post-Structuralism, and Power', in M. Tymoczko and E. Gentzler (eds.): 195-218.

Godard, Barbara (1988) 'Theorizing Feminist Discourse / Translation', in David Homel and Sherry Simon (eds.) *Mapping Literature. The Art and Politics of Translation,* Montréal: Véhicule Press, 49-51. Rept. in S. Bassnett and A. Lefevere (eds.) (1990): 87-96, 2nd edition 1995.

Godayol, Pilar (1998) 'Interviewing Carol Maier: A Woman in Translation', *Quaderns. Revista de traducció* 2: 155-162.

----- (2000) *Espais de frontera: Gènere i traducció.* Vic: Eumo.

Goffman, Erving (1975) *Les rites de l'interaction,* Paris: Minuit.

Gokhale, Vibha Bakshi (1996) *Walking the Tightrope. A Feminist Reading of Therese Huber's Stories,* Columbia: Camden House.

Gouanvic, Jean-Marc (1999) *Sociologie de la traduction: La science-fiction américaine dans l'espace culturel français des années 1950,* Arras: Artois Presses Universitaires.

Grimberg, Michel (1998) *Die Rezeption der französischen Komödie. Ein Korpus von Übersetzervorreden (1694-1802),* Frankfurt: Lang.

Gubern, Roman (1981) *La censura: Función política y ordenamiento jurídico bajo el franquismo (1936-76)*, Barcelona: Península.

Gutiérrez Lanza, C. (2000) *Traducción y censura de textos cinematográficos en la España de Franco. Doblaje y subtitulado inglés-español (1951-1975)*, León: Universidad de León.

Guzmán González, T. (2002) 'Feminine Assigned Gender for Ships: Just a Metaphor?', in I. Moskowich-Spiegel Fandiño (ed.) *Re-Interpretations of English. Essays on Language, Linguistics and Philology* 1: 45-62.

Hahn, Andrea (1993) 'Therese Huber (1764-1829) Zwischen Nähzeug und Mannskleid', in Birgit Knorr and Rosemarie Wehling (eds.) *Frauen im deutschen Südwesten*, Stuttgart/Berlin/Köln: Kohlhammer. 50-57.

------ and Bernhard Fischer (1993) *'Alles ... von mir!' Therese Huber (1764-1829), Schriftstellerin und Redakteurin*, Marbach am Neckar: Deutsche Schillergesellschaft.

Halliday, M.A.K. (1978) *Language as social semiotic: The social interpretation of language and meaning*, London: Arnold.

------ (1994 [1985]) *An Introduction to Functional Grammar*, 2nd edition, London: Arnold.

------ and Ruyaiya Hasan (1976) *Cohesion in English*, London: Longman.

------ and Ruyaiya Hasan (1989) *Language, context and text: aspects of language in a social semiotic perspective*, Oxford: Oxford University Press.

Hanai, Aiko (1989) *Futari Jikan* 'Time for the Two of Us', Tokyo: Shueisha Bunko.

Hartley-Brewer, Julia (1999) 'Gay couple will be legal parents', *The Guardian*, 28 October 1999.

Hartman, Kabi (1999) 'Ideology, Identification and the Construction of the Feminine: *Le Journal de Marie Bashkirtseff*, *The Translator* 5(1): 61-82.

Harvey, Keith (1998) 'Translating Camp Talk. Gay Identities and Cultural Transfer', *The Translator* 4(2): 295-320.

Harvey, Keith (2000) 'Gay Community, Gay Identity and the Translated Text', *TTR* 13: 137-165.

Haste, Helen (1993) *The sexual metaphor*, New York/London: Harvester Wheatsheaf.

Heath, Christian (1993) 'Diagnostic et consultation médicale: la préservation de l'asymétrie dans la relation entre médecin et patient', in Jacques Cosnier and Michèle Grosjean (eds.) *Soins et communication. Approche interactionniste des relations de soins*, Lyon: Presses Universitaires de Lyon. 65-83.

Henitiuk, Valerie (1999) 'Translating Woman: Reading the Female through the Male', *META* 44(3): 469-484.

Hermans, Theo (1999) *Translation in Systems. Descriptive and System-oriented Approaches Explained*, Manchester: St Jerome.

Hermans, Theo (ed.) (1985) *The Manipulation of Literature: Studies in Literary Tradition*, London: Crown Helm.

Herter, Lori (1996) *How Much is that Couple in the Window? / Shoo Uindoo no Hanayome* 'The Show Window Bride', Tokyo: Harlequin, 1998. Trans. Rutsu Minami.

Hinck, Walter (1965) *Das deutsche Lustspiel des 17. und 18. Jahrhunderts und die italienische Komödie*, Stuttgart: Metzler.

Homel, David and Sherry Simon (eds.) (1988) *Mapping Literature. The Art and Politics of Translation*, Montréal: Véhicule Press.

Houdebine, Anne-Marie (dir.) (1998) *La féminisation des noms de métiers: en français et dans d'autres langues,* Paris: L'Harmattan.

House, Juliane (1981 [1977]) *A Model for Translation Quality Assessment*, Tübingen: Narr.

House, Juliane (1997) *Translation Quality Assessment. A Model Revisited*, Tübingen: Narr.

House, Juliane (1998) 'Politeness and Translation', in Leo Hickey (ed.) *The Pragmatics of Translation*, Clevedon: Multilingual Matters, 54-71.

Johnson, Barbara (1985) 'Taking fidelity philosophically', in Joseph F. Graham (ed.) *Difference in translation*, Ithaca: Cornell University Press. 142-48.

Kadish, Doris and Françoise Massardier-Kenney (eds.) (1994) *Translating Slavery: Gender and Race in French Women's Writing – 1783-1823,* Kent State University OH: Kent State University Press.

Kaminsky A. K. (1993) *Feminist Criticism and Latin American Women Writers*, Minnesota, Minn.: University of Minnesota Press.

Kaplan, C. (1976) 'Language and Gender', in *Essays on Culture and Feminism*, London: Verso, 69-93.

Keenaghan, Eric (1998) 'Jack Spicer's Pricks and Cocksuckers: Translating Homosexuality into Visibility', *The Translator* 4(2): 273-294.

Kelsky, Karen (2001) *Women on the Verge: Japanese Women, Western Dreams,* Durham & London: Duke University Press.

Kolias, Helen Dendrinou (1990) 'Empowering the Minor: Translating Women's Autobiography', *Journal of Modern Greek Studies* 8(2): 213-221.

Koller, Werner (1979/2001) *Einführung in die Übersetzungswissenschaft*, Wiebelsheim: Quelle and Meyer.

Köpke, Wulf (1988) 'Immer noch im Schatten der Männer? Therese Huber als Schriftstellerin', in Detlef Rasmussen (ed.) *Der Weltumsegler und seine Freunde. Georg Forster als gesellschaftlicher Schriftsteller der Goethezeit*, Tübingen: Narr, 116-132.

Korsak, Mary Phil (1992) *At the Start. Genesis Made New. A Translation of the Hebrew Text*, New York & London: Doubleday.

Kövecses, Zoltán (1988) *The Language of Love: The Semantics of Passion in Conversational English,* Lewisburg: Bucknell University Press/London &

Toronto: Associated University Presses.

La Bible. La nouvelle traduction (2001) Paris & Montréal: Bayard/Médiaspaul.

Lakoff, Robin (1975) *Language and woman's place,* New York: Harper and Row.

Lambert, José (1993) 'History, Historiography and the Discipline. A Programme', in Yves Gambier and J. Tommola (eds.) *Translation and Knowledge. Actes du 4e Symposium Scandinave sur la théorie de la traduction (Turku, 1992),* Turku: Grafia Oy, 3-26.

------ (1995) 'Literatures, Translation and (De)Colonization', in Theresa Huyn and José Lambert (eds.) *Translation and Modernization,* Tokyo: Tokyo University Press, 98-117.

Lane, Andy and Paul Simpson (1998) *The Bond Files,* London: Virgin.

Laviosa-Braithwaite, Sara (1998) 'Universals of translation', in M. Baker (ed.): 288-291.

Lefevere, André (1992) *Translation, Rewriting and the Manipulation of Literary Fame,* New York & London: Routledge.

Lemke, Jay L. (1995) *Textual Politics: Discourse and Social Dynamics,* London: Taylor and Francis.

Leonardi, Vanessa (n.d.) 'Gender Issues in Translation Studies', *Centre for Interdisciplinary Gender Studies. E-papers.* (http://www.leeds. ac.uk/gender-studies/epapers/leonardi.htm)

Leuschner, Brigitte (1995) 'Einleitung. Therese Huber und Karoline Pichler – Schriftstellerinnen und Schwesterseelen', in Brigitte Leuschner (ed.) *Schriftstellerinnen und Schwesterseelen. Der Briefwechsel zwischen Therese Huber (1764-1829) und Karoline Pichler (1769-1843),* Marburg: Tectum, 7-21.

Levine, Suzanne Jill (1991) *The Subversibe Scribe: Translating Latin American Fiction,* Minneapolis, Minn.: Greywolf Press.

------ (1992) 'Translation as (sub)version: On translating Infante's *Inferno*', in L. Venuti (ed.): 75-85.

Lewin, Kurt (1947) 'Group Decision and Social Change', in M. Macobi (ed.) *Readings in Social Psychology,* New York: Holt, 197-211.

Littau, Karin (1995) 'Refractions of the Feminine: The Monstrous Transformations of Lulu', *Modern Language Notes* 110(4): 888-912.

Liturgiam authenticam. On the Use of Vernacular Languages in the Publication of the Books of the Roman Liturgy , Fifth Instruction 'For the Right Implementation of the Constitution on the Sacred Liturgy of the Second Vatican Council' (Sacrosanctum Concilium, art. 36), www.vatican.va/ccdds/documents/rc_con_ccdds_doc_20010507_liturgiam-authenticam_en.html

Lotbinière-Harwood, Susanne (1994) 'Acting the (Re)Writer: a Feminist Translator's Practice of Space', *Fireweed* 44/45: 101-110.

------ (1989) 'About the *her* in other', in Lise Gauvin, *Letters from an Other,*

Trans. Susanne de Lotbinière-Harwood, Toronto: Women's Press, 9-12.

------ (1991) *Re-belle et infidèle. La traduction comme pratique de réécriture au féminin. The body bilingual: Translation as Rewriting in the Feminine,* Montreal: Les Éditions du remue-ménage.

Lublin, Nancy (1998) *Pandora's box: Feminism confronts reproductive technology,* Lanham: Rowman and Littlefield.

Lugones, M. (1994) 'Purity, impurity, and separation', *Signs* 19(2): 458-79.

Maier, C. (1996) 'On translation: the translators', In R. Christ (ed.) *On translation: The Translators,* Atlanta: Atlanta College of Art Gallery. 57-67.

------ (1994) 'Women in translation: current intersections, theory, and practice', *Delos* 16(2): 29-39,

Maier, Carol S. and Françoise Massardier-Kenney (1996) 'Gender in/and literary translation', in Marilyn Gaddis Rose (ed.) *Translation horizons: Beyond the Boundaries of 'Translation Spectrum'. Translation Perspectives IX,* Binghamton: Center for Research in Translation (State University of New York, Binghamton), 225-242.

Maltz D. and Borker R. (1982) 'A cultural approach to male-female communication', in John Gumperz (ed.) *Language and social identity,* Cambridge: Cambridge University Press, 195-216.

Markley, Robert (1984) 'Language, Power and Sexuality: Cleland's *Fanny Hill*', *Philological Quarterly* 63(3): 343-356.

Marsiglio, William (1995) 'Artificial reproduction and paternity testing: Implications for fathers', in Mirjam van Dongen, Gerard Frinking and Menno Jacobs (eds.) *Changing fatherhood: a multidisciplinary perspective,* Amsterdam: Thesis Publishers, 159-78.

Martin, Emily (1987) *The woman in the body: a cultural anlysis of reproduction,* Boston: Beacon Press.

Martínez de la Hidalga, F. *et al.* (2000) *La novela popular en España,* Madrid: Ediciones Robel.

Massardier-Kenney, Françoise (1997) 'Towards a Redefinition of Feminist Translation Practice', *The Translator* 3(1): 55-69.

Matsumoto, David (1996) *Unmasking Japan: Myths and Realities about the Emotions of the Japanese,* Stanford: Stanford University Press.

Maynard, Senko K. (1997) *Japanese Communication: Language and Thought in Context,* Honolulu: University of Hawai'i Press.

McCarthy, Mary (1981) 'Acts of Love', *The New York Review of Books* 28: 3.

McGloin (Maguroin), Naomi Hanaoka (1997) *Shuujoshi* (Sentence final particles), in Sachiko Ide (ed). *Joseigo no Sekai* (The World of Women's Language), Tokyo: Meiji Shoin, 33-41.

McKinstry, John A. and Asako Makajima McKinstry (1991) *Jinsei Annai 'Life's Guide': Glimpses of Japan through a Popular Advice Column,* Armonk NY & London: M.E. Sharpe, Inc.

Meaney, Gerardine (1991) *Sex and Nation: Women in Irish Culture and Poli-*

tics, Dublin: Attic Press.

Messner, Sabine and Michaela Wolf (eds.) (2000) *Mittlerin zwischen den Kulturen – Mittlerin zwischen den Geschlechtern? Studie zu Theorie und Praxis feministischer Übersetzung*, Graz: Institut für Translationswissenschaft.

------ (eds.) (2001) *Übersetzung aus aller Frauen Länder. Beiträge zu Theorie und Praxis weiblicher Realität in der Translation,* Graz: Leykam.

Mills, Sara (ed.) (1995) *Language and gender: Interdisciplinary perspectives*, London: Longman

Mira, Alberto (1999) 'Pushing the Limits of Faithfulness: A Case for Gay Translation', in Jean Boase-Beier and Michael Holman (eds.) *The Practices of Literary Translation: Constraints and Creativity*, Manchester: St. Jerome, 109-123.

Morgan, David (1997) *Focus Groups as Qualitative Research*, Newbury Park: Sage.

Mounin, Georges (1963) *Les problèmes théoriques de la traduction,* Paris: Gallimard.

Mulhern, Chieko (1989) 'Japanese Harlequin romances and transcultural woman's fiction', *The Journal of Asian Studies* 48(1): 50-70.

Newmark, Peter (1999) 'Taking a Stand on Mary Snell-Hornby', in Christina Schäffner (ed.) *Translation in the Global Village* (special issue), *Current Issues in Language and Society* 6(2): 152-154.

Nikolaidou, Ionna and María López Villalba (1997) '*Re-belle et infidèle* o el papel de la traductora en la teoría y práctica de la traducción feminista', in Esther Morillas and Juan Pablo Arias (eds.) *El papel del traductor*, Salamanca: Ediciones Colegio de España, 75-102.

Norris, Pamela (1998) *The story of Eve*, London: Picador.

O'Brien, Mary (1989) *Reproducing the world: Essays in feminist theory,* Boulder, CO: Westview Press.

Occhi, Debra J. (2000) *Namida, Sake,* and Love: Emotional Expressions and Japanese *Enka* Music, Ph.D. dissertation, University of California, Davis.

Parker, Alice (1993) 'Under the Covers: A Synaesthesia of Desire. Lesbian Translations', in Susan Wolfe and Julia Penelope (eds.) *Sexual Practice, Textual Theory: Lesbian Cultural Criticism,* Cambridge: Blackwell, 322-339.

Pethica, James (1988) "Our Kathleen': Yeats's Collaboration with Lady Gregory in the Writing of *Cathleen ni Houlihan*', in Gould Warwick (ed.) *Yeats Annual No. 6*, London: The Macmillan Press.

Potter, Evan (ed.) (2002) *Cyber-Diplomacy. Managing Foreign Policy in the Twenty-First Century*, Montreal & Kingston: McGill-Queen's University Press.

Pym, Anthony (ed.) (2001) *The Return to Ethics*. Special Issue of *The Translator* 7(2).

Quirk, Randolph, Sidney Greenbaum, Geoffrey Leech and Jan Svartvik (1985) *A comprehensive grammar of the English language*, London: Longman.

Rabadán, Rosa (1994a) 'Traducción, función, adaptación', in Purificación Fernández Nistal (ed.) *Aspectos de la traducción inglés/español*, Valladolid: Universidad de Valladolid, 31-42.

------ (1994b) 'Traducción, intertextualidad, manipulación', in Amparo Hurtado (ed.) *Estudis sobre la traducció*, Castelló: Universitat Jaume I, 129-139.

------ (2000a) 'Modelos importados, modelos adaptados: Pseudotraducciones de narrativa popular inglés-español 1955-1981', in R. Rabadán (ed.): 255-78.

------ (ed.) (2000b) *Traducción y censura inglés-español; 1939-1985. Estudio preliminar,* León: Universidad de León.

Radway, Janice A. (1984) *Reading the Romance: Women, Patriarchy, and Popular Literature*, Chapel Hill & London: The University of North Carolina Press.

Ragoné, Helena (1994) *Surrogate motherhood: Conception in the heart*, Boulder, CO: Westview Press.

Rankin, Ian (1986) 'The Role of the Reader in Italo Calvino's If on a Winter's Night a Traveler', *The Review of Contemporary Fiction* 6(2): 124-129.

Riabova, Marina Yu (2001) 'Translation and Sociolinguistics: Sexist Language as a Translator's Problem', in Marcel Thelen and Barbara Lewadowska-Tomaszczyk (eds.) *Translation and Meaning. Part 5,* Maastricht: Hogeschool Zuyd/Maastricht School of Translation and Interpreting, 141-145.

Rich, Adrienne (1996) 'Compulsory heterosexuality and lesbian existence', in Stevi Jackson and Sue Scott (eds.) *Feminism and sexuality: A Reader*, Edinburgh: Edinburgh University Press, 130-43.

Risco, Vicente (1926) 'A Moderna Literatura Irlandesa', *Revista Nós* 26: 5-9.

------ (trans.) (1923) 'Our Lady of the Hills', by W.B. Yeats, *Revista Nós* 15: 11-13.

Rivera Garretas, M. (1994) *Nombrar el mundo en femenino: pensamiento de las mujeres y teoría feminista*, Barcelona: Icaria.

Roberts, R. P. (1992) 'The Concept of Function of Translation and its Application to Literary Texts', *Target* 4(1): 1-16.

Robyns, Clem (1994) 'Translation and Discursive Identity', *Poetics Today* 15(3): 404-428.

Roche, Geneviève (1994) "Völlig nach Fabrikenart'. Handwerk und Kunst der Übersetzung bei Georg Forster', in Rolf Reichardt and Geneviève Roche (eds.) *Weltbürger – Europäer – Deutscher – Franke. Georg Forster zum 200. Todestag. Ausstellungskatalog*, Mainz: Universitätsbibliothek, 101-119.

------ (1997) 'Übersetzen am laufenden Band. Zum Beispiel Ludwig Ferdinand Huber and Co', in Hans-Jürgen Lüsebrink and Rolf Reichardt (eds.) *Kulturtransfer im Epochenumbruch. Frankreich - Deutschland 1770-1815,*

Leipzig: Leipziger Universitätsverlag, 331-359.

Rose, Mark (1988) 'The author as proprietor: *Donaldson v. Becket* and the genealogy of modern authorship', *Representations* 21/24(23): 51-85.

------ (1993) *Authors and owners: the invention of copyright*, Cambridge, MA: Harvard University Press.

------ (1998) 'Mothers and authors: *Johnson v. Calvert* and the new children of our imaginations', in Paula A. Treichler, Lisa Cartwright and Constance Penley (eds.) *The visible woman: Imaging technologies, gender, and science*, New York: New York University Press, 217-39.

Roy, Cynthia (2000) *Interpreting as a Discourse Process*, New York: Oxford University Press.

Sager, Juan Carlos (1994) *Language Engineering and Translation. Consequences of Automation*, Amsterdam & Philadelphia: John Benjamins.

Saito, Ayako (1996) *Vaajin Byuuti* 'Virgin Beauty', Tokyo: Shincho Bunko.

Sánchez Benedito, Francisco (1997) 'Pragmatic Presuppositions in Translation: Henry Miller's *Tropics*, a Case in Point', in Karl Simms (ed.) *Translating Sensitive Texts: Linguistic Aspects*, Amsterdam: Rodopi, 267-271.

Santaemilia, José (2000) *Género como conflicto discursivo: La sexualización del discurso de los personajes cómicos*, Valencia: Universitat de València.

------ (2001) 'Some Linguistic Facts and Formulae in Erotic Subliterature: John Cleland's *Fanny Hill*', in A. Ballesteros and L. Mora (eds.) *Popular Texts in English: New Perspectives*, Cuenca: Ediciones de la Universidad Castilla-La Mancha, 287-297.

------ (2002) 'Towards a pragmatics of gendered conversation: A few general considerations', In J. Santaemilia, B. Gallardo and J. Sanmartín (eds.) *Sexe i Llenguatge: La construcció lingüística de les identitats de gènere*, Valencia: Universitat de València, 93-113.

------ (ed.) (2003) *Género, lenguaje y traducción*, Valencia: Universitat de València/Dirección General de la Mujer.

Schäffner, Christina (ed.) (1999) *Translation in the Global Village* (special issue), *Current Issues in Language and Society* 6.2.

Schwartz, Hillel (1996) *The culture of the copy: Striking likenesses, unreasonable facsimiles*, New York: Zone Books.

Scliar, Moacyr (1995) 'Notas ao pé da página' In *Contos Reunidos*, São Paulo: Companhia das Letras, 371-375.

Scott, J. W. (1992) 'Experience', in J. Butler and J. W. Scott (eds.) *Feminists theorize the political*, London: Routledge, 22-40.

------ (1996) *Feminism and History*, Oxford: Oxford University Press.

Sharpe, Andrew N. (1998) 'Institutionalizing heterosexuality: the legal exclusion of 'impossible' (trans)sexualities', in Leslie J. Moran, Daniel Monk and Sarah Beresford (eds.) *Legal queeries: Lesbian, gay and transgender legal studies*, London: Cassell, 26-41.

Shibamoto, Janet S. (1985) *Japanese Women's Language*, Orlando, FL: Academic Press.

Shibamoto Smith, Janet S. (2003) 'Gendered Structures: Japanese', in Marlis Hellinger and Hadumod Bussmann (eds.) *The De/construction of Gender Roles through Language Variation and Change: International Perspectives*, Amsterdam & Philadelphia: John Benjamins.

------ (2004) 'Language and Gender in the (Hetero)Romance: 'Reading' the Ideal Hero/ine through Lover's Dialogue in Japanese Romance Fiction', in Shigeko Okamoto and Janet S. Shibamoto Smith (eds.) *Japanese Language, Gender, and Ideology: Cultural Models and Real People*, Oxford & New York: Oxford University Press.

Simeoni, Daniel (1998) 'The Pivotal Status of the Translator's Habitus', *Target* 10(1): 1-39. *uses Bourdieu (habitus /field)*

Simon, Sherry (1992) 'The language of cultural difference: Figures of alterity in Canadian translation', in L. Venuti (ed.): 159-176.

------ (1996) *Gender in Translation. Cultural Identity and the Politics of Transmission*, London & New York: Routledge.

------ (2000) 'Gender in translation', in Peter France (ed.) *The Oxford Guide to English Translation,* Oxford: Oxford University Press, 26-38.

Simons, Margaret (1983) 'The Silencing of Simone de Beauvoir: Guess What's Missing from *The Second Sex*', *Women's Studies International Forum* 6(5): 559-564.

Singy, Pascal (2002) 'Médecins Femmes ou femmes médecins?', *Médecine et Hygiène* 2385: 655-657.

------ (ed.) (1998) *Les femmes et la langue: L'insécurité linguistique en question.* Lausanne: Delachaux & Niestlé.

------, P. Guex and O. Weber (2003) 'Le migrant face au système de soins: une expérience à Lausanne', in H.-R. Wicker, R. Fibbi and W. Haug (eds.) *Les migrations et la Suisse,* Zürich: Seismo, 528-547.

Society of Authors, The (1995) 'Quick guide 3: Literary translation', London: The Society of Authors.

------ (1996) 'Quick guide 1: Copyright and moral rights', London: The Society of Authors.

Spivak, Gayatri Chakravorty (1992) 'The Politics of Translation', in Michèle Barrett and Anne Philips (eds.) *Destabilizing Theory*, Stanford, CA: Stanford University Press, 177-200.

------ (1993) 'The Politics of Translation', in *Outside in the Teaching Machine,* London & New York: Routledge, 179-200.

Stanton, Elizabeth Cady (1898) *The Woman's Bible,* introduction by Dale Spender, Part 1 first published in 1898, Part 2 published 1898 by European Publishing Company, NewYork. Re-issued in Edinburgh: Polygon Books, 1985.

Steiner, George (1975) *After Babel*, London: Oxford University Press.

Stratton, Jon (1987) *The Virgin Text: Fiction, Sexuality and Ideology*, Brighton: Harvester Press.

Sturken, Marita and Lisa Cartwright (2001) *Practices of Looking*, Oxford: Oxford University Press.

Suleri, S. (1992) 'Woman skin deep: feminism and the postcolonial condition', *Critical Inquiry* 18: 758-59.

Susam-Sarajeva, Şebnem (2002a) 'A 'Multilingual' and 'International' Translation Studies?', in Theo Hermans (ed.) *Crosscultural Transgressions. Research Models in Translation Studies II: Historical and Ideological Issues*, Manchester: St. Jerome, 193-207.

------ (2002b) *Translation and Travelling Theory: The Role of Translation in the Migration of Literary Theories across Culture and Power Differentials*, Unpublished PhD thesis, University College London, University of London.

Talbot, Mary (1998) *Language and Gender: An introduction*, Cambridge: Polity Press.

Thorne, B., Kramarae, C. and Henley, N. (eds.) (1983) *Language, Gender and Society*, Rowley, Mass.: Newbury House.

Todo, Shizuko (1992) *Saredo, Kasumisoo 'Baby's Breath'*, Tokyo: Shincho Bunko.

Toledano, Carmen (2002) 'Recepción de *Fanny Hill* en España: Estudio preliminar', *Atlantis* 24(2): 215-227.

Toury, Gideon (1980) *In Search of a Theory of Translation,* Tel Aviv: The Porter Institute for Poetics and Semiotics, Tel Aviv University.

------ (1991) 'What are Descriptive Studies into Translation Likely to Yield apart from Isolated Descriptions?', in Kitty Leuven-Zwart and Ton Naaijkens (eds.) *Translation Studies. The State of the Art,* Amsterdam: Rodopi. 179-192.

------ (1995) *Descriptive Translation Studies and Beyond*, Amsterdam & Philadelphia: John Benjamins.

------ (1997) 'What Lies Beyond Descriptive Translation Studies, Or: Where Do We Go From Where We Assumedly Are?', in Miguel Ángel Vega and Rafael Martín Gaitero (eds.) *La Palabra Vertida: Investigaciones en torno a la traducción,* Madrid: Editorial Complutense/Ediciones del Orto, 69-80.

Translators' Association, The (1994) 'Model translation/publisher agreement', London: The Translators' Association.

Tymozcko, Maria (2000) 'Translation and Political Engagement: Activism, Social Change and the Role of Translation in Geopolitical Shifts', *The Translator* 6(1): 23-49.

------ and Edwin Gentzler (eds.) (2002) *Translation and Power*, Amherst & Boston: University of Massachusetts Press,

Unterbeck, B. and M. Rissanen (eds.) (2000) *Gender in Grammar and Cognition. I Approaches to Gender. II Manifestations of Gender*, Berlin & New York: Mouton de Gruyter.

Venuti, Lawrence (1992) 'Introduction', in L. Venuti (ed.): 1-17.

------ (ed.) (1992) *Rethinking Translation – Discourse, Subjectivity, Ideology*, New York & London: Routledge.

------ (1995) 'Translation, authorship, copyright', *The Translator* 1(1): 1-24.

------ (1998) *The Scandals of Translation – Towards an Ethics of Difference*, New York & London: Routledge.

Villar Ponte, Antón (trans.) (1921) 'Cathleen ni Houlihan', by W.B. Yeats, *Revista Nós* 8 (5 Dec. 1921): 8-13.

Wadensjö, Cecilia (1998) *Interpreting as interaction*, London: Longman.

Walter, Ulrike (2002) 'Die Anfänge weiblicher übersetzerischer Erwerbsarbeit um 1800', in Nadja Grbic and Michaela Wolf (eds.) *Grenzgängerinnen. Zur Geschlechterdifferenz in der Übersetzung*, Graz: Institut für Translationswissenschaft, 17-30.

Weber, Doris (2000) 'On the Function of Gender', in B. Unterbeck and M. Rissanen (eds.) *Gender in Grammar and Cognition. I Approaches to Gender. II Manifestations of Gender*, Berlin & New York: Mouton de Gruyter, 495-510.

Weigel, Sigrid (1985) 'Double focus', in G. Ecker (ed.) *Feminist Aesthetics*, Boston: Beacon, 59-80.

Weiss R. and R. Stuker (1998) *Interprétariat et médiation culturelle dans le système de soins,* Neuchâtel: Forum Suisse pour l'étude des Migrations.

West, C. and R. Frankel (1991) 'Miscommunication in Medicine', in N. Coupland, H. Giles and J. Wiemann (eds.) *Miscommunication and Problematic Talk*, Newbury Park: Sage, 195-214.

West, Candace (1984) 'When the doctor is a lady: Power, status and gender in the physician-patient encounter', *Symbolic Interaction* 7: 87-106.

------ (1990) 'Not just doctor's orders: Directive-response sequences in patients visits to women and men physicians', *Discourse and society* 1(1): 85-112.

Wolf, Michaela (1997) 'Translation as a Process of Power: Aspects of Cultural Anthropology in Translation', in Mary Snell-Hornby, Zuzana Jettmarová and Klaus Kaindl (eds.) *Translation as Intercultural Communication,* Amsterdam & Philadelphia: John Benjamins, 123-133.

Woodmansee, Martha (1984) 'The genius and the copyright: Economic and legal conditions of the emergence of the 'Author'', *Eighteenth Century Studies* 17(4): 425-48.

Yano, Christine R. (2002) *Tears of Longing: Nostalgia and the Nation in Japanese Popular Song*, Cambridge: Harvard University Asia Center.

Yeats, W.B. (1935) 'Cathleen ni Houlihan', collected in W.B. Yeats (1982) *Collected Plays*, London: Papermac, 75-88.

Yuikawa, Kei (1997) *Kisu yori mo Setsunaku* 'Crueler than a Kiss', Tokyo: Shueisha.

Zuber, R. (1968/95) *Les 'Belles Infidèles' et la formation du goût classique*, Paris: Albin Michel.

Zubin, D. A. (1992) 'Gender and Noun Classification', in W. Bright (ed.) *International Encyclopedia of Linguistics* Vol. II, Oxford & New York: Oxford University Press, 41-43.

Subject Index

Author Index

Alcoff, L. 28, 30, 32, 37
Allen, B. 40
Allen, R. 159
Alvarez Rodríguez, R. 73
Andermahr, S. 151
Anzaldúa, G. 9-10
Aphrodite 88
Aristotle 153, 155, 159
Arrojo, R. 2, 6, 35-36, 81-82, 94, 177
Ayako, S. 99

Bachleitner, N. 20
Baker, M. 29
Banting, P. 34
Barthes, R. 3, 85, 88, 89, 118
Bassnett, S. 34
Battersby, C. 154
Baumgarten, N. 2, 6, 58, 62, 69, 177
Beauvoir, S. de 137, 169, 172
Becker, A. L. 116
Bell, L. 28
Benjamin, W. 86
Berman, A. 44, 47
Bey, K. 61-68
Biber, D. 55
Blum-Kulka, S. 68
Borges, J.L. 81
Borker, R. 138
Böttger, C. 58
Bourdieu, P. 40, 139
Branigan, E. 58
Brossard, N. 119
Browning, D. 106
Butler, J. 4-5, 14, 151, 153

Calvert, C. 157-158
Calvert, M. 157-158
Calvino, I. 3, 81-82, 86-95
Cameron, D. 5, 7, 36, 137
Caneda Cabrera, T. 73

Carbonell, O. 30, 33-34
Cartwright, L. 62
Castro, P. R. 75
Chamberlain, L. 3, 6, 11, 27, 79, 82, 149, 155-156, 171
Chartier, R. 155
Cixous, H. 12, 169
Cleland, J. 3, 117-136
Coates, J. 138
Connolly, J. 77
Constant, B. 19
Cronin, M. 168

Davidson, B. 138
Delisle, J. 44
Dent, N. 150
Derrida, J. 86
Destouches, P. 17
Díaz-Diocaretz, M. 71
Diderot, D. 16
Doherty, M. 55
Donald, R. 111
Du Plessix Gray, F. 91
Dülmen, A. von 16, 20-21
Dumas, A. 88
Duras, Mme. de 46

Eckert, P. 5
Ekberg, A. 61-62
Even-Zohar, I. 72-73

Fielding, H. 120
Fink, I. 90-91
Firestone, S. 152
Fischer, B. 19
Fishman, P. 138
Flannery, S. 87, 90
Flotow, L. von 2, 6, 28, 35, 119, 124-125, 169, 177
Forster, G. 18
Foucault, M. 85-86
Franco, F. 124-125
Franco Aixelà, J. 29

Get *Savvi*  ™

*The Transformation of an Unfulfilled Wife, an Entitled Son
and a Preoccupied Businessman*

I hope this book
inspires you!

Rita Chowdhry

Dedication

This book is dedicated to my father, whose love for me was cut short so cruelly but whose legacy will always be with me;

To my mother, my first love and teacher. It is the loss of her that motivated me to write this book;

To my husband Jeff, my rock and my biggest supporter, whose selfless love and support is never ending. Thank you for encouraging me in all my heart's desires;

To Raju and Sunny, who have supported me in this venture;

And to my children, Reece, Leah and Anya, who motivate and challenge me every day and make me proud to be their mother.

First print, August 2019

Preface and Acknowledgements

I have 32 years' experience of working with a wide variety of people in professional and personal development, coaching, teaching, training and mentoring environments – in helping others to grow and transform their lives, to be the best they can be and to succeed. I believe that success comes in many guises. In my story and in those of my clients – and, hopefully, in yours – success means personal happiness, loving relationships, good health, career satisfaction, wealth, charitable giving and a nurturing spiritual life. I work with private and public sector businesses, in groups such as boards of directors and management teams, and with individuals ranging from businessmen to housewives, in one-to-one sessions as a coach, trainer, Certified Behavioural Consultant and DISC (psychometric profiling) accredited corporate trainer. I draw on my own experiences and on those of my clients throughout this book.

This book makes use of real-life case studies based on successful people, who epitomise SAVVI principles, including politicians, billionaires and individuals who have achieved success in the face of adversity. The information within each one is used with the express permission of the individual concerned.

Zara, Jay and Arun Sharma – the central characters – are based on real clients and their experiences, but names have been changed for confidentiality reasons.

My gratitude goes out to those who have inspired me and have agreed to be honest and open in sharing their wisdom, stories and thoughts for this book. It would not have been possible without you.

In no particular order, my heartfelt thanks to:

- Lord David Blunkett
- Jasminder Singh OBE, Chairman of Edwardian Hotels
- Nicky Morgan, MP and cabinet minister
- Sunita Arora, Director of Arora Group and Littlebrook's Nurseries
- Raju Tuli, Chairman of Tuli Holdings
- Sunny Tuli, Managing Director of Tuli Holdings
- Avnish Goyal, Chairman of Hallmark Care Homes
- Raj Kohli, Chief Superintendent, Metropolitan Police.
- Anila Chowdhry, journalist and TV producer
- Nitin Passi, CEO of Missguided

Contents

Get *Savvi*, get successful

SAVRAN

S
SELF-AWARENESS
"Exploit your strengths and overcome your weaknesses"

a
ACHIEVER'S MINDSET
"Developing the right mindset to achieve your life and work goals"

v
VALUES AND BELIEFS
"Understand your values and belief systems and how they ultimately influence your performance"

v
VERBAL COMMUNICATION
"Learn how to adapt your communication for successful outcomes"

i
INSPIRE AND MOTIVATE
"Know how and where to get yourself and others motivated and inspired"

Introduction

Rita's Story

*F*ive years ago, at about 30,000 feet in the air, I finally understood how to change the course of my life. Until then, tragedy, pain, fear and loss had become recurring themes in my family's story. In fact, I was flying out to India because of another tragedy – or *two*. This time, though, I vowed to turn the pain around. The minute I landed at Mumbai airport, several thousand miles from my home in Surrey, I took action to implement that change. Today, I can honestly say I am living my life to the best of my ability – even against adversity – because I have become what I would now call 'SAVVI'.

This book is a guide to becoming SAVVI yourself, through: **S**elf-awareness; an **A**chiever's mindset; the power of **V**erbal communication; being guided by the best **V**alues for you and seeking **I**nspiration and inspiring others. I want to share with you my journey to becoming SAVVI.

For years, my characteristic coping mechanism had oscillated between fear and anxiety, a temporary mask of control, then back to fear and anxiety. I was labelled "the worrier", the emotional member of the family and my learned strategy wasn't helping anyone – least of all the people I loved and wanted to support and inspire. Once I understood, however, that pain and loss can be the greatest triggers for change, I reflected on my former struggles – and faced up to new ones – as valuable companions on my journey towards self-awareness and developing an achiever's mindset. It marked the beginning of my transformation into a fulfilled and successful businesswoman, coach, mother and wife guided by the SAVVI principles.

When I began to reflect, I remembered that I hadn't always been so fearful. In 1965, my family moved from northern India to the West Midlands. Both my parents were teachers in India and in the 1960s, when the British government was offering voucher visas to fill the skills shortage in professions such as teaching, my father seized the opportunity and we resettled in England. My father always wore a shirt and tie, with a pen ready in his top pocket. Though he wore a stern expression, he had one of those faces where you could still see the smile in his eyes – although few dared to challenge him! Fiercely ambitious, my father managed to build up an investment portfolio of 16 properties while working as a full-time teacher. He was also quite the trailblazer, becoming amongst the first of Wolverhampton's close-knit Indian community to move us from our inner-city terrace into the uncharted terrain of the suburbs, where he bought a semi-detached house with a front and a back garden and its own driveway.

From a young age, I was aware that my father was different from the other Indian dads I met in 1970s Wolverhampton. We were part of an Indian community, in which most of the men were bus drivers and steel workers; my father had come over on a voucher to teach. He was passionate about learning and was even an early scholar of personal development books. I can vividly remember walking past his prized copy of Dale Carnegie's *How to Win Friends and Influence People* on a bookshelf and thinking what a boring book that must be! Little did I realise then how influential this book would become in my family's lives.

As a result of my father's forward thinking, I wasn't the stereotypical demure Asian daughter. I challenged things; I was up for trying anything; I expressed my views. My mother, who was more conformist, would always say: "Rita should have been the boy in the family."

When I was 10 years old, my father visited India in the August summer holiday to see his parents. Waving goodbye to him as he left for the airport, was the last time I saw this remarkable man. En route from Delhi to his home town of Ludhiana, the taxi he was riding in had a head on collision with a truck. My father suffered internal injuries, which could probably have been treated back in England. But instead of receiving help from passers-by, my 42- year-old father was robbed of his watch and the contents of his suitcase and abandoned at the roadside. It's a desperate image that haunts me to this day.

After the accident, one of my aunts in Wolverhampton came running, out of breath, to the back door of our house to break the news that somebody had telephoned from India to say that my father had died. *How could that even be possible?* In those days, my only notion of death came from the news on TV about IRA bombings and casualties. No one in my real life had ever died. I couldn't begin to comprehend the implication of losing a very real and powerful presence in our lives. Soon, my mother was packing her suitcase and leaving for India with my youngest brother, and the rest of us were packed off to stay with family in Birmingham, Wolverhampton and Leicester. Regretfully, she never made it to India in time for her husband's funeral. The intense Indian heat and lack of mortuaries meant that, left too long, his body would have rapidly decomposed, so his Hindu cremation went ahead without my mother or any of his children. In the end, it was left to his own father, my grandfather, to light the flame of his son's pyre – an act that no parent should ever have to endure. The fact that none of us saw his body again means that, to this day, I dream of my father, still alive and wandering parts of India.

Not surprisingly, three weeks after my father's passing, my mother returned from India a changed woman. Like my father, she was unusual for her time: a graduate and a qualified, practising teacher who didn't marry until she was 25, which was late for an Indian bride. She even went on working after the birth of my eldest brother, another rarity in India in 1960. When she returned from India after my father's death in 1974, she appeared in a traditional widow's white sari; she had lost weight, her face was cut and bruised and she had lost a tooth as a result of falling out of a rickshaw. It was shocking to see the transformation in her. With one unpredictable strike, each one of us had lost our footing.

After 5th August 1974 (the day of my father's death), my mother never wore make-up again and only ever dressed in the white or pale saris suitable for a grieving widow, despite them being inadequate against the harsh English winters. Acquiring a newly vulnerable mother at the same time as losing a formidable father turned me into a worrier overnight. I became unsure of myself, fearful about the future, my head was flooded with *what ifs*? Despite this sense of foreboding, for our mother's sake, my siblings and I knew we had to step up and support her in any way we could. So, each of us fell into new family roles, making the best of our respective skills. As the daughter who – according to Mum – should have been the boy in the family, I naturally became her mini co-parent, sternly ensuring that my younger brother did his homework and, house-proud like both my parents, cleaning and organising our home. In my teens, I learned how to wallpaper and decorate rooms. My siblings and I all become our mother's protectors – even our three-year-old brother. When he accompanied her to India after our father's death, he pushed away any one who unwittingly made Mum cry. All of us children became highly adept at never mentioning Dad's name again for fear of upsetting Mum. Quite often, we could hear her crying herself to sleep at night and so we believed that our silence over Dad might at least alleviate some of her hardship. We understood that none of us could just be children any more – particularly not grieving ones.

Despite growing into a teenage worrier, fretting about adult problems, like the household bills and losing my surviving parent, I was a natural at dealing with telephone calls, visiting the local support agencies and placing rental adverts in the local paper, when my mother took over my dad's property business. However, turning into an adult before I was old enough meant that for years my paper mask was prone to slipping each time my inexperienced mind ran wild, imagining that whatever could go wrong would go wrong. I was a strange mix of determination and anxiety. It was my unconscious armour against pain and loss, as I fooled myself that worrying enough in advance meant that I would be prepared for any eventuality. Whilst I realise now that I possessed elements of the SAVVI principles, even back then (the beginnings of an achiever's mindset, and the inspiration of my parents' teachings and successes, despite their hardships), I was too young to distinguish between nurturing values that would help me grow and the values imposed on me (by the Indian community) that held me back. It would be some time before I would be able to work that out for myself.

In the years following our father's death, our family – which had been raised on our parents' independent and strident values – suddenly became dependent on our community of Hindus, Sikhs and Pakistanis. My mother had been an educated, working mum in India; in Wolverhampton, she was widowed at the age of 36, isolated and unable to drive in the suburbs, with four children under the age of 11. Initially, she was clueless about running my father's business and people took advantage of her. She needed the support of the Indian community and a handful of its members delivered for her – but at a price: "Do as we tell you." She had to act and dress appropriately, and despite her loneliness, she never remarried. She always listened to her community's advice, even when it conflicted with her own ideas.

We understood that the freedoms she allowed us at home weren't for public display. Whilst my closest friends were English, I had to conform so that my mother was never judged for any deviation by her children. We were part of the West Midlands' Indian community of bus drivers, shop keepers and steel and manufacturing workers, and many of these Indians wouldn't let their daughters go away to university, let alone think about short haircuts and high hemlines.

In time, my mother, the new breadwinner of the family, had to change – or revert to aspects of her former self – to find her compass to go on. After seven attempts, she passed her driving test. She learned to be financially literate so as to deal with accountants and lawyers, and even became the rent collector and property manager, maintaining the upkeep of my father's properties. But at the same time, she still wanted to please and flatter the Indian community for its main attraction: suitable marriage introductions for her children. As a result, I spent much of my youth confused about my true identity. Beyond gaining a university education – as long as it was at the local university so that I could continue living at home – I wasn't being encouraged to go out and set the world alight. I am certain this would have been different had my father still been alive, but my mother wasn't able to move with the times, since she had to live within the confines of the community.

Looking back, the instability of my coping strategies, coupled with my conflicting public and private identities, held me back from giving and receiving life to the fullest. I couldn't celebrate life. I spent special occasions such as birthdays, Christmases and Diwali in tears, dwelling on my father's absence.

At the same time, I wanted to make my father proud of me. So, unlike my younger sister and female cousins, who all married before me, I graduated because I was determined to become a secondary school teacher. Today, I can reflect on this as early evidence of my achiever's mindset. My plan looked like this: go to university; marry (before it was 'too late', in the Indian sense) a professional; have children and live in a beautiful home. Yet all the time I thought I was different from the other Indians around us, I was in truth being led by my community's traditional values. I had even allowed the scope of my ambitions to shrink, by agreeing to attend a place of study, just a 15-minute bus ride from home.

The ambition I did realise, however – when reality exceeded all my expectations – was in the man I ended up marrying. It was the stuff of Jane Austen novels. His sister had met me at an earlier wedding and wanted to introduce me to her brother, Jeff. Despite his name, Jeff is also Indian. An English woman, who was his parent's lodger at the time, had suggested the name. When sadly, she didn't live to see him born, they named their baby son Jeff in her honour and also to celebrate the life of this woman, who had predicted that my mother-in-law – after four daughters – would finally have her longed-for son.

As soon as I met Jeff, I saw that he was well-read, polished – despite being a Geordie, we would joke – and an all-round gentleman. He worked as an analyst in the City, at a time when it was tough for Asians to work in London's financial square mile. Like my father, Jeff was doing things that few Asian men were doing in the early 1990s. Eventually, I discovered that whilst I could be outwardly confident and direct, Jeff was gentle and quietly strong. He made me feel secure and protected. He understood that my hard exterior was just a front to protect myself and my family. In the absence of my father, I had to appear tough to protect my mother from other people, and from the harsh realities of life. This armour became my public face. But Jeff's strength and love encouraged me to discover the person I really wanted to be. He was offering me a new perspective: I could be happy and successful on my own terms, rather than in the ways defined by others, such as the Indian community. In Jeff I had found my other half; I knew he was 'the one'. However, in the build-up to our wedding day, another milestone in my life, I once again became preoccupied with what was missing: my father. When I should have been savouring one of the happiest times of my life, I became absorbed in emotions that held me back. I hadn't yet learnt how to live fully.

Meanwhile, to the outside world, my life was going to plan: I had graduated, married a professional and started my career as a teacher. A couple of years' later in 1989, we had a son, Reece, followed by two daughters, Leah in 1992 and Anya in 1999. I was ticking through my checklist of goals, yet I remained restless and – despite all Jeff's attempts to free me from fears and insecurities – there were still times when I found something new to fret about. Like many children who lose a parent, I began to fear losing my partner: *Gosh, what if anything happens to Jeff? I would never be able to live without him.*

Looking back, I can see that beyond achieving my initial goals, I didn't have a plan of progression. I ignored the fact that Jeff had always loved my career-mindedness, independence and ambition. My early achiever's mindset had stopped reaching out for new goals, but I wasn't self-aware enough then to appreciate why, having achieved my initial goals, I couldn't help feeling there was something else missing – like many women conditioned from childhood to build their goals around supporting others. I recognised that my fear of the unknown was holding me back, but I just didn't know how to tackle it. I was unable to stop this mental chatter of dissatisfaction. I thought I had to live with it.

Externally, however, I was still confident and successful. I had grown up pretending, so it was easy to wear a brave face. My first teaching job was at a girls' school in Surbiton in 1986, where I taught Business Studies. I was among the first wave of teachers trained to teach the subject, and it was a pioneering and exciting subject to teach to teenage girls. After 15 years there, I went on to work at a predominantly Muslim school in a deprived part of Woking with many social challenges. I was the only member of its Business Studies department, and I made a considerable impact on results because of my specialism in specific learning difficulties and encouraging young people to find the best strategies for successful outcomes. I was passionate about teaching and enabling others to achieve their full potential – though I wasn't very good at doing it myself.

It was when my son Reece was diagnosed with dyslexia at age six, that my strategies for myself and parenting began to unravel. Today, many schools still fail to adequately support dyslexic pupils; in the 90s, teachers had even less expertise. So my professional inexperience, coupled with my characteristic anxiety, meant that I was imagining every difficult situation ahead of my son and its effect on his life chances. When I had calmed down, my achiever's mindset kicked in and I had an end-goal in place: finding the best education to personalise and support Reece's learning, which helped me keep my fears at bay. I also made the decision to do a postgraduate diploma in Specific Learning Difficulties. In the meantime, I applied what I already knew about the link between the self-esteem of students and their success and focused on Reece's strengths. Even at the age of three, he had an astonishing memory for the makes and models of every car we passed. He was clearly a visual learner, so I ensured that the appropriate strategies were incorporated into his learning at home and at school. He was brilliant at IT and, importantly, he loved it. So, we built IT and audio recordings into everything he did at home.

The process of supporting Reece's dyslexia was my first baby step towards my self-awareness and the acceptance that my previous coping mechanisms had failed me and my family. But just a year later, I was derailed again when Reece was diagnosed with vitiligo, an incurable condition where pale patches develop on the skin. I became ill with anxiety and depression; I even became preoccupied with what the community might think about his appearance. Soon, I was back to where I'd started.

In one of my stronger moments, I sought out alternative medicines for Reece and came across homeopathy. When I met the practitioner, she looked at me and said, "Well, first of all, let's sort you out." A homeopathic remedy literally fixed me overnight. It lifted my mood and I became more positive. But I thought, *I can't keep doing this – going backwards and forwards*. Deep down, I've always believed that my natural style is to go out and find solutions, but the events of my childhood and the influence of my mum as a worrier kept pulling me back. As Confucius counsels, "We should feel sorrow, but not sink under its oppression." And if I wasn't careful, I knew that I would drag my family down with me. I realised that I had to stop being so fearful and accept that some of the values I had inherited from the Wolverhampton Indian community of my youth were failing to make me happy. Above all, I wanted to be an inspiring role model to my son, to help him form a positive attitude in order to face his medical and learning difficulties. So, the solution-driven side of me took control – only this time, equipped with a better knowledge of my strengths, I could develop a plan of action. I went on a quest that stretched from Harley Street to India (via the internet and family connections) to find a solution for Reece's skin condition. In the end, we sourced a herbal treatment from a remote village in Punjab that cured almost all of his vitiligo. The ability to turn my emotional reaction to a family crisis into a practical response reminded me of what I could achieve when I put my mind to something; it was the catalyst for yet more self-awareness and development.

I looked for solutions and devoured personal development books in search of new possibilities for a better version of myself. The first book I turned to was

How to Win Friends and Influence People, the book that had sat on my father's bookshelf all those years ago. I had never read it until after I was confronted with Reece's issues. Maybe on some level I had imagined that it was going to be too painful to pick up, but reading it changed my life. It made me see just how much control we have at our disposal, and the knowledge of this reduced the influence of external circumstances and people on my goals. In some ways, the book's title is a misnomer as it speaks about the far-reaching control our thoughts and behaviours have upon others. As a result of reading it, I was even more determined to inspire my children by projecting my own positive mindset.

Before my journey towards self-development, I had neither the language nor the self-knowledge to describe how I had been dealing with pain and loss. Although my mother was an incredible role model, coping and surviving in very difficult times, I had outgrown my learnt impulsive responses to crises and required some alternative strategies as an adult – not least so that I could enjoy life's happier and lighter moments. Soon I was absorbing new ideas from further reading, training and workshops, such as those run by Tony Robbins, and was beginning to learn how to use pain to propel change in my life in order to nourish happiness and success.

My growing appetite for personal development also made an impact on me professionally. At first, I saw parallels between what I was learning and my teaching career, in which I enjoyed equipping young minds with the tools to go out into the world. The deeper I delved, however, the more I was driven by ideas about self-development – about developing and training both the mind and the person on the road to fulfilment – and, unfortunately, this holistic approach wasn't being practised in mainstream education at the time. I began to find teaching, which had always been my dream job, increasingly limiting, and I realised I was ready for a career change. I wanted to extend my teaching skills

11

into coaching individuals about how to control their mind positively, and how to use pain as a force for happiness and success. I had found my second and true vocation: self-development coaching.

After I embarked on this personal and professional journey, I sat down with Jeff and our children and explained to them what I had learnt about myself, and that I now had a template, which was not only helping me to steer my growth, but was also forming the basis of what I was coaching others to do. I wanted my family, particularly Jeff at that time, to support me on this journey. I knew that if I was changing, there was a risk that we wouldn't stay aligned, which has always been our strength. Seeing the positive impact of the personal development on me, Jeff of course wanted to share in and support the experience, so we applied the SAVVI principles to our goal-setting, our values as a family and our communication. I particularly wanted to share one of the main lessons I had learnt: keep worrying and you are supplying energy and direction to your problem. Doing so merely feeds the problem whilst sapping energy required to create solutions. In the words of Mahatma Gandhi, *"Your beliefs become your thoughts; your thoughts become your words; your words become your actions."* If your outlook is positive, your actions become positive. The same mantra applies if your outlook is negative! So, by focusing on the positive, you will always thrive.

The test of how SAVVI my family and I had indeed grown, individually and together, was challenged a couple of years' later, when we had to face my mother-in-law Rani's grave illness. I remember sitting with my husband and his siblings in the hospital corridor, sensing it was serious, waiting for the doctor to call us in. I felt that familiar, sinking dread growing inside me. I started imagining all the worst possible outcomes for my mother-in-law. And then, I just snapped out of it. I reminded myself that things were different – *I was different*

– now. I knew I had to quell my worry and direct my energy into supporting Jeff and his mother. If I'd learnt anything in those past few years, this was the moment to walk the walk.

When the doctor gave us the diagnosis of lung cancer, untreatable at Rani's age, I managed to stay composed and focused on comforting Jeff. I surprised myself and everyone else in the room with my new-found strength. Within days, my mother-in-law contracted pneumonia and her health rapidly deteriorated. The hope of another few months of life for her suddenly diminished into days and then hours, as we kept a vigil at her bedside. Soon, each of her grandchildren arrived from different corners of the country to whisper their final goodbyes. I can still picture her lying in her bed, an oxygen mask covering her face, when she beckoned Jeff, her only son, to her side. As Jeff brought his face close to his mother's, she raised her hand slowly, drawing on every last drop of energy, to touch his head in the Hindu custom of an elder giving their blessing for long life and happiness to a loved one. We were witnessing more than just a ritual; we watched tearfully in the knowledge that she was saying goodbye to her cherished son. The following day, my mother-in-law took her last breath in Jeff's arms, with her head resting on his shoulder. According to my mother, who was at the hospital when Jeff's mother died, dying in one's son's arms is considered particularly fortunate as it symbolises the child carrying the parent into the next life.

Despite the weight of sorrow, it was satisfying to feel myself living and breathing my SAVVI principles so that, instead of falling apart, I was able to support the family. I comforted Jeff, usually my rock, reminding him that his mother had wanted to leave the world with dignity. She had lived a full and fruitful life, known her great-grandchildren, and had been pain-free and independent until just a week before her death.

In Hindu families, it falls on the daughter-in-law, or a close female relative, to bathe and dress the body of her deceased mother-in-law in preparation for her funeral. The task is believed to be too emotionally burdensome for the grieving daughters. Holding the cold body of a beloved relative, who had so much pride in her appearance – who never wanted to be seen with a hair out of place, who was fiercely independent and never wanted to be a burden on anyone – was one of the hardest challenges of my life. Prior to her death, my mother-in-law had told her daughters that although she wanted me to carry out the bathing ritual, "Rita's a really emotional person. I don't know if she'll be able to carry it out." The knowledge that my mother-in-law had wanted me to do it gave me the strength I needed, and my mother accompanied me to lend support. After that very difficult day, I believed I could face anything. My coping reflexes were getting stronger and I was becoming more SAVVI.

A few days later, I was able to help Jeff and Reece write an emotional eulogy for Rani. As I listened to my eldest daughter Leah read a poem for her grandmother, and my younger daughter Anya read in Hindi, "*Dadima* (paternal grandmother), we love you and will miss you, but know that you will be happy as you will be with *hunammaji* (a Hindu god) and *dadiji* (grandfather)", I believed that I had genuinely developed. Previously, I would have found this event too emotional.

However, my challenge was far from over. I still had a niggling doubt that maybe I was only managing this well because I was focused on Jeff. I wondered if I could have been this strong had it been my own mother who had died. Shockingly, the answer to my question came just three months later.

My mum feared death – not for herself, but out of concern for how her children would cope. (This was typical of her personality: considerate, selfless, always putting others' needs before her own.) She became depressed after my mother-in-law's death. They were close friends and my mother witnessed her friend drawing her last breath. In the course of a few weeks, my siblings and I watched our mother's health deteriorate dramatically. On reflection, I believe that my mother's focus on negativity was the trigger for her rapid decline. Numerous tests and visits to the doctors did not reveal why she was losing weight and suffering panic attacks. I recall her saying in a telephone conversation, "Since your mother-in-law's funeral, I feel a sense of unease and am constantly low." Eventually, medical tests indicated that urinary infections were causing her delirium. For the next few weeks, she was in and out of hospital, always refusing to stay long for fear of dying in hospital.

During one of her hospital stays, Mum knocked her head and lost consciousness. She was transferred to a high-dependency unit in another hospital. When I reached Edinburgh, I was horrified by the sight of all the tubes attached to my mum. Now she was also suffering from hypothermia and in a critical condition. We were all stunned. Our mother had had no previous health issues – yet a spell of depression, followed by a urinary tract infection, had spiralled into this.

Overwhelmed by more pain, I had to stay positive and strong for my family and for my mum's sake. This time, I wouldn't give oxygen to my fears. I tried hard not to dwell on the awful moment when my mum had grabbed my hand inside her own frail hand and begged me to take her back to London with me. These would be her last words to me, and it was heart breaking to abandon her. Somehow, though, in the swirl of all my emotions, I knew I had to focus on my strengths to get through it all. I questioned myself in the same way I would question my clients: *What do I want for my mum?* The answer was that I wanted her to be pain-free. Having identified my goal, I drew on the family values that our mother had taught us – to be there for one another – and her Hindu values about the last rites. So, when we learnt – just three months after losing Jeff's mum – that my mum wasn't going to pull through, I prayed that God would take her without too much suffering, surrounded by her family and listening to her favourite hymns and religious readings. Instead of falling apart in the face of losing my only surviving parent, I had managed to apply strength to the situation, inspired by my mother's own values.

On one of our hospital visits, we left the room for the nurses to change the bed and wash our mother. From outside the room, we heard a cry. Our mother was too weak to even whisper by then, so we assumed it was someone else. When we stepped back into the room, we saw our mother lying motionless, the colour drained from her face. She had taken her breath and left this world. For almost three weeks, we had kept a constant vigil at our mother's hospital bed but, in the end, it was as if she hadn't wanted any us to suffer by seeing her slip away. Although we hadn't been right beside her, it was still an antidote to the way we had lost our father. In contrast to his remote death in another country, my mother had died a few feet away from us and we were able to perform the last rites on her. As I did this, I sought inspiration from her legacy to pass on to my children. We had to salvage something positive from her passing.

When my mother was alive, she had worried that a traditional Hindu funeral was going to be too difficult for her children to organise because, as foreigners, we would be exploited in India. Hindus are always cremated: the fire is said to free the soul so that it can be reincarnated when it is ready. Traditionally, the ashes are then scattered into the River Ganges, or into flowing water. My mother would say, "Just sprinkle my ashes in Edinburgh, in a local stream." But when we remembered that she had sprinkled our father's ashes in India, we knew that she would have wanted to follow him there. My mother never liked being alone; she would have cherished the company of Rani, her friend of 27 years, down her last journey on the banks of the Ganges, so our families took both our mothers' ashes to India, whilst my siblings and I dedicated a bench to my mother in front of a stream near their homes in Edinburgh.

In those three months, I surprised myself with my ability to deal with the deaths of first my mother-in-law and then my mother. I enjoyed my new sense of control, and felt strong enough to collect my mother-in-law's ashes from the funeral directors in Southall. But the sight of my mother-in-law's life reduced to the size of a small wooden box hit me hard. Was this all that was left of her lifetime?

The next day, on the plane journey to India, Jeff and I felt hollow inside. We had lost both sets of our parents. I had always pictured the love of a mother like an umbrella that protects against the rain and offers shade in the heat of the sun. Jeff and I had lost that love and protection. Sharing this thought with Jeff made us both realise that we needed to focus on our mothers' respective legacies and use them as a catalyst for further change in our family. By then, I was finishing my coaching training and I knew that my first course of action would be to choose a name for my coaching consultancy. Finally, I was going to overcome my self-limiting fears about being an Asian mother and wife, too old to set up a business. I toyed with the idea of using my children's names and even 'ISIS Coaching' (after the Greek Goddess of Knowledge). But then it became obvious to me. In the Hindu faith, life and death are part of the same concept: *samsara*. The loss of our mothers was inextricably tied to new beginnings, so it was obvious that my business had to be named after them. Thus, 'Savran' (from Savitri, my mother's name, and Rani, my mother-in-law) was born.

The minute we landed at Mumbai airport, Jeff went online to see if Companies House had already registered the name Savran. To my delight it was still available, and we started the registration process. From that day, I vowed to apply my strengths to drive my business forward. I would be doing what I valued (helping others to achieve) and, in the process, inspiring my children. Accompanying our mothers on their journeys to a secluded place along the Ganges, and also visiting the place where my father's ashes had been scattered, completed a circle for me. Out of it sprang a clear sense of how I was going to face the world.

On our return to England, I finished my coaching training and started to build Savran. Within six months, I won a contract with the London Metropolitan Police to help develop the potential of its 300 Black and Minority Ethic officers. One year later, I was nominated for Best Newcomer by the Coaching Academy. I was ecstatic. And after the sadness of recent family gatherings, I was able to bring together my family for a happier occasion at the awards ceremony. Most people take a plus one, but I booked the entire table – Indian style! I felt privileged to be nominated and I felt whole-hearted gratitude for it – a new feeling for me – and I was going to make sure I relished every minute of it. When they announced the winner of the award (…"Savran!"), I felt the sunshine of our mothers' legacy and, for the first time, I didn't worry about my parents missing another milestone. This was a defining moment for me. At the age of 50, I was experiencing new feelings: I knew I was living and still growing!

Our table screamed the loudest; my daughters were in tears and my son witnessed with his own eyes how his mother, a middle-aged Indian woman, had overcome her stereotype and her fears. On that night, he turned to me and said, "Mum, if you can do it, so can I." (It would be the impetus for him to leave his job to grow his own business.) When my younger brother Sunny posted on Facebook, "Proud of my big sis," my heart just melted. Far greater than my pride at public recognition for my achievement was the knowledge that I was inspiring my children and my family.

It was then that I knew just how far I had travelled, because I was only looking forward to the future. The Indian mystic Sadhguru says, "You cannot suffer the past or the future because it does not exist. What you are suffering is your imagination and your memory." I was no longer limiting myself by suffering the past; I was happy imagining what I could achieve next.

I set up Savran to help others make positive changes in their lives. Blending business theory and my research into the common traits of successful individuals, I have discovered that they all possess the five principles of the SAVVI framework. In my consultancy work and in my private practice, I encourage clients to embrace these principles to become the best, most fulfilled version of themselves, in every aspect of life.

Get SAVVI explores the five principles of my SAVVI framework. In my extensive experience as a coach, working with individuals and businesses, I have helped many clients like Zara, an unfulfilled wife, Arun, a self-entitled son and Jay, a successful businessman struggling to find a healthy work-life balance, to achieve a more fulfilled life.

This book charts the true stories of people, who have made transformative journeys guided by SAVVI principles: of real-life SAVVI people, who epitomise these principles, or who have achieved success in the face of adversity. I truly believe that you can be one of them.

1

Self-Awareness

The Story of the Unfulfilled Wife

*I*n my day-to-day work with clients, I like to contextualise and flavour the lessons of coaching by using the real-life stories and anecdotes of people – from all walks of life – who have overcome personal obstacles through self-awareness, and have built on that awareness to move forward happily and successfully. Some of these real-life stories are derived from the journeys of my former clients (who have kindly given me permission to model their experiences), as well as of inspiring business leaders and politicians, whom I have interviewed in order to learn how they have become SAVVI.

I am often invited to charity events and award ceremonies to celebrate other people's success stories. It was at one of these events, at a smart central London hotel, that I came across Zara and Jay Sharma. As soon as I stepped into the banqueting suite, I could hear loud, hearty laughter emanating from a small, appreciative crowd. Jay Sharma stood at the centre of it, visibly savouring the intoxicating attention he was receiving. He looked and sounded like a winner, even before the nominations' announcement for the UK's Entrepreneur of the Year award. Jay Sharma flitted easily from one group to another, purposefully working the busy room. Everything he said was said with a flourish. I watched him turn the heads of the guest speaker – a junior trade minister – and a couple of TV celebrities, who all stared in his direction as cameras flashed around them. It was no exaggeration to say that Jay Sharma looked like he owned the room.

However, it was the elegant woman standing beside him – whom I guessed was Mrs Sharma – who caught my attention. She was certainly eye-catching, in her ice-white evening gown, and her bejewelled hand sparkled like an expensive accessory on Jay Sharma's arm. I noticed that each time Jay Sharma's body leaned in to talk and laugh loudly with the men in the group, his wife's hand was temporarily left in mid-air before quickly moving to join her other hand in clutching her Chanel purse. As her husband leaned back again, the hand shot back up to catch the elbow of his tuxedo. She looked every inch the supportive wife, and I was intrigued by her quiet yet steady demeanour.

As expected, Jay Sharma won the most prestigious award of the evening, and when he rose from the table, I couldn't help but compare his appearance to his much younger self as portrayed in the programme photograph. His wealthy lifestyle had certainly impacted on his features, not to mention his waistline but that didn't shush the women around me, who cooed how George Clooney-handsome he was as he stepped up to accept his award. Meanwhile, there was no contesting that Mrs Sharma would have won the 'Most Glamourous Woman in The Room' award hands down. The Sharma brand was a carefully constructed and formidable sight to behold.

As soon as Jay Sharma was back at his table, well-wishers flocked to congratulate him. He shook hands with them and posed for photographs, aware of his good side, carrying his award in the crook of his arm like a baby he was showing off. I looked for his wife, who remained seated at the table, behind the place card that announced that she was *Mrs Jay Sharma,* while her husband took centre stage, lapping up all attention.

Noticing that she was sitting alone, a mutual friend brought her over to our table and introduced her to me.

"Congratulations, Mrs Sharma," I said, offering her my hand.

She took it, but replied, "No, the business is Jay's baby."

Shaking her hand, it was hard not to be overwhelmed by the array of rings she wore. But her handshake was delicate and unpractised. For Jay Sharma's spouse, she was a collection of contradictions and I was intrigued.

"I know that success requires sacrifices from the *whole* family," I said, sensing some vulnerability.

She smiled, but still wouldn't take any credit. "My friends call me Zara," she said.

She became quiet, so I moved the conversation onto the subject of children. (Jay Sharma had mentioned their son in his acceptance speech.) "I bet your son will be proud of his dad's award. It looks like an Oscar!" Luckily, I had uttered the magic word: "son". Zara's face brightened and her eyes softened as she started talking about her son, Arun. In no time, her mobile phone was out and she was scrolling through photographs of her pride and joy: Arun playing cricket for the county; Arun in the school rugby team; Arun standing in the 'attack' fencing position, pointing a sabre. Clearly, her son was her most valued prize.

"What school year's he in?" I asked.

"No, these are old photos I keep as my screensavers. Arun hates it when I bring them out. He works for the family business now." Then she held up some recent photographs of Arun: dangling car keys in front of a gleaming four-by-four; looking up from behind a pair of pilot sunglasses, with slicked hair and the perfect trace of a holiday beard, sitting poolside on board a yacht. He was a handsome younger version of his father, carrying on the Sharma trademark of good looks and wealth.

"He looks like his father," I commented.

She smiled at the photograph then slipped the phone back into her handbag, snapping it shut.

"It isn't easy growing up today, is it?" she said, sounding as if she was asking for reassurance. She stared into the near distance, where her husband was standing like the birthday boy at his own party.

"But he's following in his father's footsteps?" I asked.

She smiled again and replied, "My husband wears racing shoes – let's hope Arun can keep up with him!"

When Zara opened up, she was warm, and I wanted to know more about her. "Do you work?" I asked.

She took another sip of her prosecco and shook her head adamantly. For a woman who was so striking, she avoided any real focus on herself and deftly turned the subject round to my son. I showed her the obligatory proud mum's photographs of him. One of them was an old photo of Reece looking like a miniature Harry Potter, bespectacled in a blazer and school cap.

"He looks very studious," said Zara.

"He's made a real success of his life. But we've had our share of issues. He had a stern headmistress, who wrote him off at school because of his learning difficulties."

As soon as I said this, I could see that I had Zara's full attention.

I carried on, "But Reece proved his headteacher wrong: he got great A level results despite his dyslexia and went off to Durham University. He's just launched his own venture capital business."

She had stopped drinking, and was full of questions about my work and my son and listening to the changes my family had made. I detailed the five principles of success that I call the SAVVI framework, starting with self-awareness and looking within oneself to make a change. When she asked if I saw any male clients, my first thought was that she was referring to her husband. On the surface, he had just won a prestigious award; to most people in the room, he walked and talked success. But then I remembered rumours about demoralised staff members at his call centre business. I knew it was not uncommon to see people, who appear to epitomise success (usually financially) overlook other areas, such as personal and professional relationships and their own health and wellbeing.

I explained to Zara that while my private clients were usually women, my corporate clients were usually men, who saw me about professional development and growing their business. "Women," I said, "tend to see me for guidance around relationships, and for a better work-life balance."

Zara was suddenly back on her Louboutin heels and I realised I had lost her attention. Her focus was on her husband, who was beckoning her to join him for photographs. "I have to go," she apologised. But before she walked away, she added, "I think I need a bit of help – I'm concerned about my son. I'm interested in how your son turned things around with the five principles."

Two weeks later, Zara Sharma telephoned me; she sounded anxious and unhappy, nothing like the charming, self-possessed woman I had met at the awards night. She had called wanting to learn more about my practice methods and whether they could help her troubled son. "We gave Arun every opportunity, but now, at the age of 26, he's not making anything of himself. He's late for work – sometimes he doesn't even make it in. Though he'll get out of bed for a night out partying, or flying out to the Balearics with his friends. All they're interested in is chasing the next party or girl, or shopping for cars and designer clothes. And of course, we end up paying for it – in every sense."

Zara went quiet for a moment. "I don't know what to do. I don't recognise him anymore. But deep down, I know he is a good person. He thinks he's fine. He says it's just me worrying too much.

"I wanted him to come and see you, but he refused. What can I do to help him change?"

Listening to Zara on the telephone, I recognised the behavioural traits: she was preoccupied with worrying and overprotecting her son, and was spiralling into a state of negativity. Although Zara asked for my guidance to help her son, I explained that my techniques could only help the individual who actively sought help to make a change in their life. Arun would have to come to see me himself. Furthermore, Zara could not solve her son's problems; she could, however, learn to channel her energy, her emotions and her time into the areas of life that *were* within her control. Once she started to look at herself and her responses to situations concerning Arun, she could begin to foster the change she desired in her life.

I suggested that her first step should be to take actions that were personal and positive for her, to change her anxiety around parenting Arun. But to do this successfully, she was going to have to practise applying an open mind, in the way a parachute only works if it is open. Any parent or business manager has a profound effect on the people they nurture and lead. By striving for positive changes within herself, Zara could guide her son more effectively whilst also enjoying a more productive relationship with him.

Before meeting Zara again, I asked her to take the first step in the SAVVI process by completing a tried and tested online profiling system called 'DISC' (a tool that I will describe in greater detail later). Created by psychologist William Marston (famed for his development of the polygraph, or lie detector test), this online questionnaire helps to identify our individual behavioural pattern and illuminate the way they influence our responses to life and work situations, and towards different types of people. I often stress to clients that knowing oneself in this way is true wisdom and offers the power to bring about real change. Some of my clients have referred to seeing their DISC results as a revelatory moment, as if the blinkers have been cast off. The profiling test would enable Zara to achieve some self-awareness about the way she instinctively responded to personal situations, such as her relationship with her son, and would in the longer term improve aspects of her wider life and would help her understand other people's behaviour.

When Zara Came for Coaching

People come to my practice for all kinds of reasons, but they are all driven by either pain or pleasure. Tony Robbins, in his book *Unleash the Giant Within*, sums it up precisely, explaining that all our decisions are to derive pleasure or to avoid pain. Zara's decision to see me derived from her pain at seeing her son lost and unhappy. It would turn out that her pain was rooted deeply in her own frustrations.

At the initial session with a new client (before revealing their DISC results), I ask them a series of questions designed to reveal their inner truths and challenges. The purpose of the client's reflection is for them to articulate their strengths and weaknesses and discern what they value most, as part of their journey towards self-awareness. From there, they can start to plot a course of action for the future.

When I met Zara face-to-face again, true to form, she described how she was feeling in terms of her anxiety about Arun. From the outset, she stressed that she was seeing me to help solve his problems. If Arun was happy, she too would be happy. Her identity was so entwined with her son's, and I realised that it was difficult for her to see herself as a separate entity. I tried, however, to hold the mirror up.

RITA: Can you recall your happiest memory?

ZARA: Undoubtedly it was the birth of Arun. We'd tried for a long time to have him, and I gave up believing it was going to be possible. I can still remember holding him for the first time, and staring at him all through our first night in the hospital bed. I miss being that close to him.

RITA: What are your most fulfilling accomplishments?

ZARA, without a moment's hesitation: Arun, Arun and Arun! To please my parents, I married relatively young and didn't go to university, but having Arun made the sacrifice worthwhile. It gave me a sense of fulfilment that I'd never dreamed possible. Even my marriage to Jay was fulfilling back then. I loved setting up our first home, decorating it the way I wanted, and – as Mrs Jay

Sharma, with an image to maintain – I could shop for jewellery and designer labels to my heart's content.

In the early days of Jay's business, I did some part-time secretarial work in the office, which made me feel as if we were building something together. But as the business took off, Jay wanted me to make sure that our home – where he entertained a lot of his clients – ran as smoothly as his business. He told me to hire all the domestic help I needed. So now we have efficient staff around our home and the parties take care of themselves, whilst I mill around looking like the perfect hostess.

RITA: You are a supportive wife and mother. What helps you to be successful at what you do?

ZARA: I don't consider myself remotely successful. I wish I'd gained some qualifications. And I can't even take credit for organising our parties anymore – it's all done by staff. I'm just there to look pretty on Jay's arm. Sometimes, with all our business contacts, I feel I should do my bit for charity, but I'm so de-skilled now. And I don't want to end up to hanging around like a spare part, which I already do at Jay's parties.

After a pause, Zara continued.

ZARA: A while back, I would have said that I was a successful mother, but I can't claim to be that now. Frankly, Arun hasn't turned out the way we hoped. And I blame myself for that since I spent more time with him than his dad did.

I feel like a failure for raising a young man with all the wrong priorities. All Arun cares about is status and playing hard – without any of the *working* hard. His dad isn't perfect, but he works hard. Arun knows his dad worked hard to give him everything his grandparents couldn't provide for him – always the best and latest of everything, and then this prestigious job as his dad's second in command. But I still wake up every morning to make sure Arun's heard his phone alarm – otherwise he'd sleep right through it. Sometimes I'll find he's not even in his bed because he's spent the night out – and then I have to track him down before his dad finds out. I'm successful at keeping Arun out of trouble. But how do I get him to have half the motivation that his dad has?

RITA: I want to go back to discussing you, Zara. What motivates you?

ZARA: I know I sound like a broken record, but it's always been Arun. He used to be my driving force. But now he doesn't need me, I feel empty. I suppose waking him up in the morning gives me some sense of purpose – sad as that sounds! But I worry about what he's become. I expected so much more from him as a son – I want to be able say I'm proud of him after everything I've poured into him. You sounded so proud talking about your son at the party. I suppose that drove me to come to see you.

Apart from him, nothing else makes my life meaningful. I know I'm surrounded by luxuries, but I don't enjoy any of them. I used to shop 'til I practically dropped for Arun and me. Now, though, I don't bother as I'm always buying him the wrong brand or label. I'm not interested in buying new clothes for me because I hardly socialise now, unless it's at one of Jay's business parties. And those people aren't friends; they're acquaintances.

My close friends, the people I grew up with, used to motivate me. We used to talk about what we'd become and do and see when we were older. But to be honest, I've seen all the places I used to dream of. Now I just wish I saw my friends more, but they live miles away. I haven't seen any of them in a long time. I miss them. But everyone's so busy with their own lives.

RITA: Where do your thoughts usually wander, Zara? To the past, the present or the future?

ZARA: Doesn't the past always look rosier as you get older? I had all kinds of hopes and dreams for Arun, and for my marriage. These days, I think a lot about what I could have done differently. Like I wonder what I did wrong with Arun. His dad says I smothered him.

When you spoke about your son's learning difficulties, I wanted to know how he managed to turn things around for himself. I'm convinced Arun's dyslexic; Jay says it's nonsense, but Arun struggled at school, and while everyone else's children came home with certificates for 'excellence in circle time', 'excellence in handwriting', 'excellence in times tables', I was getting phone calls about his disruptive behaviour and incomplete work. One of his teachers did suggest testing him for dyslexia and dyspraxia, but his dad wouldn't allow it. He said I was being over-protective and there was nothing wrong with his son, that he just needed to pull his socks up. But I didn't want him to fail at school, so I used to sit up late helping him do his homework, well into secondary school. I enjoyed it actually. It made me wish I'd paid more attention at school.

Arun didn't want to go to university – although he didn't tell his dad that – then, somehow, he scraped high enough grades to get a place at uni. I think he only accepted the offer because he was so shocked. But at uni, he wouldn't admit that he was struggling with the course work – and this time I couldn't do the essays for him. So he dropped out at the end of his first year before they made him leave.

RITA: Tell me about your family life and you and Jay as parents.

ZARA: Jay says I focus my whole life on Arun. I think he's jealous that Arun always comes first with me. Jay spoils him in his own way – with gifts and money.

RITA: Tell me what happens when Arun isn't successful at something. How do you react?

ZARA: When he was little, Arun often came home crying that he wasn't as clever as the other kids in his class. He'd say he wasn't as good a writer or speller as his friends, or any good at maths, and that the teacher never picked him to read out his work. And it broke my heart to hear the disappointment in his voice. I vowed then that I would never let him feel a failure again. We got him tutors and I sat down with him for hours, helping him with school projects and with his reading and writing, until he left secondary school. When we got married, we promised ourselves that we'd give our family everything we'd lacked. So the whole point of our existence – of Jay's hard work, our money – is to give our son a life free from hardship. Isn't that what you're meant to do? Even if you're poor? Isn't it the law of nature for kids to do better than their parents?

RITA: I want you think about the word 'better'. In what way is Arun's life *better* than yours was?

ZARA: He lives far more comfortably. He's always dressed well, has all the latest accessories. He can be proud of his home. He's travelled and seen the world. He's had experiences that Jay and I never dreamed of.

RITA: You said you remembered how it felt 'not to have'?

ZARA: Yes – it didn't feel good, and I don't want the same kind of life for my child. Is that so bad? It sounds like you're saying that if we had let Arun suffer, like we had in our childhood, he wouldn't be suffering like he is now. But surely, he would be suffering, because we'd be depriving him?

RITA: No one wants to watch their child suffer. But there are degrees of suffering and deprivation. Is it possible for you to see that 'not having' motivated you to make things happen for yourself and not to rely on others doing everything for you later in life? If you had let Arun fail in his homework, for example, what's the worst he could have suffered?

ZARA: I guess he would have suffered a few bad grades. But he would also have felt awful about them, and so would we. It felt like failure when his teacher suggested the dyslexia text.

RITA: What other outcomes could have arisen from letting Arun do the dyslexia test, or even fail a little in his school work?

ZARA: If they'd found him dyslexic, I suppose they might have supported him better. If more teachers had seen Arun struggle to complete his homework, maybe alarm bells would have rung and they might have given him more help. I just never wanted him to feel stupid, so I covered up his weaknesses for him. But he can't seem to help himself now.

ZARA: When I first met you at the party, you told me about your son's learning difficulties. How did you help him to help himself?

RITA: Before I could genuinely help my son, I had to become more self-aware; I had to address some of my own strengths and weaknesses. To do that, I had to reflect – just as you are doing – on myself without bias through DISC psychometric testing.

Self-awareness is the first and most important step on the road to self-development. In the workplace, for instance, research has shown that high-performing managers have higher self-awareness than low-performing managers. According to Church (1997), high-performing managers were able to assess their own behaviour more accurately than low-performing managers. Self-awareness allows us to see our own limitations and blind spots, and to make choices based on our capabilities. Gandhi famously said, "Be the change you want to see in the world." If you want to make a transformation in your life, you have to look within yourself before you can enact any change in your external world.

Becoming self-aware helped me face the fact that, frankly, I should not mollycoddle my son, that this would not help him at all. But I also acknowledged my strength as a teacher and as an individual who enjoys inspiring and helping others grow and develop, with a proven record of helping struggling students. Once I recognised both these sides to myself, I came up with a model that I called 'Paint the road to success'. This is a great way of illustrating the first stage in the SAVVI framework: self-awareness.

In this model, the destination at the end of the road is success. To get there, we need to learn to use all of our strengths to the maximum. Sometimes our strengths can lie dormant, and we need to be reminded what they are; sometimes our weaknesses can hold us back. The key is to develop a conscious awareness of both our strengths and our weaknesses, so that we can exploit our strengths and overcome our weaknesses – and, by doing so, reach our destination.

Weaknesses can come in many different guises. Paralympians are a prime example of a group of people who have typically had to overcome significant physical weaknesses. There are a number of double amputees, for instance, who can run twice as fast as many able-bodied individuals. Just as a blind person makes use of other heightened senses, such as hearing and touch, a Paralympian double amputee does not let their weakness hold them back. They learn to overcome it by exploiting their strengths – in the case of a double amputee runner, they strengthen other parts of their body to compensate.

This is precisely what I taught my son Reece to do. To overcome his numeracy and literacy challenges, we exploited his strength of being a good visual learner by using mind maps to help him retain large amounts of factual information, as well as his passion for and talent in IT through making use of speak and write software and touch typing.

When it came to painting my own road to success, I knew that I had to exploit my strengths – in this case, as a teacher – to overcome my weakness as an anxious over-protector who enjoyed being in control. That was the best I could do for my son; he did the rest.

So, I want to start by holding up the mirror to you, Zara, to see who you are. Describe a typical day for *you*.

ZARA: Well, since Arun's back living with us, it's a bit like the old days. I like to do his washing and give him lifts, even though he has his own car. When he was little, I didn't actually mind all the driving and the school runs; it meant that we could enjoy more time together. I used to love our conversations and little jokes in the car. But as he got older, he usually had his earphones in. And now he's always on his phone.

RITA: How much of your day is left for you to spend on just yourself?

ZARA: Well, I go to the gym for two hours every day. Jay likes me to look after myself. I wish he'd do the same – he's putting on weight – but he complains he doesn't have time. I have a weekly manicure; I watch TV in the evenings, mostly on my own. I probably spend too much time on Facebook, looking at other people's happy photographs with their happy kids. I used to like reading for Arun's school work. I remember loving *Jane Eyre*; he hated it.

I used to love cooking, but Jay eats out with clients most nights now and Arun eats standing at the fridge when he gets in late, after seeing friends. When we have parties for Jay's business guests, we get caterers in. He doesn't want them thinking his wife's done all the cooking because we can't afford to hire caterers.

I guess I'm what they call a lady of leisure, but it's not what I expected it to be like. I can't complain. My mum worked her fingers to the bone, and complained about it all the time! I don't have to lift a finger. So running around after Arun – doing his breakfast, his laundry, making sure there's food in for him, chauffeuring him whenever he wants – keeps me busy.

RITA: What happens when you say no to Arun?

ZARA: I don't think I've ever done that. Not since he was a toddler and I told him not to run out into the road. When he asks me for something now, it makes me feel like he still needs me, so I can't say no. I like doing things for him.

RITA: Even though you say you do nothing it sounds as if you're the doer in your relationship with Arun.

ZARA: But Arun seems so dissatisfied right now. I find it hard to deprive him of what he wants if it will put a smile on his face. Growing up, I knew I wanted to be a different parent to my parents. They were too busy working and trying to make ends meet to have time for me. I understand that they didn't have a choice, but I always knew I wanted to be available for my family.

RITA: Parents at both ends of the economic scale can end up neglecting their children when they're working too hard and are absent from them.

ZARA: To be honest, I don't think we've ever actually taught Arun the value of hard-earned money – apart from telling him that we didn't have most of the things he takes for granted. I suppose it seemed obvious to us. We thought seeing his father work hard and long hours would be enough. Also, we didn't want to bore him, reminding him about the cost of everything – which is exactly what our parents did.

When my parents waved bills in our faces, telling us how hard life was, I genuinely believed that money was a magic wand that would make everything better. But now I'm confused. I'm questioning what I've done in the belief that I was making life happier and easier for Arun. It sounds like you're saying that, despite everything we've done for him, wealthier parents are doomed to be worse parents.

RITA: You're not a worse parent – but the challenges of parenting increase with more wealth. Malcolm Gladwell has a theory about 'advantage' and 'disadvantage' as twin ideas. Viewed like this, 'disadvantages' or problems – when faced and overcome – can become advantageous. So, an obstacle (like a learning difficulty or a tendency to over-protect, or to be anxious) when faced and understood, can be conquered to one's advantage. For example, high numbers of successful businessmen are dyslexic.

Whilst wealth can be a great advantage, opening all kinds of doors, it can also turn into a disadvantage that kills ambition and self-esteem. So many wealthy children, with seemingly everything at their fingertips, can seem lost and inexplicably unhappy.

ZARA: Yes, that's how I'd describe Arun. And to be honest, I can identify with it too. I thought I was unhappy because of Arun's problems, but I can't blame him for the way I feel. I realise it's not just about him. I've also got everything, so why do I feel so empty? Is this how Arun feels?

RITA: You've told me that he is vague and lost; workshy and without motivation. I can't coach him about overcoming whatever is holding him back unless I speak to him directly, but I can advise how you, as his parent, might respond to him in this state. I can also help you, as an individual, paint your road to success, so that you can exploit your strengths to overcome your weaknesses and become happier in who you are.

 ZARA: I've never felt like an 'individual'. I belonged to my parents, and then to Jay, and then to Arun. And for a long time, being a wife and mother was all I needed to be happy. I don't know when it stopped being enough. Maybe it's because that's all they see me as – a wife and mother. They imagine I just sit around waiting for them to click their fingers – which sums it up, really. I can't remember the last time either of them took time out of their day just for me. Jay buys me things for my birthday, but we don't do things any more to celebrate it.

I can see why you asked me how I spend my days. None of it's for me. I do the gym to look good as Jay Sharma's wife. I know I should do something for myself – maybe Arun and his dad would be more respectful, kinder to me, if they saw I could be someone else besides a wife and mother – but I've got no idea what I'd do. I've got no hobbies; I can't play any sport. I'm not skilled at being anything but Mrs Sharma, and I'm even finding that tough right now.

RITA: Sometimes when we're feeling stuck, in order to move forward it can be helpful to reflect on the beliefs that have carried us up to this point. It's useful to examine whether they can propel us forward, or whether we need to let go of some beliefs that are holding us back. Can you tell me how your beliefs and attitudes have changed over the last decade?

ZARA: 10 years ago, I thought that my bond with my son was unbreakable. I considered myself to be a good mother and wife.

Jay's money has meant that we've been all over the world, but I haven't felt close to anyone in my immediate world for years. 10 years ago, I had some close girlfriends, but I hardly see them now. They still live in my home town, miles away.

I was intrigued that Zara rarely mentioned her husband outside of the context of being a co-parent – one who was mainly absent from Arun's childhood, and from her life now, apart from when they appeared together at parties. I began to wonder about the kind of marriage they had.

ZARA: It's funny that we can afford to go anywhere, do anything, but there doesn't seem to be a place that feels right for anyone. I get to see all these beautiful places, I put up our holiday photos on Facebook, but I don't feel connected to where I've been, what I was doing there, or who I was doing it with. Money answered so many of our problems in the early days. It was fun to have – but not anymore.

This pattern of behaviour is common among many parents. All parents have commendable and individual reasons for providing a comfortable – even privileged – life for their children, but intervening too much to protect one's children from pain, an emotional fall or failure is often described as 'helicopter parenting'. I have seen it in the lives of many of my private clients and throughout my teaching career. Many parents believe that a better life for their children means releasing them from any kind of hardship and shielding them from any kind of disappointment

As the education reformer John Dewey summed up wisely, "We only think when confronted with a problem." If Arun had been allowed to face his literacy problems, in time – with the right support – he could have learnt strategies to deal with his difficulties. Zara was beginning to see the consequence of her helicopter parenting and the ways in which it had prevented Arun from thinking through problems for himself.

This is why I asked Zara to consider what was better about Arun's life. For children's lives to be better, parents must ensure that they are helping them to acquire priceless life skills alongside all the latest accessories that money can buy. Preparation for life can begin in small ways, like allowing a child to make their own journey to school from a certain age – just as we had to do in our youth.

I shared with Zara, Malcolm Gladwell's findings in his book David and Goliath, when he urges parents to swap, "No we can't" to, "No we won't". And even when you are in the position of being able to afford something or do something for your child but choose not to, you do still need to explain to them why you won't give them what they want. This requires a conversation with them – so you can't just say, "No, I won't" and walk away. A little deprivation like the occasional no can go a long way. But to do it meaningfully, you need to have in place certain family values around how you want to spend your time and wealth, which are shared with each of your family members. We will examine how to do this later.

Research shows that effective parents don't have to say no all the time. The danger lies in saying yes to everything. Thanks to his parents, Arun had it all. However, saying yes to everything on top of that had created an abundance of side effects. Whilst Zara and Jay had worked so hard to improve Arun's material life, ironically, they had turned wealth into their son's adversity. By never denying children, many parents have become, according to psychologist Dr Madeline Levine, "overly concerned with what our children do rather than who they are." As a result, privileged children like Arun can do as they please, at their parents' expense, but many – like Arun – aren't developing on the inside to become self-sufficient and resourceful. And why would he bother doing anything for himself when his parents have done everything for him his whole life – from writing his essays to getting him a job to getting him home from a party in the middle of the night?

Preventing your child from 'doing' for themselves eventually creates an emptiness inside them, caused by a lack of personal fulfilment. Zara and Jay had been so overly concerned about providing a 'better' life for their son that they had deprived him of learning who he was outside of his material status, and finding out what he could do for himself. In fact, wealth had become an obstacle to Arun's sense of fulfilment and his development of life skills, which are entwined with personal satisfaction.

It may sound outrageous to suggest that less money can make parenting easier, when a lack of money can cause severe anxieties. However, too little money and too much money both present problems when raising children. Furthermore, researchers have observed that in wealthier societies, after a certain threshold, the more money coming into a household the less effectively people parent. Even 'happiness' researchers have found that a family's income makes parenting easier only up to a certain level, which is about £40,000 per annum. After this point, wealth stops making much of a difference and then triggers the law of diminishing marginal returns.

Zara's statement about a shift in an old attitude, and an understanding of her disengagement, marked a pivotal point in her self-realisation. She could now start to map out a road to fulfilment. Awareness of one's strengths and weaknesses, is the bedrock of my practice with clients, and the key to unlocking the potential for a happier life. Self-awareness and careful thought about your behaviour, strengths and beliefs enables you to use your skills differently to become the best possible version of yourself and to reach success. Through self-examination, you can exploit your strengths to the fullest, whilst recognising your weaknesses and then overcoming them using your strengths. Reflection then helps you to develop your skills and review their effectiveness, rather than simply acting as you have always done. It is about questioning, in a positive way, what you do and why you do it, and then deciding whether there is a better or more efficient way of doing it in the future.

Zara's initial reflections on her responses to the intake questions marked the first steps of her growth in self-awareness. She appeared to recognise that her own – not just Arun's – lack of motivation was an obstacle to fulfilment in her current life. Once Zara could face her own obstacles, and the fact that they went beyond Arun's problems, she could begin to think about strategies for tackling her difficulties that exploited her existing strengths. To begin to do so, she would need see the twin side to her 'weaker' characteristics. For example, her over-protectiveness, seen positively, stemmed from her strong, nurturing personality. Once Zara (like me, on my own journey of self-awareness) had recognised the problems of over-protectiveness, she could transform this 'weakness' into her more positive nurturing trait, thus enabling her son to grow for himself so that he could fall over and pick himself up again. From my own parenting experience, I have learnt that nurturing does not mean wrapping a loved one up in cotton wool, or else they will be unprepared for the challenges of the wider world.

The journey to self-realisation is a continuum: the road doesn't reach an end once you have succeeded along one path; it should take another turn towards a new destination. In the words of philosopher and education reformer John Dewey, "Arriving at one goal is the starting point to another." Thus, we keep our motivation burning.

There's a Spanish proverb I like: "He who doesn't have it, does. He who has it, doesn't." Once Zara had had an opportunity to reflect on how her attitudes and motivations had shaped her as a parent, I wanted her to hear about the experience of a family much less privileged than hers, whose members had been driven by scarcity to overcome some unimaginable obstacles in order to achieve far-reaching success. I often share this family's story with my clients as an inspiring lesson for teaching the model of self-awareness.

Through the Eyes of Lord David Blunkett

'We are only as blind as we want to be.'
—Maya Angelou

RITA: I want to tell you a story about overcoming obstacles by using strengths to conquer weaknesses. You described holding your son for the first time as your happiest memory. I agree that that moment when the midwife delivers this tiny, helpless, screaming bundle into your arms is the most precious and daunting moment of a parent's life. Nothing, not all the baby books in the world, the scans nor other parents' advice, prepares you for the eruption of conflicting emotions – pride, joy, fear and the primitive desire to protect – the instant you lay eyes on your baby and hear it scream as it takes its first independent breaths. You know you're witnessing the start of an incredible adventure.

Remember the relief of hearing your baby cry for the first time, and the relief of knowing that he was healthy? Imagine that relief evaporating when, in the next breath, you are told that your baby is blind. This happened to a mother I find inspirational. Having carried her son in the safety of her body for nine months, she learnt that he was going to have to face the world – the less inclusive society of the 1940s – blind. It turned out that the optic nerve behind each of the baby's eyes had failed to develop properly due to a genetic incompatibility between his parents. The mother's hair is said to have turned white overnight after hearing the news. Yet somehow, over time, she and her family conquered this enormous obstacle – an obstacle that she always drummed into her son was a mere 'inconvenience' – and he grew up to state that his mother had been the driving force behind his determination and success.

The family came from a rough and tough background in the city of Sheffield, in Yorkshire. They didn't possess any of the economic resilience required in the face of such challenges. The mother had left school at 14, but she and her husband wanted to give their son access to opportunities that had been beyond their reach – a perennial and universal desire in every loving parent, regardless of their economic background. At that time, in their part of the country, the only way a blind child had access to braille, so that they could learn to read and write, was to go to a special boarding school for the blind. So, at the age of four, the boy was sent off to Manchester Road School for the Blind, where his parents were permitted to visit him on one Saturday a month – but not take him out. The child was only allowed home once a month. In accordance with conventional wisdom concerning character building at the time, once the children were installed in the school assembly hall, their parents were instructed to say goodbye and leave as promptly as possible!

These parents could have taken the easy route: kept their son at home and protected him from the harsh world. It was heart-breaking to send their four-year-old away and, for years, they were plagued with guilt about their decision. But they believed that education was a route out of poverty and the challenges of blindness. In later life, the boy would reflect on his days at the school as one of the worst experiences of his life, where he felt "totally abandoned and terrified", thrown into unfamiliar, unseen surroundings. Overnight, the boy had to learn to do things for himself that his parents had done for him at home, like "dressing and undressing, washing, keeping track of possessions". In the absence of his parents' love, the boy's only affection came from the house-mother, a 16-year- old, who tucked the boarders into bed at night with a goodnight kiss. It was also this girl's role to make sure that the children, when brushing their teeth and washing behind their ears, didn't fall into the open coal fire that warmed the bathroom. It was only through his friendships, sport and the radio that the boy managed to keep his spirits up and, in time, he learnt the laborious task of reading and writing on a wooden braille writing frame, which had been his parents' goal for him.

On his treasured visits home, the boy would enjoy walks with his father, who painted the landscape around them with words and made sure that his son's mind was kept agile by firing general knowledge questions at him. Most importantly, his father taught him not to regard blindness as a disability that stood in the way of achievement. He was urged to treat it as an inconvenience, and encouraged to focus on what he wanted out of life rather than on what he currently lacked – despite the fact that he was clearly going to have to work harder than many to overcome his physical 'weakness'.

Then, as if the odds weren't already stacked up against him, he was dealt two further blows. The first occurred when he was just nine years old: his mother was diagnosed with breast cancer, a disease that, in those days, had a desperately bad prognosis. Thankfully, despite the bleak outlook, she managed to survive.

The second blow was truly devastating. When the boy was 12, his father died in a work accident, falling into a giant vat of boiling water as the result of a co-worker's negligence. After a month in hospital, his father died of severe burns. Awarded only a woeful compensation, his mother was plunged into further poverty and was unable even to buy the headstone for her husband's burial.

Of course, this story is set in a simpler age, and the family's deprivation seems unimaginable to many of us today. But armed with the right set of timeless values and parental nurturing – along with a healthy dose of his own "sheer bloody mindedness" – he learned how to swim (calculating the safety of the sea by listening to the rhythm of the waves) and ride a bicycle and a horse. He attended night school for a total of six years, three of them after leaving the school for the blind and taking a business qualification on day release from work, while doing A-levels in the evening. He then went on to university and became the first in his family to graduate. Despite all the odds, he had used his skills to climb out of the poverty trap and overcome the perceived limitations of his blindness. Today, we understand much more about the challenges of disadvantages such as dyslexia on children's life chances, but can you imagine the difficulty of equipping your child in the face of blindness when, as a parent, you are poor and uneducated? This boy's parents confronted the problem of blindness – even when it was so painful to watch their son go off to boarding school – and taught him from an early age to focus his mind on the possibilities of his enquiring mind and determination. This formed one of the principle paths on his road to success.

After graduating, he worked for what was then the East Midlands Gas Board and, with his wages from his first job, was finally able to buy a headstone for his father's grave. He then took a postgraduate certificate in teaching (adults) and taught for seven years, before becoming Leader of Sheffield City Council prior to his election to Parliament in 1987. To this day, he continues to work towards social reform. The hero of this success story is Lord David Blunkett.

The former politician is, for me, a wonderful example of *SAVVI* achievement, and one that I refer to in many of my seminars and private sessions. He and his parents really did paint a road to success that was clearly signposted with parental awareness and Lord Blunkett's knowledge of his strengths and weaknesses, and he navigated himself through it. At boarding school, for example, he was reprimanded for being attention-seeking and making too much noise, but he turned these negative traits into strengths by debating and championing causes, such as healthier school meals at two of his schools, rehearsing for a future life in politics.

In his late teens, he was also aware that whilst his verbal skills were strong, he wasn't as effective in the written word. So at university he used the support of tutors to help him improve his essay structure, in order to become more fluent and persuasive.

As a young man, he recognised that he was socially awkward and prone to agoraphobia. But he forced himself to join a youth club to bring him out of his shell, and even learned to dance there despite his obvious setback. Later, in the world of work, his blindness meant that he was more vulnerable to public embarrassment in front of colleagues: once, in the town hall in Sheffield, he even walked into a broom cupboard, believing he was leaving the room through the exit. It was a lesson that made him rethink his decision not to have a guide dog, and he acquired the first of a series of guide dogs, all of whom became loyal companions helping to steer him around some of his daily obstacles.

What's more, Lord Blunkett has never allowed his limited vision to stop him communicating with people, which is clearly a vital part of his public role. Rather, he has learnt to listen to the subtleties in the way people breathe to understand them better; in addition, every letter he receives is recorded for him, and he then dictates his replies. Lord Blunkett knows himself and his physical challenges and has overcome them by applying existing strengths and learning new ones, in order to power through towards successful outcomes.

The headline to the Lord Blunkett story is that you really can achieve anything – even in the face of the greatest adversities – once you understand what is holding you back. Only then can you channel your strengths to overcome your obstacles.

In addition to the family's poverty, there were three major obstacles in Lord Blunkett's life: his blindness, his father's workplace accident and the end of his grandfather's life, neglected on a hospital ward. Blunkett took these three great adversities head on and turned them into his motivation to make a difference to himself and to British society. His experience of school drove him to make an impact on the education of deprived children; his father's accident incited him to ensure changes in health and safety legislation in the workplace, and his grandfather's tragic neglect inspired him to improve care for the elderly in the UK. Lord Blunkett used his adversity as a driver for change, with phenomenal results.

ZARA: That's such a humbling story. We have everything, while the Blunketts had nothing. And yet their son has been so successful. They suffered real adversity, whilst we've ended up raising Arun with a sense of entitlement and emptiness, because we didn't say no enough.

These are hard lessons to hear. I thought I was being a good mother by always being available, by not working and giving him whatever he wanted 24 hours a day, seven days a week. When Arun was younger, he really did seem appreciative of things and I was the best mummy ever for giving them to him. And I can't deny loving that smile on his face whenever I say yes.

But isn't it easier to say no when you have less or nothing? Surely that made it easier for the Blunketts and even my own parents to say no. That's what I heard all the time growing up. What about other parents like me? Parents who are wealthier. You said you've seen other clients with similar issues. Is it really possible to be wealthy and say no to your children?

RITA: I can't discuss my clients in any depth, but let me tell you more about the mother who said no to sleepovers for her daughters. Imagine trying to exclude your teenage girls, desperate to fit in as all teenagers are, from a significant aspect of their social life? Sleepovers were what all their friends were doing, and it must have been incredibly tough for her to say no. However, by establishing this rule and sticking to it, she knew that her children would be more able to focus on school work or other responsibilities the next day.

This person is not a client, but someone I interviewed as the case study of a successful businesswoman and mother who overcame the fact that she, like you, had not gone to university because she was expected to marry before she was 20 and quickly settle down with children. Like you, Sunita Arora is the wife of a very successful businessman, but she has emerged as a successful businesswoman in her own right, all whilst raising three children. She's an example of a mother who has raised happy and successful children whilst being a working mum.

Sunita and her husband, Surinder Arora, built their chain of 16 hotels, which they still call a family business, from a couple of guest houses located near airports. Neither Sunita nor her husband would say they had much of an education, so a good education became a priority for them when it came to their own children. Like you, Sunita didn't have to work once the business took off, and they moved from living off Southall Broadway into successively bigger houses, further out into the leafy suburbs. However, Sunita's drive and determination for her family also extended to herself and her journey towards self-fulfilment. So when her children were young, she did an Open University degree in Psychology, Health and Social Care; true to the successful SAVVI model, once she had achieved that goal, she created a new challenge for herself and grew a nursery business alongside the hotel business. Today, she owns three private nurseries and advises on the interior decoration of the family hotel business.

Despite their great fortune – as a result of which it is arguably more difficult to say, "No, we don't" – Sunita remains humble and has worked hard to ensure that her children stay grounded. She also ensured that she continued to thrive alongside her growing family. As she developed personally and professionally, she got involved in charity work because she likes to give back to people with less than she knows she is lucky to have. Sunita has planned two major charity events and raised £1.3 million for charities like Cancer Research, the Caron Keating Foundation, Macmillan Nurses, UNICEF and some other charities abroad.

Sunita is an alternative to the equally well-motivated stay-at-home mother. As Sunita's children grew up, she organised her work around them, but they and her husband acknowledged the fact that her professional time away from the family was valuable, and enjoyed seeing and hearing about her role in other spheres. Whilst there is inconclusive evidence on the impact of working mums versus stay-at-home mums on the wellbeing of children, if work does not necessitate excessive absence, working mothers are healthy models for their children, who see them as fulfilled and successful outside of the family. Sunita's children have grown up to be successful in their own careers. One of her daughters is a lawyer; the other is in management. Her son has an MBA and, having worked first for another company, is now part of the family hotel business.

Sunita states that, in her opinion, it's important for a husband like hers, who is driven and ambitious, to see his wife as goal-oriented too, in all kinds of spheres. This, she argues, commands greater respect from him. She explained to me, "What I've achieved makes my husband proud of me. And the by-product is that it does make me more attractive."

ZARA: "OK, I'm understanding that I should have reflected on myself more and developed myself in other ways. But I believed that I was correcting the fact that I'd missed out on a lot from my own mother. I suppose I reflected on my own past and came to the conclusion that I needed to be a full-time mother.

RITA: Of course, that's a very admirable aim, but do you think that somewhere along your journey to being the best mother you could be, you lost a sense of your purpose, and of who you are, particularly when Arun grew up?

ZARA: To be honest, as I said before, I don't think I've ever really had a strong sense of who I am separate to my family, and it never really bothered me before. But the emptiness I'm feeling now could be because, without my family and my old friends, I don't know who I am. You've told me about using one's strengths to overcome weaknesses. But I'm struggling to know who I am, and I don't know my strengths – only my weaknesses.

I can see that I have things in common with Sunita, but I don't have any of her strengths, like her confidence to go out and set up a business. I've left it too late to get any qualifications.

I just don't think I've ever had the same determination to be successful, like Blunkett or Sunita. Not for myself anyway.

RITA: You've possessed determination to facilitate your son's success and Jay's success. I saw first-hand your ability to make your husband shine. You've focused your energy on helping them to achieve. Now it's time to reflect on yourself and get to know yourself better so that you can overcome whatever's holding you back. Then you can paint your road to success. Let's take a look at the results of your DISC profiling.

What Is DISC?

Before coaching any new client, be it a business or an individual, I ask them to complete the DISC personality style profiling as a fast-track method to bring them closer to both self-awareness and an awareness of others in their personal and working life.

DISC is an easy-to-understand profiling tool that identifies your natural style, as well as how you adapt in relationships and in the workplace under stress. It was devised by the inventor of the lie detector test, psychologist William Marston, so there is scientific methodology behind the approach. The outcomes of the questionnaire reveal key personality traits; for example, some require harmony, others need to be in control; some need to be liked, others need rules. DISC analysis also uncovers the ways in which you approach your goals in life and identifies your strengths and weaknesses, your fears and motivators and your communication style.

In the words of the ancient Chinese philosopher, Lao Tzu:

> *Knowing others is intelligence;*
> *knowing yourself is true wisdom.*
> *Mastering others is strength;*
> *mastering yourself is true power.*

Getting to know who you, your family members and colleagues are through DISC profiling helps you understand different personality styles, and to check whether you are using your skills to their maximum potential and your strengths to support others to overcome their weaknesses.

Getting to know the other people in your life through their DISC personality style gives you strength in your relationships with them. Mastering the art of self-awareness through DISC gives you true power towards attaining your goals.

RITA: Zara, before analysing your specific DISC type, I'll share an overview of the four different types with you. DISC is made up of the dominant **D** type, the influencing **I**; the steady **S** and the compliant **C**. To simplify matters, I'll just be outlining the typical 'pure' traits of each type. It's important to remember that most people are more than one type. In reality, people are a combination of styles – usually two, but sometimes more – and there is usually a dominant style and a secondary style. For example, someone might be a **DS** – which means they are mainly dominant, but also steady. We all possess different degrees of the characteristic strengths and limitations of our specific DISC types. Importantly, no one type is better or worse than another.

DISC types can also be categorised into those who are active (in the outgoing, fast-paced sense – this is a typical DI), and those who are more passive (slower-paced, reflective thinkers – this is a typical SC). Additionally, you might be task-oriented (like a DC) or people-oriented (like an SI). Knowing your type, how you deliver and what motivates you are all key to becoming SAVVI.

Understanding all the DISC types helps you to see that different life situations can require us to adopt aspects of another personality type. There will be times in life when we need to adapt, and this is what successful, SAVVI people learn to do. They know what they are, and they know that some areas of life may be more difficult for them than others; that they will need to adapt to achieve the best results. When you decide on an immediate or longer-term goal, combining your strengths (in varied shades and nuances) will paint your road towards achieving any goal.

Let's start with the first of the DISC types (see the DISC profile chart above): D. A typical D is dominant. This individual likes to take the lead, is very driven and demanding, is goals-orientated and determined. This type looks for a challenge; they like change and get bored without it. D managers have high self-confidence, are risk takers and problem solvers. Their motivator is power and control. As they work hard and drive themselves, their key 'stressors' (triggers that cause stress) are feeling that they're being taken advantage of, and a fear of loss of control and failure. **D**s are active and outgoing. **D**s' area for development is that they are opinionated and blunt.

ZARA: Jay sounds like a **D** type to me. If he likes the look of something – anything, a beautiful car, a set of golf clubs he'll never use, new technology – he'll just buy it. And of course, he's dominant and likes to speak his mind – at any opportunity! He's been promising to cut back on his working hours for years, but I know he enjoys the control he gets at work. It's interesting that you say he's motivated by a challenge. I know he's like that at work.

RITA: Precisely. You're already seeing Jay's strength and how he uses it to overcome a problem. Also, be aware that Jay's **D** type stressor is a lack of control, wasting time and being taken advantage of.

ZARA: Yes, he's started to feel that way about Arun not showing up for work; he can't bear for people to think he has no control over his son, or that he's being taken advantage of.

RITA: Remember that people are usually more than one personality type. So, whilst **D** may be Jay's dominant style, he's likely to have an element of another style too.

Let's now turn to the **I** type. They are instinctive communicators who inspire and influence others. They are innovators, motivated by recognition. **I**s are outgoing, so they think quickly and are people-centred, and need a friendly, fun and flexible work environment. Their stress trigger is rejection and not being recognised for their contribution. Growth areas for them to work on include being less impulsive, talking less and listening more. They also need to concentrate more on following through on their actions.

ZARA: I'd say that Arun is a natural influencer and communicator. He may have trouble reading and writing, but he's always been a natural at talking to people and winning them over. He's quite the charmer, which is why I can never say no to him. Even though he can be monosyllabic with us at home – unless he wants something – I've heard him get very passionate arguing with his friends. And he loved playing for the cricket team and the football team when he was younger, winning trophies and medals – they still have pride of place in his bedroom. I wish we saw more of his old passion these days. What I do see is one of the **I** weaknesses, around planning and following through – that's why I had to help him at school. Maybe that's why he struggled so much at university: because he didn't have my help.

RITA: The knowledge that his passion and ability to be a team player are part of his personality type means that these elements can be drawn out using his other traits. It's useful for you and Jay to know they're there to tap into. The weaknesses of the **I** type is that they can make spontaneous decisions and lack follow-through; they don't listen fully and are very fast paced. Their stressors are social rejection, being excluded from activities, negativity, deadlines and disapproval.

ZARA: Ah, yes. He can't bear missing out on a party; sometimes he'll pack two or three into one night. He wouldn't open up about his reading difficulties at uni because he was so worried about what his friends would say. And we always call him Mr Last Minute.com. I'm starting to see the link between Arun's type and why he behaves the way he does. I want him to understand his traits as well.

RITA: Before you can help him, we need identify where you fit into the DISC profile, so that we can see how your type influences your behaviour and interactions with others.

ZARA: I don't recognise myself in the either the **D** or the **I** type. I must be an **S** or a **C**, then?

RITA: Even if you don't see yourself in them, it's important to observe the strengths in opposite types that you could learn to adopt if the need arose.

ZARA: It's funny that one of Arun's strengths is that he can create a caring environment. I suppose he is supportive of his friends. He likes to make sure they're properly looked after when they visit. I'm proud that he's a caring friend.

RITA: From your responses, you're both an **S** and a **C**, with **S** being your dominant style. Remember, there is no better or worse type or combination. I'll go through your **S** side first. **S** stands for *Steady;* an **S** is also supportive and sensitive, with a desire to maintain the status quo, peace and harmony. Pure **S** types are people-centred, enjoy being a team player, and are *Passive* in that they are reflective thinkers, needing more time to process. Stress triggers for a pure **S** are change and the loss of security. Areas of growth are to be less accommodating, be able to deal with confrontation and to increasing their pace.

As an **S**, you're motivated by making others feel comfortable, team work and building relationships, so long as you're given time to process information. What do you think? Do you recognise yourself as an **S**?

ZARA: I am supportive, and I do like peace and harmony. And I can't bear for others not to feel comfortable – even at my own expense. I think that's why I don't like to ask for things. I'd rather not ask in case it embarrasses them to say no. I am a team player, which is why I miss having a role working with others – to organise our parties, for example. I just make the phone calls to the caterers and the florists. I feel in the way when they arrive. I used to enjoy being one of the school mums – I was on the PTA. But I don't belong to any type of team any more.

RITA: To feel fulfilled we need to be utilising our strengths, or we risk levels of dissatisfaction.

ZARA: I'd forgotten how much being in a team made me happy and gave me a sense of purpose.

RITA: This might be an area for you to work on. Some areas of weakness for **S** types include needing assured security, being indecisive, being too reflective about completing tasks, and having difficulty multi-tasking. Stressors for them are change, confrontation and pressure. Being aware, now, that you possess these traits as am **S**, can you think of ways in which they could have impacted on your life?

ZARA: Yes. I hate change and I can't deal with confrontation. I've found it hard watching Arun grow distant from me – that's a big change after we used to be so close. I avoid any kind of confrontation with him, or his dad, and then I suppose I disconnect from them and from what I'm trying to do. I do feel a bit let down by some of my old friends, to be honest, but I couldn't tell them that. I don't want to embarrass them, and I don't want to argue with them. So it's been easier – but painful too – to let those friendships fall by the wayside.

RITA: Let's look at your strengths as a **C** type. Pure **C**s are compliant, will follow rules set by others and will strive to do the right thing. **C**s are strong organisers with well-defined plans. They are task-focused, motivated by a steady environment and clear processes and plans. Stress triggers for pure **C**s are not having enough information or a clear direction, multi-tasking and criticism without justification. Personal growth areas include being less self-critical and critical of others, being decisive and concentrating less on facts and more on people.

ZARA: Really? I have well-defined plans? I don't recognise that part of me.

RITA: From what you've told me, you decided as a child on the type of parent you aimed to be. Your plan was to create a more comfortable life for your child. You have achieved that. Now, with the benefit of self-awareness, it's time to define a new set of goals to motivate you.

ZARA: But that's been my problem. I don't feel driven by any goals.

RITA: As a **C**, you tend to work at a steady pace, you can be overly cautious, and you can fixate on faults and rather than solutions. It's crucial to look at the **C** type's motivators to get you back on track. The **C** type thrives in a steady environment with clear processes and plans, and brings quality to what they do.

ZARA: If my **S** personality style is telling me I'm motivated by being part of a team, maybe that's why I feel so aimless. I enjoyed it when Jay and I worked together, starting up the business. I was doing the accounting books and, you're right, I found it quite satisfying chasing up invoices and settling accounts. I know that that was when we were just a small business, but Jay knew I was good at it. I think he's forgotten what I can do. Actually, even I had forgotten what I'm capable of.

RITA: There will be certain points in your life – like now – when you find yourself stuck and unable to prioritise to move forward. This is why knowing who you are through your personality type – your strengths, weaknesses and motivators – will help you deliver to your strengths and overcome your limitations. Understanding what makes you tick – working as part of a team, or supporting and nurturing, for example – will help you lay down some new goals.

ZARA: I'm trying to support Arun, but I'm not feeling fulfilled by it.

RITA: As an **S**, you're motivated by working as a team supporting others around you.

ZARA: But right now, I feel like I'm supporting Arun when he doesn't need it, and I don't feel as if I'm working in a team with Jay in our marriage.

When you told me David Blunkett's story, I did admire the way his parents worked as a team to support him. Even when they had so few resources, they were effective together as a team. Jay and I have been effective together as a team in the business in the past, and working together at it again might give us both the strength to say no to Arun.

I know I don't have any formal qualifications, but Jay once thought I was valuable in the office. He trusted me above everyone else. I want him to see me as a collaborator again. I know that working together on Arun isn't work, but it'd be a start.

I want them both to see my strengths again – I'd forgotten them myself until you reminded me. We have so much more than people like Lord Blunkett's family. I'm going to find a charity, maybe for the blind, that I can help. We know lots of wealthy people, so perhaps one day I could persuade Jay to let me organise a party to raise money for a charity. Maybe then he would see me achieve more than still getting into a size 10 party dress.

I wouldn't dare to dream as big as Sunita, but I do know I have a good eye for quality. I can already imagine the party. If I make it fun and sociable, I can get Arun involved. My first goal, though, would be to identify the charity.

RITA: Zara, I see you creating a new energy around herself. Already I'm seeing the difference in your drive. How does it make you feel?

ZARA: I feel as if I'm waking up after a long sleep. I'm ready to start moving again. Moving forward. Seeing who I am and remembering who I was makes me want to reconnect with my old school friends. I think seeing friends who've known me all my life will help me move forward. Maybe there was some part of me that didn't want them to see who I'd become – even though my life looks so perfect on the outside. They would've known I wasn't happy inside, even when I didn't.

One of the most powerful aspects of my coaching practice is working on this self-awareness principle. Once clients recognise their characteristic strengths and limitations, and can see them plainly in black and white, then can also see the person they want to become. Clients often describe this moment of sudden realisation of their own and others' personality styles as an 'out-of-body experience'. Once Zara could see for herself her strengths alongside her weaknesses, and understand the different personality styles, she was embarking on her journey towards becoming SAVVI.

At certain points in your life, you may need to shake up your natural styles and, for example, become more of a dominant **D** to get things done, or learn to be a bit of an **I**, who naturally inspires. But this requires self-knowledge and the knowledge of those you want to influence or work with. Gaining a deeper understanding of the motivations and behaviours of different DISC types can significantly improve communication in teams and in personal relationships with partners, children and wider family members. In teamwork and collaboration, it is proven that different and complimentary personality styles can generate better outcomes.

RITA: Moving forward, I want you to think about some outcomes and resolutions that you're going to take away from our first session. Part of the SAVVI process is that you commit to taking actions. What will your actions be?

ZARA: I can see that I need to learn to say no to Arun, and that if he fails as a result, he'll learn from his mistakes. I'll tell him what I learned from you today, and perhaps he'll be inspired to come and see you himself.

RITA: What are you going to say no to him about?

ZARA: I'm going to say that I won't be chauffeuring him around anymore. I'll also sit down with Jay and introduce the idea that Arun gets a monthly salary as opposed to just having free reign of the credit cards.

Also, now that I've started thinking about my old friends, I want to get on the phone to them and arrange to visit them as soon as possible. I'll use my love of organising to arrange a get-together. I could book a house for the weekend to treat them all.

Then, like I said, I really want to look into some charity work. I've been really inspired and humbled by Lord Blunkett and Sunita's stories. I'll shortlist two charities that I want to work with, and then perhaps one day I'll be able to convince Jay to let me organise a party.

I saw your daily quote on Instagram this morning: *'The best way to predict your future is to create it.'* I feel like I've begun the journey towards doing that.

Zara had come to see me in the belief that her happiness sprung from her son's happiness. By the end of our first session, she had started to understand that she needed to turn this idea on its head. Once she held up a mirror to herself and began to get a better sense of who she was – of her strengths and the things that motivated her so that she could overcome her weaknesses – she was on the road to adapting herself, when necessary, to see positive changes in events and people around her. She had developed increased self-awareness – the first step in becoming SAVVI.

2

Achiever's Mindset

The Story of the Entitled Son

A couple of weeks after Zara's first session, she contacted me to give feedback on how she was progressing with her action plan. On the telephone, her tone sounded more upbeat. She was keen to tell me about an old friend with whom she had reconnected through Facebook, and then visited back in her home town. The trip had turned into a reunion with some other friends Zara hadn't seen in years. She reflected that it had been the first time in her married life that she had gone away on her own. The physical distance from her daily life had helped her to reconnect with aspects of her former, younger self, and remember some of her former personal ambitions.

Zara went on to describe that when she returned home, she noticed a difference in Jay and Arun – they had both been more attentive. Arun had driven to the station to pick her up, and they had laughed about the role reversal. She could get used to being chauffeured, she had told him. Arun even joked that he'd discovered the whereabouts of the dry cleaners and that after a week of takeaway meals, he was really missing her home cooking. Zara had enjoyed observing her son realise that his mother wasn't just his cook, chauffeur and cleaner.

Zara went on to explain that her husband Jay was also different after her trip. For the first time in years, he had remembered their wedding anniversary and booked a table for them at a local restaurant, and Arun had asked to join them. After Jay's initial interest in his wife, however, he was soon habitually checking his phone at the table. So, she had talked to Arun about seeing her old friends, what they were doing and how it had reminded her of what she had missed out on. She had described how she had come home energised and brimming with ideas about what she wanted to do with her spare time. On the phone to me, she recalled the moment that she had raised the idea of finding a charity to support; Jay had finally put his phone away, and had given her a perplexed look. Before she had even had a chance to explain what she had in mind, she could tell that Jay was already mentally dismissing it, which had knocked her confidence. She explained to me that this was a regular pattern in her interactions with Jay – but that for the first time, she was starting to become aware of the extent to which he was impacting on her self-belief.

The next day, Zara did her own research into some charities that she was interested in, and asked for Arun's advice about using the internet and social media to decide who to support and how to do it. In the past, she had berated her son's screen time wasted on chatting and socialising, but she tried to see it more positively – after all, he had a few thousand followers on Instagram.

Zara told me that Arun had been surprised by the change in her, and told her he was proud of his mum and her new-found energy and enthusiasm. Her son's affirmation gave her a confidence boost, and she admitted to him that she was consulting a coach who had given her a new sense of purpose. She didn't know whether Arun was just being polite, but he had wanted to know more about the coaching. Zara was delighted to hear his interest in self-development and was on the verge of making an appointment for him, but she stopped herself. Instead, she handed him a contact number to arrange it for himself. When Zara reported back to me, she was proud that she had exercised another new skill: helping her son to help himself.

In fact, it didn't take long for Arun to contact me. "I've seen the difference you've made to my mum," Arun began, in a warm, friendly tone. "She's happier. She's got a spring in her step and she's more adventurous. I've never seen her like this. My dad and I are both intrigued. She keeps talking about how she's becoming 'SAVVI' and mentioned a personality test that turned things around for her. I'm interested in finding out more."

So we arranged a session and, in advance, as I do for all new clients, I sent Arun the DISC profile to complete so that we could identify his characteristic strengths and weaknesses. Zara had guessed that her son was an **I** type: an influencer and natural communicator, who was motivated by recognition and a sociable environment even at work. From our initial phone conversation, Arun sounded open and talkative, so I too believed that he was likely to be an **I**. Also, in my experience, it is often **I**s who are most inquisitive about their profile type.

When we met face-to-face for our first session, Arun insisted, "To be honest, my mum seemed so pleased when I asked about you that I had to follow through. My main issue is that my parents keep going on about my so-called problems. But my dad is the type who will never be satisfied, and my mum's always worrying – even when there's nothing to worry about. After seeing you, at least she's busy researching her charity project and it was nice to be asked to help out for a change. Unlike at work, where nothing I do feels useful to my dad."

I was beginning to detect some of the traits of Arun's character that Zara had described to me. Our conversation continued.

ARUN: As far as I'm concerned, I'm still young and meant to be enjoying life – when I'm not chained to a desk at my dad's business. I know my parents have given me all kinds of options, a life they never had when they were my age, but now they expect me to be like my dad. I'm fed up of listening to the same old rags-to-riches story about how my dad became a millionaire despite coming from nothing.

RITA: As you are here, let me explain why I like to DISC profile people. Then we can go through your personality results. Knowledge of whether you're a **D, I, S**, or **C**, or a combination of them, furthers your self-awareness and helps you become what I term 'SAVVI'.

I recapped the strengths and challenges of the different DISC types:

D

Strengths: leader, forceful, direct, dominant

Challenges: impatient, poor listener, insensitive

I

Strengths: influencer, sociable, friendly, talkative

Challenges: gets bored, lack of detail, short attention span

S

Strengths: steady, patient, loyal, considers others' needs

Challenges: over-sensitive, dislikes change, working at a fast pace

C

Strengths: precise, sensitive, analytical

Challenges: perfectionist, critical, unresponsive

After going through the DISC personality types with Arun, I asked him if he recognised any of the traits in people he knew.

ARUN: Well, I'd guess my dad is a **D** type. He has that drive and he's demanding of himself and the people around him. His challenge is that he's a poor listener and overlooks others' feelings. I don't know how my mum puts up with him.

I'm sure Mum is an **S** – she's loyal, and she always puts other people's feelings ahead of her own. That's why it's been so refreshing to see her put herself first for a change. While she was away, I could see that Dad hated not having control over her for the first time. Mum also hates conflict, so she'll always make sure that Dad and I make up after one of our disagreements. We're both headstrong and neither of us wants to back down. But Mum's the peacemaker, and we've got used to her resolving things for us. I think that's why we were so relieved when she came home after her trip.

Arun's own profiling revealed that he was in fact an ID type. As an I, he enjoyed being around people, but found it challenging to be left alone in a work situation without any social interaction. As a D, he was also a natural leader, dominant and fearless. Interestingly, these were not traits that his mother had recognised in her verbal assessment of him.

RITA: Arun, what personality type do you think you are?

ARUN: I like being around people. In fact, I'm useless on my own. I bounce off other people. Am I an **I**? Friends and my social life kept me going for the short time I was at university. Even now, my friends come first with me. They all say I could sell anything, and I do enjoy influencing others. I'm sure I'm an **I**, an influencer. When I was at school, if I started wearing a brand, everyone else would follow – silly things like that. These days, I know I always get my way when my friends and I are deciding where to go out. And I can always persuade my dad to buy me the latest gadget because, secretly, I think he enjoys them as much as me. Getting a date with a girl comes easily too. I'd say I'm an **I** type.

RITA: Yes, you've identified your type based on some of your strengths. Can you also identify with the challenges of the **I**?

ARUN: Yes, I do get bored and lose interest easily. I found studying difficult because I was bored by it, especially if the style of teaching wasn't dynamic and interactive. On top of that, I'm dyslexic, so I was doomed as a student. I'm not good at writing, even though my dad insists on sitting me down at a desk, on my own, writing company reports for him. Seeing my profile, no wonder I'm so unhappy working for him. You're right: as an **I**, I do need to be interacting with people or I'm bored and unmotivated. But I can't be the high-flying achiever that my dad wants me to be. I'd love to be just like all his friends' successful kids, but I can't.

RITA: Before coaching I was a school teacher, and I often heard the 'I Can't' mindset amongst certain students who believed that intelligence was fixed for life. But with **I** type students, for example, I found that their skills actually grew when they worked with a study partner or in small groups in an interactive way. Changing one's environment can turn 'I can't' into 'I can'.

ARUN: Yes, I would have done better in that environment. I can't work in isolation for too long. It seems really clear to me now. Maybe if I'd worked alongside others, I wouldn't have dreaded studying. I might not have left uni. But I didn't tell any of my friends there that I was dyslexic, and I ended up trying and failing to work on my own. Even at school, it was a very traditional setup and the teachers were all talk and chalk – no one there engaged me. So I preferred subjects like Business Studies and Psychology because they were about people and business behaviour, real-life situations. That's where my interest lies: real and relevant things. Not facing a computer screen all day that can't talk back to me.

RITA: What does the knowledge that you're an **I** type tell you about yourself in your personal and working life?

ARUN: That I have to get out of my dad's office and interact with other members of staff.

RITA: Is have a tendency to be impulsive and don't like social rejection. Does this describe you?

ARUN: My mum says I need to slow down and think things through. I know I can be impulsive, and it sometimes gets me into trouble. You're right, I can't bear social rejection! I need to be liked by everyone, not just girls. If I'm not invited to a party, I take it badly.

RITA: Your profiling also reveals that you're a **D** type, which is how you identified your father. Do you see that?

ARUN: I hadn't seen that before… But maybe that's why we're always clashing. Possibly I just didn't *want* to see that I'm like my father. But my friends do always leave it to me to make plans, and I do prefer it when I'm in the driving seat, planning, organising parties and holidays. So, in that respect, I can see the **D** side of me.

RITA: As a **D** personality, you also have competitive leadership traits. How does this manifest in you?

ARUN: I don't think my parents would ever say I was leadership material. My dad controls everything. I feel like a spare part working for him. He makes all the decisions at work, and everyone knows it. Everyone knows I'm his son and that I've only got the job because of him. I just end up agreeing with him. I do what he wants me to do for a quiet life, and then I get to go out and play hard with my friends, who do see me as more of a leader.

I don't understand my dad's hunger for work. Honestly, the only thing I get competitive about is having the best cars and clothes, and getting into the right parties. That feels real, it's something I care about. I once drove three hours to get hold of the latest, limited edition D & G shirt. I wanted to be first person I knew to own it!

RITA: How do you fund your lifestyle?

ARUN: I'm not on a salary as such, but my monthly credit card bills for expenses like clothes and going out are all paid for me. There's enough family money to do that, and my parents enjoy hearing people compliment my clothes and whatever car I'm driving, so it's a two-way street. I enjoy my lifestyle and my parents enjoy giving it to me. What else are they going to do with the money?

In typical D fashion, Arun was very direct about his sense of entitlement to his expensive lifestyle – arguably even insensitive. A key strength of Ds is that they also possess direction in terms of setting and achieving goals.

RITA: What results and goals are you interested in achieving in your life?

ARUN: I'm not focused on achieving results and goals in my career. In fact, I've never been given a choice about what I do at work, so I haven't felt the desire or need to create a plan for myself. I just agree to my dad's goals for me – even when I hate them – but I keep focused on enjoying my social life. That's what I want to achieve the minute I leave work behind.

I used to want to make difference, but I feel my hands are tied. My dad controls everything. But I can see that my mum is changing since she's started seeing you. I wish I'd known earlier about my need to be in sociable working environment. It explains why I'm so unhappy cooped in an office behind a desk. It's given me a real understanding of my parents, especially my dad and why we clash. I can't believe that self-awareness of my personality style and my parents' can bring such clarity. It seems so easy.

RITA: This is just the beginning! Your increased self-awareness will help you adapt your style to achieve what you want in life. A 2010 study by Green Peak Partners and Cornell's School of Industrial and Labour Relations showed that a high level of self-awareness is the strongest predictor of overall success.

It's clear to me that you're sociable and have already achieved what you value in your personal life, which has had a positive impact on your friendship circle.

ARUN: So now I need to apply some of these strengths to my professional life. Will my profile always stay the same or can it change?

RITA: People's profiles can change over time, according to their environment and in times of stress. For example, sometimes you might need to flex more of a **C** trait in logical thinking to achieve your goals.

Developing an Achiever's Mindset

After the DISC analysis, I highlighted three main areas of development for Arun. Firstly, he did not take personal responsibility and was complacent in the face of obstacles. As a result, he had become self-entitled. Secondly, he suffered a lack of drive in his professional life and hadn't created a vision for his future because he had relied on others – chiefly his father – to do it for him. But the goals he had been assigned as a result, did not align with his own values, and therefore led to frustration at work. Finally, he needed to overcome his 'I can't' attitude, which had spilled over, from his academic life to his professional life.

As the famous quote by Theodore Roosevelt goes, *'Believe you can and you're half way there.'* Half of succeeding is believing that you can, and ensuring that your mind does not become one of your biggest obstacles.

By applying his increased self-awareness and reflectiveness, Arun would be able to use his strengths to give him a greater purpose, satisfaction and recognition, as well as a sense of achievement – all of which are motivators for his personality type.

The next step on one's journey towards any type of success – be it in business or personal relationships – is to develop an achiever's mindset. Neither Zara nor Arun had revealed this mindset because both had, in various ways, described themselves as failures. There is a great difference between saying, "I am a failure," and, "I have failed." The first statement links the failure to one's identity and treats it as fixed and unchangeable; the latter detaches failure from one's identity, so that it is a fixable outcome that can be changed in the future. When I am developing the **A** in SAVVI with my clients, I introduce the GRIPP model. Before you can possess the mindset of an achiever, you need to break down into smaller steps exactly what you are aiming for and how you are going to achieve it. GRIPP provides a step-by-step plan: begin by setting your **Goal**, be **Reflective**, employ an '**I Can**' attitude; recognize, as Albert Einstein said, that '***Perseverance** is priceless*', and develop thoughts that help you to **Progress**. All five steps – though in varying orders – are necessary in order to get what you want.

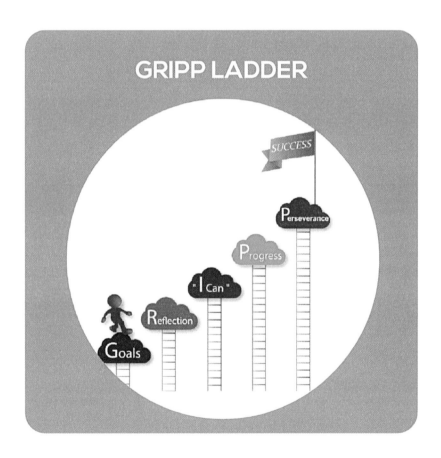

Goals: The G in the GRIPP Ladder

'If you want a happy life, tie it to a goal. Not to people or things'
—Albert Einstein

It is vital to set goals so that you have something to focus on. When you make them 'SMART' goals (which I will explain in detail shortly), they will keep you motivated and hold you accountable for following them through. Goals encourage you to think about what you are doing in your everyday life and consider whether your actions are helping you to get closer to them. Goals give you the confidence to understand in which direction you want to take your life and they force you to think about how your actions will help you get there. The ancient Chinese philosopher Lau Tzu said, *'A journey of a thousand miles begins with a single step.'* Likewise, the first step of acquiring an achiever's mindset is to set a goal – but they must be SMART goals, which are personal to you and are framed positively. For example, don't set yourself the goal, *I don't want to be poor.* Set yourself the SMART goal, *I will earn £50,000 over the next 12 months.*

So, what are SMART goals? SMART goals are:

Specific
- This one is fairly straightforward: be precise about your goal. Focus on a *specific* goal. For example:
- *D*on't just say: I want to lose weight.
- *D*o say: I will drop two dress sizes by my next birthday.
- *D*on't just say: I want my business to grow.
- *D*o say: I will increase my company's profits by 8% in the next financial year.

- *D*on't just say: I want to write a book.
- *D*o say: I will write a self-development book in 12 months.

Measurable

There is a famous saying, whose origins are widely debated (some argue that it goes back to Rheticus in the 1500s): 'What gets measured gets done.'

Your longer-term goals should be measurable in terms of clearly defined criteria, such as time (as shown in the above examples). However, you can motivate yourself with some shorter-term goals so that you have mini milestones to celebrate, whilst moving towards your longer-term goals. Creating short-term goals makes the bigger picture appear less daunting. Keep your overall number of goals relatively small, as studies show that people can't really focus on more than five to seven goals at one time.

Achievable

Your goals should be challenging and not too easy – yet they must be achievable. Of course, the definition of achievable varies from person to person. One individual's achievable goal may seem unrealistic to someone else. Importantly, the study Goal Setting and Task Performance, by Locke, Shaw, Saari and Latham (1969-1980), states that, 'Specific and challenging goals lead to higher performance than easy goals, "do your best" goals or no goals.' In other words, your goal must be challenging and demanding. In fact, business academics Locke and Latham in their Goal Setting Theory mark a strong correlation between difficult goals and high performance. They found that the performance of those who set themselves challenging goals was 250% greater than those people who hadn't really stretched themselves.

In the process of goal setting, assess any potential barriers you might have to overcome in order to achieve your challenging goal. It's important to make this assessment early on to help you realise it.

Relevant

Make sure your goals are relevant to what you're actually trying to achieve. Sometimes, we blindly pursue a particular goal in the belief that it will take us down the path of fulfilment. For example, one of my client's goals was to be married, so she remained in an unhappy marriage to fulfil that goal. Through coaching, however, she came to understand that her goal of being married was no longer relevant – that it was based on a goal dating back over 20 years, and was only relevant to other people's desires and expectations. Her old goal was making her deeply unhappy. In time, she recognised that it was more relevant for her to be in a happy marriage or relationship. So, after a year, she took the difficult step of leaving her marriage in the pursuit of her goal of being in a loving relationship.

Another client came to me expressing his goal to develop his hair salon business. He believed that he could achieve this by increasing his number of salons. However, after identifying his specific goal – to increase profits – he realised that to be more profitable, a more relevant goal for him would be to close down two of his underperforming salons.

Timely

You must have a timeframe for every single goal you set yourself. Make sure you set a 'to-do by' date, which includes the exact date and month by which you want to have achieved your goal. As American self-help author Napoleon Hill wrote, *'A goal is a dream with a deadline.'* Time limits and deadlines ensure that you're more likely to push yourself towards achieving your goals. Jim Carrey was a struggling actor in 1985 when he wrote out a cheque to himself for $10 million for 'acting services rendered', dated Thanksgiving 1995. By 2000, he had been signed for the blockbuster movie *Dumb and Dumber* and had actually doubled his $10 million goal.

Once you have identified your SMART goals, you need to commit them to paper – write them down – so that you are setting the ball rolling to actualising your intentions. People with written goals are 50% more likely to achieve to them. You should write your goals down somewhere that you will see them regularly. Take a photograph of them and keep them in your phone to remind yourself of them, and to enable you to easily check that you're still doing what you need to do to make them happen. Once you have a set of written goals, tell a few well-chosen people about them. Select the people who want the best for you. They make you accountable because, knowing that they know your goals, you'll feel obliged to make each one a reality, thereby giving you a sense of purpose.

At the start of every new year, my family and I use a holiday together to set aside dedicated time to write down our individual goals for the year ahead. Once we've written them down, we read them aloud for everyone to hear. In this way, each family member has to set themselves goals that are challenging, relevant and timely – or the rest of the family pushes them harder. Making one another aware of our respective challenges means that we are accountable to one another for achieving our goals, and that each member of the family supports each other to move forward.

Finally, once you have your SMART goals written down, follow Walt Disney's advice: *'Quit talking and start doing!'*

Reflection: The R in the GRIPP Ladder

'Ask yourself if what you're doing today is helping you get to where you want to be tomorrow'
—Unknown

Reflection is the next rung on the GRIPP ladder. Stopping to reflect on our day, our months and our years helps us to learn how to move forward tomorrow and the next day. By habitually pausing to reflect on current or prior experiences (positive and negative), we can learn valuable lessons to help us make better decisions in the future. This is known as 'reflective learning'.

Personally, I use reflection for emotional cleansing. Reflection helps me to recognise and then overcome any emotional blockage that is affecting my thoughts and actions. If I reflect, I will see that my energy is too dispersed and unfocused – like having too many tabs open on your computer screen – until things become overwhelming and difficult to process. This is when we risk becoming disconnected or negative, so that it becomes impossible to be productive. Reflection can help you to turn negatively into positivity so as to get yourself back on track and even accelerate your progress.

One easy way to reflect and learn is to keep a journal. Robin Sharma, the author and motivational speaker, claimed that, 'Keeping a daily journal has not only changed my life – it saved it.'

I myself started keeping a journal during one of the most challenging times in my life: when my mother was in hospital with her health deteriorating. I sat in the hospital keeping a journal, through which I was able to stop and reflect on what would be our final days together. Reflection taught me to value time and my mother's achievements, and filled me with gratitude for her life and for everything I already had. It stopped me focusing on what I was losing. Writing it was emotionally cleansing for me. On reflection, this journal was also an early blueprint for the change in direction that I would make in my life – from a negative outlook to a positive one; it also gave me the confidence and clarity to set some myself some SMART goals. A few months later, I set off on my journey to build my business, Savran.

So, my first journal was written during an unpredictable time in my life, and it became a way of anchoring my thoughts and feelings. Once I was back into a more regular routine, I wrote my journal at a set time, every evening. This time of the day works best for me, although some people prefer to write in the morning. Most importantly, journal writing should be a sacred part of your daily routine. Record every day in writing. In the beginning, I would often think that I had nothing to write, but then fragments of my day would start coming back to me. I suggest recalling even the smallest step, or interesting or thoughtful thing – positive or negative – that you've seen, heard or learnt that day. The main purpose is to celebrate the positives, however small, and even if you've had challenging issues in your day, to reflect on what you've learnt from them and what you could do better next time. When I used to have tennis lessons, my coach would only let me finish after I had served a good shot, however difficult I'd found the rest of my lesson. In a similar way, it's vital to always end your journal on a positive note, even after reflecting on any negative aspects of the day. Each year, I now treat myself to a leather-bound journal with a lock and key so that I can write freely and openly about my successes, failures and future hopes without any judgement from others.

'I Can': The I in the GRIPP Ladder

'Your I Can is more important than your IQ.'
—Robin Sharma

A positive 'I Can' mindset is a fundamental step of the GRIPP ladder. Without flexibility and openness, the mind will focus on past failures and they will become barriers to achieving future goals.

Your 'I Can' attitude can be developed through affirmations and working with a coach to challenge your restricting beliefs about yourself. As a teacher, I understood that a child's negative self-belief hinders their progress. When my son Reece's teacher gave up on him, I knew it was important that he didn't pick up on that. The priority was to help Reece believe in his own ability. As a parent and a manager, you have a huge influence on your children or staff, so, it is important to deliver empowering messages that nurture the 'I Can' attitude. This requires a positive tone and supportive words, but even more crucially it requires positive self-talk and affirmations for yourself.

It is no surprise that children who are consistently praised grow up to feel better about themselves than children who have been constantly criticised. Consistent positive statements, or affirmations, help to reinforce a positive outlook and belief in oneself. They also help us to overcome any self-doubt and negative thoughts and feelings. Over time, repeated affirmations help to hardwire positivity and possibility into our brains. Positive affirmation is like exercise for the mind, training us and getting our outlook and focus into shape so that we can move towards success and fulfilment. You could either write down your positive statements – for example in your journal or onto post-it notes displayed around your home or workplace – or you could make your affirmations by looking at yourself in the mirror. Importantly, think about affirmations in the present tense, so that the positive statement applies to the here and now. ***I am a good public speaker***; ***I am*** *a positive person*. If you repeat an affirmation over and over again, like a mantra, in time, your words will indeed become your actions.

However, switching your mindset from one that's negative to one that's positive doesn't happen overnight – not when you are re-programming potentially years of ideas about yourself. Affirmations and mind management are keys tools to helping you understand what is holding you back from achieving what you want in life. Mind management is about managing the thoughts that we have from different parts of our brain. There is the human side, which is logical and uses facts and experience to make decisions; the other side has been termed the 'chimp' side by Professor Steve Peters in his book *The Chimp Paradox*. According to Peters, *'Everyone has an inner chimp. Yours can be your best friend or your worst enemy... This is the chimp paradox.'* Both sides co-exist inside your brain, and the key is to manage them so that they work for you rather than against you. My client Zara's inner chimp told her that she was unintelligent and incapable; Arun's inner chimp made him act impulsively; my inner chimp sabotaged even my happiest moments, like my wedding day, with my preoccupation with my father's absence. Our over-feeling, over-emotional inner chimps were holding us all back.

The key is to recognise and accept that your inner chimp will never go away. So how do you ensure that it doesn't ruin your prospects of happiness? Like a difficult child, the inner chimp needs recognition and praise. It needs to be let out in safe places, among close friends. So share your fears and insecurities with supportive people, or a coach – it can be challenging at the beginning to do this your own. Hear out the negative words of the chimp, but avoid engaging with them. Remember that you are not the chimp; you are separate from the chimp, even though it occupies a space in your mind. Manage your inner chimp through affirmations and you will be steering your mindset towards growth and abundance.

Perseverance: The First P in the GRIPP Ladder

'I am not afraid of storms, for I am learning how to sail my ship.'
—Louisa May Alcott

Whilst it may not feel like it when you're in the eye of the storm, difficult times in our lives can make us stronger. An achiever's mindset weathers the storm. You will avoid making certain mistakes again, and you will see challenges or failures as an opportunity to learn and grow. Parents may often say that they don't want their children to make the same mistakes as they did, or they may worry about the impact of failure on their children, but it is impossible to protect one's children from the failures and challenges that life will inevitably throw at them. Those challenges are out of our hands. What is within our control is the ability to share the achiever's mindset, view failure as a way to grow to new heights of self-knowledge and success. SAVVI people are the ones who don't give up, because you only fail when you give up! No successful entrepreneur gave up at the first hurdle. In fact, research by Sigrun Gobel and Michael Frese found that the characteristic of 'action orientation after failure' (which, simply put, means picking yourself up after a knock back) is always prevalent among successful people.

Following the GRIPP ladder is a process of practice and repetition of all the steps. Recently, I reminded my daughter Leah about perseverance for success, when she was struggling with one of her goals. In 2017, Leah set herself the phenomenal goal of swimming the English Channel to raise money for a cancer charity and a project helping victims of child trafficking in India. I should point out that Leah has grown up swimming competitively, so although many would consider the Channel swim an unrealistic challenge, for Leah, a very strong swimmer, the goal was an achievable, if difficult, challenge. A year after starting her rigorous training, and four months before the actual swim, Leah went to Croatia for a qualifying swim. The Channel swim takes 14 hours to complete so, in preparation, she had to swim six hours non-stop, without any human contact, in just a regular swimsuit, in water temperatures of 12 degrees. Leah managed to swim for two hours on day one, but on day three she failed to complete the three-hour swim, pulling out after two hours. She was meant to be completing a six-hour hour trial by the fourth day, but after training for 12 months, she felt she had made the wrong decision and was unable to achieve her goal.

Leah had underestimated the size of the ordeal. It was on the three-hour swim that she faced the reality of being so isolated – with only sea creatures like poisonous jellyfish for company – in the midst of the vast sea, with no hope of seeing land for hours and miles. Even as a highly capable swimmer, she hadn't realised just how cold and tired her body would become. She was about to give up on her dream to raise more money than she'd ever raised before.

Leah phoned me in tears, on the verge of literally throwing in the towel. After listening to her express her fears, I could see that the SAVVI principles could help her get back on track to achieve the goal she had spent a year working towards. We started with her self-awareness, revisiting her strengths and weaknesses. Her strengths are that she's a powerful swimmer, that she's young, fit and healthy, and that she had the determination to commit herself to all those hours of training. Then we examined her weaknesses: she was not a long-distance swimmer – but she had overcome this by successfully adhering to a strict training programme, which demonstrated that fatigue wasn't an issue for her. The other weakness she had overcome was that she had previously been too thin to undertake such a long swim. Weight is an important issue because being underweight would have put her at risk of hypothermia, the most common cause of death in cold water for such as long distance. Again, she was so committed to achieving her goal that she gained 14lbs. When I asked her if she had been too cold in the sea, she told me it hadn't been unbearable. So physically, her body was prepared.

Then we moved on to the next element: her achiever's mindset, starting by examining her goal. Did she have a clear goal? Yes! At the time, she wanted to swim the channel and raise £75,000 (of which she had already raised £38,000) for charity. Her other personal goal was to be the first Asian woman to have swum the Channel. Reminding Leah of her goal kickstarted her motivation once again. She realised that she possessed the strength to swim the distance, and a compelling purpose. What was letting her down was her mindset: she had turned her 'I Can' attitude into 'I Can't' through negative self-talk and not managing her mind.

That evening, she wrote down some positive affirmations in her journal and reflected on them: "I am a world-class swimmer. I am strong in mind and body. I am going to raise £75,000 to help poor, sick and disadvantaged children." She also listened to some online motivational talks. Then she devised a plan to distract her inner chimp so that her mind was busy. Leah is a Disney fan and loves all the music, so she came up with a plan: when she was all alone in the sea, she was going to sing to herself all the Disney musical songs. She couldn't wear headphones to listen to the music, so she would have to sing in her head to manage her mind and distract herself from negative thinking and her fears about isolation and the dangers of jellyfish. The distraction from negative thoughts would also help to increase her pain threshold so that she wasn't preoccupied with the physical toll the swim took on her body. Through reflection, Leah believed that she might need more open water training in lakes and seas, and should postpone her Channel swim to later in the year. As a result, she reduced her short-term goal for the next day's swim to three hours instead of six.

I was ecstatic when I received a phone call from Leah the next day to tell me that all the techniques had worked. What's more, by managing her mind and her fears, Leah had in fact managed to swim for six hours and qualify easily for the longer Channel swim. What a turn-around after just one day – and all because she had changed her 'I Can't' attitude to 'Yes, I Can'!

Leah exceeded her target and has raised a total of £152,000. She continually works on her mindset to keep her eye focused on her goals. She's already got her eye on her next goal: influencing 1000 other people to challenge themselves to do some fundraising for charity.

You will find countless stories of well-known successful people who understand the art of falling down, sometimes several times, before finally achieving their goals. I want to share some inspiring quotations with you. Write them down in your journal, as I often do, or place them around your home to keep you striving onwards, whatever storm you find yourself in.

'Success is no accident. It is hard work, perseverance, learning, studying, sacrifice and most of all, love of what you do or are learning to do.'

—Pele

'Failing is a crucial part of success. Every time you fall and get back up, you practice perseverance, which is the key to life. Your strength comes in your ability to recover.'

—Michelle Obama

'I look in the mirror and see the hardest thing I've ever had to go through is now my strength. Scars may be permanent but I am who I am today. Take back the power and live your best life. Never allow anyone to control or attempt to silence you.'

—Katie Piper

(known for her campaigning work for burns victims since suffering an acid attack by her ex-boyfriend in 2008)

'It's not that I'm so smart, it's just that I stay with problems longer.'

—Albert Einstein

'Where there is no struggle, there is no strength.'

—Oprah Winfrey

'You always hear about a 'long road to the top', but perseverance isn't limited to the early stages of a person's career. Oftentimes, failure can occur after a long period of success.'

—Steve Jobs

'Maybe your third, fourth, 50th song, novel or painting will be the one that 'makes it', that wins the plaudits… But you'd never have got there without finishing the others (all of which will now be of more interest to

your audience). Do not ever quit out of fear of rejection.'
—JK Rowling

'Making your mark on the world is hard. If it were easy, everybody would do it. But it's not. It takes patience, it takes commitment, and it comes with plenty of failure along the way.'
—Barack Obama

Progress: The Second P in the GRIPP Ladder

'A little progress every day adds up to big results.'
—Satya Nani

To make progress, you need to take a small step each day towards your goal. Do this by revisiting your goals; keep them constantly at the front of your mind and look at your list on a daily or weekly basis. My family revisits our new year goals three times a year to see what progress we're making towards them. Journal writing ensures that you are regularly reflecting on how far you've come towards achieving your goal, and whether you need to make any changes. Importantly, acknowledge your successful steps along the road to achieving your goal. From there, you can start to set yourself new goals for constant life-giving growth. Like a plant, or any living organism, if we're not growing, we're dying!

David Blunkett could have been satisfied with managing to enrol at night school for a couple of qualifications – which was a great achievement in itself for a blind, working class young man in the 1960s. But he didn't stop there: he set himself the goal of going to university, and even went on to pursue a political career that impacted on health and education policies.

Later in the book, I will look at how inspiration and support from others, and professional development through books and training, can also help us to progress towards the cycle of success and then growth to fuel even more success and growth.

Put simply, the achiever's mindset is about adopting an 'I Can' attitude. For Zara, it meant reframing her old mantras of *I am a failure* and *I am not qualified to do anything* into, *I now recognise my strengths and can use them to help others, as I have in the past.*

Having taken him through the GRIPP Ladder model, I explained to Arun that, after the acquiring and building on their self-awareness, successful people (not just those defined by their wealth, but people who are successful in other areas of life) need an achiever's mindset to help propel them towards becoming SAVVI.

Barman to Billionaire: Jasminder Singh, Chairman of the Edwardian Hotel Group

RITA: I want to share with you the story of someone who has a highly developed sense of self-awareness and has possessed an achiever's mindset from an early age. You may have already heard of him: Jasminder Singh. I have met him on a number of occasions and interviewed him as part of my research. He started out with just one guest house, which he built up into 14 hotels. Today, he is Chairman of Edwardian Hotels London, one of the major hotel chains in the UK.

ARUN: Of course! My father told me about him. He's now one of the wealthiest Asians and most influential Sikhs in the UK, and he's on the Forbes Rich list.

RITA: Yes, most people know Jasminder Singh for his wealth, but he has other credits to his name: for example, he has an OBE for his services to the hotel industry, and he holds an Honorary Doctorate from the University of Stirling.

ARUN: I find it difficult enough trying to follow in my dad's footsteps. Jasminder sounds like an impossible act to follow. I am intrigued by how much genuine respect he receives from my father, his business circle and the Asian community. I've spent years hanging out with them, and all of them – including my dad – are in awe of him.

RITA: Well, I want you to think about the Jasminder Singh beyond the headline. He's an inspiring model for you because, like you, he presents **DI** traits. Whilst in many respects he presents classic **D** type characteristics (he is determined and driven to achieve his goals), like you, he also demonstrates an **I** personality, so that he wants to take people along with him on his road to success and enjoys making an impact on the wider community. Crucially for you, Jasminder proves that it is possible to be people-focused, social and successful – so long as you possess an achiever's mindset.

One businessman client of mine describes him as god-like because of his power and authority in business circles. I can see why some people say he reminds them of Morgan Freeman's God character in the film *Bruce Almighty*: in real life, Jasminder has a persuasive and larger-than-life presence. But for someone of his status, he's a modest man who, despite arguing that he's not academic, is very articulate, especially in areas such as personal development and growth, and consciously practices the principles of self-awareness. For example, early on, he recognised that school wasn't his forte, but that he had an aptitude for maths. So he capitalised on that strength, worked hard to push his average grade up and, eventually, went on to qualify as an accountant at Hacker & Young.

Jasminder also realised that – like you – his working style was best suited to encouraging other people to succeed. Although he was the one with the vision, he realised that it was everyone in a company, who drove that company towards achieving success. His flair for communication involved direct and meaningful interaction with staff and clients – and not just writing reports and emails. We'll talk later about the way different personality styles effect communication.

So, Jasminder exploited his natural communication skills. Listening to him, you can't help but be drawn to him by his words. In this respect, he's a great influencer. But when he listens to others, he's also an active and intent listener. He's not just listening to further his own agenda, which is a rare quality in most successful entrepreneurs (usually pure D personalities), who may be good talkers but find it challenging to listen to others, when it's not going to help them achieve their own goals. Jasminder listens and actively engages in conversation, which suggests he is an **ID** personality, like you: he is motivated by influencing the people around him, including his family and employees. One of his employees, for example, started out with just one O level but, with Jasminder's support and influence, went to do an MBA at Oxford University and has risen to the position of Commercial Development Director for Edwardian Hotels. Jasminder is a leader, who takes people along with him on his journey and this feeds into his achiever's mindset.

Most people assume that Jasminder is very serious, but he has a good sense of humour and an infectious laugh. He has a powerful voice, yet he is also a very private person who does not seek attention. Even when his business is awarded accolades, he shies away from publicity and rarely appears to collect any of his awards. Instead, he usually sends in his place his son or his commercial director. When Jasminder does speak, he gives great thought to what he says. When he enters into a conversation, he has a desire to make a difference to the person he is speaking to. For example, when my husband was diagnosed with cancer, Jasminder urged both of us to keep a positive mindset, to find a way to relax, and he reminded me to make the most of my support network and to share my concerns with them. On his recommendation, we also visited a wellbeing clinic in Germany where we fasted for 10 days, living on fluids alone to detox our minds and bodies, to allow our cells to heal and to declutter our minds. We returned from this trip energized and 10lbs lighter, and made lasting changes in our eating habits as a result – most notably, we both gave up eating meat.

At one of his own birthday parties, Jasminder screened a speech given by Robert Kennedy after the assassination of Martin Luther King. The speech was about unity in times of racial division, and asked for "love, wisdom, compassion and justice". It was also a reminder that, "We will have difficult times. We've had difficult times in the past. And we will have difficult times in the future." I found this a very poignant message in light of the ever-increasing uncertainties, posed by acts of terrorism, facing our society today, and the extreme reactions they can naturally provoke in people. The message, it seemed to me, was 'Stay united.' Even at a social event, Jasminder was looking to help people grow from the lessons in the speech. This is the type of successful, sharing communicator he is, which in turn drives his focus and mindset.

ARUN: Wow – I don't know anyone who would think of using a party as an opportunity to inspire people. All my friends and I think about at parties is having as good a time as possible! All I inspire people to do at parties is drink more!

RITA: I wanted to share Jasminder's journey with you because he is a wonderful example of an alternative model of success, who has grown – and keeps on growing – in a style that makes the most of his inner strengths.

Self-awareness, as we've already discussed, highlights our strengths and weaknesses so that we can identify what it is that we desire and need for happiness. Jasminder has been self-aware from an early age, growing up in 1950s' and 60s' Dar es Salaam, Tanzania, where his father worked on the East Africa railway and also ran a small family bar and restaurant. It was there that 14-year-old Jasminder learnt some fundamental business skills in his spare time, in the company of uncles, older boys and men, who worked at and frequented his father's business. Since these older role models didn't see the young Jasminder as a threat, they shared their knowledge with him and, in turn, he delighted in every opportunity to learn from them. In his own words, Jasminder was a "lazy teenager" with a "laid-back attitude", so hanging out at the restaurant bar was much more fun than going to school. He may have been lazy in his academic learning, but young, entrepreneurial Jasminder was already putting himself into situations where he could learn key business and life skills that would build on his strengths. His most important education came from observing and listening to his father and people such as local senior police officers, politicians and businessmen. So, in his formative years, he spent his evenings with his uncles and other adults, learning how to hold conversations and enhancing his influencing skills. In time, Jasminder was deputising in his father's absence and the staff were always happy when he was on duty. This early start in the family business taught Jasminder that his strengths lay in his charm and influence, his people skills, and his focus on staff. Understanding these skills and the satisfaction he derived from exercising them helped him to foster his achiever's mindset. So, having acquired the S and A of SAVVI, he was already on the road to success.

However, in 1968 Jasminder – and in 1972 his family – decided to leave Kenya because of new laws that prevented Indians living there, from working or owning businesses; they were, however, allowed to resettle in England as British citizens. Despite difficult circumstances in a new country, the young Jasminder never lost his drive, vision and goals, and it was in England that he channelled his aptitude for maths into training to be an accountant. As in Kenya, Jasminder and his family faced the racial prejudices and stereotyping of the 1960s and 70s in the UK; however, he decided that he wasn't going to allow it to be a limiting factor for him, so he changed his belief system – his mindset – to keep him on the road to achievement. He stepped out of his comfort zone and changed the goal posts for himself. So, in 1971, at a time when most Asians (skilled and otherwise) in the UK were being hired as bus drivers, factory workers or manual and semi-manual labourers, Jasminder decided to be an entrepreneur. His uncle, chief executive of Sarova Hotels, gave him invaluable advice and experience over the next 18 months, after which he invested a modest amount of money in a small hotel in west London because he thought it would be "more exciting than being an accountant!" As Jasminder says, "You write your own life script, you're in control of your own destiny." Jasminder knows he must enjoy what he does at work, and the investment didn't seem too big or too risky. Then, by placing himself in a people-centred environment, which he knows is also is a motivator for him – where he is learning as much as he is leading, and where he encourages the people around him to develop themselves to the fullest – he exceeded his own expectations. His idea of a little excitement grew into a healthy, growing hotel business that, over 41 years, has acquired 13 top London hotels, including The Vanderbilt, Radisson Blu Edwardian Sussex (formerly The Savoy Court) and The May Fair in central London.

Jasminder's management style is proof that you don't need to be desk- or office-bound to be a business success. In fact, his main 'office' is in the bar at one of his central London hotels, where he maintains an open-door policy to encourage staff to talk to him and resolve issues, before they become too big or lead to further problems. In the spirit of a hands-on approach, he also encourages his assistant managers to sit amongst their staff, rather than have their own offices. All heads of department work together to run the hotel, which is very important to Jasminder. He also considers what his staff want, and how he can fulfil their needs to keep them happy and productive. As a result, his employees are loyal and long-term. He personally visits his hotels and encourages his management and his children involved in the business to be champions for the employees. He urges them to eat in the staff restaurant, to hear staff perspectives and learn how to meet their demands within a budgetary frame, such as improved toilet and locker facilities.

ARUN: That's interesting. I've spent all this time believing I'm a failure because I feel stifled and restless staring at figures and paperwork at my dad's business. I just can't do that kind of work. When I sit there, I feel like I'm being set up to fail. I hadn't imagined I could be successful – in my dad's sense of the word – if I wasn't sitting behind a computer at a desk. I like the idea of interacting with the staff. I think I could be good at that. Jasminder displays such a different style of management to what goes on at Dad's business. It's also interesting that Jasminder learnt by observing other people, and took the risk of leaving a well-paid job to set up a business in an industry he knew nothing about at the time – and has become a billionaire in just 40 years! He just went for it – he's got the mindset that he can do anything he puts his mind to. I think you call that the 'I Can' attitude. I spend my days in the office telling myself I can't do anything. I want to learn how to become more like Jasminder. I'm intrigued that someone my dad respects, who operates very differently to what I've experienced at Dad's business, manages to be so successful and wealthy.

RITA: Jasminder understands that for him wealth alone isn't a motivator. Whilst he may have accumulated enough wealth that his future generations never need to work, he remains driven by the desire to continue growing and learning, and leave a legacy. His achiever's mindset is oriented around more than just acquiring wealth and status.

ARUN: So you're telling me he doesn't do it for the money?

RITA: If he had carried on doing it purely for the money, he wouldn't be SAVVI. Something would have had to give. His happiness, or his relationships, or his sense of purpose. He might at some stage have suffered a loss of purpose if it was all about the money. He once told me, "What drives me is a sense of purpose. What do responsible people do with their life? They reach fulfilment through helping others. I don't want to lose that trait."

Jasminder's approach is that even if you have wealth, you don't just stop there. He explains, "When I started out, my drive and motivation was to provide security and stability for my family. Once that was achieved, I realised I could make a difference in my community." Nowadays, Jasminder is motivated by the aim of achieving longer-term success and happiness through leaving a legacy, which includes the aim of raising £300,000 a year for cancer research, as well as other charity work. His next biggest project is The Londoner in Leicester Square, an iconic building that will make a difference to London's landscape. This will, of course, bring in more wealth and job creation.

For Jasminder, true wealth and happiness come from constantly growing and not just achieving more material things. He believes that if you're fortunate enough to start off wealthy, then your starting line is different, so your goals must be higher. He says, "I believe my children have been given a head start, so making a difference to the community is their duty." Jasminder and his wife parented their children to aspire to be more than just wealthy; they wanted them to be socially responsible. For example, his wife wanted to buy second-hand school uniforms for their children that were just as good and less wasteful, which shocked his parents.

Whilst Jasminder has created enough wealth in his lifetime so that neither his wife, his children nor his grandchildren need to work, he has instilled in his children a strong work ethic and independence. As parents, they want their children to achieve things for themselves and his wife, Amrit, often reminds their children, "If you earn it, you burn it." Her message to them is that they are free to spend their own hard-earned money on whatever they want. What they don't have, though, is an open cheque book from their father, which leaves them with regard for money. In this way, Jasminder's children don't have the sense of entitlement that others in their privileged position may have.

Amrit herself was already successful in her own right when they met, a graduate working in Japan. After having children, Jasminder encouraged his wife in her decision to study interior design, and now she's responsible for interiors at his hotel group. The whole family works. Two of his daughters and his daughter-in-law returned to work after they had children. His son works in the family business and is now the managing director of The May Fair Hotel. But on top of the professional satisfaction derived from a successful career, Jasminder wanted his children to enjoy the sort of fulfilment that you can't acquire with money: making a positive difference to others.

Inevitably, wealth handed on a plate means that children of wealthy parents may not possess their drive and hunger. Whereas Jasminder made a difference to his parents, his family and his community, he wants his children and his business to make a difference to the country and to the wider world. So the whole family is involved in charity mentoring for under-privileged children, and his son Inderneel is on the board of the Francis Crick Institute, which researches into cancer.

ARUN: I can't imagine my parents sending me to school in second-hand clothing. That was what their childhood was like because their parents couldn't afford things. I know they've always bought me the best and the latest of everything – and I'm grateful for it. I don't need to reach for anything, which is what I thought parents were meant to do for their kids. I never thought of it in this way: that because I've started out on the same financial footing as my parents, my goals need to be extended beyond that. I've never had goals at all – I didn't think I needed them. I've always had everything I could ever want. But hearing about Jasminder's family has made me realise that goals are important – and more than that, because I've had such a privileged starting point, the goals I set need to go beyond what I've got right now. That thought is quite exciting! I've never viewed my dad's success as a motivator to achieve my own goals. I've always just seen it as something to measure up to, and I never felt I could measure up, so I didn't really try. If you don't climb very high, you don't have far to fall, is how I always thought.

RITA: Since Jasminder's children started off in life with existing material comforts and rewards, he knew they needed a different kind of drive to motivate them; he encouraged them to pursue social responsibility to make a difference to their community and to the wider world. Jasminder also sees himself as a father figure to his staff, and derives his inspiration for nurturing staff from ideas in nature. He says, "If you want to grow world-class tomatoes, it's no good just having world-class tomato seeds. You need to nurture the plant every day, to nourish it, provide the right environment for it to grow. You won't instantly see results, so you need to be ready to delay gratification."

He sees his responsibility to cultivate the right environment for his employees, business partners and family, and he accepts that the results might take time, but he doesn't give up on the seeds. Some of the seeds might never grow, but he understands that perseverance is key. Importantly, he takes time to reflect on the needs of people and the impact of his own actions. When he sees that a client needs extra assurance, for example, he gives them his mobile phone number and offers to be available to them. However, he argues that the seed itself needs to want to grow. Small, daily improvements are key to long-term progress – otherwise you risk a bad crop. If that happens, you reflect on what you have learnt from the experience.

ARUN: My dad isn't a father to his staff. If he was, maybe they wouldn't keep leaving. Even I can see that we have high staff turnover and that it's having a knock-on effect on profits, but Dad won't accept that it's a problem for us. He just thinks it's a 'bad crop' and part of a general problem in the industry. But I know just through walking through the car park that our staff don't want to stay because they aren't happy. I've overheard people complaining that we never promote within the company, we just bring in new people.

RITA: This is why I share Jasminder's story as an alternative model of good leadership. He's aware that he first learnt the ropes of business through the generosity of people around him, and he repays that by helping others. Looking back, he explains, "I wanted to build a company where everyone could feel they could do much more than they thought." From his own experience of stepping out of his comfort zone, he encourages others to prove that they "can do a lot more than the world is telling them". If you think back to the G – or GOALS – in the GRIPP ladder, this is what he's talking about here. But it shouldn't stop there: next, they should develop a desire for continual evolution and curiosity (this is the Progress part of the GRIPP ladder). To this day, Jasminder surrounds himself with people who stretch him, from whom he can develop and learn. For example, as part of a recent conference, he surrounded himself with the likes of

Bill Clinton and Bill Gates. Jasminder never wants to stop learning: "Discussion is important; it's the best type of learning."

Jasminder keeps on learning by persevering. (The other P in the GRIPP ladder!) He explains, "Persevering is far more difficult than getting started," which is true whether applied to a business or personal context. In the 1990s, his hotel group suffered financial business troubles to the extent that even if he was ill, he had to keep on going. During the worst global recession in recent history, his perseverance meant that his fortune grew by £85 million. He believes that this ability to persevere came from his mother, who would always make him go to school even if he was ill. It was how his family worked, and he's passed this attitude down to his children. At his son Inderneel's wedding, Jasminder read a letter penned by Ronald Reagan to his own son about the importance of perseverance in a marriage, urging, "It does take quite a man to remain attractive and to be loved by a woman, who has heard him snore, seen him unshaven, tended him while he was sick and washed his dirty underwear." It's the weak man that wanders or gives up.

Someone who perseveres as hard as Jasminder doesn't like to be taken advantage of (a characteristic of the **D** personality). It was, therefore, particularly difficult when he felt betrayed by his parents and siblings in a well-publicised court case in 2012 about company assets – and again, more recently, in 2018. Remember, Jasminder and his family fled Kenya to resettle in the UK. They were a close family with strong family values, united in adversity and the desire to rebuild their lives. Jasminder's focus on that dream, and his years of hard graft and capitalising on his innate skills, formed the backbone of the hotel group. For many years, Jasminder was the unpaid CEO of the business but did the lion's share of the work, whilst his siblings were sleeping partners and his elderly parents lived in his home. In 2012, Jasminder felt it was time to reflect on his contribution to the business and divided company shares accordingly. However, his father and siblings challenged the new distribution of shares and took Jasminder to court. Furthermore, his father was considered too frail to travel to court, so the court was forced to travel to the May Fair Hotel, owned by the family, to hear his evidence. Jasminder felt that the taxpayer should not have to pay for a special hearing, and so covered the cost himself. Whilst Jasminder was determined not to be taken advantage of, equally he is a family-centred man who was very troubled at having to face his parents at home and in 'court' during the trial. Even though the judge found in favour of Jasminder, it was a distressing reminder for Jasminder about the dangers of valuing material happiness over emotional wealth in family life, which runs against his own parenting principles. He reflects with sadness that, in the end, for his siblings, "it was the size of the gift that defined their value, not the love."

For a businessman who, by his own admission, can't relax or sit still, Jasminder always ensures that he does stop for what he calls his 'daily mirror test'(a technique for Reflection – or the R in GRIPP), when he figuratively holds up a mirror at the end of each day and asks himself, "What did I do today? What went well? Where have things gone wrong? What have I learnt from it?" Through this reflection technique, he positively acknowledges what has happened and identifies ways to move forward. This openness towards success and failure means that he doesn't shy away from talking about areas of improvement – such as the criticism one of his hotels received in a TV documentary – because he takes ownership of even "the messy things", which are part and parcel of running a large business. For him, it's important to face up to failure in order to achieve self-improvement and self-awareness. He goes further to say, "I avoid people who say you're OK – that doesn't help with self-improvement."

In my observations and experience of Jasminder, I can tell that he is naturally SAVVI. For him, terms like 'self-awareness' and 'achiever's mindset' are just everyday concepts that he acts on intuitively, without any formal training, and which have turned him from a bar boy in Kenya to a successful billionaire – with his (and his children's) feet firmly on the ground. In his own powerful words, "The truth is not to be grand," and he fixes his mind on this key principle in his personal and professional life.

So, the question is: how could you apply lessons from Jasminder's story to your own search for meaning at work or in your life?

ARUN: I thought I felt uncomfortable about work, even bored by the idea of it, but I suppose the reality is that I haven't been pushed to do anything out of my comfort zone. Jasminder would say I've been too comfortable, that I haven't taken control of my own destiny and persevered to set and achieve goals. If I don't like the feeling something gives me, I move on. That's the story of my life – school, uni, work. But it's always been OK because my parents have had a back-up plan for me. It sounds tough being one of Jasminder's children, but I like the sound of him. He sounds like he enjoys life and has found a way of combining what he likes doing with being a success at work. That sounds easier in his line of business. I have no interest in my dad's call centre business.

RITA: It does sound like you're interested in why your father's employees are losing interest too, though. Maybe, like Jasminder, your forte is relating to people, communicating with them and encouraging them.

ARUN: But I don't get to be that person at work. It's not the culture at all. My dad never does it. It sounds so much better than what I do at the moment, but I can't see my dad letting me do it. Though if I could tell him that his business hero takes the time to talk to staff in such a hands-on way, he might agree to let me try it out. I could introduce an open-door policy to start to get staff to come and tell me why they're dissatisfied. I'm starting to feel as if I could contribute something. It makes me feel nervous though. I'm not sure Dad will be on board at all.

RITA: It sounds as if you're moving out of your comfort zone.

The Wheel of Life

Jasminder's story had made Arun think. Jasminder was a financially successful and respected businessman who also appeared to be having fun doing what he loved. Observing his father at work, Arun had never equated business success with a sense of happiness *through* work. Consequently, for Arun work represented the opposite of the enjoyment he derived from his successful social life. However, Jasminder's story presented Arun with a model of success built upon taking advantage of and developing his own strengths, despite the fact that they may be different from his father's. Working closely with people, developing them and interacting with them were all activities that would come naturally to Arun. Arun could see that a key part of Jasminder's business strategy was to seek out opportunities so that he, and the people around him, could grow and become better versions of themselves. Arun now needed to learn to apply the GRIPP Ladder model in order to develop his own achiever's mindset, the way that Jasminder has been doing for years. Intrigued by Jasminder's methods, Arun was willing to listen to his journey to success: Jasminder not only had goals, he stretched those goals further (see G in the GRIPP Ladder). He doesn't let failures set him back, but learns from them and takes time to reflect on them (see R in the GRIPP Ladder). Jasminder worked out early on in life what he was good at (creating vision and driving, influencing and inspiring others) and could see how he was going to apply that skill to help grow his business, without letting his weaknesses limit him. Even when things become tough, Jasminder still maintains his 'I Can' attitude (see I in the GRIPP Ladder). I wanted Arun to reflect on these lessons early on in the process of his own self-development.

To move forward, I asked Arun to complete the Wheel of Life chart (see overleaf).

Wheel of life

Instructions to complete the wheel of life:

- Look at each segment and mark a line across each one to indicate your level of contentment in that area.
- The lines nearer the centre of the circle represent lower contentment (0), and the lines at the outside of the circle represent greater satisfaction (10).
- This should be completed with the first number you think truly represents you and not how you believe it should be.

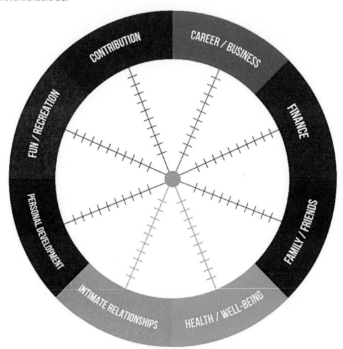

Example of completed wheel of life:

The Wheel of Life gives a visual representation of how you are currently leading your life. Developed by Paul J Meyer, founder of the Success Motivation Institute, this wheel represents the eight main areas in your life. These are commonly areas like: Health; Wealth; Family and Friends; Playing, Hobbies and Fun; Intimate Relationships; Career and Business; Personal Development; and Contribution and Spirituality. Each area is divided up by spokes – like the inside of a wheel – and by plotting along the different points of the eight spokes and joining them up, you can identify the way your life is currently balanced between the eight areas. We dedicate different amounts of time and space to, for instance, Health, Wealth and Family and Friends at different stages in our lives. The wheel offers an effective way of seeing how you currently balance your life and, if you're feeling levels of dissatisfaction about the distribution, is a way to help you re-plot your priorities.

To identify how you currently balance your life, take each of the eight areas and, on the corresponding wheel spoke, mark on a scale of 0 (low) to 10 (high) how much attention you currently give that aspect of your life. (Be aware that a healthy, balanced life doesn't mean giving five to each area; it depends on what's going on in your life at that time.) Then join up the marks inside the wheel and decide from the shape of your personal wheel just how balanced your life looks. Bear in mind that for a wheel to function effectively it has to be round.

When one aspect of our life becomes the focus and others are neglected, the wheel becomes out of balance and misshapen. For instance, if you're focusing too much on wealth, and are neglecting your health as a result, this will ultimately have a negative impact on your wealth and eventually the wheel will end up completely out of shape – and on misshapen wheels, you're likely to crash. Once you've considered each area of your life, ask yourself what your ideal balance of, say, career versus hobbies should be, and write down an action plan to help you regain balance. This is particularly important when considering neglected areas in your life.

Arun's completed Wheel of Life indicated that his high scoring areas were Wealth, Playtime and Health, whilst other areas, such as Career and Business and Contribution and Spirituality scored low for him. Reflecting on how the area of Wealth was a priority for him, Arun experienced a lightbulb moment when he acknowledged that his wealth was actually his father's wealth. He recognised that unlike Jasminder's privileged children, who were raised to earn their own money despite their father's wealth, he had become reliant on his father's money, which inevitably gave his father the right to make decisions for him. He started to blame his father's hold on his life for thwarting his sense of purpose. "My dad has made me dependent on his money. I know I've enjoyed spending it, but he could've given me some guidance – like Jasminder gave his son – about running his business and developing an achiever's mindset. Jasminder even guided his son to be a good husband. My dad wants me to achieve so that he can be proud of me in public, but he hasn't shown me *how*. Telling me what to do isn't the same as developing me. That's a parent's responsibility, isn't it?"

I could see that Arun was understanding the concept of an achiever's mindset, and was starting to see how his own mindset was different – however, he still needed help to discover how to take responsibility for his own life.

RITA: Do you know what you want to achieve?

ARUN: No, I don't know what I want. I guess I've always been told what I should want. Until today, I've never stopped to reflect on who I am. I've just been pulling on my father's coat tails, with no real sense of where I was ending up. I didn't have to worry about money, so nothing ever felt urgent.

When my clients are stuck, lack goals and don't know what they want from life, I start off by asking them what they don't want. Arun knew that he didn't want to live in his father's shadow a minute longer, and that he wanted more control of his life.

ARUN: If my mum can do it, so can I. I want to run a business, but not the way my dad does. We may share **D** traits, but I can see my **I** strengths and I know I'm a good, influential communicator – so right there I'd make a different businessman to my dad. I want to be more like Jasminder, although he was driven by his ambition to make a difference to his family, and now he wants to create a legacy and, honestly, those aren't my motivators. I already have money in my pocket – and I'm not at a stage in my life when I'm thinking about leaving a legacy. Also, I live in a different era to the one Jasminder started out in; although he's a good role model, he is my father's generation, and I wonder if he's the success he is because he started out in a different, easier time, without as much competition. There are different challenges now. I'm not sure it's possible to work like that and be successful in a modern, digital and more competitive society. I need to find a motivation that's relevant for me.

RITA: Good. Now you're reflecting.

OK, let me share with you a different scenario, about a young entrepreneur who has had a similarly privileged upbringing to you. Nitin was also lucky enough to have a good start in life thanks to his father's wealth, and since money wasn't a motivator for him either, it took him time to find the source of his motivation – and he took detours and made mistakes along the way. For a year, he also worked in his dad's business, but then wanted to spread his wings and attempt to do something for himself. If we look again at the GRIPP Ladder, Nitin is another good example of someone who sets himself Goals – despite everyone assuming that he would just take over his father's business – and looks to

Progress and Persevere. I think you'll be able to identify with him. It's worth mentioning that he's also an **ID** type.

Make Work Fun: Nitin Passi, Founder and Group CEO of Missguided

RITA: Like Jasminder's children, Nitin and his brother were taught early on about the privileges of their wealth. Nitin tells the story of how he and his brother travelled first class from their boarding school in England to Hong Kong, where their parents had resettled, but had to return economy class. When the boys complained about this, their father told them, "If you like the good life, you have to work for it."

Nonetheless, Nitin, like many privileged children, enjoyed many years of partying. Finally, however, he accepted that he had to change and take back some control of his life, however difficult that might feel. After working for his dad's business supplying clothes to the high street in the UK and Europe, he decided he'd had enough. "I was selling blouses to a high street retailer, and I thought, *This is not for me. I can't do this. Let me try doing something by myself."* He was brave enough to take a risk and apply his strengths to suit his personality style.

So at the age of 25, he took a £50,000 loan from his father. This was back in 2008-2009, during the recession. Recalling the time, Nitin explains, "The only path to success I could predict was in online retail. But I had no understanding of online retail or women's fashion, and the only experience I had of online shopping was going to Selfridges in the sales, buying all the jeans and sticking them on eBay for a bit of profit."

Still, Nitin moved up to Manchester and took a little corner of his uncle's office, commissioned a website for £3000, then went out, bought some clothes and started selling them online. He remembers that the first two years of running his own business were probably the hardest times he has ever endured. In his first month, he turned over £1000 and came home to tell everyone. While his mum said, "Well done!", his dad said, "Is that all?"

ARUN: That's exactly what my mum and dad would say. My dad's never satisfied, and that's what has stopped me taking risks.

RITA: According to Nitin, he always experienced this same pressure at home – and he struggled, because he wanted and needed to be successful but didn't know to achieve it by starting off so small.

So, understanding the importance of goal setting, Nitin set himself turnover goals. Having launched his online fashion website Missguided in March 2009, he managed to turn over £100,000 by the following November. Then, in his first year, he turned over £1 million, which grew to £3 million, then £10 million and then £100 million. He also encourages his staff to keep stretching their goals. He urges them to "always be happy and never be satisfied." He perseveres even when the going gets tough and the competition, such as Topshop, attack him from every angle. He says that these kinds of problems only drive him to be more successful.

Like you and Jasminder, Nitin is a social creature who needs to enjoy his work and his working environment. He is motivated by recognition and driven by results, but his motto around work ethic is, "Work hard, but let's have fun while we're doing it." His office environment epitomises this value: in his own office, he has two floors for his personal space and a spiral staircase connecting to a bar downstairs. For staff there are meeting rooms with swings, as well as sleep pods, blossom trees and palm trees. He enjoys the fact the office "is a bit crazy."

ARUN: Yes, I can really identify with Nitin. I'm impressed by the way he's made his workplace fit his personality. That's inspiring. I can see that he's someone else who has managed to be successful by using his strengths. I didn't think that my talent for socialising could be a strength in business, but I'm thinking differently now – I just need to convince my dad. In the past, I thought that there was just one route to business success and it didn't suit me, so that always put me off being at ACE – my dad's call centre.

RITA: So, having heard these stories of alternative routes to success and fulfilment, what goals will you put into action?

ARUN: First, I need to take on personal responsibility and set some goals of my own. I have to persuade my dad that it would be better for the business if I had a more interactive role with the staff. I enjoy talking to people when I get the chance at work, but he's neglected them and they're leaving the business. I know I can see things on the people side of business that he misses. If he wants me to write a report, I could do an employee survey to understand why people are leaving. That kind of information feels like the real world to me. I'd be motivated to find out about that. When I look at my Wheel of Life, it's clear that the Career and Business area needs some serious attention. Maybe this is how I could start working on getting my wheel into a decent shape!"

RITA: Remember that your father is predominantly a **D** type, so he's goals-focused, which means he's more likely to accept your proposal to interact with staff if he can link it to better results for the business. He needs to see a tangible reward.

ARUN: At uni, I read about a survey on employee engagement and its impact on profits. I should dig that up and use it to help me write one for ACE to show my dad how important it is to keep your staff happy.

RITA: How could you turn that into a SMART goal for yourself?

ARUN: I'm going to do a survey at ACE about levels of staff engagement and how they link to our profits. That is a goal that is both 'Specific' and 'Measurable', and it will be 'Achievable' if I do most of it as an online questionnaire, with a smaller number of face-to-face interviews. I'm interested in conducting this survey because it's 'Relevant' to my wish for a happier workplace, which I believe will make ACE more productive and profitable.

RITA: How long do you think it will take?

ARUN: If I do about 40 interviews face-to-face, that's 10 a week. So, realistically it's going to take me a month to do those, as well as analysing the online results. I actually feel quite excited about getting involved in my own project at work. It's the first time I've felt driven.

3

Values and Beliefs

Mother and Son Design their Lives

'It's not hard to make decisions when you know what your values are.'
—**Roy Disney**

Zara and Arun had come to me at different life stages, with different problems. Their common thread, though, was their overlapping home-grown values. Whilst values are personal to the individual, they do not just appear out of nowhere: our values are shaped by factors such as our parents and families, our religion, our community and even external forces like the media. Some values and beliefs help us to move forward; some hold us back. Zara and Arun's next step would be to examine how the values they currently lived by, and the beliefs they had acquired, were affecting their lives.

Values are defined as the 'moral principles and beliefs or accepted standards of a person or social group' (*Collins English Dictionary, 12th Edition*, October 2014, HarperCollins Publishers). They provide the principles by which we live our lives; they are the emotional and physical states that we consider important in order to lead a meaningful life – for example, the states of good health, wealth, status, spirituality, democracy, love, honesty, family or marriage (see appendix for a fuller list). It's important to recognise that when we say we value family, for example, we're talking about what family represents. For example, valuing family could mean that we are actually seeking security and support; placing a high value on love is also about desiring intimacy with your loved one. We often juggle a combination of values and they help us to achieve our life goals.

The co-existence of our values and beliefs offer us an interpretation of the world behind us and in front of us. Beliefs are distinct from values in that they are the thoughts we hold onto unquestionably. Beliefs, like superpowers, have the potential for good or bad: they can make us soar or they can destroy us. Arun, for example, believed that he was unacademic – a belief that was limiting him, and that he needed to challenge. Our beliefs influence our attainment of goals. Fundamentally, our beliefs make or break our ability to live according to our values – so for example if you *value* the idea of marriage but *believe* that you are unlovable, or have given up on ever meeting the right person, it becomes harder for you to uphold that value. This mismatch of values and beliefs (and self-belief) creates unhappiness and dissatisfaction.

Through our beliefs, words, actions and habits, we make our invisible internal values and beliefs visible to the external world.

I am very fond of the saying, '*Show me your friends and I will show you your future.*' During my 20-year career in teaching, I saw a lot of situations in which teenagers were at odds with their parents, or where parents were completely shocked by their children's behaviour. My first piece of advice was always to look at who and what was influencing them. The chances were that they were picking up values and beliefs from those around them. These days, it's not just friends that influence young people's values – social media exerts a huge influence.

When I thought about who was influencing Arun – where his values and beliefs stemmed from – I realised that some of his mother's own limiting beliefs – especially those originating from her cultural background – were holding him back just much as they were her. At the same time, however, Zara had raised Arun with some of the more empowering beliefs absorbed from her traditional upbringing – such as loyalty and a strong connection with friends and family. Arun's popularity and success in his social life were clear indicators of that.

All values and beliefs can have both positive and negative impacts on our lives, depending on how we associate with them. I often share my mother's life story to illustrate the way her values of love for family and friends, a social contribution and gratitude, impacted both positively and negatively, on her personally and on us as a family. Stephen Covey's book *The 7 Habits of Highly Effective People* identifies the second habit as, *'Beginning with the end in mind.'* Covey advocates use of a powerful exercise: visualising the funeral of someone you love. He writes, *'Notice the flowers, the soft organ music... the faces of friends and family... feel the shared sorrow of losing, the joy of having known. As you reach the front of the room, look inside the casket. You suddenly come face-to-face with yourself. This is your funeral, three years from now.'* Covey goes on to ask you to imagine looking at the programme for your own funeral and reading over the list of speakers. Which area of your life do each of them represent? Consider which of your characteristics you would want others to have noticed and remembered. Did you make a difference to anyone's life? How does the final celebration of your life reflect your values?

To illustrate Covey's point, I told Arun and Zara my mother's story – starting at the end of her life.

Rags to Riches: The Story of My Mother and Raju Tuli, Chairman of Tuli Holdings

'Men are what their mothers made them'
—Ralph Waldo Emerson

For children, losing a parent at a very young age often means that the surviving parent is adored and treasured that much more. As adults, we wanted to give our mother the love and security that had been lacking in much of her life. So, on the awful day that our mother passed away, 39 years after our father, we knew we wanted to celebrate her values and beliefs on a grand scale. Although she herself had had simple tastes and was never extravagant, she meant the world to us and we wanted her funeral to reflect her importance in our lives and in those of others. We arranged for a carriage adorned with purple chrysanthemums, lavender (purple was her favourite colour) and white lilies, drawn by four horses, to carry the coffin from her home to the crematorium. After the cremation, we invited all the guests to a reception at a stunning five-star hotel.

However, the most impressive aspect of the day was the sheer outpouring of love and gratitude that guests – in their hundreds, from up and down the country and from all over world – lavished on the memory of my mother's life and on the values she had lived and breathed. Family, friends and community were her top priorities, and they all turned out – including extended family, her children's friends and employees, her builder, her gardener, people she'd only met a few times – to celebrate her life. Almost everyone, including the priest, community leaders, her grandchildren and her friends – even the shyest of them who weren't

117

used to public speaking – wanted to say a few words to pay tribute. She had showered so much love on countless people's lives that they all wanted to honour her. Friends and family remembered how she would regularly telephone them, whether they lived in India, Canada or the Midlands, and that she was always there to share in their burdens – yet was also the first to congratulate them on news of happy occasions. Many spoke of the way my mother made every single person she knew feel loved and valued, paying them close attention and remembering details about their likes and dislikes, where they went on holiday, and the ages of their children. Above all, though, my mother loved to express her love for others by cooking them their favourite dish. We even laughed on that terribly sad day as we shared stories about how my mother made each one of us feel as if we were her one and only favourite. Each anecdote about my mother shared a common reflection on her strong values of family, the wider community, and her social responsibility and contribution to the temple and charities. In fact, there were so many speakers, who all wanted to extol her values and virtues, that we had to book an extended time slot at the crematorium!

My mother always regretted not having been at her grandmother's side when she had died, so we knew that she would cherish the presence of all 13 of her grandchildren at her own funeral. The children were asked to choose a song to reflect their emotions as each of them said their final goodbye, laying a single rose on her coffin. They unanimously chose Whitney Houston's *I Will Always Love You* because they felt that their precious grandmother was leaving them just as it was their turn to serve and look after her in her fragile old age. They knew, however, that she had always insisted that she never wanted to be a burden to anyone else. The grandchildren believed Whitney Houston's lyrics summed up their grandmother's selflessness:

If I should stay

I would only be in your way

So I'll go but I know

I'll think of you every step of the way.

So goodbye

Please don't cry

We both know I'm not what you need.

My siblings and I, and our children, felt immense support over our loss of a woman whose values had left an indelible mark on everyone who met her – especially on us. The writer Robin Sharma asks, *'Who will cry when you die?'* Well, I can confirm that there wasn't a dry eye in the house on the day of my mother's funeral, and the ceremony was a fitting tribute to her values.

Looking at my mother's life, you can see that whilst some of her values were rooted in her cultural background, many were formed by enduring difficult experiences. During her lifetime, my mother used to tell me that the two greatest sources of love come from your mother and your husband. Tragically, she herself had been denied the two greatest loves of her life: her mother died just days after her birth, and she became a widow at the age of 36, having been married for only 12 years. So, her lack of these two fundamental loves in her own life underpinned her values and later her goals for her children's futures. Her first-hand understanding of devastating loss meant that she knew instantly how to support others through difficult times. She recognised that difficult times are harder to bear without the support of friends and family, whilst the good times mean nothing without people to share in them. She also made us appreciate that whilst you're never short of friends when you're successful, few stand by you through the tough times. She wanted to raise her children to count among those who *did* help friends and disadvantaged people through the difficult times. My mother

119

understood and upheld this value, not only because she had suffered the deaths of loved ones but also because she, as a child, had witnessed gruesome scenes of violence and her family's subsequent displacement during the brutal partition of India in 1947.

Until partition, her family had lived comfortably (her father was a lawyer) and they had wanted for nothing. However, partition put a dramatic end to all that. Her Hindu family was forced to flee their home in the Indian territory that became redefined as (Muslim) Pakistan, and they had to travel a long distance in trucks to the newly sectioned (Hindu) India. My mother and her family spent many nights along this journey sleeping at truck stops, railway stations and on just the bare, cold ground, using stones as pillows in case they fell asleep too deeply, which would have endangered their lives. In fact, one of her siblings drowned herself to avoid being killed or raped by Muslims in the religious feuding incited by the partition.

Once the family had finally reached Hindu India, they were allocated the same size of land that they had owned in their former home on which to build a new life. By that time, my mother's father was already remarried and had had more children with his second wife; as a result, my mother was only really parented by her eldest sister and brother, and when she herself was older she helped support her younger half siblings and did household chores. In her teens, it was my mother's responsibility to look after her paternal grandmother. The two of them enjoyed a close relationship and my mother was always at her grandmother's side before going to school – though sadly, she wasn't there when she died, and always regretted it. She, did, however complete her education, qualifying and working as a teacher, which was unusual for a woman in India in the late 50s and early 60s. Although it was a time when marriage was a symbol of societal acceptance, my mother's unsettled childhood drove her to seek the value of security through education and work. It was a value she went on to instil in all of us.

It was lucky that my mother was so driven in terms of her education and career, because she was neglected even as an adult in the matter of marriage: her family failed to actively seek a potential suitor for her. In the end, a sister-in-law found my father, an ambitious, educated man, and so my mother married at the age of 25, which was relatively late for an Indian woman. Her mother-in-law was controlling, though, and wasn't easy to live with, so my mother had to work hard to fulfil the role of a dutiful Indian daughter-in-law and keep the peace. Yet outside the family home she continued to work as a teacher, even after having two children (my brother Raju and me). She was torn between her dual values of family (in the Indian sense) and security. Ultimately, though, her value of conforming to Indian family expectations outweighed her value of gaining security through an independent career. It is a tension that causes frustration for many women.

In 1964, my parents came to England as immigrants. Once again this was a period of displacement for my mother, at a time when Britain was not a diverse country; there was at least some consolation, however, in the fact that her two brothers were already living in the UK. My parents' stay in England was never meant to be permanent: it was a case of coming over on working visas to save money, and then returning to India. Just when we were meant to return to India – in fact, we travelled all the way back there – my mother changed her mind at the last minute. She feared that her children wouldn't be able to resettle in India because we hadn't grown up speaking Hindi. This could alienate and disadvantage us, so we flew back to England. However, like many other immigrant families who remained for longer in the UK, my mother felt rooted in her new home – until the ground beneath her gave way once again with the sudden death of my father. Overnight, she became a young widow with four children and was transformed into the main breadwinner in a foreign country. Although my father had managed to build up a successful property business alongside his teaching career, my mother (like so many women of her generation) knew nothing of the details of her husband's business. She had no idea what properties he owned, what his bank account details were, where the property deeds were kept or even the name of his solicitor. Although she was an intelligent woman, she was not financially literate. She soon learned to her cost that, though she appeared wealthy on paper, having inherited her husband's 16 properties, most of them were heavily mortgaged and any remaining value was paid out in inheritance tax.

At that time we were living in the suburbs, away from most of our close-knit Indian community, so my mother was isolated, unable to drive and had four children to raise on her own. When she turned to others for support, she found it wasn't always forthcoming. Her world instantly shrank as our conservative Asian community struggled to include her as a young widow and a single mother. Meanwhile, her brothers moved to Edinburgh, leaving her feeling even more lonely. Not surprisingly, when she tried to carry on my father's business affairs, she was taken advantage of by tenants and builders. In the end, 'Uncle Abdul' my father's best friend, stepped in and regularly drove her to collect rents with an old-fashioned rent book, whilst we kids sat in the back of the car. It was gestures made by people like Uncle Abdul – alongside the absence of them made by others – that meant my mother never forgot the value of being there for people in times of great need. As her children, we witnessed her hard work and perseverance against all odds. She also ensured that we took on responsibilities around the house.

Within our tight family unit, my mother's key values became our values. However, as we grew older, we became aware that whilst her values about family love and community enriched her life, there were also times when they fell short of delivering her happiness. For example, her Hindu values meant that she never felt able to remarry after my father's death, despite being just 36 when she was widowed. In her mind, remarrying transgressed her cultural and religious values and fundamentally compromised her love for her children. At times, her cultural values also restricted her attitude towards assertive girls and women – despite the fact that in India she had worked when it was unusual for women, and in England had taken over my father's business. Still, she did struggle raising and encouraging assertive daughters. As a result, while growing up I felt the pressure to conform to an Indian ideal of femininity, which was upheld by my mother's values but which I ultimately rejected for myself and for my daughters. If, like my mother, I had lived by that self-limiting belief and value, I would have been unhappy and unfulfilled.

Reflecting on my mother's life, I can see that she was an **SC** personality like Zara. My mother also put her family and cultural expectations before her own needs. And, like Zara, there were times when my mother's values held her back, making her unhappy. I wanted Zara to recognise the importance of bestowing values onto children, but also to understand that there are times when we must challenge our values and beliefs if they no longer serve us – or else we risk unhappiness and a sense of loss of identity.

In one important aspect, my mother did manage to adapt one of her chief values in the face of a certain situation concerning my eldest brother, Raju. Although our mother highly valued education, she saw Raju failing to thrive at university and accepted his desire to leave without graduating. Her unwavering belief in Raju and his happiness helped her to cope with her conflicting values and beliefs about education, and her concern about what the community would think.

Quitting higher education did not mean stopping work for Raju. It was our mother's overarching belief in her children's ability to achieve anything with hard work, whatever the world threw at us, that Raju took to heart. Our mother encouraged him to find his own path towards fulfilment and she actively got behind it, which, combined with his new drive and purpose, ultimately led to his creation of a multi-million-pound business.

I believed that my mother's relationship with my eldest brother (who grew into a **DI** personality like Arun) and their shared values, as well as the way they resolved their conflicting values, was a good model for Zara and Arun. I wanted to impress upon them the knowledge that Raju, an award-winning multi-millionaire business leader, would never have become the man he is today had it not been for the values and beliefs – social, religious and financial – that were instilled in us by both our parents, and which he accepted and supplanted into his own adult life.

In contrast to other SAVVI role models I have discussed – such as Nitin Passi and David Blunkett – Raju was a desperately shy and introverted child. Unlike those success stories, he also lacked the benefit of having *two* nurturing parents. In fact, after our father's death Raju was placed under enormous cultural pressure to be a mini-adult from the age of 11. At the Hindu ceremony following our father's funeral, Raju appeared dressed in a tied turban to symbolise that he was the new head of the family, bringing his childhood to an abrupt end in a very public way. Growing up beside him, my younger siblings and I witnessed the enormous weight of cultural values that Raju was expected to shoulder, and which unquestionably held him back. To this day, I cannot comprehend how he coped. I would reiterate, then, that whilst some values ground us and nourish us

124

to become the best version of ourselves, certain others, upheld unthinkingly, can harm and hinder our development. Fortunately for Raju, despite the constraints of the community values placed upon him, his acquisition of our parents' other values of loyalty, respect, relationships and hard work helped him in the longer term to overcome his early inhibitions.

As well as being a quiet child, Raju was not especially academic. He left school at 16 to study for a diploma at college and never wanted to socialise outside of school. Reflecting on his later decision to leave university, he says, "It would have been three years of struggling. It was the 1980s when unemployment was high; 60% of graduates wouldn't go on to find jobs, and it felt like a safer bet to go into the world straight away to earn money." So for two years he worked in the grocery business. He recollects, "It was a just means to solid, guaranteed money, on a weekly basis, so that Mum wouldn't have to worry. It was just safe money coming in through hard graft."

Even as a teenager, Raju had adopted our mother's core values about looking after one's family and working hard. He recollects, "I saw Mum work hard. That was normal to us. She showed us that if you need to work seven days a week, so be it. Psychologically, I followed that rule every day. Even now, it's how I do business: I get up at 6.30am regardless of what time I go to bed. I knew back then that I needed to earn money, so I went into it the quickest way I knew how – by going into the grocery business – although it was hardly my passion."

Raju describes how, two years later, fate stepped in: a market stall came up at an indoor shopping centre in Edinburgh, where his uncles lived. "It was a risk," he recalls, "but Mum said, 'Go for it'." She was living out her conviction in her son. She told him, "I've got £2000, and that's all I've got to give you. You choose whether it's for a grocery shop or a clothes stall."

125

Raju knew it was a risk – he was investing the last of our mother's savings, which was more of a worry than whether the business failed. But he wasn't frightened by it; he saw it as an opportunity. Just like our father, who he remembers, "Always made the most of whatever opportunities came his way. He made the most of life."

My demure brother managed to overcome his inhibitions through self-belief – regardless of what others thought of him – and lived true to his values about supporting his family and providing our mother with a home and security. "That sticks with you," he explains. "It's an underlying motivator and becomes more important than anything else in life."

At the age of 20, Raju moved to Edinburgh to trade at a small clothes stall. It was the 1980s, the era of the Young Enterprise Allowance Scheme designed to encourage young people to come off unemployment benefits by creating their own businesses. Combining our mother's investment, which he used to buy stock in jeans and casual wear, with a state allowance of £35 per week, which underwrote part of the risk, Raju started his first business, Jean Scene. The stall was an instant hit and he soon opened a second, asking our younger brother Sunny to join him. As the money came in, they re-invested it into properties and went from strength to strength, building a chain of nearly 70 stores over 15 years. Accountants Ernest and Young recognised them as one of the fastest growing businesses in Scotland, and they attracted a lot of attention and publicity. Numerous newspapers covered what they called my brothers' 'Rags to Riches' story, and their names appeared in the Asian Rich List and in *The Sunday Times'* Young Rich List. Then, after 16 years in the business, Raju realised that the fashion market wasn't reliable and could be cut-throat, but that people's dining habits were changing and people were going out for coffees. So they diversified: first into property, then into fast food and coffee outlets. Raju is currently the master franchisee of Costa Coffee in Ireland (with over 180 stores) and has numerous KFC shops in both Ireland and Scotland.

Yet even though Raju has done so well financially, amassing millions of pounds, he has always remembered our mother's values to stay humble; build and prioritise relationships and treat people with respect. Our mother had seen people succeed around her, and saw what money could do to them. "Don't ever be like that," she used to warn us. By living our mother's values himself, Raju has succeeded in instilling them in others. For instance, Raju's senior staff from the 1980s (when they were fashion retailers) still work for the business: our mother's value of loyalty has been passed on to them through Raju. Talking about his staff, Raju explains, "They have developed with us. Rather than think of themselves as individuals who are good for one job alone, in one environment, they know that working for us means that there's a job for life in whatever business we're involved in." For example, a sales assistant started working for him in 1987, when she was at 16, without any formal qualifications. Today, she is the area manager for KFC in Scotland. Another employee was a manager of Jean Scene and is now a business director. There's another who started out as a junior surveyor: today he's a property director who's well-known in Ireland. They all know that if the business ever gets sold, or whatever Raju does next, there'll always be a job for them.

After our mother's funeral, Raju remembered the support Uncle Abdul (our father's best friend) had shown her on all those occasions when she'd needed to be driven to collect rents – and when others had abandoned her. Raju repaid Uncle Abdul's loyalty with a brand-new Mercedes, which he'd always dreamed of owning. Raju wanted to make Uncle Abdul feel special, which our mother had always believed in doing for other people. She had instilled in us the value of doing good deeds for others and a belief in the rewards of karma, which has

127

passed down to her grandchildren. My son Reece, for example, will say that if someone does him wrong, he is able to simply shrug it off and let it go in the belief that, in time, it will rebound on them. This belief has freed him from ruminating on conflicts.

Raju has also passed down both our parents' values to his own children. My formerly shy, demure brother has grown up to embrace our father's value of enjoying life, but he reminds his children, "You're allowed to go out and party and enjoy holidays – do whatever you like the night before – but you've got to get up for work in the morning." Raju knows that he can't wrap his children in cotton wool all their lives. He says, "They need to fall over. They need to make mistakes. They need to get up, and they need to learn from falling."

Given that family ranked highly for our mother, when Raju's marriage unravelled, he and our mother had to reframe values they both held dearly. In the past, our mother had always urged us never to let anybody know of our troubles. She valued her privacy: she didn't share her problems and she preferred to cry herself to sleep rather than dropping her public mask in front of the community. In the face of Raju's divorce, however, she and Raju had to challenge their values and beliefs about the appearance of family respectability – mainly to avoid his children's suffering. But throughout her life, our mother was always clear about her values and how they underpinned her actions and her hopes for us.

ZARA: Hearing your mum's story, the way she worried about what the community thought, makes me realise that I've also been limited by the values of my parents, my husband and our community. Like the belief that I shouldn't work once I was married. I've never challenged that.

RITA: A characteristic of your **S** side is that you value serving others. You prioritise your family and serve them before yourself. However, when a value is no longer satisfying – and even worse, holds you back – it's time to re-evaluate it before it's too late. My mother spent too many years playing the part of the young, dutiful widow who, each night, when no-one was watching, cried herself to sleep.

ZARA: Yes, I know that feeling. I'm living a life that's been designed for me by other people and it's making me unhappy. I can't go on acting like it's all right. I never expected to find myself feeling so empty. I feel like one of those Russian dolls: all bright and gold and smiling on the outside, and then hollow when you take away all the baby dolls inside.

Zara and her son Arun were both being held back by some of their values and beliefs. They were at a point in their lives, where they needed to examine how they were going to align their values and beliefs to what they wanted to achieve and grow together, so that they nurtured and fulfilled them. The ability to live by your values requires an achiever's mindset. If you value good health, for example, you need to make time for exercise and cooking healthily, or you won't be living by that value, which then spirals into frustration and unhappiness. If you count healthy living amongst your values – but remain unhealthy – then you are revealing that you actually value something else – rest or more family time – more highly.

There are times in life when we may decide that our values and beliefs are leading us in the wrong direction, away from fulfilment and happiness. This is when we need to question or reprioritise our values and beliefs, and even consider discarding them or writing new ones for a chance at future fulfilment. Reframing our values doesn't just happen overnight. It takes work and energy. I too had to reprioritise my values and beliefs. As my children grew older and needed me less, I could move personal growth, development and success higher up on my list of values. At the same time, I had to question my cultural value about solely being a good wife and mother, alongside my negative belief that I didn't have the skills required to run a business. These values and beliefs were holding me back. Only once I challenged them, by reprioritising my values and writing a new set of empowering beliefs for myself, did I succeed in creating a more fulfilling life.

At Zara's and Arun's sessions I wanted them to question the values and beliefs they had carried with them up until that point, and then examine how well they had served them. Just as Zara was inevitably influenced by her parents' values, many of Arun's values were shaped by his mother's – yet these clients were often at odds with one another. So, as well as encouraging them to question their own values, I sought to remind them of their common core family values and how to make them work positively in their relationship with one another.

Zara was learning how to paint herself a road to success that circumvented her usual route of designing a life around others. She had begun to exploit her strengths to overcome her weaknesses, in order to start making the necessary changes in her life. As part of this process, she had visited old friends for the first time in years and found a project to work on, giving her a renewed sense of purpose outside of caring for her family. She understood that her new achiever's mindset depended on her continually reminding herself of her strengths and new goals.

At this session, Zara explained that she had been given a boost, hearing her childhood friends say they saw the old spark return to her by the end of the weekend. Even Zara's newer friends at home started to comment on how active and alive she'd become. People complimented her on how much energy and passion she was pouring into her research into charities. Zara admitted that she'd forgotten what she was capable of – that she was a quick learner. Friendly advice from others helped her to take the skills she had gained through managing a large home and channel them into supporting charitable causes. For example, she started volunteering at a school for special needs.

The Five Root Model

I engage my clients with the Five Root Model, using the image of a tree with five roots. For me, the tree and its roots are analogous to the values and beliefs that sustain us and help us to grow. They may lie beneath the surface but they are fundamental to growth, and they influence the direction of growth. Sometimes, though, roots are limited or damaged, restricting – or causing an adverse effect on – growth. This is when we need to re-evaluate them, or even cut them loose. Once I had taken Zara and Arun through the importance of their values and beliefs, they were ready to apply them to the Five Root Model.

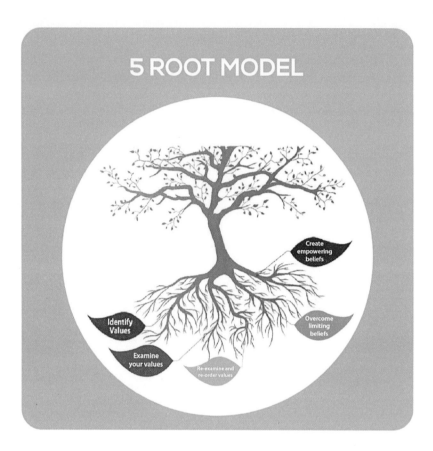

Root 1: Identify Your Values

Start by listing what you value in life: a loving relationship; recognition at work; good physical health; a less stressful job (see appendix [page 249] for a comprehensive list). Then narrow your list to the top five things you most want in life. This blueprint of values will help you in the face of dilemmas: how will a certain action or decision impact on your values?

Nitin Passi believes in working hard, but also values playing hard. So when he challenged himself to set up his own business, the value of fun became a value enshrined in his company's charter – right down to the playroom atmosphere of the staff room.

Root 2: Examine Your Values. Are They Serving You?

Even if you haven't yet defined your values in black and white, they do exist: we acquire them through life experiences. When our values are conflicting, or we are living a life that does not reflect our values, or our values are failing to serve our interests, it causes us pain, confusion or stagnation. Zara's chief value of family was costing her happiness because her belief in being, first and foremost, the perfect wife and mother had hampered her personal growth. As a result, the first time she came to see me, she described feeling hollow inside. However, by considering a new value – success – which hadn't previously featured in her top five values list, Zara started to map a new route towards happiness and self-belief.

When David Blunkett opened up in his interview about having had an affair with a married woman – despite the fact that years had passed and that he himself had not been married at the time – he clearly displayed sadness and circumspection, brought on from having behaved in a way that was incongruent with his values of honesty, loyalty and family. When we aren't living according to our implicit or explicit values, our bodies and emotions tell us about it. We need to listen to our suffering or stagnation and revisit our values. I urge my clients to revisit their values list each time they achieve a goal. Then it's time to set a new goal.

Root 3: Re-Examine and Re-Order Your Values

Values need to be flexible enough to deal with the changes and challenges that life throws at us. Now and again, you may need to re-order, or even discard, some of your values to help you deal with change. It's important to stress that this doesn't mean losing your integrity, or undergoing a personality change. Crucially, *your values are not your personality*. Just because you have deprioritised your value of, for example, community in favour of recognition, doesn't mean that you no longer value community. It may be time to re-order some of your values to help you feel rewarded.

When re-examining and re-ordering your values, you should ask yourself: *If I could only live by one value, what would it be?* Then, order your other values around this chief value.

You could also try to imagine what would happen if you turned your values upside down for a few months, and consider what changes would you expect to see.

When Jasminder Singh believed that his value of justice was being undermined by his family taking advantage of him, he made the tough decision to take them to court, despite his other value of family. In the end, Jasminder's value of justice out-ranked all his other values, thereby enabling him to make a painful decision.

Once Nitin Passi had learnt as much as he could through work experience at his father's business, he knew he wanted to achieve something independently. He was already fulfilling his value of success, but he needed a new value to move toward.

Root 4: Overcome Self-Limiting Beliefs

Adversity in life, be it at home, at school or in the workplace, can trigger a lack of belief in one's abilities. Tony Robbins calls this generalised attitude about oneself a *'global belief'* that can bring a negative shadow to every thought and action, even turning into a self-fulfilling prophecy that seeps into other areas your life. To leave it behind you, you must challenge self-limiting global beliefs because, equally, it is possible to acquire *positive* global beliefs about your abilities. Before Arun and Zara could fulfil their new values, they had to overcome the self-limiting beliefs that were holding them back. Zara lacked belief in her ability to do anything but be a wife and mother because she hadn't studied beyond A levels. Meanwhile, Arun's negative global belief about his dyslexia destroyed his enthusiasm for work. Anthony Robbins writes, 'It's not the events of our lives that shape us, but our beliefs as to what those events mean.' (Anthony Robbins, *Awaken the Giant Within,* Free Press (November 1992)) Arun and Zara needed to overcome their interpretations of past events, which had convinced them that they were shaped to fail professionally.

A positive global belief can dramatically change your outlook. It's like seeing the world and your abilities through rose-tinted glasses. Some people refer to the 'positive delusions' (the very opposite of self-limiting beliefs) of successful people who achieve beyond expectations. Everyone knows someone who doesn't allow anything – whether it's a physical difficulty (such as David Blunkett, a great example of someone with positive global beliefs), an emotional issue (in my case, the deaths of my mother and mother-in-law, and then my husband's cancer diagnosis), or an intellectual block (like my son Reece's dyslexia) – to hold them back. You can become a limitless person by seeing limiting beliefs for what they really are: merely founded on fears (which may once have served a purpose) or other people's attitudes. Once you have accepted this about limiting beliefs, you can begin the process of isolating them.

Root 5: Write Yourself a Set of Empowering Beliefs

Empowering beliefs separate the person who sees a world bursting with opportunities from the person who believes that the world is against them. Everyone can be the person with an empowering mindset, ready to embrace every opportunity. Getting there requires small, targeted steps. Begin by writing down a list of small improvements, achievable in the short term. Make these realistic targets or you'll become disheartened. For example, don't aim to become an engaging and persuasive public speaker within three months, if you've never stood up in front of an audience before. That can be a longer-term goal; in the short-term, sign up for a course in public speaking. Crucially, in the short term, you must believe that you will be able to learn new skills.

Perceiving herself as limited by her lack of formal education and career, Zara believed she was unable to hold interesting conversations at the parties she attended as Jay's wife. This negative self-belief brought her pain, which, when accompanied by a set of empowering beliefs, can be a trigger for change. Of course, without the empowering belief in the possibility of turning things around, you hold yourself back. When Zara remembered that she had enjoyed school and was a quick learner, she could start to tackle her pain, which came from social embarrassment and low self-worth. As soon as she embraced the empowering belief, *I can be a great learner,* she saw that she could transform her pain into pleasure. Once she acknowledged, *I have the ability to grasp new ideas quickly*, she could drive her re-entry into education or training. Meanwhile, a simple, short-term strategy was to educate herself about current affairs, by reading newspapers or news round-ups like 'The Week', a few days prior to a party so that she had a range of topics to discuss. Experiencing the ability to converse at parties would develop her belief in her potential to achieve her longer-term goals.

Arun's pain stemmed from his lack of identity and independence at work. The pain of frustrated values should be the trigger for embedding new empowering beliefs towards the imagined pleasure of your values and goals. To turn his pain into pleasure, first Arun had to write himself empowering beliefs such as, *I am emotionally intelligent because I understand people*; *I am creative and can think outside the box*; *I am great at influencing others*. This was the start of his progress towards the pleasure of feeling the recognition that he valued. In particular, he derived pleasure from the recognition of his father, who asked him to undertake his own project, and from the idea of building a fairer workplace for ACE employees.

Once you start taking the small steps towards fulfilling your empowering beliefs, it is vital that you acknowledge each little success along the way. Tell yourself, *I did it!* Keep a record to remind yourself that you really are changing and working towards realising your values and beliefs.

Zara and I had discussed the fact that her new-found self-belief had had a positive impact on Arun, even prompting him to make an appointment to see me himself. When I asked her about her husband Jay's response to 'the new Zara', however, her smile disappeared.

ZARA: At first, he was more attentive. He remembered our anniversary for the first time in years, and booked a table when I got back to celebrate. I think he started to appreciate me when I was away – or at least what I do for him at home. He kept phoning me to ask me where his lucky cufflinks were, or where I'd put a certain pair of shoes. In the end, one of my friends hid my phone from me, so I wasn't still at his beck and call. I found that hard, but it was the best thing for me. Jay kept leaving me messages about trivial things, which he never does. Then I got home to a big bunch of flowers. But it wasn't long – about a week – before he slipped back into his old habit of being distant and preoccupied. And always on his phone.

I have moved a few steps forward, but there are still times when I feel frustrated. I think it's because I'm working on myself when he isn't. He doesn't think he needs to change a thing about himself, that it's everyone else who is the problem. Whilst I'm noticing a shift in Arun, Jay's just stuck in his old ways. In the past this would have upset me, but since I've started the journaling and tried to keep myself busy with charity research, I've found it easier to stay positive: I can now see my own role in creating my future happiness. In the past, I was rattling around our house feeling empty inside, waiting for someone else to make me happy. Now I understand the steps I need to take to make *myself* happy.

After my minibreak with my friends, Jay and I talked about having a regular date night, but that's gone out of the window. He made it to two more dates after the anniversary – although that first one didn't count as Arun joined us for that. He was so late for the next one that I ended up watching most of the film on my own. I didn't even want to see it; it was an action movie that he had wanted to see. Then he cancelled one of our dates for a meeting with his finance director, as it was the only night she could make after work because of childcare issues. He even had the audacity to call me back to ask if he could use our restaurant reservation for his meeting. But I invited a couple of local friends to dinner instead, and had a good time – though I did feel guilty about not helping him out.

I know Jay's impressed by successful professional women – but then he won't let me work! He says it wouldn't be right for the wife of Jay Sharma to be seen 'having to work'. He'd never support my idea to work. What would his colleagues and the community say? But I've seen the attention he lavishes on businesswomen at the events we go to. That's why I don't enjoy them. I never feel comfortable when I've got nothing interesting to say; I'm just the homemaker. But now I want something else – although I feel guilty about that because my mother always told me to put my husband first, to be a good wife. "Jay works hard to support you and Arun," she used to say. And remembering her words makes it hard for me to try something new – but I do want to create a different life for myself.

As an S type, Zara needed to feel that her team – in this case, Team Sharma (her family) – was on board with any change and growth she undertook. Promoting change in her life was going to be a challenge because S types don't like change for change's sake. When there is change, they need to know that it won't have a negative impact on them. Zara needed to examine her learnt value about solely being a good wife and mother. Additionally, she had to stop seeing and valuing herself through her mother's and husband's eyes.

ZARA: When I told Jay I was researching charities to support, I thought I caught a flicker of surprise – even respect. It was like he was seeing me through a fresh pair of eyes. But in the end, it's just charity work to him – it's not real work. I've seen the respect he shows his finance director, who has an MBA from Cambridge. He's always saying she's a magician with figures. He tells everyone he'd be lost without her – and I've heard rumours that other directors call her his company wife.

*True to Zara's **S**-type profile, she had a strong sense of loyalty in conjunction with her inherited values about family life. So, when she discussed Jay's 'company wife', she was too loyal and protective of her family's unity to reveal any concern about her husband's relationship with his finance director – that is, until I explicitly asked her about it.*

RITA: What kind of relationship do you think they have?

ZARA: I'm sure some women might think she's more than just a colleague, but I'm not sure. I know she's young and attractive. She's the first and last person Jay phones each day. He speaks to her more in one day than he speaks to me in a week! But I think it's the business that Jay loves, and she helps him get the results he wants.

RITA: So Jay spends a lot of time to talking to her.

ZARA: Yes, he does. Although sometimes when I walk into the room and he's on the phone to her, it doesn't sound like it's about the business. He doesn't use that tone of voice with everyone. He laughs, and he seems happy and relaxed in her company.

When she heard herself say this aloud, Zara became emotional.

ZARA: Most of the time I try to block out my worries, and I cope with it reasonably well. But I sway between thinking it's more than just a professional relationship to thinking I'm just being paranoid.

RITA: If you could redesign your own life, how would you do it?

ZARA: I've always regretted not going to university. I'd love to go back to studying and get a paid job. I know we have more than enough money, and that I'm free to spend it however I want. That's Jay's idea of happiness. But his money's not making me happy. I have this fantasy that getting a job would help me regain my confidence, but I've been scared to do anything about it.

RITA: When you imagine yourself being happy in a job, what sort of job do you see yourself doing?

ZARA: Working for a charity. But I don't just want to be another spare part in an office, where I'm known as Jay Sharma's wife. That's why I want to study again and learn how to do something meaningful. I've thought about doing an Open University course. Then maybe Jay and Arun might look at me differently.

RITA: I want you to start examining yourself through your own lens – not through the eyes of others. It's natural and inevitable that we worry about what others think of us and compare ourselves to other people, but other people's views and opinions of us are not real. Your value doesn't decrease based on others' inability to see your true worth.

ZARA: You're right. I am bothered by what people think of me – or what I imagine that people think of me. I'm starting to see that I need to change my priorities, starting with putting myself first for once. But I don't want to give up my family values, and I get upset when Jay and Arun don't share in them.

Having said that, I don't think I've ever discussed my values with Arun, or gone out of my way to teach him about them. There's never been any time. I just expected him to pick them up by observing. It's only when we have an argument that I remind him of our expectations which, I admit, are our cultural expectations – and that means that he just turns around and tells us we're too old-fashioned.

Identifying Zara's Values and Beliefs

Early on in our sessions, Zara extolled her chief values of family, love and relationships – all of which are essentially about valuing security and loyalty. By her third session, it was time to identify her more nuanced values and beliefs by completing a values elicitation exercise. The act of recognising your values gives you the focus to make the best decisions appropriate to your life – to the situation you find yourself in at any given moment. Values are the conscious and subconscious motivators behind the way we lead our lives, and understanding their importance enables us to evaluate them and re-evaluate them as required. Our values and beliefs are immensely powerful: they can build us up or bring us down.

Identifying Arun's Values and Beliefs

Arun's journey towards becoming SAVVI also required him to evaluate and, where necessary, re-evaluate his values and beliefs. He had acquired some of his mother's values about the importance of family and community, which he was finding difficult to live up to personally and professionally. He also upheld some distinct values around status and recognition that were being unmet, which was causing him dissatisfaction. Like his mother, he needed to overcome some limiting beliefs around his education (and particularly regarding his dyslexia) in order to move towards happiness.

At the end of Arun's last coaching session, we had agreed that his next step would be to act on his concerns about low staff morale at his father's call centre business, by gathering feedback from staff focus groups. DISC analysis had identified Arun as an influencer and communicator, and he used this self-knowledge to pursue a piece of research on staff engagement and satisfaction at ACE.

Arun's value eliciting exercise also revealed that freedom, justice and fun – for himself and others – featured highly in his core values: he thrived in supportive environments, where everyone could interact and bounce off one another. It was the lack of any opportunity do this at work that frustrated him. Arun also valued status and recognition and, whilst he was highly regarded within his social group, at work he was just the boss's son; his role came without any authority or recognition, which he found limiting. Acting on his strength for engaging with people, Arun's staff research project was a way to resolve some of his current dissatisfaction at work. It also gave him some independence from his father and positive contact with employees, which helped him gain some recognition.

When Arun returned to see me, he explained that he had spent several days listening to staff describe their sense of disengagement at his father's business, which he had found fascinating and which had confirmed his own ideas about problems at ACE. He told me that it had been a new experience, wanting to go into work to hear what people had to say. He'd also felt a sense of freedom because it was his project, and had been his idea. As he put it, "I wasn't just lurking in my father's shadow, at his beck and call."

I congratulated Arun on his new mindset about work. He had used his strength in social interaction to persuade employees to talk to him about a sensitive topic, despite the fact that he represented company management.

Arun went on to explain that the staff feedback revealed that the situation at ACE was worse than he had imagined. His value of justice motivated him to delve deeper and ask more questions to tackle a problem that was clearly damaging the company.

ARUN: Staff said they were dissatisfied with the promotion process. They complained that there was very little diversity, and that there was blatant favouritism towards certain employees. Some felt that white British members of staff were being favoured over Asian staff in terms of promotion, and that most managers were white men. It's not overt racism, but there doesn't appear to be any room for promotion if you're Asian. That's the feedback I got, anyway. It looks like ACE doesn't think that Asians are good enough for management roles. Which is odd when the CEO is Asian!

When I looked at the figures, I saw that the complaints were justified. Asian employees make up 79% of our workforce because we're located in a predominantly Asian area, yet our senior staffing doesn't reflect that. 93% of senior positions are held by white staff brought in from outside the company – which, to me, looks like racism.

RITA: My experience of other organisations has revealed that unconscious bias can have a big role to play. The term 'unconscious bias' refers to the way our brains make quick assessments of people and situations, which is influenced by factors like our background, cultural environment and personal experiences, and which leads to us developing both positive and negative associations around those people and situations. It doesn't exclusively apply to race; another element commonly subjected to unconscious bias is someone's regional accent – for example, different accents are associated with varying levels of education and sophistication. Malcolm Gladwell, in his book *Blink*, examined people's unconscious bias, regarding physical height in relation to power, by polling companies in the Fortune 500 list. He found that most CEOs were just under six feet tall, which is interesting considering that the average American male at the time was five feet 11 inches. Gladwell's evidence suggests that our unconscious bias equates high status with high stature.

At ACE, there appears to be an unconscious bias that white managers make better leaders, which is part of a wider assumption that links strong leadership skills to people from certain cultural backgrounds.

ARUN: Yes, my father can't believe there might be Asian talent within the business. Not surprisingly, our Asian staff have picked up on this unconscious bias, so the good ones are leaving. They've worked out that my dad doesn't value Asian staff – unless it's his attractive finance director. He doesn't make a decision without consulting her, even if it's about the colour of his office carpet. I know they call her his company wife.

Another problem at ACE is that our sales teams won't go above or beyond their job description because they're not incentivised to – and I don't just mean at promotional level. Staff in the call centre complain that they're managed by numbers like Average Call Handling Time (ACHT). Our work culture is to sell hard and get fast results. My dad thinks that so long as we're bringing in the sales, we're doing very nicely, thank you. But staff I spoke to don't feel that their managers give them the framework to do their job properly. They told me they're not given time to listen to customer complaints; that there's no time for building a rapport with customers or providing a personalised service. As a result, ACE has a bad reputation for after-sales service and we have low repeat business. And because staff are only rewarded for delivering sales, I'm hearing reports that some of them lie to secure a sale – that it's even encouraged on the sales floor!

Arun's value of recognition was apparent in his concern that ACE staff weren't being rewarded appropriately – that ACE's focus was on financial results rather than on its people.

ARUN: There's a lot of resentment amongst staff I spoke to. Many of them talked about management having an 'us and them' mentality. It's well known that managers go out socially together – they play golf, and I know that many of their business decisions get made on the course. Most of our employees are excluded from these social events because they're not from the right background or pay scale. It's a miracle that they talked to me, actually, because I'm seen as part of that elite group. Maybe it's because the staff I spoke to felt like they were being listened to for the first time. Or maybe they just don't care because they plan to quit anyway.

Instilling Values and Beliefs in Business

RITA: From what you've revealed about ACE, it seems to me that it prioritises profitability over the wellbeing of its staff. In my experience, there is a correlation between the personal values of founders and CEOs and the values upheld by their businesses. For example, if the leader is solely profits-orientated and not at all staff-focused, employees won't believe they are valued highly and morale will inevitably suffer. Is this what's happening at ACE, do you think?

ARUN: ACE's company values are all about profiting at any cost. My father only values wealth, and that's how the company's run. My dad would never talk about his employees like Jasminder or Nitin do. He wouldn't see the value in developing staff or keeping them happy. That just isn't a motivator for him. His family was poor, and he's only motivated by the desire to leave all that a million miles behind us.

Staff repeatedly told me in these focus groups that they didn't feel appreciated. From what you've been saying about values, it sounds like people feel this way is because they're not included in ACE's – or my dad's – set of values. Even I feel undervalued by my dad because I don't fit into his ideal about having a top degree, like all his friends' kids do.

Arun was beginning to understand the need for his father's business to grapple with its values in order to improve staff morale and retention. But how – when, by his own admission, the company had no shared positive values – could he begin to have an impact on this?

RITA: You're evaluating ACE's values, and reaching that point is a big step for you. Before we address how to go about re-evaluating and redefining them, we should return to your personal values, which we established at our last session.

We know that you value relationships – being around people – which is why you undertook the staff survey. You also value fun, justice, status and recognition. Your values of justice and recognition reveal your driving principles about fair treatment: people should be rewarded for their efforts. This is clear in the way you talk about staff disengagement. Transferring some of these positive values to ACE could help to improve its working culture.

ARUN: I'm excited by the idea that I could make a difference like that. I can see that, to have any hope of re-engaging staff, ACE needs to create a set of company values that includes a focus on their needs. Fairness has definitely moved up as a priority for me since the staff survey.

I do value status and recognition, so I empathise with demotivated staff. I don't feel I have any real status at the company – not in the eyes of the senior managers or my dad. As far as they're concerned, I don't have a degree and I'm dyslexic, so I don't count as one of them and my opinion doesn't matter. When I told my dad how people were feeling, I could tell he wasn't really listening. My results didn't make any difference. How can I make a difference to the working environment at ACE if I can't make my dad sit up and listen?

At their third sessions, Zara and Arun were both gaining a better understanding of the power of personal values over longer-term happiness and success. Once they could recognise their values, they were on their way to being able to re-evaluate those that were not serving them. Zara's prioritisation of her family values had meant a strong focus on being a good wife and mother; however, this was no longer serving her, so she applied a new value of, professional success – which she'd never previously entertained – into her mix, and ranked it highly as a core value. Arun had also neglected the value of professional success, and re-ordered his values of justice and recognition to propel his success at work.

In Zara's session, I wanted to encourage her to focus more on nurturing the family values that were serving her, as well as on letting go of those that weren't. To help her in this, I decided to introduce the idea of a family charter.

When I reached a crossroads in my own life and found myself questioning my identity as a wife and mother, I sat down with my husband and children and, together, we discussed what we valued about our family and our time together, and what we hoped for as a family – even down to the holidays we wanted to go on. I suggested to Zara that she do the same with Jay and Arun.

Creating a Family Charter

'If you don't know what you stand for, you'll fall for anything.'
—Anonymous modern proverb

Knowing what you stand for as an individual is important. However, it's also important to apply this knowledge to the groups you belong to in your wider life, both personal and professional. No man is an island, as they say, and our values connect us in fruitful ways to the people – partners, children, extended family, work colleagues – with whom we share our lives.

A set of shared values has been described as a family's 'DNA imprint'. Having shared values gives families a collective identity, and helps them to occupy their shared space and time more harmoniously and productively. What's more, members of a family with overlapping, agreed-upon values can support one another in striving to live according to their respective individual values and beliefs. Having a set of shared values creates a built-in compass that keeps each family member aligned and focused as part of the family unit.

Formalising these shared values into a family charter (sometimes referred to as a mission statement) creates a powerful bond between members that doesn't exist without a shared vision. This process doesn't just happen overnight though; it takes an investment of time. The good news is that it's never too late to recognise and develop shared values to support the health of your family. My family and I first sat down to discuss our shared family values after Jeff and I had been married for 24 years, when our children's ages ranged between 10 and 20!

However, it is important to follow several steps when introducing a blueprint of values into your family's life.

1. **Make sure your family charter is the result of a collaboration between everyone**. An effective family charter has to have the buy-in of everyone it intends to support. You need shared participation in establishing shared values, or else it will be difficult to get commitment from each family member – especially children. Even when your children are very young, it is still possible to introduce values such as justice by keeping the language simple: for example, discuss living by a family value of 'fairness'.

2. **Put aside time to create your family charter.** Don't rush it. The process of negotiating your family's values can take weeks if you properly allow everyone, who will be building and living by the charter, to discuss and justify their choice of values.

Jeff, the children and I spent several weeks considering our respective values. Each one of us wrote down a list of our chief values. We then brought these to a family discussion, in which we talked about what our respective values meant to us, and then ranked them in order of priority for us individually and as a family. Only then were we able to look for our common values. Where there was any disagreement about the importance of a value, family members were able to present their arguments for or against its inclusion in the charter.

3. **Agree your shared values, then write them down**. You will find that no two people share all the same values, and that even when their values are similar, they may prioritise them differently. However, within a family you should be able to identify enough common ground on which to lay down the foundations for a family values charter. My family and I spent time debating our values and beliefs and found that, for example, one of us didn't see the value of a clean and welcoming house, whilst others argued that if the house wasn't clean and ordered, it made them feel uncomfortable and ill at ease.

Meanwhile, in another discussion about the personal values each of us sought to extend to the whole family, Jeff and I wanted to prioritise the Hindu principles we had grown up with; however, our children, who had been born and raised in secular Britain, argued that they didn't feel as if they could get behind living up to the values of Hinduism. In the end, after some debate, we all agreed that, actually, even Jeff and I weren't practising or living by all the Hindu principles. However, we could agree on the shared value of leading a spiritual life, which we would express through the values of karma (the idea that our good deeds contribute towards future happiness) and serving others.

Arriving at an agreement on shared values takes open-mindedness and negotiation. We eventually edited down our list to 10 key shared values for the collective Chowdhry unit, and wrote them down. There is immense power in seeing your values written in black and white. This was the list we drew up:

1. Love and support
2. Gratitude
3. Integrity
4. Karma
5. Fun
6. Good communication
7. Positive relationships
8. Serving others – for example, through charity work
9. Healthy living
10. Personal growth
11. Order and cleanliness at home

Having established this list of values, we followed the Five Root Model to help us live up to the values that we as a family held dear. For example, once we were all able to agree on the value of order and cleanliness at home, we focused on the goals we would need to set ourselves to enable us to live by it. We discussed the ways in which the chores should be divided up between us: for example, food shopping to be done by daughter Leah, and son Reece, to help with everyone's technical support – from buying phones and laptops to finding contractors to do jobs around the house.

When it came to deciding how we would live up to the value of karma, we defined what the word actually meant to us and decided that we all sought a life that created good karma. For example, even if we felt hurt or upset by someone's unkind actions, we would remind each other that it was not worth responding in a negative way. To this day, it's refreshing for Jeff and me, as parents, to be reminded of this value by our own children when we're feeling let down by other people. Because of our shared family value of karma, we each make a conscious effort every day to focus on creating positivity and steering away from negativity.

For my daughter Leah, applying the Five Root Model to the value of serving others has meant putting herself through a number of physical challenges in order to raise a significant amount of money for charity.

Of course, the way in which each of us lives up to the value of serving others is different, and doesn't need to be on such a grand scale – that just happens to be what motivates Leah. My own way of serving others is through voluntary work as a governor at a school for children, who have been expelled, and through pro bono coaching for underprivileged children. However, witnessing Leah's recent achievements has inspired the whole family to reflect on how we are living up to this key point in our family's charter.

Anya, the youngest of my children, was initially the most sceptical about the idea of drawing up a family charter. However, when she reached her teens and began facing issues with her friendship group, our family's values of personal growth and positive relationships prompted her to discuss her issues with her siblings and make some informed decisions, that better equipped her to avoid potential conflict. In a Savran video (which can be found on the Savran Ltd YouTube channel) about the impact of the charter on our family, Anya went on to reveal, "I found that if my friends didn't have the same values as me, such as hard work or family, we end up clashing. So, having the values there helped me to decide who I wanted to be my friends."

By following the values listed in our charter, Anya had worked out an important lesson for herself. In today's society, young people's values are influenced not only by their peers but by social media. For this reason, it's more important now than ever before to ensure that your children are supported in the wider world with a charter of family values, created with their input. If they don't know where they stand on certain issues, or what their values are, they are vulnerable to falling blindly for those displayed by other people. A well-planned and thoughtful family charter means that you're not leaving this to chance.

4. **Print out, frame and display your family charter. Seeing is believing.**
   Once we had a list of our family's core values, with a couple of sentences on how we would deliver on each one, I printed out, framed and prominently displayed *The Chowdhry Mission Statement* in our kitchen, for everyone to see and think about every day before going out into the world. (Photo of this is included on page 157).

Open and healthy communication featured highly in our charter. When, three years later, Jeff was diagnosed with cancer, his natural **S** style personality wanted to withhold the news from the children in order to protect them. I had to remind him that our family charter states that we all value open, honest communication – that there was a framed reminder displayed in the kitchen for all to see on a daily basis. Ultimately, telling the children was the best thing we could have done, because it gave them the opportunity to be wonderfully supportive and held us accountable as parents to the values we had agreed with them.

5. **Your family charter isn't set in stone; keep revisiting and re-evaluating it alongside the family's changing needs.** At the point in my life when I was examining my personal values, it was appropriate to touch base with the values of my family, because the two are intertwined – for better or for worse! Creating a family charter isn't the end goal; it

should respond to changes in your family's cultural, economic and social circumstances. From my own experience, I understood the risk of living blindly by values set for me by my community, and recognised the importance of adapting the charter to reflect developments in our family life. For example, this year (2019) we welcomed a new family member, when my son married his fiancée, Anila. We want her to feel part of the collaborative process of establishing a meaningful charter; we don't want to simply force our existing charter on to her. So, we will take time to listen to Anila discuss her personal values and examine how our Chowdhry mission statement might need revising, in order to support the new family dynamic, and so that we all still feel that we are living by our shared values.

Best Business Women Awards 2018: My first award gave me hope, my second gave me confidence

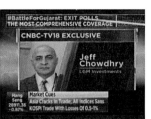

Jeff, one of the first Asians in the City, to now having a global influence as a market guru

With my husband Jeff, my rock and biggest supporter, humbled to be featured as Asian Power Couple 2018 and 2019

My inspiration for SAVRAN (Rita's mum, Savitri)

Rita's mother-in-law, Rani

Chowdhry family holiday in Mexico - living one of our family values of having fun together

My daughter, Leah, crossing the English Channel in 2018

My daughter, Anya, grilling Boris Johnson about his ambitions to be Prime Minister

My son's civil wedding, there is no greater happiness than seeing your child find love

My son, Reece, receives his first award and makes a name for himself in the venture capital business

Knocking at No. 10 to discuss how to make the workplace more diverse and inclusive

Running a SAVVI workshop with the Board of Directors at Hallmark Care Homes

Sunny Tuli, knows how to work hard, play hard and rest hard

Raju Tuli, Chairman of Tuli Holdings, he has demonstrated how valuable relationships are in creating his success

Lord David Blunkett who surpassed all obstacles to succeed

Having the pleasure of interviewing the inspiring Lord David Blunkett

Nicky Morgan, MP, making personal sacrifices for public life

Jasminder Singh, inspirational and larger than life character

Celebrating Jasminder`s daughter`s wedding

Anila Chowdhry in action interviewing high profile people like Sadiq Khan

The charming Chief Superintendent Raj Kohli keeping our streets safe

The humble Sunita Arora, who has created her own identity in the corporate and charitable world

Nitin Passi showing how fun and creativity can be profitable

Avnish Goyal creating a business culture inspired by his values

156

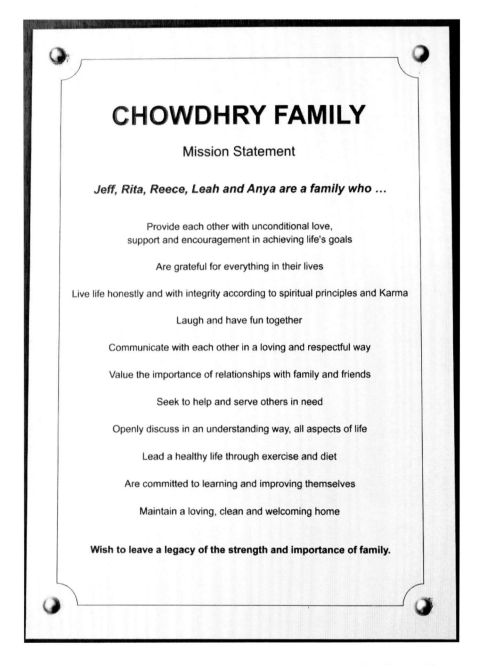

CHOWDHRY FAMILY

Mission Statement

Jeff, Rita, Reece, Leah and Anya are a family who ...

Provide each other with unconditional love,
support and encouragement in achieving life's goals

Are grateful for everything in their lives

Live life honestly and with integrity according to spiritual principles and Karma

Laugh and have fun together

Communicate with each other in a loving and respectful way

Value the importance of relationships with family and friends

Seek to help and serve others in need

Openly discuss in an understanding way, all aspects of life

Lead a healthy life through exercise and diet

Are committed to learning and improving themselves

Maintain a loving, clean and welcoming home

Wish to leave a legacy of the strength and importance of family.

Chowdhry Family Mission Statement hung up on the kitchen wall

Arun's Reflections

In Arun's session, upon hearing the stories of my mother and my brother, he quickly recognised that he and Raju had both been raised by self-sacrificing women with strong, child-centred family values.

ARUN: My mum's like yours: always fretting about how we appear to the outside world – though I can't say that bothers me. I know she always puts my needs and my dad's before her own, too – it's just how our family operates. She's always said that if I'm happy, she's happy. I feel guilty for saying it out loud, but I've never had to think about her needs. Hearing about the way Raju did things for your mother – more than that, how he *wanted* to do things for her – makes me feel a bit guilty. But our situation's not the same. My mum's got financial security. Your mum didn't.

This seemed to be the first time that Arun had ever reflected on what his mother might want from life. Like his father, he believed that Zara enjoyed a comfortable and uncomplicated existence with nothing to complain about.

ARUN: I've never thought about what else she might need. I didn't understand why she needed to get away – but when she came back from being away with her friends, I really did see a difference. She was all smiles, telling us all about what they'd been up to. I realised then that I hadn't seen her happy in ages.

I suppose anyone looking at my life would think the same about me, though – that I've got it all, so what could I possibly have to complain about? Yet here I am, sat here in front of you. Maybe I'd know my mum better if I'd had to shoulder all the responsibilities your brother had to take on after your father's death. It sounds like you and your siblings really understood you mum.

RITA: Our mother's needs were much more outwardly obvious. Plus, we all knew what she valued, so we could help her live by her values. Importantly, these are the same values – with a few nips and tucks, as some had outlived their usefulness – that my brother used to develop himself, personally and professionally. Remember that you too have absorbed your parents' values, even if you haven't realised it. What do you think those values might be?

ARUN: I know that I don't value what the community thinks, which is all Mum and Dad ever go on about. They talk about the importance of education too but, like Raju, I don't think that education is the only route to success.

RITA: So, what values do you think you share with your parents?

ARUN: I'm probably more like my mum in the way I think I should treat other people. She's always been kind and friendly towards my friends, and they like her as a result. She's good with the people who work around our house. She remembers things like our cleaner's birthday. She's had the same decorator painting for us since I was a kid.

My mum values people. Being around her friends did her a world of good. I get a lot out of being around people too. I like being there for my friends, helping them out, making a difference to their lives. I suppose it makes me feel valued, when I haven't always felt valued academically – in that respect, I can relate to your brother. And to be fair to my mum, she did calm my dad down when I dropped out of uni. She's more diplomatic than he is – she's always trying to settle our arguments. It's funny when I think about it, because I can see that I'm that person in my friendship group. I like to sort things out and, if I'm honest, I do worry about what my friends think of me. I like to be seen as someone popular, well-liked.

I've never stopped to ask myself, *What are my values?* If it's about what's important to me and what motivates me, I'd say friendships and fairness – which is where my dad and I are chalk and cheese. He could learn a thing or two from my mum about the way you treat staff. He really needs to develop a new company culture at ACE, before everyone walks out.

RITA: What values would you try to instil in order to create a new company culture?

ARUN: I like the loyalty that Jasminder, Nitin and your brother show their staff. My dad doesn't do that, certainly not among non-management staff. I would love to turn it around at the call centre so that people hang around for more than six months. It doesn't seem fair to me that people who are on the phones all day, trying to bring in the money are the least valued workers in the place. I would love to give them a voice, improve their working conditions so that they'd feel invested in the company.

RITA: One of my good friends and existing clients is Avnish Goyal, the Founder and Chairman of a healthcare business called Hallmark Care Homes. Like you, this client valued justice and fairness at work and, consequently, at Hallmark they celebrate employees' accomplishments in a variety of ways. As Avnish explained, "It shouldn't just be about celebrating team success at the end, but also celebrating it along on the way. So, we hold 'Hallmark empowerment days' and have a team recognition fund, awarded each month when staff hit certain KPIs and a Christmas party fund."

Arun looked animated.

ARUN: Those are exactly the types of things I want to bring to the call centre.

RITA: In order to lay down the foundations of staff success, the management at Hallmark encourages integrity in the way they all work together. So for example, if someone says they're going to do something by a certain date, they get it done by that date. Integrity in the workplace is about keeping your word. If it becomes apparent that it's possible to deliver a result, any affected members of staff must be notified immediately – not just five minutes before the deadline. In that way, integrity has become part of the company's shared values.

ARUN: We need to instil some integrity into our business – we don't have a culture of trust. I couldn't persuade my dad with the feedback from my staff survey, but maybe he'd listen to you explain the importance of instilling some values into ACE.

RITA: Your dad's a **D** type, which means he needs to be presented with objective evidence, rather than emotional hearsay from disgruntled employees. In order to persuade him to listen, you need to back up the findings of your survey with statistics, linking profits to levels of staff satisfaction and development. Hallmark, for example, supports the aspirations of its staff through continuous training. I was asked to deliver a series of SAVVI workshops around personal and professional development for its managers and staff teams, as a result of which, 25% of its general managers were promoted and 50% of staff demonstrated improved performance. My client reported back to me that, "It's had an impact on everyone. It's a ripple effect: you throw a pebble into the pond, and you don't know how far the ripple is going to travel."

ARUN: That's an impressive figure. It would make my dad sit up listen. Our staff need decent training and coaching. I would benefit from some coaching too, but mostly I'd love to see some of the Asian employees, who've been ignored for so long, being given opportunities to develop so that we can have some home-grown managers in the future.

RITA: Arun, you've said that you don't get recognition at the business. We can't ever control what others think of us, but we *can* control what we bring to the table. This will help you feel differently about your status in the short- to mid-term. Clearly doing the staff survey has had a positive effect on you: you feel you've contributed by listening to workers. As a next step, why don't you put together a costed proposal, backed with data, for creating a company culture at ACE based on some of your values about respect and fairness, with the aim of inspiring staff loyalty? Looking after staff inevitably benefits the longer-term financial health of a business, which chimes with your father's value for profits.

Arun's Action Plan

Arun and I worked together to devise the following SMART action plan, which was linked directly to the results of the staff survey and was aimed at improving the company culture at ACE.

- Create a rewards programme linked to quality of service, not just delivery of sales.
- Run a formal recognition scheme to reward staff by giving time off in periods of high availability (i.e., when the company is not so busy).
- Introduce an awards gala night to celebrate the achievement of staff members who go the extra mile.
- Improve the comfort of communal staff areas.
- Improve the lighting and air conditioning in the office.
- Regularly work on the telephones himself, taking calls, which would enable him to better understand the practical side of the job as well as empathise more with employees. Simultaneously, seeing a management

figure like Arun get down to the serious work of telesales would help to break down the prevalent 'them and us' mentality.

- Monitor the promotion process and invite external individuals to observe the interview process to ensure impartiality.

- Develop team leaders, encouraging them to work together instead of against each other, and ensure quality consistency. Arrange SAVVI workshops with Rita for staff and managers.

- Create a working party comprised of junior, middle-management and senior staff to generate company values, facilitated by Rita.

Zara's Reflections

Zara's value about being an ideal wife and mother left her unfulfilled, particularly now that Arun was growing older and her role as a mother was diminished. However, any notion of becoming someone other than a wife and mother, even if Jay were to allow it, was thwarted by her limiting belief about her weak education and skills.

Over the course of our sessions, Zara had made progress with her self-awareness and was working on her mindset to liberate her strengths. However, by clinging to some of her old values and beliefs, she was limiting her personal growth and preventing herself from achieving her full potential. I wanted Zara to start to question some of the values and beliefs that she was using to map out her life choices. Crucially, she had to overcome the limiting belief that she didn't have the education to pursue a career beyond being a homemaker. Being able to do so would inch her closer to success. Zara had expressed her regret at not pursuing higher education, but at the same time she had recognised that at school she'd been a conscientious student and a quick learner. This showed that she was beginning to challenge her limiting self-belief, and was another step on the road to becoming SAVVI.

Zara's Action Plan

Now that Zara was beginning to develop her sense of self-belief, she was able to work with me to devise a SMART action plan of her own focused on self-development, and on enabling her to live by the values that were serving her, whilst learning to reject those that weren't. Zara's plan was to:

- Devise a list of five charities to support and organise an event to raise money for the first on the list.
- Work together with Arun and Jay to draw up the Sharma family charter.
- Persuade Jay to attend a joint family session with Rita.

By the end of their third sessions, Zara and Arun were each able to identify the root cause of their lack of fulfilment: the conflict between some of their values and beliefs and the lives they were leading. They needed to work out which values and beliefs were serving them and which were hindering. Those that were hindering them needed to be challenged, rewritten, reprioritised and possibly even rejected. Importantly, both Arun and Zara needed to stop allowing themselves to be defined by other people's values and beliefs. Once they began to understand how to *consciously* and *proactively* carve out lives congruent with their abundant values and beliefs, they were closer to achieving their goals – and, consequently, to future happiness and success.

Acquiring self-knowledge related to our values and beliefs marks a powerful stage in becoming SAVVI. If your thoughts, actions and habits are making you feel unhappy, unhealthy, unsuccessful or lost in life, it didn't happen by accident.

It is the result of a spiralling effect, identified by Gandhi with the following words:

Your beliefs become your thoughts,
Your thoughts become your words,
Your words become your actions,
Your actions become your habits,
Your habits become your values,
Your values become your destiny.

Once you become aware of the positive and negative influence of values and beliefs on your current and future happiness, you can make them work for you rather than against you. When we find ourselves living out of step with what we value, which makes us unhappy, it's vital to remember our own power to turn things around. In the words of the American spiritual teacher Peace Pilgrim, *'If you realised how powerful your thoughts are, you would never think a negative thought.'* The power of a positive mindset will help you take control of your destiny.

4

Verbal Communication

The Pre-Occupied Businessman Who Doesn't Listen

When explaining the power of verbal communication to my clients, I describe the message behind a short film about an old blind man begging on a street in Glasgow. The man sits on a pavement with a cardboard sign that tells people, *'I'm blind. Please help.'* Throughout the morning many people walk past him, too busy to give him the time of day or any loose change. Only a handful stop to drop a few coins. Then, a woman who notices that most people ignore the blind man approaches him and picks up his sign. She writes a new message on the other side and places it back on the ground. Within minutes, every passer-by is throwing down money, several coins at a time, for the blind man. The man can't believe the sound of the heavy shower of coins. Later, the woman comes back. The man recognises her from her touch of her shoes.

- "What did you do to my sign?" he asks her.
- She replies, "It's the same, but different words."
- She had written the words: 'It's a beautiful day and I can't see it.'

This story reveals the extraordinary power of words to change human response to the same situation. It's a lesson in how we can make the greatest impact by carefully choosing our words for any given audience. This technique in communication is another key step to being SAVVI.

Once Zara and Arun had developed their respective self-awareness and achiever's mindsets and identified their driving values, it was time to flower their verbal communication skills so that they could fulfil the steps they'd taken thus far on their journey to becoming SAVVI. They were ready to start seeing the change in their lives.

I use the simple image of the lotus flower (see previous page) to illustrate to my clients the overlapping petals of verbal communication. Isolated, one petal makes little impact. Together, the petals can blossom into a fuller understanding of one another's communication skills and limitations, which makes for fruitful communication in the future. SAVVI communicators understand that effective verbal communication, adapted to one's audience, builds positive relationships and wins deals. Understanding the personality types – and the corresponding verbal communication styles—of your partner, child, family member or colleague can fundamentally alter the way you bring issues to the table and how they get resolved. Successful verbal communication – and your choice of words – really can enhance and save relationships.

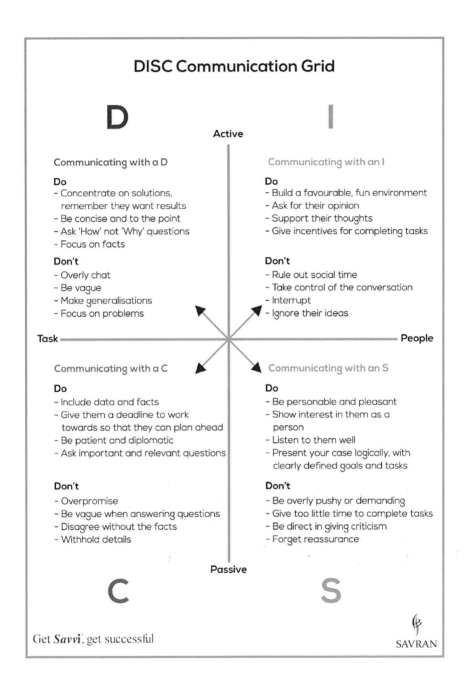

Zara and Arun had reached a critical point in their personal development: they could only progress with their respective action plans if they paused to reflect on the way they currently communicated (according to their DISC profile) and studied the ways in which other personality types characteristically communicate back.

This knowledge enables you to adapt your verbal communication style in response to others. For example, the pace of processing ideas and information varies across the personality types. A **D** type, for example, thinks and speaks quickly, whereas an **S** type is more considered and processes information at a slower pace. If you don't know that about an **S**, you may falsely believe that they are disinterested in what you're saying. Knowing the communication traits of others helps you to adapt your style for them, thereby reducing the risk of miscommunication. Another example of different verbal communication styles, is that a **D** type would typically say, "You need to do this, in this specific way." An **S** type (which is the opposite style of a **D**), is less forceful and may suggest indirectly, "Others found that this method worked well." So, a **D** type would benefit from adapting their style to meet half way and say, for example, "You may want to consider this," particularly if they're talking to an **I** type who doesn't respond well to feeling controlled. **I** types themselves are talkative and persuasive in communication, but they should be brief, direct and to the point when talking to their opposite style, a **C**. By using the right language for the right personality type, you will hear first-hand the way that verbal communication can flower between different people.

Zara had become sufficiently self-aware through her sessions to realise that she needed to reprioritise her values. But to realise them, she would soon need to have a potentially difficult conversation with Jay. **S** types seek harmony and want to avoid conflict in their personal and professional relationships, which means they tend to shy away from difficult conversations. For instance, an **S**-type manager will be reluctant to deal with tricky issues such as the underperformance of staff. In Zara's case, one of her areas of difficulty in communication was that she was unable to broach the subject of her suspicions about Jay's relationship with his finance director. However, if she was going to start making the changes that would help her live a life that was true to her values, she would need to adapt the way she communicated with her husband.

Arun, meanwhile, was full of ideas and renewed enthusiasm about changing the unhappy work culture at his father's call centre business. However, he too needed to reflect on the strengths and limitations of his **I** style communication, in order to be able to start living according to his values – in his case, by delivering his ideas for the business to his **DC** father. He needed to adapt his tendency to talk for too long, without enough hard facts and details, if he wanted to capture the attention of a direct and dominant communicator like Jay.

Furthermore, to sit down and write up their charter of family values would require Zara and Arun to demonstrate the right verbal communication skills to ensure that everyone felt they were being heard and valued. They both recognised the need to enhance their communication skills – starting at home – to fulfil the first three steps of becoming SAVVI, so they booked in a family session with me, to which they wanted to invite Jay.

Zara and Arun arrived together for the session. After 15 minutes of waiting for him to arrive, Zara made an announcement.

ZARA: Jay's not coming.

RITA: Have you heard from him?

A: No, he'd never actually tell you that he wasn't coming. I agree: he won't be coming. He does this type of thing all the time. Over-promises and never shows.

*Zara had fallen silent and I wanted to hear from her. But true to her **S** type, I could see that she wanted to avoid a difficult conversation, so it was up to me to draw her back in. Zara was being held back by this **S** trait. **I** and **D** types like Arun and Jay find these direct conversations easier.*

RITA: Zara, it looks as if Jay isn't coming. Why do you think he's not here?

I could see that Zara found this difficult to talk about.

ZARA: He's very busy right now. A big contract's just come in. That'll be the reason he's not here. He must've had to stay on at work. I'm sorry we've wasted your time.

ARUN: Mum, when are you going to stop making excuses for him?

ZARA: That's not fair on your father, Arun." *She looked uncomfortable.* Sometimes he needs to prioritise the business.

ARUN: Mum, he *always* prioritises the business. This is how it always goes. Dad constantly lets you – *both of us* – down, and you never say a word. He knew we wanted him here and I know – *he knows* – that you'll just let him get away with it.

*I noticed that Zara and Arun's communication with each other was typical of their respective personality types: Arun, the **ID** type, was a persuader – already trying to talk his mother into facing up to the issues with Jay – and did all the talking. Zara, meanwhile, became incommunicative when she felt out of her comfort zone.*

RITA: I suggest we go ahead with the session and if Jay does arrive, he can still join in. The good news is that he did complete the online personality profile and consented to sharing it in the session.

Just as you both identified, Jay is primarily a **D** type: dominant. As you know, people are often a combination of styles – usually two, occasionally more – but there will typically be a primary style and a secondary style. Jay's secondary style is **C**, which means he makes decisions based on facts and not emotions. Looking back at the DISC communication grid (see page 169), you can see both **D** and **C** styles are task-focused. He doesn't respond well to people communicating in a rambling way, or stating points and ideas without any evidence. This desire to get tangible results can make him come across as unfeeling.

ZARA: Everything you've just said describes the way I currently talk to him.

RITA: Jay's **DC** combination gives him a task-focused and problem-solving attitude. In my experience of working with teams and families, **C**s are often the last to participate in the personality profiling because they want enough time to complete the questionnaire accurately – plus, they fear the prospect of criticism.

ARUN: That's Dad through and through. He always needs to be right and he won't listen if he doesn't like it. He wouldn't have seen the point – 'the goal' – of turning up today.

RITA: Did you give him a purpose for coming to today's session?

They both explained that they had simply told him, using emotional language, that they wanted him to come along. They hadn't actually told him that by attending a family session, they could start to communicate more effectively for the benefit of the family business, for example.

RITA: In my family and team sessions, we sometimes role play to rehearse difficult or new conversations that we might need to have with people. What we say and how we say it may not chime with our usual style, but sometimes it can be useful to wear the mask of another type's verbal communication style in order to get our message across.

I'd like the two of you to be aware of how you currently communicate. This is the middle petal on the flower image – *Yours*. We then need an awareness of *Others'* communication styles. SAVVI people understand and practise this.

Let's start with Zara, an **S** type. You communicate with sincerity and you're a good listener. You naturally relate to others, helping them to belong. You're a real team player. You strive for peace and harmony, as you've shown all along in your support of Arun and Jay, and in your desire to be a dutiful daughter.

ZARA: I know it takes me time to process what's being said, but I like to take my time and think things through. I do struggle with confrontation. I avoid it and I feel uncomfortable when others force it onto me. I know I can be indecisive and reticent, and too compromising.

RITA: S types do tend to overthink the consequences of communication, which holds them back from saying what they want or don't want. However, if you don't undertake that difficult journey in the short term, the outcome may be worse in the future: you're storing up trouble.

ZARA: But I thought I was helping by not rocking the boat. I like people to think of me as easy-going. I prefer to make things easier for others. I'm not used to asking for things for myself. I worry that if I ask for something the other person will say no, and the idea of that make me feel worse. So it's easier not to ask and manage on my own.

RITA: S types have a talent for giving. Sometimes, however, it can come to define you, to the point that you don't know how to ask for things for yourself. Try adapting your behaviour to be more like a **D**: open and direct, having a clear plan or solution.

ARUN: I'm embarrassed to say, Mum, that I don't remember you ever asking anything of me that was just for you. I'm sorry.

Hearing Arun's supportive response gave Zara the burst of confidence she needed to have a go at rehearsing her difficult conversation with Jay.

RITA: Zara, shall we role play to help you practise what you might want to say to Jay about missing the session? I'll be Jay.

ZARA: Jay, I want to talk to you. I really wanted you at the session today. I'm upset that you don't think it's important enough…

RITA: You know how busy I am. What do you mean, you're not important? The business is all about you and Arun! Look around you: at your beautiful house, your car, your jewellery, your holidays.

Zara struggled to answer at first.

ZARA: Yes, you have given me everything I could materially want. But I'm not happy, Jay.

RITA: You sound ungrateful. Our parents had nothing. We have everything!

ZARA: I know we're luckier than them in so many ways, but it's not just about money. It's the simpler things. When you couldn't come today, I was really disappointed. And you made me feel embarrassed. You could have phoned or texted to tell us you weren't coming. That made it worse, because it felt that it was so unimportant to you that you couldn't be bothered to even tell us you weren't coming.

RITA: I told you, I didn't have time. I was too busy.

ZARA: Really? Too busy to text me?

I decided to check in with Zara at this stage.

RITA: That's a positive start, Zara: you opened up about what had upset you. It can seem easier to stay silent and not rock the boat just to keep the peace, but your feelings will fester and that's dangerous in relationships. Now, I want you to consider how Jay, given his **DC** style, might have responded to your words.

ZARA: I kept talking about feelings though, didn't I? He won't listen to me waffling like that. I found it hard saying all those things directly. I don't know that I could do that to his face. It makes me feel unkind.

RITA: As an **S**, you're a kind and sensitive listener. Adapting to another style of communication doesn't mean a personality change – you can still be yourself – but when you call him out on something, there are communication techniques that will help you move towards a better solution. This is why you need to learn about other people's way of communicating: so that you're speaking one another's language.

ARUN: So if I've understood right, Dad's **DC** type means that he makes decisions based on cold facts. He doesn't do emotions and he doesn't like criticism. He wants evidence-based solutions, not a problem, or he loses interest. To be honest, I've seen it happen in my conversations with him. I can't communicate with him either.

RITA: Yes, **D**s like your father are direct and unemotional in their verbal communication. You'll have noticed that his language doesn't dwell on feelings. If you want to be heard by him, you should know that he won't respond well to anyone rambling about vague ideas or emotions.

ZARA: Which is exactly what I always do. In the past, every time I've plucked up the courage to tell him I'm unhappy or feeling empty, he switches off. I clearly can't speak his language.

ARUN: Not yet.

Arun was trying to help his mother feel better, which is a trait of the I communicator.

RITA: All of us – including Jay – need to adapt our communication style to work with others, sometimes borrowing from other personality traits in order to improve the way we communicate. The two of you have some great skills that Jay could apply to his own communication.

ZARA: So we just need to use different words?

RITA: Different words, with a different style of delivery. **D** types like Jay are direct, and their highly intense communication style is sometimes seen as *too* direct. However, it works the other way too: if you don't tell Jay exactly what the issue is, he won't know there's an issue and he'll assume all's well. Learn from his direct approach: if he had a problem, he'd tell you directly, wouldn't he?

ZARA: Yes. If he needs something done, or disagrees with the way something's been done, I'm the first to know about it.

ARUN: And you let him order you around.

ZARA: Yes, I've avoided certain conversations with him for an easier life.

RITA: How does avoiding direct conversations leave you feeling?

ZARA: Very upset, deep down. And then my feelings of sadness become worse.

RITA: What do you think might happen in your relationship in, say, two to three years if things continue in this way?

ZARA: I guess we'll carry on drifting along, and grow further apart. I see him light up around successful women at parties, and I know he's an attractive man to other women. Maybe he'll be drawn to one of them – someone who's more like him, someone more outgoing and ambitious. Jay never seems thrown by a problem. He manages to shrug them off. He'd probably prefer me to be more like that. Not like me at all.

Suddenly, Zara had a moment of revelation.

ZARA: Now I see exactly why he enjoys the company of his finance director: she communicates like him. No wonder he sounds relaxed around her, why they're always laughing together.

All right, starting from today I am going to start to change. I'll admit to you – even in front of Arun – that I do worry about her and Jay. I can't stop wondering if they're having a romantic relationship – but in my typical **S** style, I've never confronted him. I've held back from saying anything because I keep worrying about what he'll say. I know I need to do this, though: I can see that my silence is giving him licence to carry on making me feel belittled.

ARUN: Mum, I'm sure there isn't really anything going on. But you're right: it's a good idea to start being more direct with him. Listening to what Rita's said about how we both tend to communicate, I do think we need structured plans in place for when we do talk to Dad, to get him to actually listen to us.

ZARA: But Rita, if you're telling me not to talk to Jay about emotions, how can I tell him I'm unhappy in the first place?

RITA: To have influence over a **D**, you need to bring solutions to the problem you're discussing. Then when you have their attention, you invite them to offer their opinions too. Ask Jay to comment on your ideas, and talk about how they could help him to achieve his goals too.

ZARA: Until I started coming to these sessions, I didn't have a plan for my next steps in life. I've got some ideas now, like going back to study and supporting a charity. To get Jay to listen, I should ask him for his thoughts on my plans and work out how they fit in with his own goals.

RITA: Well done! You're becoming SAVVI about Jay's communication style. **D**s are always looking for new challenges, new opportunities to help them achieve their goals. Someone like Jay needs to have what's on your mind explained openly and clearly. He thinks differently to the way you do, and will be focused on different things.

ZARA: I have a short-term solution to my unhappiness: getting involved with a charity. Next, I need to link it to Jay's goals. I'm still going to find it hard to be direct with him, though.

RITA: The more you practice, the easier it gets. Knowledge about yourself and Jay as communicators is a vital first step. A **D** type, for example, is motivated by a good challenge, whilst you, as an **SC**, are motivated by working as a team, which is promising for the two of you when it comes to joint projects like supporting Arun.

ARUN: So in our family, Mum is a primary **S** type. I know she doesn't open up easily and avoids confrontation. I've seen her do that all my life.

ZARA: I just want us all to get along.

A: But you end up losing out, Mum, when you don't say what's on your mind. So the way to move forward when we talk to Mum is to make sure we ask for her opinion and present her with the why and how if we want her to do something, especially if it involves change.

Meanwhile, Dad's primary **D** type makes him plain-speaking: he wants results and solutions, so when we talk to him, we need to get to the point and not focus on problems. Already I can see why he didn't listen to me when I told him about staff dissatisfaction. Then, his secondary trait as a **C** focuses him on process and quality. So, to win him over I have to back up what I say with evidence and data. Again, I didn't go in with enough solid data to back what I was telling him about the staff survey results. Finally, as a **C** he's sensitive to criticism and works hard to get things right, so if we disagree with him, we should make it about disagreeing with the facts, and not about disagreeing with him personally. Dad's a 'teller' not a 'seller'. He doesn't bother with selling people an idea – he just tells them directly. We need to adopt his way of telling it like it is. I know now that when I want to him to do something, I need to ensure that I broach the subject at the right time and in the right place. He doesn't like being interrupted or feeling as if he isn't being heard. I need to let him feel as if he's in control of the conversation.

ZARA: Can I have a go at describing Arun's communication style?

Zara was looking animated, and clearly felt much more like joining in than she had at the beginning of the session.

ZARA: He's an **I,** which makes him a natural persuader – something he's definitely always been. People are drawn to him, and he finds it easy to sell an idea. Unlike me, he'll voice his opinions, but he has a tendency to ramble and talk too much. I think both of us need to adapt the way we talk if we're going to make Jay listen.

ARUN: So now we know all this about our different communication styles, how easy will it be for us to change and make things better? You make it sound easy.

RITA: You'll experience first-hand the way your respective verbal communication styles will 'flower' when you're equipped with awareness of people's different styles of communicating.

Good Cop, Good Cop: Raj Kohli, Chief Superintendent, Metropolitan Police

Arun had worked out for himself that he needed to improve his verbal communication with his father, both at home and in the workplace. Having identified some serious concerns at work regarding staff morale, Arun needed to communicate them to his father in a way that he would listen to and act upon. In contrast to his reticent mother, Arun needed to control his tendency to talk too much and ensure instead that he listened more, and that he weighed up what he wanted to say. To communicate effectively with someone like his father, Arun (like his **S**-type mother) needed to have evidence at the ready.

However, before Arun was ready to practise a conversation with his father through role play, I wanted to share with him the story of Chief Superintendent Raj Kohli – who, like Arun, is an **IS** type. Raj is far from being your typical senior officer serving in the London Metropolitan Police: he is a charming, wisecracking Scottish-Punjabi in a turban, who sports a kilt on special occasions. Despite his colourful and outgoing personality, he admits that he's not comfortable at high-profile events or in professional networking situations. He says, "That's just not me. I'd rather a smaller setting. I need to be able to connect with somebody at a deeper level."

Raj is a fascinating mix of someone who is outwardly confident – he appeared on national television as the face of the Metropolitan Police after the tragic death of singer Amy Winehouse – but admits to being ill at ease in the spotlight. "I felt nervous after the Westminster Bridge attack. I was at the Houses of Parliament and as I walked towards the doors of Westminster Abbey, I could see that there were 600 people inside. I could also see my reflection. And I remember thinking, *S**t!* But at the same time, I thought, *I'm going to have to fake it 'til I make it.* I just burst through that door and said, 'All right, where's the microphone? I'm going to speak to these people.' But it was one of those, *My God! What am I doing here?* moments."

Raj comes from a family of strong communicators: his mother was a renowned political agitator in the 1970s and 80s, speaking out on domestic violence. His father was a teacher in the secure unit of a prison for young offenders. His two brothers are entertainers and broadcasters in the UK. All the Kohlis have a talent for communicating with the outside world, and they each enjoy successful careers as effective verbal communicators. But according to Raj, "We don't have a lot of open communication and deep conversations within our family." When he was racially and physically bullied as a child at private school, for example, and seeing the school doctor on a daily basis, he didn't tell his parents – even though he calls them his heroes. He puts it down to the times they were living in. "They were working so hard, doing 12-hour days. Dad was a teacher by day and then out buying and selling property in his own time, working exceptionally hard to put us three through private school, college and university."

After graduating, Raj quit a Master's degree just a few months short of completion and worked for a couple of years at his father's property business before joining the police on its graduate recruitment scheme. As an **IS** type with a very strong **I** side, Raj (like Arun) thrives in a sociable, people-focused work environment, which is what drew him to a police career, that sees him working with the community every day.

In many ways, though, Raj Kohli is an anomaly in the police force. "The Met" is, by the nature of its hierarchical structure and its command-and-control system, a **DC** organisation. For example, it measures success through statistics such as the number of arrests. However, Raj readily admits that, "We're a public service and you, as a tax payer, want to know where your hard-earned bucks are going, so I have no issue with it being results-driven. My issue is that we are potentially looking at the wrong results.

Certainly, Raj's **IS** strengths of human warmth and persuasion have served him well when dealing with suspects, and he enjoys a reputation amongst colleagues as having considerable talent in coaxing information out of uncommunicative suspects. Raj explains, "I chat to them, open up a bit about myself, and then they open up. I said to somebody in detention recently, 'Look, I know what you know. I don't know what you're going through, but I know you're worried about your kids. You made a mistake. We'll get it sorted, then we'll move on. Life goes on.' And he started talking; he shared criminal intelligence that I was able to pass on to the officers on the case.

"I've just been with a 17-year-old boy with significant mental health issues in police custody. After taking him through the formal bit – which I always do with juveniles – I talked to him as me, the parent. I said, 'You made a mistake; don't worry about it. It'll get fixed. Just get some help, see a doctor.' His grandmother was there and I think it touched her heart, because all they see is a police officer and the legislative stuff. But I never want them to walk away thinking, *He's just a police officer.* I want them to think, *He's a human being.* My default position is that everyone is good. Some of the criminals I'm dealing with have just made a bad decision."

Raj can be equally persuasive when communicating with some of his colleagues. "I said to someone who didn't look their usual self, 'Look, this is not a boss-to-junior-colleague conversation – this is Raj speaking. If you want to talk about what's bothering you, then let's talk.' She opened up about issues with her ex-husband, her son, work. She's a decent, hardworking person, who was having real difficulties. And because I always start off with, 'I know something's wrong,' I can take them to the place where they feel able to open up."

Whilst Raj has brought extraordinary empathy to his performance in the Metropolitan Police Force, he became aware early on in his career that some of his **IS** traits were also holding him back. For five years, he was stuck at inspector level. "I think the organisation misunderstood me. I was always starting arguments. I faced some challenges going from inspector to chief inspector. My left-wing politics didn't necessarily plug into the organisation 10 years ago, though it's vastly different now." To utilise his **IS** out-of-the-box thinking skills, and to have some influence over the perception of crime in the Metropolitan Police and the way the police engaged with the public, Raj knew he had to formalise some of his communication and borrow some **DC** traits, such as the ability to be direct and precise.

IS types like Raj can be challenged by specific issues that require a potentially difficult conversation, such as staff underperformance. Many **S**

managers need coaching in this area, and the key is to encourage them to consider the outcomes of failing to deal with a situation immediately.

After some coaching, Raj recognised that he had difficulty communicating with **C** types, his opposite in the personality chart (see DISC Communication Grid on page 169). In fact, **Cs** view **IS** types like Raj as too emotional. Armed with this knowledge, Raj needed to modify the way he communicated with others – for example, communication with his **C-** and **D**-type line managers would mean leaving out the frills of his usual style and getting straight to the point, focusing on facts, data and process.

Raj used to insist, "I don't do data. I don't do data!" But through coaching, he grasped the importance of identifying and understanding the wants and needs of his audience, which made it easier to have productive communication.

Recalling a previous boss, Raj explains that, "Whilst we were respectful and got on socially, professionally I didn't understand what she wanted from me, and I don't think she understood what I wanted or needed from her. But after the DISC analysis, I realised my colleague is a **D** and I'm an **I**, which meant that for the working relationship to improve it was up to me to change my style. However, I did it without compromising my values; all I did was to re-frame information into graphical or numerical form. What my colleague didn't want – because she couldn't feel it – was my passion. She needed to see the product. So I turned my passion into a product. I've learnt that **Cs** and **Ds** see my passion as me being emotional; this wasn't historically seen as an asset in the Metropolitan Police, though that is changing under the new commissioner. She has talked about being true to yourself, being emotional. Funnily enough, that **CD** colleague I mentioned is the one who's had to roll out this new style into the Metropolitan Police."

By adapting and flowering his verbal style, Raj can now switch easily from speaking directly with **CD** types in senior positions and being heard clearly by them, to gaining the trust of drug dealers or troubled teenage suspects, and to being sympathetic to grieving relatives.

It is testament to Raj's efforts to become SAVVI, that his ability to communicate successfully across diverse styles and backgrounds was rewarded by the Metropolitan Police: finally, after his five years of 'stalling', he started to rise rapidly through the ranks. Raj has risen to superintendent in 16 years when, on average, it takes 22 years (his progression is 60% faster than his white peers). Raj claims, however, that he didn't start off with a plan of career progression. "I've always been in the here and now. I never thought, *"This is the next step."* What spurred him on was his **I**-type fear of rejection (which means he still sometimes doubts himself and compares himself to others), which was fuelled by his desire to live up to others' expectations of him. That, along with the encouragement of mentors, friends and family, motivated him to seek promotion. Although Raj now jokes with characteristic modesty, "I got accidentally promoted," he also acknowledges that, true to his personality style, he holds back and waits to be invited before taking each forward step in his career.

Today, Raj is one of only three BAME (Black Asian Minority Ethnic) chief superintendents in the UK and one of the most influential Sikhs in Europe. He has won numerous accolades over the course of his police career, including a commendation for increasing the number of Police Community Support Officers (PCSO) from minority groups and a British Indian Overseas Award for Services to the Community.

Yet he remains modest. "When you say I've been successful, I genuinely don't see it. I look at my success through the lens of other people, who've achieved because I've been in their life. I'm driven by helping others because I've seen how much difference it's made when others have helped me."

Although Raj has adapted his communication skills, he understands what other personality types bring to the table. "I don't always think I have to change; I have to understand others and get them to do certain things for me. Whenever I need performance to be driven, for example, I know I've got a deputy who's great at driving performance. I'll say to him, 'This is why I need it to happen. Can you go and make it happen?' There are pros and cons to that, of course. The pro is that performance gets delivered, but the con is that he'll also deliver performance on something I might not even think needs measuring. I have to accept that; I have to accept that he's got an alternative view. We'll have healthy discussions as to why I don't think certain performance indicators are healthy, and we'll come to an understanding; over time I can see how he thinks, and he starts to think a little bit more like me, so we meet in the middle."

Raj Kohli is an example of someone who, over time, has undoubtedly flowered his communication and learnt from other styles, whilst managing to uphold his strong values and apply his creative thinking. In fact, the flowering of his verbal skills has enabled him to promote some of his other values, which may have gone unheard or been dismissed, had he not understood how to communicate them in a results-driven work environment. For example, Raj is currently asking charities to research treating serious youth violence as a public health issue, rather than just a crime issue. He believes that, "Something's driving young people to carry and use knives. If we look at it from the mental health point of view, we've got a much greater chance of success. You can apply coaching, mentoring and mental health support as opposed to arrest."

Employees like Raj, who may start out holding different values from their dominant work culture, have more opportunities to thrive and be heard – and even influence colleagues' ideas – once they become SAVVI communicators.

RITA: So Arun, you've heard how Raj Kohli, an **IS** like you, modified his style not only in the interest of his own career, but also in order to become best placed to advance the people around him. Like you, he's passionate about fairness at work. Listening to his story, and now that you're more knowledgeable about yours and your father's communication styles, I'd like us to try some role play to practice talking to your father and trying to engage him with the staff problem at ACE. Remember that he is a **DC,** only persuaded by tangible evidence that directly impacts on him and his goals.

ARUN: Yes, I can see where I've gone wrong in the past. Like Mum, I was speaking a different language to Dad. I know I'm a good and persuasive communicator, which goes with my **I** profile, but somehow, I've never been able to hold Dad's attention for long.

RITA: As an **I**, you are a natural communicator. You like to do business in a friendly way whilst managing to draw people into your viewpoint. However, the weakness of this style is that you sometimes don't think through your ideas, and that you can talk over others in your enthusiasm.

ZARA: Yes, that sounds familiar!

RITA: Rambling will lose you your audience – particularly with your **DC** father – and you won't make the desired impact.

ARUN: So I need to go to him with hard evidence and solutions or he'll simply switch off. I need to properly plan ahead before I talk to him.

RITA: Is and **C**s are opposite types, which you can see from the chart: **I** types are people-focused; **C** and **D** types are task-oriented. You'll have been thinking about the staff dissatisfaction; Jay will have been thinking about what he needs to do to keep the business profiting. Pure **C**s need time to analyse data, and can over-analyse to the point that decision-making takes too long and they suffer from a paralysis of analysis. Jay is not a pure **C** so he won't get stuck on the data, but that doesn't mean he doesn't need it in order to engage with what you're saying.

ARUN: To be honest, when I went to talk to him about the staff problems at ACE, I focused on people's feelings of dissatisfaction because that's important to me. I can see now that that's why his eyes glazed over. If I'd gone in armed with some solid data and not just a list of staff complaints, he might have been more receptive – and then we would have been 'flowering' our communication.

RITA: Exactly. Your father doesn't have time to listen to the complaints of others. He needs to see hard-hitting figures from your staff survey about the impact on his profits and losses before he'll make any kind of change.

ARUN: I do have plenty of data on staff retention, and about the impact of low morale on company profits, but I'd lost his attention before I had the chance to refer to those. I'll need to be quicker off the mark. I need to balance my natural persuasive skills with the right evidence to support my findings.

RITA: It sounds like you're ready to have a go at role playing.

ARUN: OK. I'll give it a go.

Dad, we've got a staff retention problem at ACE. I've put together numerical data from staff interviews and gathered some industry research to back up my findings. After you asked me to do the staff survey, I sat people down and asked them, 'In the next 12 months, where do you see yourself professionally?' I was shocked when 83% said that they didn't see themselves remaining at ACE. In the previous year, front line agents replaced 40% of our 250 staff. From my research, I've learnt that our industry is notorious for high staff turnover rates, but did you know that ACE's is higher than the national average?

A 2009 survey by Response Design Cooperation calculated an average of 26% staff turnover – we have nearly twice that figure! And compared to the results of a Gallop poll, where 55% of people report feeling disengaged at work, 74% of our staff feel disengaged. I'm convinced that staff are unhappy because they're not being led effectively or being valued for being anything more than money-making machines.

I'm talking too much, aren't I?

RITA: Your figures are compelling, so consider how to communicate them so that they make a real impact. This will require better planning of what you're going to say. I've obviously put you on the spot here. Be more concise and, yes, talk less and be sure to use accurate data. Stick to the point. But you're starting to work this out for yourself. Well done.

I'll role play your dad now: Arun, as long as profits are up, I don't see the point of worrying about what they're saying on the shop floor. If they don't like it, they can leave. Don't forget, I've just won a business award – I've been in the business for years. I know what I'm talking about.

ARUN: Dad, our staff retention issues are eating into our profit margin. It can take six to nine months for you to see that on our accounts, but it is happening. Oxford Economics calculated in 2014 that it costs £30,614 to replace an employee. I've worked out that, according to our data, we lost £3,061,400 having to re-recruit after staff had left us.

RITA: OK, interesting.

*Arun was beginning to see the difference between the way his natural **I** style wanted to communicate with his father, and the way in which he needed to communicate with him in order to get and keep his attention.*

ARUN: I can see now that I was rambling before. I was telling him about low staff morale, which bothers me (because I like a happy workplace) more than it bothers him!

RITA: Great! You've managed to link an **I**-type concern of yours – low staff morale – to one of his goals – maximising profits – which will get his attention. Remember, though, that he is a **D** style and will also want to hear solutions, not just problems. We've had a little practice here. How will you re-present your report to your father? What is your SMART goal around this?

ARUN: First, I'll book a meeting with him next week with a clear purpose, an agenda and a PowerPoint. I was too informal last time. Then, I'm going to have to reframe the way I talk about the problems, and be clear that I have three clear solutions: number one, to get a budget of £100k to improve the quality of customer service and productivity at ACE by implementing some people-centred values; number two, to get a working party up and running within a month; and number three, to persuade my dad to come to regular family meetings.

RITA: I'd suggest starting with something like, "Dad, I've uncovered an issue." Importantly, make sure that any problems or criticisms you raise are always based on facts (because **C**s are sensitive to criticism) and that you focus on the ways in which they impact on his business goals.

ARUN: I can really hear the difference in talking to him like that. I feel quite excited about trying out being a SAVVI communicator with him. I wish I'd known all this years ago. It seems so obvious now why Dad and I always kept clashing, with my poor mum sat in the middle of us always trying to keep the peace by saying nothing.

RITA: As I said to your mum, becoming a good verbal communicator doesn't happen overnight: it will take practice. However, knowledge of your tendencies – strengths and weaknesses – will at least give you a better chance of pulling communication back in your favour. You're clearly understanding the SAVVI principles of communication. I'm really looking forward to hearing about the outcomes of your meeting with your father.

Arun was well on his way to being a SAVVI communicator. Throughout Raj Kohli's story and my role play with Arun, Zara had sat quietly. I decided to bring the focus back onto her own communication.

Speech is Power: Nicky Morgan MP

RITA: Another public figure I've interviewed who holds some strong views about diversity in the workplace, particularly regarding female staff, and who's also a persuasive verbal communicator is Conservative MP Nicky Morgan, the former Secretary of State for Education and ex-Minister for Women and Equalities and current Secretary of State for Digital, Culture, Media and Sport. Zara, I think you in particular will find her interesting. Nicky comes from what many people would call a privileged upbringing: she grew up in Kingston-upon-Thames, was privately educated at Surbiton High School and went on to Oxford University. She qualified as a Solicitor before switching to a career in British politics, and managed to rise to a cabinet position in just three years.

By the expression on Zara's face, I could see that she was surprised by the example I'd chosen to share with her.

RITA: I can see you're not convinced that Nicky is relatable to your situation.

ZARA: Well yes, there's a bit of a gulf between her education and professional status and mine.

RITA: On the surface, it does look as if Nicky's had it all: she had the right start in life and was raised in a stable family home with the best education opportunities. However, she's also faced barriers as a result of being amongst the 22% minority of women in British politics. What's more, Nicky understands that not having, "A typical background… or going to a good university, doesn't mean you can't do the job." In Nicky's case, she may have had the right educational credentials but, as a working mother, she had to make a number of compromises when embarking on a political career. Her son was only two when she became an MP, and after she rose to a cabinet position, she had to be based four days a week in London, 100 miles away from her family, who moved up to live in her constituency – which left her husband to do the school runs and activities. Female politicians like Nicky Morgan and Prime Minister Theresa May become easy targets: judged for being 'unmaternal' (whether they have children or not) whilst simultaneously being seen primarily as wives and mothers. It's difficult to imagine men in public office being judged on their parental status!

Despite the pressures she faced, Nicky refused to listen to other people's perceptions of what was socially acceptable for her as a woman; instead, she remained true to her heart and her values about making a difference in society.

ZARA: That's was a brave decision; I respect her for that. If I can also learn to be true to my values, I know I can be happier, which will help make my family happier.

RITA: Having been a member of the Conservative Party since she was 16 years old, Nicky defied convention by leaving behind her stable, well-paid job for a less lucrative career in, "One of the toughest working environments." She acknowledges that to do this, she needed to have a very supportive husband. They had to work together and to communicate openly to support Nicky's career. Nicky's weekends are still filled with local events in her constituency, some of which she drags her son to. On top of that, she recalls that during her time as cabinet minister, she would get, "A red box [of documents] to read every weekend – sometimes at 7.30 in the morning – that had to go back down to London at 6pm on a Sunday night."

ZARA: I didn't know she'd left behind a better-paid job for politics. She's obviously made a lot of sacrifices to do something she really believes in – and she's made it work for her. I share Nicky's value of serving others, but it's always been about serving my own family's needs. I know I've got more in me to give to other people as well, so I need to stretch my goals. But my obstacle – which is the same as Arun's – is going to be getting Jay on board.

RITA: Achieving your goals and living by your values is much easier to do when your partner, your family and friends communicate openly and are prepared to adapt to new situations. In Nicky's experience of the world of politics, "A significant number of marriages and relationships don't survive the balance of Westminster [...because] it's almost impossible trying to maintain a social life and doing normal things like go to the cinema, hanging out with friends. That definitely takes a back seat." Nicky and her husband had to work hard on their communication to enable her to move into politics. In my own experience, I sat down with my husband and then our children at one of our weekly family meetings to discuss how my new career was going to change all our lives. I listened to their feelings about it and explained how I needed to be supported, and together we came up with an approach for dealing with this change in our family life. Openly talking like this meant that I felt supported and they didn't feel threatened.

In politics, Nicky constantly adapts her communication skills: from ensuring that her voice is heard in a male-dominated workplace, to communicating with the public. At a basic level, Nicky is, "literally knocking on doors talking to people about politics and building up an instant rapport with them."

Nicky describes herself as a naturally relaxed and articulate communicator, who adapts her language and tone for different audiences – which range from constituents who could be homeless, to school children, to local business people and institutions, to other MPs from all parties and even the media. She also has a personal team, including a secretary, a researcher and two constituency case workers. She explains that they are all very different personality styles. As a SAVVI communicator, Nicky has learnt to communicate with them according to their preferred style. "I have to give instructions in quite a different way. Sometimes you have to just say, 'No, this is the way it is going to be, this is the way I want it to happen.' This reflects Nicky's **D** style traits. Most of the time, however, Nicky brings them on board as a team by asking, "How are we going to do it?" This demonstrates her **I** style as a natural communicator and influencer.

As a cabinet minister, Nicky also worked beside civil servants who provided, "the details, the analysis, and numbers," and gave advice on detailed delivery implementation, so that Nicky could push through policy. Analytical civil servants tend to be **C** types (Nicky's opposite), but she knows how to adapt her **I** style to meet them half way. In the way that she can identify how others communicate, and adapt her own style to engage them, Nicky Morgan is a great example of someone who really flowers her communication – whether it's in dealing with colleagues, constituents or her husband – to help her live out her values and achieve her goals.

Importantly, however, she has learnt that as a minister it's vital, "to be respectful, to listen to people." She explains that she has had to learn to really listen to what her constituents are saying, rather than leaping straight in with an answer – and to even admit to them sometimes, "Actually, I don't have the answer to that; it's a very good question." In her view, if you communicate honestly, your audience is less likely to feel that they are being lied to.

Throughout her political career, Nicky has had to argue with people who disagree with her ideas. She has had to work with colleagues from opposing political sides, and she has had to convince the public about her government's policies. To persuade a sceptical audience, she explains, you need to set up plainly why you're doing something, as well as get your timings right when challenging someone else's view. "Sometimes you have to not be too dominant because [politics] is full of dominant people. You have to work out when is the right time to say, 'This is not working, let's do it differently.'"

ZARA: I need to find the right time to get Jay on board, to persuade him that I want to do something different with my life. I didn't appreciate how far my style of communication was contributing to the difficulties in my marriage. Now I can see that if I talk Jay's language and align my goals to his, we'll all be happier. I need to link what I want, to what is important to him: his business goals. If I want to go back into education and support a charity, I need to tie that in with his goals in order to make him sit up and listen. I could tell him that doing things like this will make me a better asset to him as a corporate wife, which would benefit him. I could even set up a charitable foundation linked to his business, which would be good publicity for ACE.

RITA: Great. This is 'flowering' your language. Let's rehearse some of the things you would like to him – about being late today, for example, or even missing the session."

ZARA: He wouldn't know how important it is to me. I haven't shared that with him.

RITA: So that's about being more open in your communication. How might you begin to open up about what it meant to you that he should show up?

ZARA: I know I can't be emotional about it, or he won't hear. Plus, he thinks that I should be satisfied, that I have nothing to complain about. We have more than enough money. I don't think he'd understand that I want things that money can't necessarily buy.

RITA: So how can you say that in a direct way to Jay?

ZARA: Jay, I want to support you when you're busy at work – I'd like to be better at accompanying you to work parties – but the three of us don't ever have a chance to sit down to find out what we're all doing or would like to do. I've met someone who works with business clients and families to help people collaborate more effectively, and be more goal-oriented at work and at home. She's won a coaching award. It would mean a lot to me if we could meet her as a family.

RITA: Is there any other action you want to take around improving communication with Jay?

ZARA: Well, I'll have to ask him directly about his relationship with his finance director.

RITA: How do you feel about this?

ZARA: To be honest, it fills me with terror. I don't know what I'm leaving myself vulnerable to.

At this point, I reminded Zara of the simple diagram showing how the different DISC types prefer to communicate.

RITA: To get the answer to your concerns about Jay's relationship with his finance director, you need to understand that you, like Arun, will need to communicate more like Jay. Just as Arun needs to be more concise and direct in his language when talking to his father, you too will need to adopt a more direct approach.

ZARA: OK, I can see that leaving the question unanswered about what's going on between them for any longer just makes it harder for me and is worse for our marriage in the longer term. I have to know what's going on now. He's generally a bit less preoccupied with work on Sundays. I'll ask him this Sunday.

RITA: Zara, if you and Arun can flower your communication skills with one another and with Jay, you can become a family of SAVVI communicators, which will make everyone happier.

ARUN: I can see that Mum and I need to adapt the way we talk to Dad, but it feels like we'll be doing all the work – which is how it already feels with him. Doesn't he need to adapt his style to suit ours, too?

RITA: You're right. In an ideal situation, it's more effective when an entire family is flowering its communication skills together. But as your father is not here – and until we can get him on board – let's see how you and your mum adapt your communication styles, and then observe the impact it has on him. Longer-term, yes, Jay will also need to adapt his style because you all need to meet in the middle. In the meantime, I suggest arranging regular family meetings.

Family Meetings

ARUN: Are you suggesting that we meet formally, as a family? I can't see my dad making time for that. He'll say he's far too busy.

RITA: I've had people argue that, with so many competing distractions, it's difficult to make time for regular family meetings. I always respond with one of my favourite Oprah Winfrey quotes: *'If you don't have time for one night or at least one hour during the week where everybody can come together as a family, then the family is not the priority.'*

Use your first family meeting to establish your family charter and set some individual goals. In my family, we have weekly meetings.

ZARA: How do these meetings work? What do you talk about?

RITA: I suggest that people organise family meetings in the following way:

Find a regular time to meet
We do ours on Sundays at 6pm, and we commit to clearing the diary for it. Even after the children have moved away from home, technology makes it possible to

carry on upholding your family values, making one another accountable and supporting each other wherever in the world you're living.

Avoid distractions at the meeting

No phones or television in the background. It's all about the family and showing respect, giving each other undivided attention. This encourages the art of listening and improving communication, something lost amongst younger family members when phones and devices are around.

Have a schedule

For example, ask family members to share things like, 'Something I've learned or experienced this week is…' or, 'A goal I would like to achieve by the end of the month is…' If I'm struggling with a goal – for example, losing the motivation to exercise – I tell my family about it at these meetings and they come up with ideas to get me motivated again, such as encouraging me to walk to the station with them each morning.

At one family meeting, my youngest daughter shared her experience of coming across girls she knew taking drugs, and admitted that she was troubled by the question of how to react if she was offered some. Her older siblings were able to give her advice that we, as parents, weren't as well placed to give. In this way, family meetings can provide mentorship in which members provide each other with constructive and useful advice. After the goal-setting at another meeting, my son helped his younger sister look into local sixth forms.

Reflect on the previous week

Ask each other what worked well and what could have worked out better for this in the previous week. By doing this, you are instilling in your children the practice of reflection, which is a key element of the achiever's mindset.

Reflect on values from your family charter

Share the actions you've taken that week in order to live by your family's values. One way to encourage a more reticent family member to contribute is to ask them to select the particular value (serving others, for example) to be discussed that week.

Allow each person time to speak and be heard

Encourage members to apply the W.A.I.T strategy – ask themselves Why Am I Talking? – and then listen to others before jumping in, which is far more effective than everyone just chatting. We all tend to feel consumed by our individual lives, and family meetings are a great opportunity for us all, particularly busy parents, to stop to listen to our family's needs and hear how we can support one other. For example, after listening to details at a family meeting about my daughter Leah's gruelling training for her charity swim, her brother Reece reached out to some of his contacts to support her fundraising efforts.

Adapt your style of communication

Remember, your family members or partner will have their own communication style; SAVVI communicators will listen and respond accordingly. With a diversity of styles in my own family, we have all learned to appreciate how best to communicate with one another in our meetings and at other times. For example, Anya, a DC (task-focused) communicator, is aware that she can come across – as she describes – abrupt and direct, and so she adapts her style when dealing with her more sensitive sister Leah, an SC (people-focused).

As a fast-paced ID style, I've learned to slow down and listen more, to reflect and check in with my family to make sure that I've heard correctly from SCs (who are slower paced and reflective). I don't naturally think or communicate in that way, so our meetings are also good practice for improving the way I communicate in the wider world.

I've shared videos about the way my family meets and talks on Savran's website – go to www.savran.co.uk.

Show gratitude

For example, discuss, 'The best thing that happened to me this week'; or, 'One good thing my family has done for me.' Having gratitude for even the smallest thing that has gone well, or made us smile, helps us to appreciate what we already have, rather than constantly looking for the next thing to fulfil us, which only leads to dissatisfaction.

End the meeting on a positive note

Plan a fun activity, outing or holiday for your family. We use meetings to plan holidays and days out to places like Escape Rooms, bowling and crazy golf. In addition, use the meeting as an opportunity for all members of the family to acknowledge something that's gone well for everyone, or to celebrate individual successes. My children particularly love hearing their siblings recognise their achievements at our family meetings. Recently, upon hearing the news that Anya had been accepted into her first choice of university, her brother welled up because he'd been on that journey with his sister – from taking her around sixth forms to helping her choose universities – which was a role he'd undertaken as a result of our family meetings.

ZARA: I want our family to try having family meetings. Arun, what do you think about sitting down as a family like the Chowdhrys do?

ARUN: I think it's a brilliant idea. If I could have an impact on Dad at home, he might start listening to my ideas at work too. It's not going to be easy persuading Dad to come along, though.

RITA: What will you do if he doesn't agree to attend family meetings?

ARUN: We should still go ahead.

ZARA: I agree.

RITA: Arun, the principles you'll be developing at your family meetings will apply just as well to team meetings at work, and to the ideas that you have for engaging people at ACE. I'm always surprised by the number of teams I come across, where members don't meet each other regularly. I don't just mean staff meetings, but meetings in which staff from all levels of a business come together to have a say and be heard. Until I'd coached one particular sales manager, he'd never met with his team on a regular basis; once he introduced regular meetings, all staff had the space to share their successes and failures, in order to support one another and find solutions to common problems. He then hired dedicated technical support staff to free up time for generating sales. Team meetings were also an opportunity to acknowledge those members who performed well.

ARUN: Yes, I can see how the model of family meetings could be adapted for use in the workplace and be beneficial. After hearing the negative staff feedback, about the culture we have at ACE, I really want to establish meetings involving staff from all levels of the business – from the cleaners to the directors. We could use these meetings as a basis for how we set up efficient working parties to improve motivation, satisfaction and productivity in the business.

Over the course of several months and sessions, it was clear that Zara and Arun had made significant progress on their journey towards becoming SAVVI. Significantly, both had shifted from an attitude of helplessness about their respective situations, to one that saw them starting to take responsibility for bringing about the changes they wanted to see in their lives. They understood that they had to adapt their verbal communication skills in order to achieve their desired outcomes.

5

Inspiration

Who Gets Savvi?

'If I have seen further it is by standing on the shoulders of giants.'
—Isaac Newton

*T*he next time I saw Arun and Zara, they'd had several weeks to put into action their individual SMART goals and to start to adapt their methods of communication, in order to get the results that they desired. I was looking forward to hearing about any changes and improvements they might already be experiencing in their lives.

A: Looking back on where I was in my life, I can see that I was stuck and feeling resentful. I blamed other people for not giving me a chance. The minute I stopped to think about the way I communicated, and how other personality types like my dad communicated – and realised that I need to adapt my communication depending on who I'm speaking to – I felt like I was holding a magic key that would unlock a problem I've always had – with my dad in particular. I went away from our last session armed with the knowledge that my dad's direct **D** personality means that he only really listens and responds to facts and figures. To be honest, I've always known that about him, but I didn't think to communicate back to him in the same way and nor did I want to – it just wasn't my natural language. Now that I've started adapting my language when I talk to him, though, I'm actually becoming really successful at getting through to him. He's listening to me. It seems so obvious now that I can't believe it's taken me this long to work it out. In a funny way, it's a bit like going abroad to do a deal with a foreign investor and learning a few polite phrases and practising the appropriate customs, to make you seem a worthy and respectful business partner. I'm using dad's language of facts and figures to explain my fears about low staff morale being our biggest problem at ACE, and I'm finally making an impact with him and the other directors!

Dad was shocked when he saw my data about how much staff turnover was costing us. I'd worked hard on making sure the data was thorough, and I could see that he was impressed by the effort I'd put into pulling it all together. Seeing the numbers in black and white got him hooked. I saw the difference in his expression when I was talking his language. He was genuinely interested in what I had to say – I haven't seen him like that with me in years. Then I did something I know I'm good at: I got persuasive. Once I'd hooked him with the figures, I was able to buy him into my ideas for ACE, like the staff awards night to recognise good employees and the team meetings. By the end of my presentation and after hitting Dad with hard, direct facts to answer some of his questions, he gave me a budget of £100,000 to get my ideas for having a more people-focused atmosphere at ACE off the ground.

I've already started the nomination process for staff that have given a long term of service to ACE, or who have provided exceptional customer service. I'm also keen to acknowledge the staff who are good at customer service on top of being good at sales: all our staff are good at selling, but as I explained to my dad, negative customer feedback has compromised our returning sales. Also, the staff who are good at customer support don't feel valued, and ultimately leave, because ACE doesn't seem to value customer service. Now that Dad can see it's not just a hunch of mine – because he's seen the sales figures – or just complaints from a few disgruntled staff, he's decided to let me look at ways of addressing our customer service issue.

As well as showing our staff that we value customer service, we're now focusing on the importance of teamwork across the business. I'm spending time in the call centre to see how they do it. The sales team was a bit wary of me at first, but I think it's helped to break down some of the them-and-us mindset between management and staff. At least they can see that I'm trying – plus it's been a good opportunity for me to experience first-hand some of their concerns. For example, I can see that the communal staff area needs to be made more comfortable, and that the lighting and air conditioning in the office need upgrading. My showing interest in our staff's needs has created a new energy and buzz around the office. Even my senior colleagues can see we're onto something here, and they're starting to talk about arranging team nights out to improve staff morale.

I've also set up a working party with representatives from different departments. At our first one, there was a discussion about monitoring the promotion process. There was a suggestion that we invite external people to observe the interview process to ensure impartiality, which I'm looking into. For the first time, I'm getting to flex my muscles at work and am being heard. I'm loving my job right now!

RITA: It's wonderful to hear your enthusiasm, Arun. And remember, you've turned things around for yourself at work by being a skilled SAVVI communicator. In order to keep the momentum up, you're going to need to keep inspiring yourself and your team – which is the final element, the 'I' for Inspiration, of being SAVVI.

Before we start discussing that, I want to ask you about your father. Where has he been whilst you've been bringing in all these changes at ACE?

ARUN: To his credit, he's stood back. He hasn't interfered. He's just observed, which is a real change for him: usually he's straight in there with his opinion on how I should do things. Having that autonomy has given me the space to raise the idea of a charter of company values with some of his senior colleagues.

RITA: It's interesting to see the change in your dad in response to your new style. How has this extended to way you all communicate at home?

ARUN: Well, he was reluctant to come to our first family meeting because he said he had work to do.

ZARA: But he did sit in the same room, in the background, when we had our first meeting. I could tell he was listening in on us even though he didn't look up from his paperwork – well, not until Arun brought up the girlfriend issue, and incompatible values!

ARUN: If you'd told the teenage me that I'd be talking about my girlfriend with my mum, I would've squirmed. But honestly, discussing it at our first family meeting really helped me work out why the relationship with this girl was going nowhere. After I'd sat down to identify my values, I realised that she and I just don't share any.

ZARA: That was when I looked round and caught Jay looking at us. I knew he was dying to say something. Funnily enough, he made himself available for the second meeting the following week – and the big news is that he's agreed to come in for a session on his own with you.

RITA: That's great! What do you think has changed Jay's mind?

ZARA: He likes results, and he can see how coming to see you has impacted on Arun and me. I think he wants to come and see for himself what SAVVI is all about.

RITA: It sounds like communication barriers are really starting to break down in your family, just as Arun said earlier.

Zara, let's move on to you. Tell me about the outcomes of your SMART targets and the work you've been able to do on your own verbal communication.

ZARA: I was nervous about my targets, because to meet them I knew I would have to really step out of my comfort zone. One of my targets was to persuade Jay that my enrolling on a further education course would be a positive thing for him. I was worried about bringing it up with him; however, once I explained that some further education would help me feel more confident talking to his colleagues at business events, and would help me in my role supporting him, he was open to the idea. And starting the course – I chose psychology – has been better than I ever imagined. I wake up every day with a new purpose. I've got a new routine, in which I try to spend four hours during the day on my course studies, while Jay and Arun are out at work. By doing it during the day, I don't feel it's impacting on our family life.

Because Jay had been so positive about my personal development, I decided to tell him about my idea for an ACE charitable foundation. I knew I could get his buy-in if I could link my goal of setting it up to his goal of getting good PR for his company. He even suggested I contact one the banks he uses for help setting it up. I know that that's his **D** trait coming into play, steering the direction of my idea, but if it helps make it happen then I'm happy to adapt how I talk to him.

RITA: At the moment, it's you and Arun who are learning SAVVI skills, but Jay has also developed indirectly as an off-shoot of your development. When everyone in a family or team practises SAVVI communication, they make even more progress.

ZARA: I can already feel that I'm becoming happier through achieving. I offered to host a dinner party for all of Jay's directors, which he really appreciated, and I actually enjoyed it – which was a first for me at that sort of event! The difference was that this time, I revised for the dinner party conversation, which I usually dread. I spent the week before the dinner reading newspapers, and knew I had two topics that I could talk confidently about. I read a couple of opinion pieces about the US government and I was particularly interested in an article about schools banning all phones. I know so many parents who worry about the impact of phones and social media on children, and about the best age to give children a phone. All that reading, and then my new experience of being in a school, even when it's only part-time, meant that I could really contribute to the conversation. It's like going into an exam: you have to do a little revision first.

It was a really successful party. I know Jay thought so too, because I overheard him telling some of his directors about the ACE foundation I wanted to set up. That was his way of giving the night his stamp of approval.

The only one of his directors, who wasn't so positive was his finance director, who I thought looked miserable most of the night. At one point when Jay was explaining my idea, I heard her interrupt him, saying that it could be 'difficult' and 'time-consuming' to set up a foundation right now. I know Jay always listens to her and, true enough, when I asked him later what she'd thought about the idea, he was a bit vague and started to backtrack a bit – even though, earlier in the evening, he'd been so positive. I was furious inside. It just proved that I was right about his relationship with her. In my eyes, he was choosing her over me. When the guests left and I told him what I thought, he told me I was talking nonsense. He said he couldn't be emotional about running a business. When I pointed out that he always listens to her over me, he said I was being silly and overdramatic. Then, when I reminded him that he hadn't listened when I'd asked him to come to the family session, he said that that was completely different. I told him, "If there was a crisis meeting at work because the company was going to lose a client, you'd turn up. Well, our marriage is in a crisis. You need to start taking steps to change things, just like I am. You should go and see Rita – that would show me that you're serious about improving our relationship, and it will help you to understand me better." Well, he agreed! I was so happy that he agreed to see you. He wants to come alone, though. I hope he keeps his promise and turns up.

Zara and Arun had made significant progress towards becoming SAVVI. However, to sustain that growth and keep learning, they needed some inspiration to keep them motivated in the longer term.

Being SAVVI is an ongoing process. It doesn't end once you have self-awareness, the achiever's mindset, established values and beliefs and have learnt to flower your verbal communication. Successful SAVVI people keep nourishing all these elements using different methods of inspiration, such as books, role models and networking events. They also continue to inspire others. As well as sustaining their progress, seeking and providing inspiration helps SAVVI people to overcome obstacles to their development – for example, resistance from family or friends who don't want them to change. As Cesar Chavez once said, *'True wealth is not measured in money or status or power. It is measured in the legacy we leave behind for those we love and those we inspire.'*

We have all experienced loss of motivation in our personal and professional lives. At work, it might feel as if opportunities are no longer coming our way and that there is no room for progression. We may have plateaued or stagnated in our role. Like Zara and Arun, we may feel that we're not achieving our full potential and find ourselves experiencing a lack of fulfilment. In our personal lives, we may be lacking the motivation to improve our health and wellbeing, even when we know it would make life better. We might feel stuck in a loveless marriage or relationship and have lost the motivation to make it work, meaning that we stop trying. Alternatively, we may have developed in one area of our lives – such as our careers – at the cost of others, such as our health and relationships. This was Zara's view of her husband Jay.

These are the times when we could all do with some inspiration to help us get back on track or stay on track, whether we're trying to make a change, raise our game or seek fulfilment. After 25 years of teaching, I realised that I had stagnated and was feeling unfulfilled professionally; so despite the fact that I loved teaching, I looked for inspiration and ideas for a change of career.

You don't have to look for inspiration just because you are stuck. Like Arun and Zara, you may have already taken several positive steps in order to grow and develop; staying inspired, and becoming an inspiration to others in order to sustain your own growth, is simply the next challenge. Many of the SAVVI people I've interviewed talk about those who have inspired them. David Blunkett was motivated by his parents' determination; my brother Raju and I hold our mother's work ethic as our chief inspiration; Nitin Passi was inspired by his father's drive and optimism. Even someone as successful as Oprah Winfrey, widely regarded as an impressive businesswoman, as well as a TV personality, could not have become who she is today without some inspiration. For Winfrey, it was the writer Maya Angelou. Nelson Mandela is another example of someone, who was a role model extraordinaire in his own right, yet who found inspiration himself in Mahatma Gandhi and his strategy for non-violent protest.

Becoming SAVVI is not the end of the journey: SAVVI people keep on growing through inspiration, and recognise that they always need to be reaching outwards, growing upwards, towards new heights and in new directions, just like the branches of a tree. As Tony Robbins says, *'If you're not growing, you're dying.'*

When I talk about inspiration with clients, I describe the 'BRANCH Out' model (see overleaf).

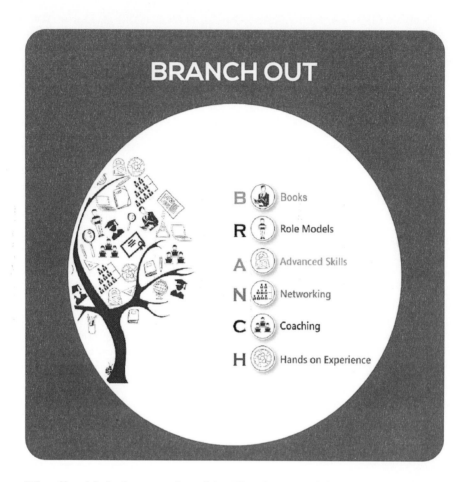

Visually, this is the opposite of the Five Root model (see page 132). Books, role models, advanced skills, networking, coaching and hands-on experience (in no particular order) are tools that all play an important part in inspiring us to become more successful at what we do. They keep us growing and help us to stay SAVVI.

Just as the branches of a real tree change with the seasons – sometimes bare, sometimes in full bloom – the rate of our own growth changes at different times in our lives. Zara's son, at one time her life's primary focus, had grown up, and she was therefore beginning to branch out and look for new routes towards fulfilment. In order to find them, and in order to keep on growing, she needed to look around for inspiration. At the same time, she needed to prune back some old habits in order to encourage new growth.

If you're stuck and struggling to grow, you're probably in need of some inspiration. One idea is to learn from people, who have already made the journey towards success and have experienced failure along the way. Learn from them when is the best time to shed leaves or to cut back in order to promote optimal growth. Inspirational people, books, ideas and words of wisdom hand us a range of techniques to help fast track our growth. I often say to my clients, "Why reinvent the wheel? There are plenty of tried and tested formulas already out there. Seek them out and use them to your advantage."

Feeding the mind with new information, knowledge and experiences helps you to develop. Simply reading a motivational book, or working with a coach for three hours, may be the only kick-start you need to start taking the sort of action that you never imagined you could. In the words of Maya Angelou, *'Do the best you can until you know better. Then when you know better, do better.'* Never settle for what you already know: there's always more to learn and understand to help you reach greater personal and professional heights. Importantly, learn to view your mistakes as part and parcel of branching out. Sometimes, the best lessons come from learning from our – and others' – failures.

However, nourishment of the mind isn't just about acquiring knowledge through academic books and information. Hands-on experience can be underestimated, which is why I'm so glad to see more businesses offering apprenticeships and internships. There's great value in learning through hands-on work: it's not just about learning a skill or trade, it's also about learning social, communication and teamwork skills, gaining confidence and experiencing responsibility. As a teacher, I would often witness just how much a 16 year-old

215

could develop with two weeks' hands-on work experience. My students always returned with new knowledge, having interacted with people from different backgrounds and having learnt first-hand about the reality of a particular career. The students who hated their work experience placement came back having realised how much harder they'd need to work to get a job that they'd enjoy. Those who loved their experience returned thinking, *I've found my perfect career!* and were driven to work harder to get the results they needed to pursue it. A survey cited by UCAS revealed that two thirds of employers seek graduates with relevant work experience, because preparation for a work environment equips them with a degree of business awareness.

Hands-on experience isn't just for young people, either. I urge many of my clients to shadow or gain work experience with people already in positions that they aspire to themselves. When I worked at the University of Surrey teaching motivation theory to students, I would periodically shadow HR directors to keep abreast of industry trends and take real-life case studies back into the classroom, to keep my teaching up to date and relevant.

When I heard that Jay Sharma had agreed to come in for a session with me – on the condition that I saw him on his own – I began to reflect on what I thought would be Jay's areas of growth, and the methods I was going to use to engage him. From my observations in Zara and Arun's sessions, and after analysing Jay's profile, I believed that he would want to work on his relationships with his family and employees, and also address his health and work-life balance. Whilst high-intensity **DC** people like Jay can achieve great success in certain areas, such as wealth and career, their task-focused **D** and **C** traits mean that they are prone to overlooking personal and professional relationships. Listening to Zara and Arun, I'd identified that one of Jay's areas for growth would concern his need to be less controlling, become a better active listener (attentive to other people's ideas, feelings and desires), and to learn how and when to seek consensus. Clearly, Jay needed to invest more in personal relationships and team support.

Interestingly, since working with the Sharmas, I'd been struck by the fact that Jay shared the same **DC** personality profile as my brother Sunny who, over 20 years, has gone from an 18 year-old without much formal training to a multi-million-pound businessman behind the world's largest Costa franchise. In Jay's case, the limitations of his personality type had led to a lack of attention being given to his relationships, both at work and at home, which had caused a high staff turnover at his business and engendered feelings of neglect in his wife and son. Sunny, however, has grown into an unconventional **DC** type who, through being SAVVI, has overcome some of the limitations of his profile. Having left formal education relatively early on, Sunny had to branch out to find his inspiration, in order to become a successful business leader. For him, the three elements of hands-on experience, books and role models have had the most significant impact on his professional and personal development. Through this inspiration, he's managed to create a nurturing, positive and loyal environment for his staff by learning to value the importance of investing in his team and understanding what motivates them. Sunny is a SAVVI business leader who really does have it all!

I hoped that using a case study based on someone like Jay would help me to build a rapport with him during our session. I believed that Sunny's story could be the catalyst to encourage Jay to branch out and grow in areas beyond his business life, enabling him to grasp a wider definition of success.

Sunny Side Up: Sunny Tuli, Managing Director of Tuli Holdings

Sunny, the youngest of my siblings, never properly knew our father, being only three when he died. However, he shares the same personality style: stern and driven, a planner, needing a meticulous home and an ordered lifestyle. Our older brother Raju enlisted Sunny into his clothes business when Sunny was 18. The two of them proved a successful double act because of their complementary **I** (people-focused) and **C** (task-focused) traits. Whilst both are primary **Ds** (driven by goals), Sunny also likes attention to detail and processes, and is a meticulous planner. Raju's secondary trait as an **I**, meanwhile, meant that they were able to build strong relationships with suppliers, bankers and employees. Sunny's profile meant that he was drawn to the finance division and ended up as the finance director, whilst Raju became the managing director. Raju has now pretty much retired, and Sunny runs their multi-million-pound business as Managing Director.

At the age of 29, Sunny appeared in *The Sunday Times'* Rich List as one of the UK's youngest millionaires. Unusually for his profile type, Sunny not only enjoys success in his business life but – through being SAVVI – is also an active 48-year-old father who looks after his health. By actively branching out, Sunny has managed to escape the paradox of modern-day living, described by the Dalai Lama: *'Man [...] sacrifices his health in order to make money. Then he sacrifices money to recuperate his health. And then he is so anxious about the future that he does not enjoy the present. The result being that he does not live in the present or the future; he lives as if he is never going to die, and then dies having never really lived.'* In contrast, Sunny has succeeded in achieving a good balance across his Wheel of Life.

When Sunny first started out in our older brother's fashion business, he didn't have any formal financial training (most finance directors working for companies that generate as much revenue as Tuli Holdings have at least 10 years of accountancy training and many years of experience). Following the BRANCH Out model, Sunny learned everything he knows about accountancy through hands-on experience. "You have to learn on the job," he says. "You look at ways of constantly learning from those who are smarter or more skilled around you. Don't see them as a threat."

In the early days of their business, Sunny employed the best accountant, asked him lots of questions and watched him work. It was knowledge acquired through hands-on experience and from lessons learnt from other people in the business that helped inspire Sunny to grow. Reflecting on this, he says, "You're always learning, every day is about learning, but it took me at least 10, 12 years." He became astute enough about the fashion market to know when it was time to diversify; they invested in a property portfolio and later moved into the fast food sector, becoming Ireland's only Costa franchise. Over 14 years, Sunny has overseen growth from one Costa outlet to 150 branches across Ireland, and the business is still growing. Today, as finance director of Tuli Holdings, Sunny can spot errors in the company accounts that even his qualified accountants miss.

At the start of his career, then, Sunny's business knowledge was founded on observing the people around him and learning on the job. Once he had branched out through hands-on experience, I suggested he read *How to Win Friends and Influence People*, the book that had inspired our father. Sunny says that he was keen to read the book because he "wanted to know" our father and understand how an academic, with a Master's degree but without any entrepreneurial experience, could become an "amazing businessman who acquired a big property portfolio in a short space of time."

I thought the book would help Sunny in the area of professional and personal relationships. Reading the book, Sunny himself realised that its message wasn't just about being an entrepreneur. "It's about knowing how to get your wealth in everything in life – not just in your business, but in your relationships. I want my children to read this book too, and study it."

Despite remaining task-focused, Sunny learnt from Dale Carnegie's techniques of winning and influencing, and adapted his communication style at work – which is rewarded by the fact that 75% of his senior managers have remained with him for over 20 years. This demonstrates that Sunny, a **DC**, has worked to overcome and adapt some of his natural traits. He identifies one of the techniques he's taken from that book as *'arousing in the other person an eager want.'* "It's about getting your staff excited about what's in it for them. I go to one of my teams and say, 'We're opening 100 stores, which will be demanding, but you're going to get something – a bonus, a car, a villa – at the end of it.' Learn about your staff's ambitions in life, learn what motivates them, then try to fulfil their desires to ensure that they stay. For instance, once I found out that one of my directors wanted to buy a house in Spain, I told him, 'Work well for me for the next 10 years and you'll get £200k at the end of the year to buy your house in Spain.' It's a win-win situation: I win because it's motivating him, so it's driving my business growth."

Sometimes, of course, you have to let good staff move on to pastures new. However, if you've managed to make your staff feel like part of a team, and have managed a successful exit, you can enjoy loyalty even from former employees. Sunny explains, "I lost one person who'd been with us from the early days. She was a head trainer and was going to a completely different kind of job. She left us on really good terms and I told her that our door remained open to her, and that if it didn't work out for her, she had two months to come back. She came back. She said the new place just didn't have the same family atmosphere as ours. We're all about family, and staff here are part of the family." By listening to his employee and supporting her growth – even if it meant her spreading her wings elsewhere – Sunny, ultimately, retained her in the longer term.

Another influential technique Sunny applies to inspire loyalty is showing staff appreciation through public recognition. "When one of my directors goes on trips to regional business seminars, he's one of the most important people in the room. I don't go. I let him take that recognition and appreciation. So, most people think he runs the business, but that's fine. He gets a high from going around having people think he owns all the Costa stores and I let them think that. I want my staff to feel as if the business is their business.

"I praise staff a lot more than I probably used to. I realise it's important to thank everyone, from the lowest-ranking to the highest-ranking person in the company. Everybody wants to be thanked, and the bigger you get in the business the more you can forget to thank people." In Sunny's view, it's vital to "praise every improvement in the business and create a culture where every single person is praised in one way or another." If Sunny is aware that one of his staff has displayed outstanding dedication or effort, he'll phone their line manager and ask them to praise them directly. "I'm role modelling how I want my managers to behave. Our KFC stores, for example, put up photos of staff who've given the best customer service that month."

There are different ways to encourage and recognise staff. Sunny advises: "Let them talk in meetings; let them get things off their chest; let them feel valued in the meeting. When people come to see us for a meeting at the head office, I always let them do their presentation first. I say a brief couple lines and then tell them: 'It's all about you, you, you.' The best thing you can do as an employer or manager is to spend time with your people. Take 30 or 45 minutes to have lunch with them, eat together and talk together. It's a gesture of your appreciation. They'll go away feeling that you looked after them, and that's what fosters a happy staff culture.

"When things go wrong in the business, it's still important to encourage staff. Don't talk about things being someone's fault; talk to the person about how they can fix it."

As a **DC** personality, Sunny recognises that his natural style is to "be blunt and straight to the point"; as a result, he's had to work hard to adapt the way he communicates, both verbally and in written form, to win people over. In the past, he admits, "I didn't think to write emails in a warm way. I would never open with a friendly line."

True to his type, Sunny seeks perfection: "I want everything in life to be perfect; everything has to have high standards." However, Carnegie's book has also taught him not to *'criticise, condemn or complain'* if he wants to nurture positive relationships. There are other ways to communicate criticism more effectively and still get what you want. Sunny admits, "I still complain when I go into a restaurant, but I've learnt *how* to complain. Now I'll get the waiter to allow me to speak to the manager. Then I'll start by pointing out all the good things he's done before mentioning the bad things, so that I've given them some positive recognition. So, I might say something like, 'It's been fantastic, the service has been great and I appreciate that you're busy, but the food was really not up to standard today.'

"I've learnt that you get better results if you complain correctly – and that applies to being on the receiving end of complaints. We have 150 Costa stores; I see five complaints come in a day. There are some people who complain all the time, and then there are those who just like writing in, whilst others complain for the sake of complaining. But when you get a complaint like, 'I'm a regular customer, I come in regularly and the service is usually fantastic, but I've just had a bad experience on a particular day,' then that person will get all kinds of vouchers. That's how our staff has been trained. I want a culture of constructive criticism within our company and in our customer service."

AD personality is never happy doing the same thing: they enjoy new challenges and new opportunities. Unsurprisingly, this applies to Sunny's reading habits: once he got a taste for growth through reading Dale Carnegie's book, he looked to other books for more inspiration. "Everyone should read as many books as possible and ask other people about books," he says. Sunny is also a fan of audiobooks, saying, "You can spend years of your life in traffic jams and on trains and planes. Imagine filling up all that empty time learning from other people's wisdom." The next book that made an impact on Sunny was Robin Sharma's, *The Monk Who Sold His Ferrari*. "It taught me about prioritising space, and about time management. It's helped me understand about the importance of better time for yourself; better time for your family, and better time for everybody. It made me reassess my life and re-evaluate what I'm doing: whether I'm living healthily; whether I'm spending enough quality time with my family; seeing how and what the kids are learning and what I'm actually teaching them.

"The book has taught me to re-prioritise my life every five years. If you find you've reached a point where one area of your life looks faulty, you should re-order your priorities so that it looks like: 1. Health; 2. Legacy; 3. Money. That makes you frame your life more positively.

"Sharma writes about the need to appreciate what you have in the here and now. A lot of people don't appreciate what they've got. It doesn't matter if they've got a million or two million, they're always looking at the person who's got more. You need to look at yourself and be thankful for what you have and appreciate what you have in this moment. I realised that I've got wealth, cars – everything. I thank the universe for everything I have each morning. All that's left for me is the legacy that I want to leave behind. Your legacy is your family – nobody's bothered about how much money you're leaving behind. I've had to think, *How am I going teach my kids?* I can only teach them by spending time with them."

These days, Sunny carves out time for his young family (a 14-year-old daughter and 11-year-old twins) and includes watching his children's sports matches amongst his weekly highlights. If his son is playing rugby, Sunny says, "I'll drop any meeting to go and see him. That's the priority now, nothing else." In the morning, he enjoys taking his daughter Diya to school; on these trips, he tries to have as much conversation as possible with her. Sunny's family doesn't just spend time together on holidays: he ensures it's part of their daily routine.

He takes the time to teach his children how to cook and they enjoy family meals together. He says, "We eat together every single night as a family – or nine times out of 10. The people who eat together stay together."

Sunny has also re-prioritised his own health as a result of Robin Sharma's book. "Nowadays, I exercise at least five times a week and think I look younger for it." Making time for health and wellbeing, gratitude and appreciation has given Sunny the headspace and distance from work for a fresh perspective on the business. "I take mornings off. I used to work from 9am and I'd be active all day, finishing around 5pm. Now, I go in at 11.30 after spending two hours of my time either exercising, planning, reading books and papers or listening to audio books. Those two hours in the morning are my time." In fact, he was sitting in the sauna when he had one of his best business ideas. "I had two hours by myself, sitting in a steam room. My mind was totally clear. I was working on an important deal and I thought, *What does this other person want out of this deal?* I put myself in their shoes, and remembered that you've got to make both sides of the deal work; that no deal works if one person gains too much." The space to think that through, earned Sunny a £12m deal. Now, he reflects, "Some of the best deals in my life have come from times when I've just sat by myself."

Going into work later in the day gives Sunny time to reflect and, as a result, his mind is decluttered and he's become a better decision maker. "Very early on in business, we were defrauded of £250,000 by an ex-employee, but I didn't allow it to stress me. I took time out to think about ways to improve our system so it was fool-proof. Indirectly because of her, the profit margin went up."

Recommended Reading

Throughout this book, I've discussed the importance of *How to Win Friends and influence People* for my family. This started with my father, then me and later my brother. My husband and our three children have all read the book, and Sunny wants his children to read it when they're older. Sharing is inspiring.

Dale Carnegie's book is good for **D** and **C** types, who are more task-oriented. It gives them strategies on how to handle people within both personal and professional relationships.

For Sunny, the key lessons that he's learnt from the book about influencing and winning people over are:

- Avoid belittling people, giving unhelpful criticism or unnecessarily complaining.
- Look for the positives in someone or in any interaction, and acknowledge them.

- Understand what motivates people and use that knowledge to influence them.

- Smile when communicating with people and demonstrate sincere interest in them –

- notably by remembering their name, asking them about themselves and actively listening to what they say.

- Be respectful of other people's views, and never tell them they're wrong.

- When you're in the wrong, be sure to own up to it as soon as possible.

- In a conversation, allow others to do most of the talking and to take ownership of ideas.

- Make conscious attempts to genuinely see things from other people's points of view.

I also recommend some other books to my clients when they are starting to turn to books for inspiration:

- *Who Moved My Cheese* - Spencer Johnson, 1998
  This book is good for **S** types, who prefer stability and security and doesn't like change for change's sake.

One of my **S** clients, who runs his own catering business, found that whilst at one point he'd been a market leader, his competitors had caught up and were growing faster than him. He knew that he had loyal customers but saw that, after 20 years of business, his sales and profits had stagnated and he was barely making ends meet. Reading *Who Moved My Cheese* inspired him to make changes even though they were out of his comfort zone. As a result, his business began growing as he entered new markets and invested in property – all of which increased his income.

- *The Chimp Paradox* – Steve Peters, 2012

  This is good for all types, especially Cs, who worry about getting things right, and people-focused I and S types, who are overly concerned about what people think of them and fear rejection.

  Another of my clients, an S type, was holding herself back professionally through her struggle to get promoted. Although she achieved great results at work, she was reluctant to express her opinions in meetings and, as a result, was overlooked by her seniors. When asked to express her thoughts, she came across as rambling because her anxiety about speaking up made her mind fog. By reading the book, she realised that she was sabotaging her own success by allowing her 'chimp' mind to take control. This book helped her learn strategies to manage her mind so that, at her next performance review, her boss commented on her new-found confidence.

- *The Secret* – Rhonda Byrne, 2006

  This is good for over-analytical **C** types, or those who have experienced adversity in their personal or professional lives – such as relationship breakdown, bereavement or career failure. It helps the reader to focus on changing a negative mindset into an achiever's mindset.

- *Rich Dad, Poor Dad* – Robert Kiyosaki and Sharon Lechter, 1997

  This is good for all styles. It has helped clients who are looking to increase their wealth and need the motivation to take the step to the next level of income. A personal trainer client of mine talked for a while about leaving his job at a gym, but didn't take any action. After reading this book, he left his job and started his own business. Within three months, he'd increased his income threefold. Now, he uses a quote from this book as a mantra: *'The poor work for money and the rich make money work for them.'*

Another element of the BRANCH Out model that Sunny uses for success is role models. A friend, colleague, family member, celebrity or even an institution can be a role model, showing us a formula for success if we follow their advice and learn from their mistakes. Positive role models boost motivation because they hold up realistic illustrations of desired success. It's been proven that a role model 'significantly influences... performance regardless of the goal set.' Sunny has been inspired by a number of role models – most notably the yoga guru Sadhguru, who has modernised teachings from Hindu scriptures to guide people through management of the mind and body. This, coupled with lessons from *The Monk Who Sold His Ferrari,* has inspired Sunny to make reflection an integral part of his daily routine. Now, he says, "I make better decisions. Before, I never actually had my own time, so I followed everything up in my head and there was no space left for anything else. When I was that busy, I didn't have time to see the future. I didn't have time to think of the bigger deal. But if you don't clear your mind, how are you going to dream about what your life should be like? According to Sadhguru, if you clear your mind, everything is created twice: once in your mind and once in reality. So when doing a deal, I have to mentally stand back, listen to the other person's point of view and think about what they want before I give my opinion."

Sadhguru has also had an impact on Sunny's family life. Through Sadhguru's example, Sunny and his family have radically changed the way they eat. As well as eating together, they have cut their meat intake by 60% and eat more raw fruit and vegetables. "I've learnt from Sadhguru that meat is fine if you need it to survive in harsh conditions, but it shouldn't be consumed daily, especially when there are other choices. I've also learnt that just before an animal is killed, it goes into shock, releasing negative chemicals that we ingest when we eat its meat." It can also take cooked meat 48 to 52 hours to be digested. When food remains in the gut for so long, it will rot and cause unnecessary levels of bacteria. Even levels of depression show some improvement when a vegetarian diet is followed. Fruit takes just one and a half to three hours to be fully digested; cooked vegetables take 12 to 15 hours. Cooked cereals take 24 to 30 hours to be digested. As a result, Sunny has transformed his diet and made his and his family's health his number-one priority.

I was delighted and moved to learn that a person closer to home who has become a role model to Sunny is my husband, Jeff. I'd had no idea of this until he told me! Sunny explains, "For the first 30 or 40 years of my life, it was all about money: if I could get money, then I could do this or that. But money's become number three for me. Health comes first. I don't care if I don't earn any more money. Because of the inspiration I've taken from books and having a role model like Jeff, I'm no longer bothered if some things don't turn out the right way. I've seen that Jeff has a balanced, successful career and a united, happy family – even after you all went through his cancer. I've heard his reply when people informally ask him for investment tips: 'The best investment is your wife and your children, because if your children screw up, they'll be a liability, and if you don't look after your wife or your marriage, your wife will take half of everything!' Joking aside, I know what he means: what's wealth if you don't have a loving partner to share it with? Wealth can't buy your kids real happiness. For Jeff, it's always been about health, welfare and family. I admire his values and the Chowdhry family mission statement. I know the importance of legacy to him.

"Jeff has unity in the family; his kids actually want to spend time with him. When I look at your family values, the things that you have in the world, the way your kids treat you, the way they are their own driving forces for getting up and working hard, I'm inspired. Even Leah has inspired me with her charity work: swimming the Channel and running the London marathon. I'd love to do something like that one day, to give back the way she's done. Imagine Leah saying to her child one day, "I swam the Channel," and her child being inspired by that. That's how legacy keeps on working. If my kids can respect me, be inspired by me and carry on that legacy, I'll be happy."

When it comes to a business role model that Sunny has been inspired by, it has to be the McDonald's fast-food chain. However, Sunny wanted to surpass them when they launched the Costa franchise in Ireland and, with all his SAVVI tools and principles, he's been able to achieve that. In this regard, he's managed to uphold Sadhguru's inspiring words: *'The greatest thing that you can do in life is to live to your peak and to set the example that there is a way to live beyond all limitations.'*

Another way to branch out is by learning advanced skills. For Sunny, this has meant understanding ideas and practices in Feng Shui, the art of balancing the energy around you to make it work positively for you. Sunny applies this at work and in his family life. "It's about having positivity around myself, in my environment, as well as keeping my mind positive through the gratitude principle I've learnt from *The Monk Who Sold His Ferrari*."

To help Zara to realise her hopes for a future career in charity administration, she decided to undertake further education through the online Open University route, which meant that she was still at home with her family. It was important to her that she was able to continue with her other responsibilities, so advanced skills acquired through virtual learning was a perfect solution. Meanwhile,

Arun's next step at work, so that he could deliver as an effective manager and actualise his ambitions for a more positive work culture at ACE, was to take on some management and HR training. Continuing professional development is crucial for anyone looking to progress in their chosen field, and there have never been so many different ways to branch out in this area.

Sometimes successful SAVVI people make their jobs look easy, when in fact they work hard at them behind the scenes for many years. For some time, I'd been impressed by a young British TV presenter, Anila Chowdhry, who, at 27 years old, has already worked with some of the biggest companies in the industry, making appearances on the BBC, ITV, Channel 5 and Zee TV. At 22, Anila already had her own live TV chat show, interviewing inspirational people and celebrities - including Bollywood legends Kajol and Kabir Beddi and the journalist Jon Snow – and covering topical issues that aired across Europe on the world's largest South Asian network, Zee TV. She then moved into mainstream media, presenting current affairs on BBC Asian Radio Network when just 2.2% of British Asians work in radio, and only 12% of BAME staff were represented in the UK's top five media broadcasters (the BBC, Channel 4, ITV, Sky and Viacom, which owns Channel 5). Anila has covered important stories such as the Westminster and Manchester terror attacks, Grenfell and the General Election. She has also worked on Channel 5's *The Wright Stuff.* Furthermore, at the age of 24 she made her mark in the world of politics by standing as London's Mayoral Candidate for the Women's Equality Party. I was curious to learn about the background of Anila's success, as she comes across as such an inspiring case study.

When I met Anila, I saw an example of someone who applies some of the branch-out elements to her life. Importantly, I learnt that she never stops working to advance her skills. After gaining an MA in Philosophy and Literature at the

University of Warwick, Anila started freelancing for ITV News, London Live and the BBC and continues to "keep training, keep gaining and keep moving, because you can never know enough." In her field, this has meant advanced skills training in media law, journalism, editing film footage, learning how to use a professional camera and being taught (as well as learning through hands-on experience) how to plan and set up a story for reporters. Anila's advanced skills are built on a foundation of years of hard graft gaining hands-on experience. She was 15 when she first decided that she wanted to be a journalist, after having undertaken work experience at a local radio station. "At school, I joined a journalism organisation for young people called Headliners, which trained me in all areas of presenting; it allowed me to interview MPs and spotted my talent for presenting in front of a camera."

Another of the branch-out elements is networking. Whilst some people have an aversion to the idea because it can feel like you're selling yourself, when used effectively it can be a vital tool to career advancement and professional growth. Networking can be an opportunity to meet others in your field and widen your support network. Networking can be done in person at real events, such as conferences and gatherings, which can be an enjoyable alternative to anonymous email and telephone communication and could even open new doors for you in the future – for example, it might enable someone to put a face to your name in an email or on your CV.

Networking is also effective through social media, such as Twitter, LinkedIn and blogs. It can help raise your profile in your industry, and can also present you with potential inspirational role models. It's also an excellent way to keep up-to-date with news, ideas and changes in your industry.

Different professions have their own entry points and requirements. Some professions are known to be more difficult to break into than others, and it's not always about the quality of your CV. This is where networking can give you an edge. It's a well-known fact that the media industry can be tough to break into, and Anila did not know anyone in it; she was also the first in her family to embark on a career in the field. She had to do it on her own, and explains, "I had nobody to tell me who I should know, who was at the top, which networks to join or events to attend. So I contacted everybody and attended every event I could find. Attending networking events alone was daunting, but I knew what I wanted and I wanted it badly enough to throw myself in the deep end. I knew that no one could help me but me, so I went for it. I once attended an event with top media professionals and said to a man, 'Hi, I'm Anila, a budding journalist.' He replied, 'You're either a journalist or you're not. And your handshake isn't firm enough.' He then tasked me with introducing myself to someone as 'Anila, a journalist,' with a firm handshake. It not only worked but made me feel confident. That day, I learnt how to present myself with conviction and integrity, which helps me now when I'm meeting celebrities, guests and people from all walks of life for my job in TV."

Networking, for Anila, is a cyclical process that not only inspires her, but helps her to be an inspiration. "I create relationships with people who inspire and empower me so that I can inspire and empower others in turn." Very often, opportunities that arise from building broader relationships across your field or industry don't become apparent until further down the line. Anila, for example, approached a producer and kept in regular contact with him via email. Then, she recalls, "Around five years later, I had a call from some documentary makers who were considering me as their presenter; they were working with the producer who knew my name from my emails, but had never met me. My perseverance over email had paid off."

After meeting Anila, I told my family about a young SAVVI television presenter I'd interviewed. Several months later, my son Reece met her at an event. It did not take him long to realise that she has similar values and the same drive and ambition as him. To my delight, they dated for two years and are now married.

Before Anila became part of our family, she and Reece took the DISC profiling test and found that they shared similar traits and values, which was important to them both. Anila has started to participate in our family meetings, and we now look forward to revisiting and rewriting our family charter in order to take into account her values and traits, enabling us to continue to support each member of our growing family.

Another key element of branching out is to seek personal or professional coaching. Sessions with a coach offer a safe environment for people to see themselves more clearly. A study by Anthony M. Grant, Linley Curtayne and Geraldine Burton at the University of Sydney found that life coaching in non-work settings can reduce anxiety, stress and depression and enhance hope, wellbeing and resilience, as well as help with goal attainment. A coach can provide you with the emotional distance you might need to identify any blind spots that are blocking your goal setting; they can then help you to develop some strategies to stay focused and edge closer towards your goals.

Here are some of the results experienced by my coaching clients:

- Over three months, one client (a fitness instructor) saw his earnings increase by over three times once he left his job to start his own business.

- Another client (a hairdresser) made drastic changes to his business strategy that resulted in an increased net profit of 25%.

- 33% of my executive coaching clients have been promoted within six months.

- A female client who had been struggling in a loveless marriage finally gained the courage to admit that ending the marriage would be the best outcome for her, her children and her husband.

I, in turn, have been inspired by the incredible journey made by my clients Zara and Arun, the subjects of this book. Zara first came to see me for coaching when she was feeling unfulfilled and unable to understand why. Arun soon followed, inspired by the change that he saw coaching had made to his mother. By then, Zara was already displaying the benefits of her coaching because rather than telling Arun to develop – as she had done in the past – she had inspired him to begin the process of personal development.

Over a number of sessions, the coaching developed Zara and Arun into SAVVI individuals and into a SAVVI team at home, where their family meetings were like group coaching sessions that helped them to inspire and motivate one another. Observing a couple of these family meetings played a part in Jay's decision to come to see me for his own session – not realising that he had already started on his own journey to becoming SAVVI. Clearly, Zara and Arun had come a long way, and it was going to be interesting to see just how open Jay was to growth for his own professional and personal benefit – in particular for the benefit of his family.

However, after Jay's failure to appear for his last session with Zara and Arun, I couldn't be certain that he would actually come. Regardless, I knew that Zara and Arun were already enough of a supportive SAVVI family unit that, whilst it would be valuable to have Jay on board, it would also be possible for them to continue on their own SAVVI journey without him. When the family had arrived at this crossroads, waiting to see whether Jay would be joining them, I felt it was a good time to ask Zara and Arun to reflect on how they'd both developed since the start of their coaching sessions with me.

Zara's Reflections on Her SAVVI Journey

'Now, I'm the creator of my life.'
—Zara

ZARA: Looking back, I realise that I was sleepwalking through life, blindly leading a life designed by my family and my culture, so much of which was unfulfilling. I'd limited myself. I didn't realise the impact that my values and beliefs were having on me, whether they were positive or negative. I didn't have the distance from my situation to look at what was happening to me. Actually, I always believed that things were *'happening to me'*. I didn't see my part in allowing these things to happen.

Then, you shared an inspirational quote with me: *'I am not a product of my circumstances, I am a product of my decisions.'* This has really stuck with me, and I've written it down and put it up on the wall where I can see it every day. Now I see that my sense of frustration was partly my own doing! These internal voices had had a huge impact on my actions my whole life, but once I'd started looking inwardly, and had faced up to the mental limitations that were my inner demons, I realised that I could take control of my own destiny. It's not Arun's job or Jay's job to make me happy! Now I can say proudly that I'm the creator of my life.

These days, I have the courage to consciously work towards being the person I want to be, and I can express that to others by flowering my language. For me, that's meant changing the negative thoughts I used have and the words I used to speak. Now, instead of saying 'might' or 'hopefully', I use words like 'absolutely' and 'sure I will', and I say yes more often.

The SAVVI principles have helped me find my purpose. The first step of self-awareness has helped me focus on my strengths – not on my weaknesses, which I did before – and to see that I can use them to serve others. What's great is that I can do that without compromising my strong family values. In fact, this knowledge has enhanced my relationship with my family, especially my son. I have more self-love and self-respect and, in turn, I can feel my family's renewed respect for me. I know that Arun has been inspired by me to come and see Rita. I hope that Jay goes through the same transformation – not for my sake or for our family's sake, but for himself – just like our son has done.

I used to feel hollow inside, but now I feel so much new information and energy flowing through me. I'm constantly being inspired and learning through the charity work I'm doing. I can honestly say that I'm finding fulfilment in ways I couldn't have imagined.

I wouldn't have believed it if you'd told me six months ago, but I'm truly living a life now that allows me to grow and develop every day, so that I feel like I'm alive! I'm continually moving towards becoming a better version of myself, which leaves me feeling younger in mind and in spirit.

Above all, I've got the confidence to open up and express my feelings – particularly to Jay. I recognise that some of my problems in the past were down to my own failings in communication, expecting Jay and Arun to be mind-readers. They didn't know how I felt because I didn't really share my emotions. Recently, when reflecting on how disappointed and hurt I was that Jay had missed our family session, I could see myself bottling it all up in the way I used to do. I felt myself becoming anxious again, wondering about Jay's relationship with his finance director. So, in no-nonsense terms that Jay would understand, I applied my new communication skills to telling him that I wanted him to attend a session with you, and that otherwise I would challenge the finance director about their relationship directly. My SAVVI training has opened up so many possibilities, and has given me the confidence to understand that being direct in my communication won't destroy my options, but rather will give me more routes towards my desired outcomes. It'll be interesting to see how Jay responds."

Arun's Reflections on His SAVVI Journey

ARUN: Before I started seeing you, I was lost in the fog. I didn't know my destination, let alone which route to take. I lived in my father's shadow and felt I'd never be successful at anything, and that it was safer to do nothing. I'd become risk-averse because I was worried about failing; this was based on past experience of failure, like dropping out of uni. Unfortunately, money wasn't a motivator for me as I'd always had free access to my dad's wealth and didn't have to work for it. Ironically, I ended up with a sense of entitlement to the fastest cars, the best clothes – just like many of my friends – even though I hadn't really earned any of it. A big change for me is that now I'm finding giving far nicer than receiving.

Using the SAVVI framework, I was reminded of my strengths around influencing and inspiring others. By examining my values properly for the first time, I understood just how important justice and equality are to me. For years I had felt unfairly treated because of my dyslexia – I felt judged as a failure because of it. It definitely held me back. However, by identifying my chief value of justice, and then switching my mindset from 'I Can't' to 'I Can', I turned things around for myself and for others: I injected fairness into our workplace with the introduction of a working party. I want to create a business that values corporate and social responsibility, with a culture of diversity and inclusivity. I love the difference I'm making to the working lives of ACE's employees. In addition, whilst I enjoy making money for the business, I want to use the profits to create a positive impact on the lives of our staff and the community. I'm finding this far more rewarding than acquiring material possessions. I've done that; it doesn't motivate me anymore.

Something that does drive me now is reflecting on how I could do something better. I used to be paralysed by fear of failure, of not doing something well enough. But reflection through journal writing has helped me to see failures as valuable lessons without knocking my confidence. Now, I talk about 'lessons learnt' rather than failures, and encourage staff to do that too. It's been a really powerful shift in our attitude to success.

The GRIPP ladder techniques (particularly those based around goals and reflection) have helped me stay focused on my goals, and have given me clarity and drive. I've ended up re-prioritising some of my goals. Before, my sole goal was to go out clubbing at the weekend, but I've lost that drive to party. I don't take any pleasure from it anymore. Now, I look at my goals and see that clubbing doesn't serve any purpose; it only distracts me from my purpose. I know some of my friends feel I've betrayed them, but I'm on a different journey now.

Frankly, these days I'd rather spend an evening having dinner with a company director and getting to know what's happening in the marketing team, with a view to helping me progress with the business. Or if I go out socially, I want to spend time with a girl or a friend with similar values to me. Becoming

SAVVI has a had a holistic effect on me: it's affected both my work and personal relationships. Ultimately, I've learnt to have an attitude of gratitude. I look around the business that my dad has created and worked hard to build, and I'm grateful to him for the comfortable life he's given me. Now, it's time to create my own wealth – and that's a new motivator for me.

I'm inspired to carry on growing and developing in the business by using some of the BRANCH Out methods. For example, I've joined a couple of networking groups and recently started looking for a mentor in the HR field.

Becoming SAVVI (even though I know it's not the end of the journey!) has been transformative for me. Interestingly, because I work with my dad and know him as well as I do, I'm using my strengths to help overcome *his* weaknesses at work. This has been really fruitful for the business, which has become more financially successful with our introduction of corporate social responsibility and strong ethics and values; importantly, it's improving my relationship with ad at home too. It's funny: now that I've stopped worrying about getting my dad's approval, I'm getting it in abundance!

The SAVVI journey has done so much for my mum and for me. I'd like to see my dad taking in some of the guidance. He can definitely see the difference in the two of us. I'd love to see him take the plunge for himself.

It was a privilege to guide Zara and Arun on their SAVVI journey. They were not only experiencing the benefits for themselves, they were also observing that Jay had, without realising it, begun his own journey of transformation, as evidenced by his allowing Arun more control at work, attending family meetings and showing more interest in both Arun and Zara's lives. Now, it was only natural that both of them wanted Jay to accompany them on that journey so that they could be a SAVVI family, held together by common values and goals.

Mother and son were already enjoying the benefits of strength and unity from being a SAVVI team; if Jay were to follow in their footsteps, he would need to face some challenging questions along the way – just like his family and the SAVVI business leaders I've coached and interviewed. For example, would he be able to understand the value of carving out quality thinking time for himself in order to become a smarter businessman? Could he learn the lesson of being less controlling of his business in order to support Arun and his directors in performing better? Would he address his work-life balance to make his marriage work? Would he open up about this relationship with his finance director?

I was sat contemplating the fact that Jay's SAVVI journey would certainly be different to his family's when I noticed a text message appear on my phone: *Jay's on his way. – Zara.*

There was a knock at the door.

Conclusion

Staying SAVVI

I used to be a worrier, someone plagued by insecurities, who had limited herself in certain areas of her life. It took a series of events – culminating in my mother's death – for me to realise that I needed to turn to a new page. The saying goes, *'You have the power to say: "This is not how my story will end."'* Once I'd made the decision to take power into my own hands, I changed the course of my life forever.

Consequently, I've grown and achieved things I'd never dared dream of – like being invited to the House of Lords and 10 Downing Street! Creating and living by the SAVVI framework has enabled me to write a transformative new chapter in my life, that has helped me reach unexpected heights and has had far-reaching effects on my family and the people around me.

For many years, I've shared the SAVVI principles with private clients, such as Zara and Arun, and many private and public sector businesses, from SME businesses to London's largest employer and the largest local authority in the UK, the Metropolitan Police. As a result, I've had the privilege of taking others along the journey towards achieving greater personal fulfilment, career progression, business growth and enhanced performance.

In this book, I've sought to share the inspiring stories of some of my clients (whose names I have changed) in order to demonstrate to readers how SAVVI principles have been put to practice in real people's lives.

As I've stressed throughout, the SAVVI journey is cyclical and constant. I myself continue to use the framework in my own life. Staying SAVVI is a life-long journey.

As a SAVVI family, we work on maintaining an achiever's mindset by reviewing our family charter twice a year. On a daily basis, all of us try to live by Roosevelt's words, '*Do one thing every day that scares you.*' While writing this book, my family has reached some real milestones; we have grown and developed in our careers and personal lives, and have overcome adversity.

Inspired by my journey, my son Reece and my eldest daughter Leah have both left their Ernst & Young jobs to set up their own businesses. In Reece's words, "Mum, if you can do it so can I." Now he is running his own venture capitalist business, RLC Ventures, which invests in FinTech businesses – an industry he's always had a passion for. It's incredible to see Reece, the boy who was written off by his teachers, now a SAVVI role model. He's already made a significant mark on the venture capitalist industry. He says, "I've used the principles of an achiever's mindset, from the GRIPP ladder. I've created goals that stretch me; I maintain an 'I Can' attitude, and when things go wrong, I don't let them get me down – I just work out other ways of progressing."

Today, Reece speaks at a number of technology events and has won an award for Top Asian Angel Tech Investor in the UK by KPMG. Last year, he met and fell in love with Anila, one of the SAVVI subjects I interviewed for this book, having met her at a Women's Equality Party event at Ernst & Young. Apart from being drawn to her obvious beauty, intelligence and charm, Reece applied the SAVVI principles of self-awareness and values to learn that the two of them were a good match.

Last year, Leah combined her passion for helping children and fundraising with her swimming skills and became the first British Asian girl to swim the English Channel, raising £155k. She's now in the second year of her business, which provides on-site pop-up child care for shared office spaces, weddings, members' clubs and exclusive restaurants. SAVVI principles have helped a childlike Leah, whose natural **S** style meant that she was limited by insecurity and a desire to stay in her comfort zone, to put herself through immense emotional and physical pressure to complete a Channel swim in 14 hours and 44 minutes, all to help others. Reflecting on her achievement, Leah says, "Self-awareness was key: knowing what my fears were meant that I could work out how to overcome them and achieve what I'm really passionate about, which is helping disadvantaged and sick people."

My youngest daughter Anya identified her passion for drama and politics and has followed it. As a result, she's been awarded a drama scholarship and has had the opportunity to appear on Sky TV, grilling Boris Johnson about his ambitions to be Prime Minister. Last Autumn, she started a degree at Bath University in Social Science and Politics, and is aspiring to a political career. She has strong empowering values and beliefs and dreams of being, as she says, "The first Asian female Prime Minister." Even at four feet 11 inches, Anya doesn't lack confidence around anyone. Meanwhile, she continues to grow within herself using an achiever's mindset, through which she recognises her need to work on her communication skills.

Like Anya, I remain mindful of my verbal communication, especially when preparing to deliver my SAVVI Managers workshop. When I analyse the DISC profiles of attendees, I make sure I've adapted my verbal communication to keep my audience engaged.

244

I'm delighted to say that my husband Jeff has responded well to his chemo, and that his cancer has been in remission for over two years. A principled man guided by his strong values, he has continued to develop his expertise in sustainability and is now one of the world's most renowned experts in the field of responsible investments in emerging markets. He says, "I always choose businesses that want to make profit with principles. It's about what they can do to reduce poverty, or improve climate change, or deal with water and food shortages." His fund, launched in 2010, recently crossed the $500m threshold of assets. Jeff continues to have a good work-life balance, spending time with our family whilst carving out time for himself to improve his golf handicap.

This year our family has grown with the addition of a new member: my son's wife, Anila. We'll be revisiting the shared values that we drew up in our family charter to ensure that we retain mutual respect for each other's values, when the two families come together. Looking into our family's future, we will need a new charter to help serve and support everyone in leading a fulfilling life.

My mother and mother-in-law's legacies continue to inspire the work I do. I feel such pride when I hear someone else call out the name Savran (say at an awards night, or when I hear my head of client services call up a client to make arrangements for a workshop). Hearing my mother and mother-in-law's names being used on a daily basis means that their legacies live on; I feel they're both still here with me. I hope they are proud of the work I continue to do in their name – particularly when I receive industry recognition for it (Best Newcomer of the Year at the International Coaching Awards 2015; Best Small Business Coach at the International Business Awards 2016; Best Coach at the Best Business Woman Awards 2016; Service Award Finalist 2017 at the Toast of Surrey Business Awards).

It was my mother who instilled in me the value of giving back and helping others. I'm passionate about using all of my strengths to uphold that value. It has led me to search for new causes to support outside of my coaching: I am now a governor for a short-stay school for pupils who have been expelled from mainstream education. I also provide pro bono leadership coaching (through the Uprising programme) for young adults from minority ethnic groups. I am in the process of setting up a mentoring system for children in India, and look forward to offering pro bono services to school teachers there. All these projects and their respective challenges inspire me as a coach.

However, there are times when I too can feel stagnated in some area of my life. That's when I look to the BRANCH Out model for inspiration and ask myself, "What can I do next?" For example, it might be a good time for me to attend a networking event, such as Women Empowered, to share ideas with other businesswomen and learn from other women's success stories. The importance is to keep on looking outwards – as well as inwards – in order to keep growing.

Writing this book had been part of my personal SAVVI journey, and stemmed from my desire to communicate with a wider audience and to inspire others. I'm happy to report that it's also been a great year for Savran. The business continues to flourish, and soon we'll be sharing an online training platform offering interactive support with the SAVVI principles.

In the meantime, I hope this book will help you get started on your SAVVI journey.

Bon voyage! Get SAVVI, get successful!

Bibliography

- Peters, S., 2012, The Chimp Paradox: The Mind Management Programme to Help You Achieve Success, Confidence and Happiness, Vermillion, UK

- Locke, E. A., Shaw, K. N., Saari, L. M., & Latham, G. P. (1981). Goal setting and task performance: 1969–1980. *Psychological Bulletin, 90*(1), 125-152

- Carnegie, D., 1936, How to Win Friends and Influence People, Simon and Schuster, UK

- Gladwell, M., 2013, David and Goliath: Underdogs, Misfits and the Art of Battling Giants, Allen Lane, UK

- Gladwell, M., 2005, Blink: The Power of Thinking Without Thinking, Allen Lane, UK

- Alcott, L. M., 1868, Little Women, Roberts Brothers, USA

- Covey, S., 1989, The 7 Habits of Highly Effective People, Free Press, USA

- Sharma, R., 1997, The Monk Who Sold His Ferrari, HarperCollins Publishers, Canada

- Johnson, S., M.D., 1999, Who Moved My Cheese? An Amazing Way to Deal with Change in Your Work and in Your Life, Vermillion, UK

- Byrne, R., 2006, The Secret, Simon and Schuster, UK

- R Kiyosaki and S Lechter, 1997, Rich Dad, Poor Dad, USA

- Collins English Dictionary, 12th Edition, October 2014, HarperCollins Publishers, UK

- M. Grant, L. Curtayne and G Burton, Executive coaching enhances goal attainment, resilience and workplace well-being: a randomised controlled study, Coaching Psychology Unit, School of Psychology, University of Sydney, Sydney, NSW, Australia (Received December 2008; final version received June 2009) The Journal of Positive Psychology Vol. 4, No. 5, September 2009, 396–407

SAVRAN

Appendix

What are Your Values?

Achievement	Adventure	Art	Balance
Challenge	Community	Creativity	Democracy
Effectiveness	Fame	Health	Helping others
Honesty	Independence	Family	Friendships
Growth	Knowledge	Laughter	Learning
Love	Loyalty	Money	Nature
Order	Pleasure	Power	Recognition
Relationships	Religion	Responsibility	Reward
Security	Self-respect	Serenity	Stability
Status	Success	Time	Truth
Connection	Wisdom	Spirituality	Understanding
Co-operation	Risk taking	Spontaneity	Openness
Awareness	Patience	Integrity	

About the Author

Multi-award-winning coach **Rita Chowdhry** has always been passionate about developing others. She started her career as a teacher of business and economics at secondary school and university level, at the same time as running her own property business. Her focus on changing the mindset of her students enabled them to go well beyond academic attainment towards achieving their full potential in all areas of their lives. She wanted to offer this expertise to a wider audience and took the decision to undertake further training to become a professional personal development coach and behavioural consultant.

In her personal life, watching both her mother and mother-in-law take their last breaths made her reflect and take action to enter the business world. Rita's loss and her training as a coach acted as a catalyst to overcome obstacles and gave her the courage to form her own coaching company, Savran. which offers a blend of training, coaching and profiling. Organisations such as the **Metropolitan Police, KFC, Spelthorne Council** and healthcare providers have benefitted from her ability to help their people accelerate performance, sales, leadership skills and improve recruitment and retention. Rita also supports private clients, particularly women and minority ethnic groups to help fulfil their personal and career goals and promote positive change.

Born in India, Rita came to the UK in 1965. She currently lives in Surrey with her husband Jeff and three children. She absolutely loves interior design, good food, music and travelling. She strongly believes in giving back and offers pro bono coaching to several charitable organisations and is a school governor.

She was recently given two International Coaching Awards as 'Best Newcomer' and 'Best Small Business Coach' *and* 'Most Inspirational Businesswoman' and 'Best Coach' by Best Businesswomen Awards.

www.Savran.co.uk